⊚ Harden's

London
Restaurants
2007

From the publisher

Other Harden's titles
UK Restaurants
London Party, Event & Conference Guide

www.hardens.com
The launch of this guide coincides with a major upgrade to the Harden's website. Apart from restaurant information, the site now includes details of thousands of rooms for parties, conferences and events, plus related services. Please do visit us and have a look.

Corporate and promotional gifts
Harden's guides are available in a range of specially customised formats for corporate gift, promotional and marketing purposes, in quantities from 10 to 1,000,000. Where appropriate, we can even research and incorporate non-standard listings and other bespoke editorial.

Further information
For further information on any of the above, please call (020) 7839 4763 or visit www.hardens.com.

© Harden's Limited 2006

ISBN 1-873721-76-5
(13 digit version: 978-1-873721-76-6)

British Library Cataloguing-in-Publication data:
a catalogue record for this book is available from the British Library.

Printed in Italy by Legoprint

Research manager: Shannon Doubleday
Research assistants: Rachel Black, Jessica Hindes, Lianna Hulbert, Matthew Millson

Harden's Limited
14 Buckingham Street
London WC2N 6DF

CONTENTS

Ratings & prices
How this guide is written

RATINGS & PRICES

Ratings

Our rating system is unlike those found in other guides (most of which tell you nothing more helpful than that expensive restaurants are, as a general rule, better than cheap ones).

What we do is to compare each restaurant's performance – as judged by the average grades awarded by reporters in the survey – with other restaurants in the same price-bracket.

This approach has the advantage that it helps you find – whatever your budget for any particular meal – where you will get the best 'bang for your buck'.

The following qualities are assessed:

> **F** — Food
> **S** — Service
> **A** — Ambience

The rating indicates that, *in comparison with other restaurants in the same price-bracket*, performance is …

> **❶** — Exceptional
> **❷** — Very good
> **❸** — Good
> ④ — Average
> ⑤ — Poor

Prices

The price shown for each restaurant is the cost for one (1) person of an average three-course *dinner* with half a bottle of house wine and coffee, any cover charge, service and VAT. Lunch is often cheaper. With BYO restaurants, we have assumed that two people share a £5 bottle of off-licence wine.

Telephone number – all numbers should be prefixed with '020' if dialling from outside the London area.

Map reference – shown immediately after the telephone number.

Rated on Editors' visit – indicates ratings have been determined by the Editors personally, based on their visit, rather than derived from the survey.

Website – the first entry in the small print (after any note about Editors' visit)

Last orders time – listed after the website (if applicable); Sunday may be up to 90 minutes earlier.

Opening hours – unless otherwise stated, restaurants are open for lunch and dinner seven days a week.

Credit and debit cards – unless otherwise stated, Mastercard, Visa, Amex and Maestro are accepted.

Dress – where appropriate, the management's preferences concerning patrons' dress are given.

Smoking – given the state of flux as the statutory ban approaches, we have felt it best to omit any information relating to smoking restrictions.

Special menus – if we know of a particularly good value set menu we note this (e.g. "set weekday L"), together with its formula price (FP) calculated exactly as in 'Prices' above. Details change, so always check ahead.

HOW THIS GUIDE IS WRITTEN

Survey

This guide is based on our sixteenth annual survey of what Londoners think of their restaurants; it is by far the largest annual survey of its type. Since 1998, we have also surveyed restaurant-goers across the rest of the UK. The out-of-town results are published in our guide 'UK Restaurants', published in association with Rémy Martin Fine Champagne Cognac. This year the total number of reporters in our combined London/UK survey, conducted mainly online, was nearly 8,000, and, between them, they contributed some 90,000 individual reports.

How we determine the ratings

In most cases, ratings are arrived at statistically. This essentially involves 'ranking' the average rating each restaurant achieves in the survey – for food, for service and for ambience – against the the average ratings of the other establishments in the same price-bracket.

A few restaurants – usually too recently opened for the survey – are rated by the editors themselves. To emphasise the personal basis of such assessments, we include a small-print note – "Rated on Editors' visit".

How we write the reviews

The tenor of each review is broadly determined by the ratings of the establishment concerned (derived as described above). We also pay some regard to the proportion of positive nominations (such as for 'favourite restaurant') compared to negative nominations (such as for 'most overpriced'). To explain *why* a restaurant has been rated as it has, we extract snippets from survey comments ("enclosed in double quotes"). A short review cannot possibly reflect all the nuances from, sometimes, several hundred reports, and what we try to do is to illustrate the key themes which emerge.

Editors' visits

We have, anonymously and at our own expense, visited almost all the restaurants listed in this book. However (except in the case of new restaurants, as noted above), we use these experiences only to help us to interpret reporters' views. We do *not* superimpose our own opinions: how well (or poorly) a restaurant is rated is determined by the survey results.

Please help us to make the next edition even more accurate. Register for free updates at www.hardens.com and you will be invited to take part in our next survey in the spring of 2007. **If you take part in the survey, you will, on publication, receive a complimentary copy of *Harden's London Restaurants 2008*.**

Richard Harden   **Peter Harden**

SURVEY – MOST MENTIONED

These are the restaurants which were most frequently mentioned by reporters. (Last year's position is given in brackets.) An asterisk* indicates the first appearance in the list of a recently-opened restaurant.

1	J Sheekey (1)
2	Hakkasan (2)
3	Gordon Ramsay (4)
4	Chez Bruce (9)
5	The Wolseley (5)
6	Bleeding Heart (6)
7	The Ivy (3)
8	Gordon Ramsay at Claridge's (8)
9	La Poule au Pot (11)
10	Andrew Edmunds (12)

11	Oxo Tower (10)
12	Le Gavroche (13)
13	Nobu (7)
14	maze*
15	Zuma (18)
16	La Trompette (20)
17	The Cinnamon Club (15)
18	Tom Aikens (19)
19	Yauatcha (14)
20	Locanda Locatelli (17)

21	Le Caprice (16)
22=	Galvin Bistrot de Luxe*
22=	The Square (21)
24	Pétrus (23)
25	Club Gascon (24)
26	Connaught (Angela Hartnett) (27)
27	Amaya (39)
28	The Anchor & Hope (33)
29	Racine (31)
30	The River Café (25)

31	Mirabelle (22)
32	Moro (32)
33=	Blue Elephant (26)
33=	The Ledbury*
33=	Chutney Mary (29)
36=	The Don (30)
36=	St John (40)
38=	Zafferano (36)
38=	Cipriani*
40	Bentley's*

SURVEY – NOMINATIONS

Ranked by the number of reporters' votes.

Top gastronomic experience

1. Gordon Ramsay (1)
2. Chez Bruce (3)
3. Le Gavroche (5)
4. Gordon Ramsay at Claridge's (2)
5. Tom Aikens (4)
6. Pétrus (9)
7. maze*
8. La Trompette (7)
9. Nobu (6)
10. Connaught (Angela Hartnett) (-)

Favourite

1. Chez Bruce (1)
2. The Ivy (2)
3. J Sheekey (4)
4. The Wolseley (3)
5. Le Caprice (5)
6. La Trompette (7)
7. Gordon Ramsay (6)
8. Hakkasan (8)
9= Zuma (10)
9= Moro (-)

Best for business

1. Bleeding Heart (1)
2. 1 Lombard Street (7)
3= The Don (2)
3= The Wolseley (3)
5. The Square (4)
6. Coq d'Argent (5)
7. Savoy Grill (9)
8. Rhodes 24 (8)
9. Bank Aldwych (10)
10. The Ivy (6)

Best for romance

1. La Poule au Pot (1)
2. Andrew Edmunds (2)
3. Bleeding Heart (3)
4. Chez Bruce (4)
5. The Ivy (5)
6. Le Caprice (6)
7. Julie's (7)
8. Café du Marché (8)
9= Oxo Tower (9)
9= Clos Maggiore (-)

Best breakfast/brunch

1. The Wolseley (1)
2. Giraffe (2)
3. Carluccio's Caffè (6)
4. Smiths (Ground Floor) (3)
5= Simpsons-in-the-Strand (5)
5= Pâtisserie Valerie (4)
7. Balans (10)
8= Electric Brasserie (8)
8= Bank Aldwych (9)
8= Chelsea Bun Diner (7)

Best bar/pub food

1. The Anchor & Hope (1)
2. The Eagle (2)
3. The Anglesea Arms (7)
4. The Ladbroke Arms (-)
5. The Engineer (3)
6. The Gun (-)
7. St Johns (-)
8= Earl Spencer (10)
8= Churchill Arms (5)
10. The Cow (6)

Most disappointing cooking

1. Oxo Tower (1)
2. The Ivy (2)
3. The Wolseley (3)
4. Tom Aikens (6)
5. Gordon Ramsay at Claridge's (4)
6. Cipriani*
7. Bluebird (8)
8= Locanda Locatelli (-)
8= Quaglino's (5)
8= Sketch (Gallery) (10)

Most overpriced restaurant

1. Oxo Tower (1)
2. Cipriani (6)
3. Sketch (Gallery) (2)
4. The Ivy (5)
5. Hakkasan (8)
6. The River Café (4)
7. Nobu (3)
8. Sketch (Lecture Rm) (7)
9. Gordon Ramsay at Claridge's (10)
10. Gordon Ramsay (-)

SURVEY – HIGHEST RATINGS

FOOD	SERVICE

£70+

FOOD	SERVICE
1 Gordon Ramsay	1 Gordon Ramsay
2 Pétrus	2 Pétrus
3 Rasoi Vineet Bhatia	3 Le Gavroche
4 One-O-One	4 The Lanesborough
5 Pied à Terre	5 Foliage

£55-£69

FOOD	SERVICE
1 Chez Bruce	1 Chez Bruce
2 Assaggi	2 Roussillon
3 The Ledbury	3 Smiths of Smithfield
4 J Sheekey	4 The Ledbury
5 Club Gascon	5 Assaggi

£45-£54

FOOD	SERVICE
1 Morgan M	1 Oslo Court
2 La Trompette	2 Lundum's
3 Hunan	3 Le Caprice
4 Yauatcha	4 La Trompette
5 Amaya	5 Archipelago

£35-£44

FOOD	SERVICE
1 Tsunami	1 Bombay Palace
2 Bombay Palace	2 Lamberts
3 Moro	3 Indian Zing
4 Inside	4 Caraffini
5 Ottolenghi	5 Il Bordello

£34 or less

FOOD	SERVICE
1 Mirch Masala	1 Mandalay
2 Café Japan	2 Uli
3 Sukho Thai Cuisine	3 Agni
4 Mangal Ocakbasi	4 Tandoori Nights
5 New Tayyabs	5 Yming

AMBIENCE

1 Blakes
2 The Lanesborough
3 The Ritz
4 Taman gang
5 Hakkasan

1 Les Trois Garçons
2 Rules
3 Cheyne Walk Bras'
4 Babylon
5 Smiths of Smithfield

1 Archipelago
2 Crazy Bear
3 Blue Elephant
4 Julie's
5 Belvedere

1 La Poule au Pot
2 Lightship
3 Pasha
4 Café du Marché
5 Mr Wing

1 Gordon's Wine Bar
2 The Wine Library
3 Andrew Edmunds
4 Bar Italia
5 Wright Brothers

OVERALL

1 Gordon Ramsay
2 Pétrus
3 Le Gavroche
4 Blakes
5 Pied à Terre

1 Chez Bruce
2 J Sheekey
3 The Ledbury
4 Roussillon
5 Assaggi

1 La Trompette
2 Le Caprice
3 Notting Hill Brasserie
4 Lundum's
5 Archipelago

1 Lamberts
2 Café du Marché
3 Bombay Palace
4 Il Bordello
5 Moro

1 Wright Brothers
2 Andrew Edmunds
3 Comptoir Gascon
4 Eriki
5 Santa Maria de Buen Ayre

SURVEY – BEST BY CUISINE

These are the restaurants which received the best average food ratings (excluding establishments with a small or notably local following).

Where the most common types of cuisine are concerned, we present the results in two price-brackets. For less common cuisines, we list the top three, regardless of price.

For further information about restaurants which are particularly notable for their food, see the cuisine lists starting on page 242. These indicate, using an asterisk (*), restaurants which offer exceptional or very good food.

British, Modern

£45 and over
1 Chez Bruce
2 The Glasshouse
3 Notting Hill Brasserie
4 Origin
5 Lindsay House

Under £45
1 Inside
2 The Havelock Tavern
3 Lamberts
4 Franklins
5 The Barnsbury

French

£45 and over
1 Gordon Ramsay
2 Morgan M
3 Pétrus
4 La Trompette
5 Pied à Terre

Under £45
1 Comptoir Gascon
2 Cellar Gascon
3 Le Cercle
4 Lou Pescadou
5 The Food Room

Italian/Mediterranean

£45 and over
1 Assaggi
2 Quirinale
3 Zafferano
4 Tentazioni
5 Locanda Locatelli

Under £45
1 Il Bordello
2 Pappa Ciccia
3 Salt Yard
4 Latium
5 Aglio e Olio

Indian

£45 and over
1 Rasoi Vineet Bhatia
2 Amaya
3 Zaika
4 Chutney Mary
5 Deya

Under £45
1 Mirch Masala
2 New Tayyabs
3 Kastoori
4 Lahore Kebab House
5 Bombay Palace

Chinese

£45 and over
1 Hunan
2 Yauatcha
3 Kai Mayfair
4 Ken Lo's Memories
5 Hakkasan

Under £45
1 Mandarin Kitchen
2 Jenny Lo's
3 Royal China
4 Yming
5 Royal China

Japanese

£45 and over
1 Zuma
2 Nobu
3 Matsuri
4 Tatsuso
5 Roka

Under £45
1 Café Japan
2 Jin Kichi
3 Tsunami
4 Yoshino
5 Sakura

British, Traditional
1 Fuzzy's Grub
2 Wiltons
3 St John

Vegetarian
1 The Gate
2 Food for Thought
3 Mildred's

Burgers, etc
1 Haché
2 Gourmet BK
3 Lucky Seven

Pizza
1 Il Bordello
2 Pappa Ciccia
3 Delfino

Fish & Chips
1 Fish Club
2 Golden Hind
3 Nautilus

Thai
1 Sukho Thai Cuisine
2 Amaranth
3 Patara

Fusion
1 Tsunami
2 Nobu
3 Ubon

Fish & Seafood
1 One-O-One
2 Fish Club
3 J Sheekey

Greek
1 Kolossi Grill
2 Daphne
3 Costa's Grill

Spanish
1 Moro
2 Salt Yard
3 Navarro's

Turkish
1 Mangal Ocakbasi
2 Kazan
3 Shish

Lebanese
1 Fairuz
2 Fresco
3 Maroush

TOP SPECIAL DEALS

The following menus allow you to eat in the restaurants concerned at a significant discount when compared to their evening à la carte prices.

The prices used are calculated in accordance with our usual formula (i.e. three courses with house wine, coffee and tip).

Special menus are by their nature susceptible to change – please check that they are still available.

Weekday lunch

£60+ Nobu
The Ritz

£55+ Gordon Ramsay

£50+ Connaught (Angela Hartnett)
The Capital Restaurant
Le Gavroche
Gordon Ramsay at Claridge's
The Greenhouse
The Grill
Hakkasan
Pétrus
Savoy Grill
Sketch (Lecture Rm)

£45+ Asia de Cuba
Bibendum
Dorchester Grill
The Lanesborough
L'Oranger
Oxo Tower (Rest')
Pied à Terre
The Tenth
Toto's

£40+ Aurora
Axis
Berkeley Square
Cocoon
Rasoi Vineet Bhatia
Tom Aikens
Umu

£35+ Aubergine
Belvedere
Boisdale
Boxwood Café
Clos Maggiore
5 Cavendish Square
Giardinetto
L'Incontro
Locanda Ottoemezzo
Mirabelle
Orrery
Santini
Tamarind

£30+ Albannach
L'Aventure
Beauberry House
Benares
Les Coulisses
Deep
L'Etranger

Fino
Kensington Place
Launceston Place
Lucio
Montpeliano
Mosaico
Notting Hill Brasserie
Papillon
La Porte des Indes
La Poule au Pot
Quaglino's
Roka
Sardo Canale
Le Suquet
La Trouvaille
Villa Bianca
Zaika

£25+ L'Accento Italiano
Baltic
Bank Westminster
Blue Elephant
Bluebird
Boudin Blanc
Bradley's
Brula
Café des Amis du Vin
Café Fish
Cantina del Ponte
Canyon
Le Cercle
Cheyne Walk Bras'
Chez Liline
Chisou
Circus
Cru
Eight Over Eight
Electric Brasserie
Enoteca Turi
Esenza
Frederick's
Galvin Bistrot de Luxe
Greig's
Island
Joe Allen
Kew Grill
L-Restaurant & Bar
The Light House
Lobster Pot
Malmaison Brasserie
Mediterraneo
Mon Plaisir
Monza
Orso
Patara
Rivington

Royal China Club
Sam's Brasserie
San Lorenzo Fuoriporta
Sargasso Sea

£20+ The Anglesea Arms
Balham Kitchen & Bar
Le Bouchon Bordelais
Boulevard Bar & Dining
Room
Busabong
Café du Jardin
Le Chardon
Cross Keys
Le Deuxième
Elephant Royale
Il Falconiere
El Faro
The Fire Stables
Florians
Franklins
Garbo's
Gastro
Grumbles
Lilly's
The Palmerston
Soho Spice
Sophie's Steakhouse
Stratford's
Sugar Reef
The Terrace
Thai Elephant
Tugga

£15+ Al Bustan
The Arches
Chiang Mai
The Han of Nazz
Lime
Lowiczanka
Monty's
Namo
Pasha
Le Petit Auberge
Le Sacré-Coeur
Sakura
Sonny's

£10+ Anglo Asian Tandoori
Il Cantuccio di Pulcinella
Carnevale
Chutneys
Don Pepe
Fish in a Tie
Fresco
Galicia
Inshoku
Newton's
El Pirata
Sagar
Sree Krishna

Pre/post theatre
(and early evening)

£50+ Connaught (Angela
Hartnett)
Browns (The Grill)
Hakkasan

Savoy Grill

£45+ Asia de Cuba
Lindsay House

£40+ Axis

£35+ Astor Bar & Grill
Indigo
Matsuri

£30+ Albannach
Bank Aldwych
Bank Westminster
Beauberry House
Benares
Christopher's American
Bar & Grill
L'Etranger
Launceston Place
Quaglino's
Quo Vadis

£25+ Al Duca
Baltic
Café des Amis du Vin
L'Estaminet
Frederick's
Joe Allen
Luigi's
Orso
Redmond's
Tuttons
Veeraswamy

£20+ Café du Jardin
Le Deuxième
Ginger
Loch Fyne
Mela
The Portrait

£15+ Mon Plaisir
Yming

Sunday lunch

£50+ Connaught (Angela
Hartnett)
Gordon Ramsay at
Claridge's
Hakkasan

£40+ 5 Cavendish Square
Savoy Grill

£35+ Boxwood Café

£30+ Chutney Mary
The Greyhound at
Battersea
Quaglino's
Sargasso Sea

£25+ Baltic
Bradley's

£20+ Sonny's

£15+ Galicia
Lowiczanka
Pescador Too

THE RESTAURANT SCENE

Riding for a fall?

This year, we record 136 new openings – 4% fewer than last year's record figure of 142. The number of closures, 65, is similarly just fractionally behind the number recorded 12 months ago (67). (Openings and closings are listed on pages 20 and 21.)

Although it has received relatively little PR, the year has been notable for the opening of *Gilgamesh,* which – at £12m – is one of London's most expensive restaurants ever. Given both its humungous scale – 800 seats in total – and also pricing that is ambitious by Camden Town standards, it is a very brave venture. It is, perhaps, of the type one might expect to have been conceived somewhere around the 'top' of a market.

So is the market now sliding into a period of consolidation? One measure of its health is the ratio between the numbers of openings and closures we record each year. Since 1991, this ratio has risen to over 3:1 (during the late-'90s restaurant boom) and fallen as low as 1.2:1 (during the after-shock of the second Gulf War). What is most interesting about the ratio, however, is that it has always followed a clear cyclical pattern, with each cycle to date lasting between four and six years. The ratio is currently at a peak, and it may well be that – in line with the reduction seen in the number of new openings – the market is set to enter a softer period.

Market trends

The London restaurant scene seems to be in a phase which might crudely be described as 'back to basics'. Specific trends appear to be as follows:

• Asian cuisines are no longer all the rage. From a low base, the number of Japanese restaurants (in particular) has expanded hugely over the past decade. Now that the former under-provision has largely been addressed, the excitement about oriental food has calmed down. No new oriental restaurants, for example, have recently entered the survey Top-40 (see page 9).

• To the extent there is a new East, it is Latin and South America. At present, though, this looks like a major fringe development, not The Next Big Thing.

• Another sector where London is still playing catch-up (when compared to almost all major European cities) is bread and pâtisserie, and we are at last seeing the creation of a quality 'super-café' sector. This may be divided into places which are traditional, grand and French (*Ladurée, Maison Blanc Vite* and the growing *Paul* chain) and home-grown concepts which tend to be more humble in style (*Gail's Bread, Hilliard*).

- Honesty and simplicity are 'in'. The year since the last edition has seen a good number of interesting 'plain vanilla' openings, ranging from *Galvin Bistrot de Luxe* at its start to *Arbutus*, *Bar Shu* and *Dragon Castle* at its end.

- The division between restaurants and food retail continues to blur, most recently between steak house and butchers (*Butcher & Grill*).

Each year, we choose what we see as the ten most notable openings of the past twelve months. This year's selection – which, as it happens, illustrates many of the themes above – has been relatively straightforward. It is:

Arbutus	Galvin Bistrot de Luxe
Bar Shu	Gilgamesh
Butcher & Grill	Green & Red
Canteen	maze
Dragon Castle	Yakitoria

Paris... New York... Ramsay-town

For the 11th year running, Gordon Ramsay was again acclaimed by reporters as the capital's top chef. No news there. But what is new is that his group now accounts for no fewer than five of the top 10 places that reporters nominated for their best meal of the year (page 10) – up from just three last year. In some cases, this reflects the intrinsic merits of the restaurants, but in others it is just a function of the power of the Ramsay PR machine to generate footfall. It is no criticism of Gordon – or his vaulting international ambitions – to say that for one man, or brand, to achieve such dominance over London's top-end restaurant scene risks becoming stifling.

Out of the limelight, some restaurateurs continue to perform top-quality marvels, such as Nigel Platts-Martin (with a stunning collection of 'neighbourhood' restaurants headed up by *Chez Bruce*), Will Ricker (with a collection of hip, quality fusion-tapas bars, headed up by *E&O*) and the *Club Gascon* team (Messieurs Aussignac and Labeyrie) who also now run the three best sub-£45 French restaurants in town (page 14). But – even recognising these and other successes – a few more 'public' champions among the capital's restaurateurs might be no bad thing.

Prices

The average price of dinner for one at establishments listed in the guide is £37.72. Prices have on average risen by 3.0% in the past 12 months – this is in line with retail prices generally, and not, in contrast to recent years, outpacing them. At the top end of the market (£50+) prices are up 3.2%. This is the first time in seven years that prices at the top end have not increased substantially faster than prices generally.

OPENINGS AND CLOSURES

OPENINGS

Agni
All Star Lanes
Ambassador
Amici
Anakana
Arbutus
Asadal
Astor Bar & Grill
L'Atelier de Robuchon
Bar Shu
Barnes Grill
Bavarian Beerhouse
Bedford & Strand
Bistro 1 *Frith St, W1*
Bodeans *SW6*
Boulevard Bar
  & Dining Room
La Brasserie Ma Cuisine
Browns Hotel, The Grill
Butcher & Grill
The Cabin
Café Mamma
Canteen
Caramel
The Club Bar & Dining
La Collina
Cottons *EC1*
Les Coulisses
Cowshed
The Cuckoo Club
Curve
Dine
The Diner
Dragon Castle
Duke on the Green
L'Entrecôte Café de Paris
Everest Inn
El Faro
Fish Hook
Flat White
Franco's
Frankies *W4, W1, SW15*
Fuego Pizzeria
Gail's Bread
Galvin at Windows
Gilgamesh
Grafton House
Green & Red
  Bar & Cantina

The Han of Nazz
Hara The Circle Bar
Hawksmoor
High Road House
Hilliard
Hosteria Del Pesce
Hummus Bros
Imli
Indian Zing
The Inn at Kew Gardens
The Island
Jindalle
Kaz Kreol
Kensington Arms
Konstam at
  the Prince Albert
L-Restaurant & Bar
Ladurée
Leon *SW3, E1, EC4*
Lillo e Franco
Lime
Living Room *W1*
The Lock Dining Bar
Luciano
Ma Goa *SW6*
Maison Blanc Vite *W1, EC3*
The Marquess Tavern
Memsaheb on Thames
Mews of Mayfair
Mika
Mocoto
Mooli
The National Dining
  Rooms
La Noisette
Old Vic Brasserie
Origin
Ottolenghi *W8*
Pacific Bar and Grill
Papillon
Parmigiano
Le Petit Train
Pho
Pigalle Club
ping pong *W1, W2*
Raoul's Café *W11*
Real Greek Souvlaki *W1,*
  WC2, SW15
The Rivington Grill

OPENINGS (cont'd)

Rocco
Ronnie Scott's
Rossopomodoro
Roundhouse Café
Royal China Club
Royal Oak
Sagar *TW1*
Saki Bar & Food Emporium
Santore
Saran Rom
Sauterelle
Scarlet Dot
Scott's
Sea Cow *SW6*
Siam Central
Somerstown
  Coffee House
Souk Medina
The Spencer Arms
Sushi Hiroba
The Table
Tamarai
tamesa@oxo
The Terrace
Theo Randall
Thomas Cubitt
Tom's Kitchen
Tosa
The Trading House
Trinity
Trinity Stores
Ultimate Burger Company
  W1, WC1, N10
Upper Glas
Upstairs Bar
Via Condotti
Village East
Vinoteca
White Hart
William IV
Wright Brothers
Xich-lô
XO
Yakitoria
Zero Quattro

CLOSURES

Atlantic Bar & Grill
Bar Meze
The Belsize
Brasserie de l'Auberge
Broadway Bar & Grill
Bu San
Burnt Chair
Coco
Cotto
Criterion Grill
Crivelli's Garden
Cross Bar
The Crown
Cube & Star (now a bar)
Dan's
Del Buongustaio
Demera
Destino
Exmouth Grill
La Finca
La Fontana
Four Regions *SE1*
Graze
Grocer on Warwick
Halepi *NW3*
Iniga
Lola's
Lomo
Luc's Brasserie
Mao Tai *SW3*
Marechiaro
Mesclun
Michiaki
Murano
MVH
Noble Rot
Novelli in the City
Panzella
The Pen
Pengelley's
Le Petit Max
Le Petit Prince
Polygon Bar & Grill
Pomino
Il Pomodorino
Poons

CLOSURES (cont'd)

Pucci
Quod
Real Burger World
Relais de Paris
Rowley's *W1*
Rusticana
Le Soufflé
South
La Superba
Tartine *TW9*

Tas Pide *EC1*
Tiger Lil's *SW4*
The Vale
Wheeler's of St James's
Whole Hog Canteen
Windows on the World
Yas on the Park
Zamoyski
Zucca

EATING IN LONDON – FAQs

How should I use this guide?

This guide can be used in many ways. You will often wish to use it to answer practical queries. These tend to be geographical – where can we eat near…? To answer such questions, the Maps (from page 302) and Area Overviews (from page 264) are the place to start. The latter tell you all the key facts about the dozens of restaurants in a particular area in the space of a couple of pages.

But what if you'd like to be more adventurous and seek out new places purely for interest's sake or for a truly special occasion? That is the main point of this brief section – to give you a handy overview of London's dining scene, and also some thoughts as to how you can use the guide to lead you to eating experiences you might not otherwise have found (or perhaps even contemplated).

What makes London special?

London is not Paris, Rome or Madrid, which are mainly of note for their French, Italian and Spanish restaurants respectively. British cuisine lost its (individual) way over 200 years ago, and only tourists nowadays look for 'English' restaurants.

What London is particularly good at – like New York – is cosmopolitanism and range, usually in depth. Always an entrepot, London is now a culinary melting pot, too, and it offers most of the world's major (and minor) cuisines, at most levels of ambition.

More specifically, London does have a particular strength, and it is as THE worldwide centre of Indian restaurants. 'Indian' cooking now comes at every price level, in every part of town, in eating-places of every style and level of grandeur, and with a vast range of different regional influences. Just like French or Italian restaurants, it is pointless to generalise about them. The difference from these two cuisines, however, is that Indian is done better and more comprehensively in restaurants here than in any other city in the world. (And, yes, that includes Mumbai.)

Which is London's best restaurant?

Cosmopolitan as London may be, it still recognises the pre-eminence of Gallic cuisine, and the capital's three top restaurants are French. The best place is clearly *Gordon Ramsay* – the Chelsea flagship of the UK's leading chef. Just behind Ramsay, there is stablemate *Pétrus* and then *Le Gavroche*, London's longest-established grand restaurant.

If you just want to find the very best restaurants, without regard to cuisine, look at the survey results on the double page spread on pages 12 and 13. This will tell you – whether it's top food, top service or top ambience that you're particularly looking for – what are the capital's very best names.

What's 'in' at the moment?

The obvious question is: "in with whom?" The all-purpose, business-to-media haunt of recent times has been the famous *Ivy*. From a very high starting point it is currently in decline, but it remains a legendarily hard place to book.

Sharing some of the same cachet, but easier to reserve, are Ivy siblings *J Sheekey* and *Le Caprice*. *The Wolseley* – launched by Christopher Corbin and Jeremy King, who used to own the Ivy et al – has some claims to being a similar sort of glamour-destination.

Mayfair continues to (re-)emerge as an international in-crowd rendezvous. *Cipriani* is undoubtedly quite a 'scene' (as, in a rather lower-key way, is *Cecconi's*). *Bellamy's* has quickly established itself as an old school bastion.

The fashion (and sometimes Hollywood) crowd remains in thrall to Mourad Mazouz, with his properties *Momo* and *Sketch*. (Despite his efforts, though, the fine dining room at the latter has yet to be taken seriously as a foodie haunt by our reporters.)

Hip, young-at-heart types, with money to burn, have tended in recent times to gravitate to oriental places. It was *Nobu* which set the trend, but there are now a host of such places, including *Nobu Berkeley*, *Hakkasan*, *Roka*, *Taman gang*, *Yauatcha*, *Zuma* and *Yakitoria*.

I'm not fussed about fashionable scenes – where can I find a really good meal without spending the earth?

You're in luck! As appears from the introduction (page 18), 'back to basics' is a bit of a theme at the moment, with more places putting more emphasis on quality food in a relatively simple environment than has been the case in recent years. The central foodie favourites of the moment are *Arbutus*, *Galvin Bistrot de Luxe* and *Racine* (all, as it happens, French.)

For an all-round package such indefatigables as *Le Caprice* and *J Sheekey* should not be despised simply on the basis that they are also fashionable: for an all-round package, it is hard to beat what they offer. Away from the West End, Nigel Platts-Martin's establishments have become a byword for value amongst restaurant cognoscenti. *Chez Bruce*, his Wandsworth restaurant, is the survey's favourite, with stablemates *The Glasshouse* (Kew), *The Ledbury* (Notting Hill) *and La Trompette* (Chiswick) also inspiring raves.

Ten years ago one could not have said so, but nowadays it is pleasing to report that there are few major cuisines which do not have a number of representatives well worth seeking out for their own sake. If you're looking by type of cuisine, pay particular attention to the lists on pages 14 and 15.

What if I want the best of British tradition?

There are very few traditional British restaurants of note. Of these, the most recommendable are the very grand *Wilton's* and the mid-priced *Rules*. Most people will find the latter much more fun. Until very recently, one would have recommended some of the famous hotel restaurants as bastions of tradition, but – sadly – none of the more traditional rooms are currently of any note (except for the *Ritz,* and then only for the magnificence of the room).

The City preserves some extraordinary olde-worlde places such as *Sweetings* and *Simpson's Tavern*. Ancient taverns worth seeking out – for their charm, not their food – include the *Grenadier*, the *Queen's Head*, the *Trafalgar Tavern* and the *Windsor Castle*.

For foodies, Smithfield's *St John* continues to be an inspiration with its exploration of traditional British cooking, including lots of offal: uncompromising food in an uncompromising setting. South Bank gastropub, the *Anchor & Hope* has created a big name – it again topped the survey's list of favourite pubs this year – by offering similar (but perhaps less 'threatening') fare, in a rather similar vein. Newcomer *Canteen* is also promising, but consistency has proved elusive.

For afternoon tea, *The Wolseley* or *The Ritz* are best.

Isn't London supposed to be a top place for curry?

As noted above, London is the world's leading Indian restaurant city. At the top end, names such as *Rasoi Vineet Bhatia*, and then the likes of *Amaya, The Cinnamon Club, Tamarind, Vama* and *Zaika* are 'pushing back the frontiers'.

If you really want to eat the best-value food you will ever find in London, however, you need to avoid the 'obvious' postcodes (in which all of the fashionable Indians mentioned above are located). Two of the most accessible of the quality budget subcontinentals are the East End duo – which are, strictly speaking, not Indian but Pakistani – *New Tayaabs* and the *Lahore Kebab House*. There are, however, many brilliant options: look for the asterisked restaurants in the Indian and Pakistani lists starting on pages 258 and 260 respectively.

What are gastropubs?

Many pubs have re-invented themselves as informal restaurants in recent years. *The Eagle* was the original (1991). For the top ten current names, see page 11. The trend goes from strength to strength. There are now almost no affluent suburbs which lack pubs serving food of a quality that would have been inconceivable at the start of the decade.

Generally the pub tradition of ordering at the bar is kept, but some of the grander establishments offer full table service and have really become restaurants in all but name.

Can't we just grab a bowl of pasta?

Italian cooking has traditionally been the 'default' choice for relaxed neighbourhood dining, especially in the more affluent parts of town, and there is an enormous variety of trattorias and pizzerias. In recent years, some excellent high-level Italians have emerged – see the list on page 14.

What about the exotic East?

London has traditionally had quite a reasonable number of good traditional Chinese (usually Cantonese) restaurants. Most of these are not in Chinatown, and the biggest concentration of notable mid-range restaurants is in fact in Bayswater (including *Royal China*, *Four Seasons* and *Mandarin Kitchen*). Recently, Alan Yau has brought a lot pizzazz to the Chinese restaurant sector with *Hakkasan* and *Yauatcha*, while this year's opening of *Bar Shu* created much interest in the regional food of Sichuan.

Ten years ago, London was very backwards in Japanese cuisine, but the intervening period has seen a huge leap forward. For a while, indeed, it seemed that every fashionable opening in town was Japanese – see the 'What's In' section above – and London now has a very good range of restaurants at all levels. *Nobu* has maintained its appeal and cooking to an impressive extent, but its rival *Zuma* offers a better all-round experience.

You said diverse: what about other cuisines?

A major hit of recent years has been the cuisines of North Africa and the Eastern Mediterranean. These cuisines lend themselves well to good budget experiences.

Restaurant-goers have long rightly complained of the weakness of Mexican (and Latin American) restaurants in London, but this is currently being addressed by a wave of new or recent openings, of which the most notable are *Crazy Homies*, *Green & Red Bar & Cantina*, *Mestizo* and *Taqueria*.

Any suggestions for 'something completely different'?

How about *Archipelago*, *LMNT*, the *Lobster Pot*, *Les Trois Garçons* or *Sarastro*?

Are there any sharp practices I should look out for?

Yes: the 'blank credit card slip trick' (or rather, nowadays, its 'chip and pin' successor). If the credit card terminal gives you the option to add a tip, you should **not** assume that anything is payable. Check first – by reference to the bill, or, failing that, the waiter – that service has not already been included (usually at a rate of 10% or 12.5%). Sometimes the restaurant is simply hoping that you will, in effect, pay twice for the same service.

DIRECTORY

Comments in "double quotation-marks" were made by reporters.

Establishments which we judge to be particularly notable have their NAME IN CAPITALS.

A Cena TW1 £41 ❷❷❷
418 Richmond Rd 8288 0108 1–4A
This "lovely little neighbourhood restaurant", in St Margaret's,
is one of the few really recommendable places round Richmond,
thanks not least to its "very good" Italian cooking. / 10.30 pm; closed
Mon & Sun D; booking: max 6, Fri & Sat.

Abbaye £30 ④④④
102 Old Brompton Rd, SW7 7373 2403 5–2B
55 Charterhouse St, EC1 7253 1612 9–2A
"Lots of interesting beer" is the best feature of this "laid-back"
moules-frites duo (of which the City branch is much the more
characterful); they're "nice enough if you're passing", but "the food
could be better". / www.tragusholdings.com; 11 pm; 6+ must book.

The Abbeville SW4 £31 ④④❷
67-69 Abbeville Rd 8675 2201 10–2D
"They keep it simple, and it's none the worse for that", at this
"unpretentious" and "fairly-priced" Clapham gastro-boozer.
/ www.theabbeville.com; 11 pm; no booking.

Abeno WC1 £34 ❸❷④
47 Museum St 7405 3211 2–1C
"For alternative Japanese cooking", try this "quirky" okonomi-yaki
(fancy omelettes) restaurant, near the British Museum – the staff
are "charming", and "it's fun having the food cooked in front of you
on the hotplate". / www.abeno.co.uk; 10 pm.

Abeno Too WC2 £31 ❷❷❷
15-18 Gt Newport St 7379 1160 4–3B
It's not yet as well-known, but the "unusual and fun" Theatreland
offshoot of Abeno out-rates the original; it too offers "great"
Japanese-style omelettes and "very helpful" service.
/ www.abeno.co.uk; 11 pm.

The Abingdon W8 £40 ❸❷❷
54 Abingdon Rd 7937 3339 5–2A
This "slightly glam and buzzy" gastropub in a Kensington
backstreet has long been highly-popular for a "casual" meal;
"the dark and cosy booths are very nice if you can get one".
/ 11 pm.

About Thyme SW1 £36 ④④④
82 Wilton Rd 7821 7504 2–4B
Fans insist that this hard-edged Pimlico bistro offers "interesting
food at reasonable prices"; even they concede it's a touch
"overpriced", though, and many reports are of the "could
do better" variety. / www.aboutthyme.co.uk; 11 pm.

Abu Zaad W12 £16 ❷❸❸
29 Uxbridge Rd 8749 5107 7–1C
"Truly excellent, traditional and well-cooked" Middle Eastern food
draws both "Arab families" and bargain-seekers to this "smashing"
Syrian café, near Shepherd's Bush Market; no booze. / 11 pm.

L'Accento Italiano W2 £39 ❸❸❸
16 Garway Rd 7243 2201 6–1B
"Stick to the set menu" – the à la carte is "overpriced" – and you
can have a good-value meal at this Bayswater "neighbourhood
Italian"; "when you book, specify the front of the restaurant".
/ 11 pm; closed Sun; set weekday L £26 (FP).

Adam Street WC2 £57 ❸❸❷
9 Adam St   7379 8000   4–4D
A "hidden secret", just off the Strand – the "spacious" cellar dining
room of this civilised club (open to all at lunch) offers a "private"
venue to impress a client, with "sophisticated" dishes and well-
chosen wines; sadly, a £10 surcharge (included above) now applies
to non-members. / www.adamstreet.co.uk; L only (open for D to members
only), closed Sat L & Sun.

Adams Café W12 £25 ❷❶❸
77 Askew Rd   8743 0572   7–1B
The Boukraa family's "homely" neighbourhood spot – greasy spoon
by day, candlelit Moroccan by night – is "always cheery",
and serves "man-sized portions" of "cheap" cous cous, tagines and
so on (plus good breakfasts); BYO. / 11 pm; closed Sun.

Addendum
Apex City Of London Hotel EC3 £53 ❸❶④
1 Seething Ln   7977 9500   9–3D
Chef Tom Illic has made quite a name for himself over the years;
his new venture, at this 'fine dining' room (plus brasserie) near
Tower Bridge, has yet to set the world on fire, though, with some
reporters finding it "overpriced" and "disappointing".
/ www.apexhotels.co.uk; 10 pm.

Admiral Codrington SW3 £42 ❸❸❸
17 Mossop St   7581 0005   5–2C
This "lively" posh gastropub in the backstreets near Brompton
Cross serves "simple" but "decent" fare; "it's great in summer
when the roof opens". / www.theadmiralcodrington.com; 11 pm.

The Admiralty
Somerset House WC2 £55 ④④❸
Strand   7845 4646   2–2D
These historic rooms in London's grandest palazzo have bags
of potential, but it is still far from being realised – "slapdash"
service contributes to an "austere" ambience, and prices are on the
high side for food that's not much more than "acceptable".
/ 10.15 pm; closed Sun D.

Afghan Kitchen N1 £22 ❷④④
35 Islington Grn   7359 8019   8–3D
"It's a bit of a tight squeeze", but the "short menu" of "simple"
dishes offered by this "very cheap" and "busy" Afghani "canteen",
by Islington Green, is "full of fresh flavours". / 11 pm; closed
Mon & Sun; no credit cards.

Aglio e Olio SW10 £30 ❷❸❸
194 Fulham Rd   7351 0070   5–3B
You eat at "tiny, squashed-together tables" at this "manic" Chelsea
stand-by, and the noise level is "deafening"; everyone loves it,
though – it's "fun", and the "fantastic" pasta offers "real value for
money". / 11.30 pm.

Agni W6 NEW £22 ❶❶④
160 King St   8846 9191   7–2C
"Explode your taste-buds" with the "experimental" – but still "real"
– Indian cooking on offer at this "exceptionally good"
Hammersmith newcomer; the café-style premises give no hint
of the place's quality, but the service is "delightful".
/ www.agnirestaurant.com; 11 pm.

Al Bustan SW7   £38   ❸④⑤
68 Old Brompton Rd   7584 5805   5–2B
*"An excellent-value set lunch" is a high-point at this cramped
Lebanese restaurant in the heart of South Kensington; it lacks
ambience though (and the occasional reporter still misses the old
Motcomb Street premises). / 10.30 pm; set weekday L £18 (FP).*

Al Duca SW1   £38   ❸❸④
4-5 Duke of York St   7839 3090   3–3D
*Fans insist you get "the best value in St James's" at Claudio Pulze's
"consistently reliable" corner Italian; the food is "sound" rather than
spectacular, though, and the modern setting is quite "cramped"
and "noisy". / www.alduca-restaurant.co.uk; 11 pm; closed Sun; no jeans
or trainers; set pre theatre £25 (FP).*

Al Forno   £28   ❸❷❷
349 Upper Richmond Rd, SW15   8878 7522   10–2A
2a King's Rd, SW19   8540 5710   10–2B
*For a "cheap and cheerful" night out, these atmospheric old-school
Italians serve "reasonably-priced" grub, and "good pizza"
in particular. / 11 pm.*

Al Hamra W1   £45   ④⑤④
31-33 Shepherd Mkt   7493 1954   3–4B
*Reports of "excellent" food and "pleasant outside tables" recall the
features which once made this Mayfair Lebanese an "institution";
service can be "poor", though, and nowadays some reporters feel
there's "nothing remarkable here, except perhaps the prices".
/ 11.30 pm.*

Al Sultan W1   £38   ❸❷④
51-52 Hertford St   7408 1155   3–4B
*"Go for lots of mezze, rather than the dull grills" and you can have
a "delicious" meal at this "uninspiring-looking" Shepherd Market
spot, which fans still tout as "one of the best Lebanese restaurants
in town". / www.alsultan.co.uk; midnight.*

Al-Waha W2   £32   ❸❸④
75 Westbourne Grove   7229 0806   6–1B
*It briefly had a 'name', but there are few reports nowadays on this
"uninspiring"-looking Bayswater Lebanese, whose food
is somewhere between "surprisingly good" and "standard".
/ 11.30 pm; no Amex.*

Alastair Little W1   £52   ❷❷⑤
49 Frith St   7734 5183   4–2A
*This defiantly "ungimmicky" Soho dining room attracts less and less
attention nowadays; for the most part, however, it still wins high
praise for its "delicately simple, seasonal food", its "professional"
service and its "relaxed" ambience. / 11.30 pm; closed Sat L & Sun.*

Alba EC1   £39   ❷❷④
107 Whitecross St   7588 1798   9–1B
*"If you can look past the dour décor", this "off-the-beaten-track"
fixture, near the Barbican, is a worthwhile discovery for its "tasty"
north Italian cooking, its "helpful and welcoming" staff and its
"fascinating and informative wine list". / www.albarestaurant.com;
11 pm; closed Sat & Sun.*

Albannach WC2 £52 ④⑤④
66 Trafalgar Sq 7930 0066 2–3D
"A noisy bar below" detracts from the ambience of this "cramped" and "odd" mezzanine restaurant; its Scottish fare has "potential" (and there's "an amazing whisky selection"), but prices are "hefty", and the service can be "disastrous". / www.albannach.co.uk; 10 pm; closed Sun; set weekday L £32 (FP).

Ali Baba NW1 £20 ❸❸④
32 Ivor Pl 7723 5805 2–1A
"Al Jazeera on the TV" adds to the homely atmosphere of this "tiny" and "good-value" family-run Egyptian, behind a Marylebone take-away; BYO. / midnight; no credit cards.

All Star Lanes WC1 NEW £34 ④④❷
Victoria Hs, Bloomsbury Way 7025 2676 2–1D
For a "fun night out", this new Bloomsbury bowling alley – "decked out like a '50s diner" – has its fans; the food may be incidental, but it's "decent" enough (and "atmosphere-appropriate" too). / www.allstarlanes.co.uk; 11 pm; Mon-Thu D only, Fri-Sun open L & D.

Alloro W1 £45 ❷❷❷
19-20 Dover St 7495 4768 3–3C
"Very superior" cooking, "crisp" service and "elegant" surroundings make this "highly professional" Mayfair Italian a "great all-rounder"; it's on the "formal" side, though, and can seem "business-y". / 10.30 pm; closed Sat L & Sun.

Alma SW18 £30
499 Old York Rd 8870 2537 10–2B
This brilliant Wandsworth boozer (long run by Charles Gotto and his family) reverted to Young's Brewery in early-2006; early reporters disagree as to whether standards have "dropped" or are being "maintained", so we'll give the new régime till next year before awarding a rating. / 10.30 pm.

The Almeida N1 £42 ④④④
30 Almeida St 7354 4777 8–2D
Those who were dumfounded when Conran made a good job of launching this straightforward Gallic restaurant in Islington need fret no longer – the place is speedily regressing to the group norm, with many reporters now finding it "uninspired", "antiseptic" or "overpriced". / www.almeida-restaurant.co.uk; 11 pm.

Alounak £23 ❷④❸
10 Russell Gdns, W14 7603 1130 7–1D
44 Westbourne Grove, W2 7229 0416 6–1B
"The BYO policy makes it fun for big parties", at these "extremely reliable" and "value-for-money" Persians, where "excellent kebabs" are the menu highlight; the Bayswater branch has now re-opened after a fire. / 11.30 pm.

Amano Café SE1 £29 ❸④❷
Victor Wharf, Clink St 7234 0000 9–3C
"Excellent wraps made to order", "delicious smoothies", "lovely soups and pizzas" and "great coffee" make for happy refuelling at this busy "hang-out", near Borough Market. / www.amanocafe.com; 10.30 pm; no booking.

Amaranth SW18 £22 ❶❶❸
346 Garratt Ln 8871 3466 10–2B
*"You have to book", for the "fantastic" Thai food – at ultra-
"reasonable" prices – which has made this "bustling" café world-
famous in Earlsfield; it now has a license, but you can still BYO
(small corkage charge). / 10.30 pm; D only, closed Sun; no Amex.*

Amato W1 £32 ❸❷❸
14 Old Compton St 7734 5733 4–2A
*"A good place to start a day in the West End" – this "busy" Soho
café is also of note for its "excellent coffee and scrummy cakes".
/ www.amato.co.uk; 10 pm; no booking.*

Amaya SW1 £54 ❶❸❷
Halkin Arc, 19 Motcomb St 7823 1166 5–1D
*"A genuinely new spin on Indian cuisine" – featuring
an "innovative" open grill, and with many of its "outstandingly
tasty" dishes served tapas-style – has won wide-ranging acclaim for
this "stunning" Belgravia yearling. / www.realindianfood.com; 11 pm.*

Ambassador EC1 NEW £35 ❸❸④
55 Exmouth Mkt 7837 0009 9–1A
*This "bare-walled" Exmouth Market newcomer has quickly
impressed many reporters (and most of the press) with its "simple
but sophisticated" cuisine, its "super-friendly" service and its
"great" wine; in the early days, though, some reporters have found
consistency elusive. / www.theambassadorcafe.co.uk; 10.15 pm.*

Amerigo Vespucci E14 £38 ❸④④
25 Cabot Sq 7513 0288 11–1C
*"Good" Italian fare from an "extensive" menu helps make this
handily-located venture one of "Canary Wharf's best lunch
locations" – this is, of course, not saying very much.
/ www.amerigovespucci.co.uk; 11 pm; closed Sun.*

Amici SW17 NEW £34 ④❸❸
35 Bellevue Rd 8672 5888 10–2C
*A re-launch of Wandsworth's short-lived Pomino (RIP), this large
and "buzzy" Italian newcomer is hailed as "an improvement"
by some early-days reporters, but for others still "misses the mark".
/ www.amiciitalian.co.uk; 10.30 pm.*

Anakana EC1 NEW £30 ❸❷❶
1 Olivers Yd, City Rd 0845 262 5262 9–1C
*"A great place for a lunch with a difference" – this "funky" new
Indian bar/restaurant, near Old Street tube, is consistently praised
by reporters, not least for its "surprisingly good" food.
/ www.anakana.co.uk; 11.30 pm.*

Anarkali W6 £28 ❸❷④
303-305 King St 8748 6911 7–2B
*"Dependable over many years", this "stalwart" Hammersmith
Indian is still hailed by most reporters for dishes that are "delicious
every time". / www.anarkalirestaurant.co.uk; 11.30 pm.*

The Anchor & Hope SE1 £34 ❷❸❷
36 The Cut 7928 9898 9–4A
*Thanks to its "hearty" and "unusual" British food, this "vibrant"
and "genuine" South Bank three-year-old has become "everyone's
favourite gastropub" (and is again the survey's No 1 such);
it's "crowded", though – expect "interminable waits for a table".
/ 10.30 pm; closed Mon L & Sun; no Amex; no booking.*

for updates visit www.hardens.com 32

ANDREW EDMUNDS W1　　　　£32　　**❸❶❶**
46 Lexington St　7437 5708　3–2D
A "quaint" and "quirky" candlelit Soho "gem", whose phenomenal
popularity belies its "tiny" and "cramped" – but "wonderfully cosy"
– townhouse setting; the "homely" food is "honest" and
"good value" too, but the real highlight is the "astounding-value"
wine list. / 10.45 pm; no Amex; booking: max 6.

The Anglesea Arms W6　　　　£32　　**❷❹❷**
35 Wingate Rd　8749 1291　7–1B
"It's first-come, first-served", so arrive early if you want to eat
at this "charming" gastropub – many Londoners' favourite – where
the "seasonal" blackboard-menu is "worth a cross-town trek
to Ravenscourt Park"; service is "no longer as bad as people say".
/ 10.45 pm; no Amex; no booking; set weekday L £23 (FP).

The Anglesea Arms SW7　　　　£28　　**❸❷❷**
15 Sellwood Ter　7373 7960　5–2B
There's "always a lively ambience" – in summer the terrace
"heaves" – at this charming South Kensington boozer; the food
is straightforward, but "pretty good" for what it is.
/ www.capitalpubcompany.com; 10 pm.

Anglo Asian Tandoori N16　　　　£22　　**❸❷❸**
60-62 Stoke Newington Church St　7254 3633　1–1C
"Long-serving staff" contribute to the "welcoming" ambience of this
"attractive and comfortable" Indian in Stoke Newington, praised for
its "perennially wholesome" cooking; coming soon – a new candlelit
cocktail bar. / www.angloasian.co.uk; 11.45 pm; set weekday L £10 (FP).

Annex 3 W1　　　　£44　　**❺❺❷**
6 Little Portland St　7631 0700　2–1B
"Worth it just for the bling!"; "OTT" décor has made this
'maximalist' newcomer near Broadcasting House an instant hit with
"funky fashionistas"; overall, though – with its "dreadful" food and
unreliable service – it's "not nearly as good as siblings Trois Garçons
and Loungelover". / www.annex3.co.uk; 11 pm; closed Sun D.

Annie's　　　　£35　　**❹❷❷**
162 Thames Rd, W4　8994 9080　1–3A
36-38 White Hart Ln, SW13　8878 2020　10–1A
"Delicious brunches" are a highlight of the "homey"
(and somewhat "variable") cuisine on offer at these "very relaxed"
and "always friendly" west London hang-outs. / W4 10 pm,
SW13 11 pm.

Antipasto & Pasta SW11　　　　£30　　**❸❸❸**
511 Battersea Park Rd　7223 9765　10–1C
"The 50%-off deal on selected days is a winner" at this good
"cheap and cheerful" Battersea Italian. / 11.30 pm; need 4+ to book.

Antipasto e Pasta SW4　　　　£31　　**❸❷❸**
31 Abbeville Rd　8675 6260　10–2D
"If you go more than twice, they treat you as a friend", at this
"dependable" – if "predictable" – Clapham trattoria.
/ www.antipastoepasta.co.uk; 11.30 pm.

Aperitivo W1　　　　£30　　**❸❸❸**
41 Beak St　7287 2057　3–2D
This "attractive" modern bar in Soho offers an "Italian take
on tapas" – it's a bit "different" and makes for a "sociable" eating
experience. / www.aperitivo-restaurants.com; 11 pm; closed Sun.

Apium EC1 £23 ④❸❸
50-52 Long Ln 7796 4040 9–1B
This "decent" noodle bar, near Bart's, is hardly a 'destination';
if you find yourself in the area, though, it can make "a great
lunchtime venue". / www.apium.co.uk; 11 pm; closed Sun; no Amex.

Apostrophe £13 ❷❸❸
16 Regent St, SW1 7930 9922 3–3D NEW
23 Barrett St, W1 7355 1001 3–1A
40-41 Great Castle St, W1 7637 5700 3–1C NEW
20/20 Opt' Store, Tottenham Ct Rd, W1 7436 6688 2–1C
215 Strand, WC2 7427 9890 4–2D
42 Gt Eastern St, EC2 7739 8412 9–1D
3-5 St Bride St, EC4 7353 3704 9–2A
"Chic" (and "not cheap") French coffee shop/pâtisserie chain,
whose "inspired" "designer-sandwiches", "fantastic" coffee and
"wonderful pastries" inspire nothing but praise; "excellent bread
to take away" too. / www.apostropheuk.com; L & afternoon tea only, Barrett
St 8pm; no booking.

Aquasia
Conrad International SW10 £50 ④④④
Chelsea Harbour 7823 3000 5–4B
For an "unstressful" location, it's hard to beat the "lovely" marina-
side terrace of this Chelsea Harbour hotel, which serves "decent"
Med/Asian fusion cooking; when empty, though, the dining room
can feel "like a ghost town". / www.conradhotels.com; 10.30 pm.

Arancia SE16 £28 ❷❷❷
52 Southwark Park Rd 7394 1751 11–2A
"In the outer reaches of Bermondsey", this "intimate" and
homespun ten-year-old offers "a real taste of Italy", and its "rustic"
fare comes at "fantastic" prices. / 11 pm; closed Mon & Sun.

Arbutus W1 NEW £36 ❷❷❸
63-64 Frith St 7734 4545 4–2A
The ex-Putney Bridge team have created an "instant favourite" with
this "exceptional-value" Soho newcomer; it may look "simple"
décor, but the food ("between bistro and haute cuisine")
is "very impressive", and the wines – especially with the whole list
being available by the 250ml carafe – are "brilliant" too.
/ www.arbutusrestaurant.co.uk; 11 pm, Sun 9.30 pm.

Archduke Wine Bar SE1 £34 ⑤❷❸
Concert Hall Approach, South Bank 7928 9370 2–3D
Notably "improved" service is a feature of reports on this long-
established wine bar, in railway arches near the Festival Hall; if they
can now do something about the perennially "poor" scoff, this could
become quite a destination! / 11 pm; closed Sat L & Sun.

The Arches NW6 £34 ④❷❷
7 Fairhazel Gdns 7624 1867 8–2A
"Fantastic" wines at "reasonable mark-ups" are the main point
of all reports on this "magnificently idiosyncratic" Swiss Cottage
wine bar – "the food is fine, but not why you go". / 11 pm; no Amex;
set weekday L £18 (FP).

Archipelago W1 £49 ❷⓿⓿
110 Whitfield St 7383 3346 2–1B
"Weird and wonderful food in a ravishing setting" inspires "sheer
delight" in visitors to this "exotic" one-off near the Telecom Tower;
the "bizarre" menu – scorpion, bugs, kangaroo... – is "funky,
but actually rather well-cooked", and service doesn't miss a beat.
/ 10.30 pm; closed Sat L & Sun.

The Ark W8 £42 ❹❸❷
122 Palace Gardens Ter 7229 4024 6–2B
This "attractive shed", "tucked-away" near Notting Hill Gate, is a
"private and intimate" destination; fans of its "modern Italian" food
query "why it isn't more popular" – perhaps because it can seem
"pricey for what it is"? / www.thearkrestaurant.co.uk; 11 pm; closed
Mon L & Sun.

Arkansas Café E1 £25 ❷❹❹
107b Commercial St, Old Spitalfields Mkt 7377 6999 9–1D
For "first-class" burgers, steaks and ribs, "Bubba's your man!" –
his "rough and ready" American BBQ, in Spitalfields Market,
has many admirers. / L only, closed Sat; no Amex.

Armadillo E8 £34 ❷⓿❷
41 Broadway Mkt 7249 3633 1–2D
It's now operating as "a tapas-style bar", but this Hackney
"favourite" is "still the best place locally"; its Latin American dishes
are always "good value" and sometimes "amazing".
/ www.armadillorestaurant.co.uk; 10.30 pm; closed Mon, Tue L - Fri L & Sun.

Artigiano NW3 £44 ❹❹❹
12a Belsize Ter 7794 4288 8–2A
Fans praise its "consistency" and "good atmosphere", but critics –
who are becoming more vociferous – just find this Belsize Park
Italian "overpriced". / www.etruscarestaurants.com; 11 pm; closed Mon L.

L'Artista NW11 £25 ❸❷❸
917 Finchley Rd 8731 7501 1–1B
"Real Italian" style and "tasty", "basic" scoff make this "hectic"
pizza/pasta stop – "under the arches opposite the station" –
a long-standing linchpin of Golders Green life. / 11.30 pm.

L'Artiste Musclé W1 £34 ❹❷❷
1 Shepherd Mkt 7493 6150 3–4B
Being "slightly seedy and rather ramshackle" is all part of the
charm of this "friendly" and "very French" Shepherd Market bistro;
no one cares that the food is "nothing special". / 11 pm.

Arturo W2 £41 ❹❹❹
23 Connaught St 7706 3388 6–1D
"Off the beaten track" in Bayswater, this "smart and comfortable"
Italian yearling offers some "simple and well-executed" cooking;
"for the quality", though, it can seem "rather expensive".
/ www.arturorestaurant.co.uk; 10 pm.

As Greek As It Gets SW5 £22 ❹❹❺
233 Earl's Court Rd 7244 7777 5–2A
This Earl's Court café/take-away – originally planned as the
prototype of a chain – seems to have lost its way; fans say it offers
"a more modern approach to Greek food", but other reporters
"hoped for better". / www.asgreekasitgets.com; 11 pm; no Amex.

Asadal WC1 NEW £45 ❸④④
227 High Holborn   7430 9006   2–1D
*This new Korean basement beneath Holborn tube (a spin-off from
a long-standing New Malden establishment) is a "find" for most
reporters, thanks to its "good and authentic" food (in an area
"hardly overflowing with quality"); service, however, could be both
quicker and more informative. / 11 pm.*

Asia de Cuba
St Martin's Lane Hotel WC2 £73 ④④❸
45 St Martin's Ln   7300 5588   4–4C
*An "unbelievably pretentious" Covent Garden design-hotel dining
room, which offers "very exotic" – and often "delicious" – fusion
"sharing-platters"; service can be "appalling", though, and even
some fans find prices "absolutely overblown". / www.stmartinslane.com;
midnight, Sun 10.30 pm; set weekday L £47 (FP).*

Ask! Pizza £25 ④❸❸
Branches throughout London
*"Light and airy" branches and "helpful" staff are two hallmarks
of this successful national pizza chain; some tip it in preference
to PizzaExpress, but the ratings are pretty comparable overall.
/ www.askcentral.co.uk; 11 pm; some booking restrictions apply.*

Assaggi W2 £55 ❶❶❷
39 Chepstow Pl   7792 5501   6–1B
*Nino Sassu's "simple" but "truly inspired" cuisine and the
"excellent" service again makes this "amazing" room over
a Bayswater pub the survey's best Italian; the setting is "informal",
"noisy" and "cramped", but, as ever, the real problem is that it's
"impossible to get a table". / 11 pm; closed Sun; no Amex.*

Les Associés N8 £24 ❷❷❷
172 Park Rd   8348 8944   1–1C
*This "very, very French neighbourhood restaurant" offers
a "friendly" experience "like eating in someone's front room",
and "authentic" cuisine at "very fair" prices. / www.lesassocies.co.uk;
10 pm; Tue–Sat D only, closed Mon & Sun D; no booking, Sun.*

Astor Bar & Grill W1 NEW £60 ❺④④
20 Glasshouse St   7734 4888   3–3D
*If you want to check out "one of the best Art Deco interiors
in London", stick to the bar of this large basement operation near
Piccadilly Circus, which is not much changed from its days as the
Atlantic B&G (RIP) – too many reporters find its steaks and grills
"overpriced and disappointing". / www.astorbarandgrill.com; 11 pm;
D only; set pre theatre £36 (FP).*

L'Atelier de Robuchon WC2 NEW
13-15 West St   7010 8600   4–2B
*Joel Robuchon – one of the grand old men of French gastronomy –
has scheduled late-2006 for bringing his contemporary bistro
concept to the former Covent Garden site of East@West (RIP).*

The Atlas SW6 £33 ❷❸❷
16 Seagrave Rd   7385 9129   5–3A
*An "awesome" backstreet gastropub, near Earl's Court II, which –
with its "creative" Med-influenced cuisine – is often hailed as a
"true gem"; on the downside, it can be "a bit of a scrum".
/ www.theatlaspub.co.uk; 10.30 pm; no Amex; no booking.*

Atrium SW1   £40   ⑤⑤④
4 Millbank   7233 0032   2–4C
*"It's a great place for politico-spotting", but that's the only reason
to seek out this "airy" but desperately "uninspired" venture, at the
foot of the Westminster media centre.* / www.atriumrestaurant.com;
9.30 pm; closed Sat & Sun.

Aubaine SW3   £39   ⑤⑤❸
260-262a Brompton Rd   7052 0100   5–2C
*"Delicious bread and pastries aside", the food often "sounds better
than it turns out" at this South Kensington bakery/brasserie (which
is at its best for brunch); "surly but gorgeous" staff contribute to its
reputation in some quarters as "Totty Central".* / www.aubaine.co.uk;
10.30 pm.

Auberge   £35   ⑤④④
6-8 St Christopher's Pl, W1   7486 5557   3–1B
1 Sandell St, SE1   7633 0610   9–4A
31 Tooley St, SE1   7407 5267   9–4C
56 Mark Ln, EC3   7480 6789   9–3D
*A small chain (whose "handy" Sandell Street branch is "the best
rendezvous close to Waterloo"); it offers "basic" French food that's
"cheapish" but can be "disappointing".* / 10.30 pm; Sandell St closed
Sun & EC3 closed weekends.*

Aubergine SW10   £95   ❷❷❸
11 Park Wk   7352 3449   5–3B
*William Drabble's "top-notch, classic French food" ("with a few
intelligent twists"), a "stunning" wine list and "impeccable" service
come together to make this rather un-sung Chelsea fixture one
of London's best dining rooms; prices can appear "OTT", though,
and the setting strikes some reporters as "dull".*
/ www.auberginerestaurant.co.uk; 11 pm; closed Sat L & Sun; set weekday L
£38 (FP).*

Aurora W1   £38   ❸❸❷
49 Lexington St   7494 0514   3–2D
*"A nice little hideaway" in Soho – this "cramped" modern bistro
offers simple, slightly "adventurous" dishes in a "relaxed" and
"romantic" setting; there's also a "great garden for the summer".*
/ 10.30 pm; closed Sun.*

Aurora
Great Eastern Hotel EC2   £62
40 Liverpool St   7618 7000   9–2D
*The Conran empire withdrew from the management of this grand
"City lunching favourite" towards the end of the survey year, so a
rating seems inappropriate; the arrival as chef of Dominic Teague,
from L'Escargot, is a promising sign.* / www.aurora-restaurant.co.uk;
10 pm; closed Sat & Sun; booking: max 8; set weekday L £43 (FP).

Automat W1   £40   ④④❸
33 Dover St   7499 3033   3–3C
*With its "high-class American diner" looks, this "buzzy" joint
attracts a well-heeled Mayfair crowd; the food is "by no means out
of the ordinary", though, and "expensive" for what it is.*
/ www.automat-london.com; 11 pm, Sun 5 pm; closed Sun D.*

L'Aventure NW8 £50 ❷❷❶
3 Blenheim Ter 7624 6232 8–3A
"A veranda lit with sparkly lights" sets the "wonderfully romantic" tone at this "hidden-away" Gallic treasure in St John's Wood; service is "very personal" too, and the results from its "limited" menu of "French country-style" cuisine are generally "most enjoyable". / 11 pm; closed Sat L & Sun; set weekday L £34 (FP).

The Avenue SW1 £49 ④④④
7-9 St James's St 7321 2111 3–4D
It may be "impersonal" and "noisy", but the "consistent" standards of this large, '90s-"minimalist" mega-brasserie make it an ever-popular St James's business destination. / www.egami.co.uk; 10.45 pm; closed Sat L & Sun.

The Aviary SW20 £34 ❸❸❸
193 Worple Rd 8947 2212 10–2A
"Where would Raynes Park be" without this "simple" yearling? – there was the odd "disappointment" this year, but it generally provides a "relaxed" venue for "straightforward but tasty" fare in a "culinary desert". / www.the-aviary.co.uk; 9.30 pm; closed Mon.

Awana SW3 £42 ❸❸④
85 Sloane Ave 7584 8880 5–2C
This "sophisticated" new Chelsea Malaysian wins praise for its "delicious" dishes from an "interesting" menu; sceptics, though, find it "overpriced", or feel the cooking "needs work" to measure up to its ambitions. / www.awana.co.uk; 11.30 pm.

Axis WC2 £60 ❸❸④
1 Aldwych 7300 0300 2–2D
With its "convenient" location, "calm" design, "spacious" tables and "quality" cuisine, this "cavernous" Covent Garden basement makes a particularly "worthwhile business venue"; for other purposes, though, it can seem "uninspiring". / www.onealdwych.com; 10.45 pm; closed Sat L & Sun; set weekday L £41 (FP).

Aziz SW6 £36 ④④❷
24-32 Vanston Pl 7386 0086 5–4A
This "romantic" Moroccan, near Fulham Broadway is particularly of note for its "fantastic evening ambience"; like its deli-neighbour, it also makes a popular all-day stand-by for "great" (if not particularly Middle Eastern) breakfasts and so on. / www.delaziz.co.uk; 10.30 pm.

Azou W6 £28 ❸❷❸
375 King St 8563 7266 7–2B
"A long-time local favourite for excellent Moroccan food, friendly service and overall good value" – one reporter 'says it all' about this "authentic" Hammersmith café. / www.azou.co.uk; 11 pm; closed Sat L & Sun L.

Babes 'n' Burgers W11 £20 ❸④❸
275 Portobello Rd 7727 4163 6–1A
The kids' playroom (hence the 'Babes') "is no more" at this "cheap and cheerful" Notting Hill caff, which has also "dropped lots of the cranky veggie stuff from the menu" – what's left is the "willing but slow" delivery of OK burgers (and so on). / 11 pm, Sun 8 pm; no Amex; no booking, Sat L & Sun L.

Babur Brasserie SE23 £30 ❷⓿⓿
119 Brockley Rise   8291 2400   1–4D
After its recent major refurbishment, this "jewel of South East London" is "even better" – "this is no longer an upmarket curry house", but now "a fabulous Indian restaurant". / www.babur.info; 11.30 pm.

Babylon
Kensington Roof Gardens W8 £59 ④④⓿
99 Kensington High St   7368 3993   5–1A
"You can take a romantic stroll around the neighbouring Roof Gardens" after eating at Richard Branson's "elegant" ninth-floor Kensington vantage-point; the room has "wonderful" views, so it's perhaps no surprise that the food is "very average". / www.roofgardens.com; 11 pm; closed Sun D.

Back to Basics W1 £41 ⓿❸④
21a Foley St   7436 2181   2–1B
"Spanking fresh fish at very reasonable prices" has made a big hit of this "cramped" Fitzrovia bistro; "you can eat outside in summer, which is a real treat" – arrive early, though, as service gets "stretched". / www.backtobasics.uk.com; 10.30 pm; closed Sun.

Baker & Spice £35 ❷④④
54-56 Elizabeth St, SW1   7730 3033   2–4A
47 Denyer St, SW3   7589 4734   5–2D
75 Salusbury Rd, NW6   7604 3636   1–2B
"Some of the best bread and pastries in town" (and other "beautifully-prepared" fare) win acclaim for this small café/bakery chain, which has large communal tables for eating-in; service can seem "sloppy", though, especially when you consider the "astronomical" prices. / www.bakerandspice.com; 7 pm, Sun 5 pm; SW1 closed Sun; no Amex; no bookings.

Balans £34 ⑤④❸
34 Old Compton St, W1   7439 3309   4–2A
60 Old Compton St, W1   7439 2183   4–3A
239 Old Brompton Rd, SW5   7244 8838   5–3A
214 Chiswick High Rd, W4   8742 1435   7–2A
187 Kensington High St, W8   7376 0115   5–1A
For a "funky", "New York-style" brunch, these "jazzy" diners have a huge fan club extending well beyond their otherwise "predominantly gay" clientèle; at other times, though, the food "can be pretty awful" nowadays. / www.balans.co.uk; varies from midnight to 6 am; some booking restrictions apply.

Balham Kitchen & Bar SW12 £40 ④④❸
15-19 Bedford Hill   8675 6900   10–2C
It's no surprise that this "noisy and crowded" hang-out – backed by the owner of Soho House – is "chichi by Balham standards"; it seems ever-more complacent, though, attracting increasing gripes about "expensive" food and "aloof" service. / www.balhamkitchen.com; midnight; set weekday L £24 (FP).

Baltic SE1 £41 ❸❸❷
74 Blackfriars Rd   7928 1111   9–4A
"A cool bar" – featuring "fantastic home-made vodkas" – helps drive the "fun" atmosphere at this "stylish" and "airy" warehouse-conversion, "tucked-away" in Borough; the "filling" food is an interesting "take on traditional Polish cuisine". / www.balticrestaurant.co.uk; 11 pm; set weekday L £26 (FP).

Bam-Bou W1 £41 ❸❸❶
1 Percy St 7323 9130 2–1C
"Reminiscent of an opium den" – this "dark" and "stylish" Fitzrovia
townhouse makes "a perfect setting for romance"; the "eclectic"
oriental fare is "generally good" too, if rather eclipsed by the
"wonderful" cocktails in the top-floor bar. / www.bam-bou.co.uk; 11 pm;
closed Sat L & Sun; booking: max 6.

The Banana Leaf Canteen SW11 £26 ❷❷❸
75-79 Battersea Rise 7228 2828 10–2C
"Always busy and buzzy", this Battersea Thai offers "quick and
yummy" dishes and "superior" service ("for a canteen-style
operation"). / 11 pm; need 6+ to book.

Bangkok SW7 £31 ❷❷④
9 Bute St 7584 8529 5–2B
"I have been patronising this restaurant since 1972" – a report
typifying the loyalty inspired by this South Kensington canteen;
its "reliable and tasty" Thai fodder is "tweaked for Western tastes,
but none the worse for that". / 11 pm; closed Sun; no Amex.

Bank Aldwych WC2 £49 ④④④
1 Kingsway 7379 9797 2–2D
This vast, "clinical" and "noisy" late-'90s brasserie, on the fringe
of Covent Garden, remains popular as a breakfast, business lunch
or pre-theatre destination; for more serious dining, though, it can
seem plain "uninspiring" nowadays. / www.bankrestaurants.com; 11 pm;
closed Sun; set pre theatre £30 (FP).

Bank Westminster
St James Court Hotel SW1 £49 ④④❸
45 Buckingham Gate 7379 9797 2–4B
"A lack of eateries in the area" and "handiness for Whitehall" help
underpin support for this "large and buzzy" brasserie, near Buck
House; nowadays, it seems "slightly more sophisticated and less
noisy than its West End cousin". / www.bankrestaurants.com; 10.30 pm;
closed Sat L & Sun; set pre theatre £31 (FP).

Bankside £29 ④④④
32 Southwark Bridge Rd, SE1 7633 0011 9–4B
1 Angel Ct, Throgmorton St, EC2 0845 226 0011 9–2C
With their "excellent-value set menus", these functional modern
brasseries – near Tate Modern and Bank – "do the job" for
occasions such as "a work get-together"; otherwise, feedback
is rather mixed. / www.banksiderestaurants.co.uk; SE1 10.30 pm,
EC2 10 pm; SE1 closed Sat L & Sun, EC2 closed Sat & Sun.

Banners N8 £32 ❸❶❶
21 Park Rd 8348 2930 1–1C
"It's worth the trip to Crouch End from anywhere in north London",
says one of the many fans of this "exotic greasy spoon" –
a famously "excellent" place for weekend brunch. / 11.30 pm;
no Amex.

The Bar & Grill EC1 £42 ❸❸❸
2-3 West Smithfield 0870 4422 541 9–2A
A self-explanatory operation (from the operators behind 'Living
Room'), whose "stylish but affordable" charms make it a handy-
enough Smithfield "stand-by". / www.barandgrill.co.uk; 11 pm; closed Sun.

Bar Bourse EC4 £49 ④④④
67 Queen St 7248 2200 9–3C
You get "solid" cooking at this small basement near Mansion House – a "pricey" place, but one which even a critic concedes is "one of the less grey City options". / www.barbourse.co.uk; L only, closed Sat & Sun.

Bar Capitale £31 ❸❷④
The Concourse, 1 Poultry, EC2 7248 3117 9–2C
Bucklersbury Hs, 14 Walbrook, EC4 7236 2030 9–3C
"A good place for a bite after a late finish" – for overworked City types, these "authentic" Italians deliver "excellent-quality" pizza at "cheap prices". / www.mithrasbars.co.uk; 10 pm; closed Sat & Sun.

Bar du Musée SE10 £38 ⑤⑤❸
17 Nelson Rd 8858 4710 1–3D
With its "bright" conservatory and "good terrace", this Greenwich bar/restaurant is a potentially "lovely" destination; "confused" service and "disappointing" food, though, sometimes make it seem simply "appalling". / www.bardumusee.co.uk; 10 pm; no Amex.

Bar Estrela SW8 £23 ❸❸❷
111-115 South Lambeth Rd 7793 1051 10–1D
"Shut out the dreary Vauxhall view" and "you could be in downtown Lisbon" when you sit outside this ever-buzzing local linchpin; the "solid" cooking is authentically "unspectacular", but it's "tasty" and "doesn't cost the earth". / 11 pm.

Bar Italia W1 £18 ④❷❶
22 Frith St 7437 4520 4–2A
"Great people-watching" – 24/7, and especially when there's footie on the TV – plus "fast shots of excellent espresso" are what this Soho café "classic" is all about; the paninis and so on are incidental. / open 24 hours, Sun 3 am; no booking.

Bar Shu W1 NEW £37 ❷④④
28 Frith St 7287 6688 4–3A
"Sensational" Sichuanese cooking ("untempered to western tastes") has instantly made a "raging success" of this much-hyped Soho newcomer; dishes can "miss the mark", though, service is "poor", and the setting is "noisy" and "uncomfortable". / 11.30 pm; no Amex.

Barcelona Tapas £26 ④⑤❸
481 Lordship Ln, SE22 8693 5111 1–4D
1a Bell Ln, E1 7247 7014 9–2D
1 Beaufort Hs, St Botolph St, EC3 7377 5111 9–2D
24 Lime St, EC3 7929 2389 9–2D
13 Well Ct, EC4 7329 5111 9–2B
These "reliable" tapas bars offer an "authentic" ambience (which "seems a surprise in out-of-the-way Dulwich, less so in the City"); the food's "not bad" – pity the same can't be said about the "hit-and-miss" service. / 10.30 pm; City branches closed Sat & Sun.

Barnes Grill SW13 NEW £37
2-3 Rock's Ln 8878 4488 10–1A
Wozza's self-explanatory newcomer opened shortly before this guide went to press; we didn't manage to fit in a visit, but it would be surprising if it was very different from its predecessors, Notting Grill and Kew Grill. / www.awtonline.co.uk; 10.30 pm; closed Mon L.

The Barnsbury N1 £34 ❷❷❷
209-211 Liverpool Rd 7607 5519 8–2D
This "convivial" Islington spot is "a real joy" for the very many locals who comment on it – "a great gastropub, with very reasonable prices". / www.thebarnsbury.co.uk; 10 pm.

Base £33 ❸❹❸
61 Beauchamp Pl, SW3 7584 2777 5–1C
195 Baker St, NW1 7486 7000 2–1A
71 Hampstead High St, NW3 7431 2224 8–2A
"A good selection of wraps, fish dishes, pastas and meat items" make these contemporary bistros a versatile choice for a "casual" bite. / www.basefoods.com; 10.45 pm, SW3 7 pm; NW3 closed Mon D.

Basilico £30 ❷❸❹
690 Fulham Rd, SW6 0800 028 3531 10–1B
26 Penton St, N1 0800 093 4224 8–3D
515 Finchley Rd, NW3 0800 316 2656 1–1B
175 Lavender Hill, SW11 0800 389 9770 10–2C
178 Upper Richmond Rd, SW14 0800 096 8202 10–2B
Thanks to its "beautifully-made thin-crust pizza" and "swift" delivery, this remains "the best take-away pizza chain in town" for many reporters. / www.basilico.co.uk; 11pm; no Amex; no booking.

Bastille N1 £32 ❹❹❹
100 St Paul's Rd 7704 2345 1–1C
It's not without admirers, but the cooking can be "more miss than hit" at this "noisy" Gallic gastropub, in Canonbury. / 10.30 pm; closed weekday L.

Bavarian Beerhouse EC1 NEW £33 ❹❷❷
190 City Rd 7608 0925 9–1C
A feeling of promise unfulfilled hangs over this basic Bavarian basement Bierhalle, recently opened near Moorfields Eye Hospital; you might expect the food to be "subordinate to the beer", but – even on the latter front – the range can seem disappointing. / www.bavarian-beerhouse.co.uk; 10 pm.

Beach Blanket Babylon W11 £46 ❺❺❷
45 Ledbury Rd 7229 2907 6–1B
A Gothic interior that "looks like a weird film set" helps create a "lively and sociable" buzz at this Notting Hill stalwart; "go and see it", and have a drink too if you want, but "avoid the food" – it can be "utter rubbish". / www.beachblanket.co.uk; midnight; no Amex.

Beauberry House
Belair Park SE21 £46 ❹❹❹
Gallery Rd, Dulwich Village 8299 9788 1–4C
Recently revamped in pretentious contemporary style, this beautiful Georgian mansion near Dulwich Park (formerly Belair House, RIP) "still doesn't know what it's trying to be"; its "fusion-esque" French/Japanese fare can be "first-rate", but – like all other aspects of the operation – inspired very mixed early-days commentary. / www.beauberryhouse.co.uk; 10.30 pm; closed Sun D; no Amex; set weekday L £30 (FP).

Beaufort House SW3 £35 ④❸❷
354 King's Rd 7352 2828 5–3C
"A great place for Sunday brunch with the papers on a cosy sofa"
– otherwise, this year-old Chelsea operation is mainly of interest
as a bar. / www.chelseaavenues.com; L only, bar menu available at D;
no trainers.

Bedford & Strand WC2 NEW £34 ④❸④
1a Bedford St 7836 3033 4–4D
A new basement wine bar in Covent Garden that's an ideal venue
for sinking an interesting bottle (or two) of vino; on the evidence
of our early-days visit, however, we'd suggest you planned on eating
elsewhere – neither the food nor the atmosphere are up to the
prices. / Rated on Editors' visit; www.bedford-strand.com; 11 pm; closed Sun.

Bedlington Café W4 £21 ❸④④
24 Fauconberg Rd 8994 1965 7–2A
Under new owners, this "scruffy" café in darkest Chiswick is still
a "good-value" destination; it now gives no hint, however, that it
was once a Mecca for lovers of Thai cuisine; (licensed or you can
BYO). / 10 pm; closed Sun L; no credit cards.

Beirut Express W2 £22 ❷④④
112-114 Edgware Rd 7724 2700 6–1D
"It's always full, but they manage to squeeze you in" at this "lively"
Bayswater pit stop, "most frequented by locals"; it serves "excellent
value" Lebanese kebabs, salads and juices. / www.maroush.com; 1 am;
no credit cards.

Beiteddine SW1 £42 ❸❸④
8 Harriet St 7235 3969 5–1D
"A good, solid Lebanese restaurant", just off Sloane Street; fans say
"it's as good as in Beirut" – others just notice the "terrible lighting".
/ www.beiteddinerestaurant.com; midnight.

Belgo £31 ④④❸
50 Earlham St, WC2 7813 2233 4–2C
72 Chalk Farm Rd, NW1 7267 0718 8–2B
"Amazing" Belgian Beers are "the reason to go" to these "quick",
"noisy" and "busy" moules-frites halls, decked out in '90s
"industrial chic"; the food can be "barely satisfactory", though,
and the staff "often seem to be in a bad mood".
/ www.belgo-restaurants.com; 11.30 pm, Mon-Thu 11 pm.

Bellamy's W1 £63 ❸❷❸
18-18a Bruton Pl 7491 2727 3–2B
Gavin Rankin's "discreet" mews brasserie yearling has become
a popular troughing spot for well-heeled Mayfair types –
its "very professional" staff serve up "proper straightforward food"
accompanied by "top wines with remarkably low mark-ups".
/ 10.30 pm; closed Sat L & Sun.

Belvedere W8 £52 ❸❷❶
Holland Pk, off Abbotsbury Rd 7602 1238 7–1D
A location "to die for" and an interior "straight out of a glamorous
'40s movie" make MPW's Holland Park "oasis" a notably "grand"
place to eat (especially for lunch); "top-class" service and
"competent" cooking play honourable supporting rôles. / 10 pm;
closed Sun D; set weekday L £37 (FP).

Ben's Thai
The Warrington Hotel W9   £24   ❸❹❸
93 Warrington Cr   7266 3134   8–4A
It's the setting – on the first floor of a palatial Maida Vale pub –
which makes this Thai fixture of note; the food is generally
"reliable". / 10 pm; D only; no Amex.

Benares W1   £50   ❷❷❸
12 Berkeley Hs, Berkeley Sq   7629 8886   3–3B
Atul Kochar's "subtle" modern cuisine makes his "hidden-away"
Mayfair three-year-old one of London's better 'nouvelle Indians';
the "windowless" first-floor setting is "luxurious", but can seem
a little "sterile". / www.benaresrestaurant.com; 10.30 pm; closed Sun L;
set weekday L £34 (FP).

Bengal Clipper SE1   £31   ❸❸❷
Shad Thames   7357 9001   9–4D
"An airy yet intimate setting, with regular piano accompaniment"
creates a "calming" ambience at this popular South Bank Indian;
it generally offers "high-quality" cooking and "efficient" service,
but both can be "patchy". / www.bengalclipper.co.uk; 11.30 pm.

Bengal Quay E14   £27   ❸❷④
1-2 Beauforts Ct, Admiral Way   7515 3378   11–1C
An inexpensive Indian, where the setting is contemporary, but the
cuisine is pretty traditional; it's a useful informal lunch venue, a few
minutes' walk from Canary Wharf. / 11.45 pm.

Benihana   £53   ④④④
37 Sackville St, W1   7494 2525   3–3D
77 King's Rd, SW3   7376 7799   5–3D
100 Avenue Rd, NW3   7586 9508   8–2A
This "pseudo-Japanese teppan-yaki entertainment" is beginning
to look rather tired – the "antics of the chefs" can still be a hit with
kids, but you pay a "high price" for "mediocre" service and food
that's "average at best". / www.benihana.co.uk; 10.30 pm.

Bentley's W1   £55   ❷❷❸
11-15 Swallow St   7734 4756   3–3D
"Great to see a grand old dame back on top form" – Richard
Corrigan's "splendid revival" of this "clubby" Mayfair fish specialist
has quickly gathered an enormous following; it's the "vibrant"
ground-floor oyster bar which is "the star", though – the somewhat
"stuffy" restaurant upstairs is "less consistent".
/ www.bentleysoysterbarandgrill.co.uk; 10.30 pm; booking: max 12.

Benugo   £13   ❷❸④
14 Curzon St, W1   7629 6246   3–4B
23-25 Gt Portland St, W1   7631 5052   3–1C
V&A Museum, Cromwell Rd, SW7   7581 2159   5–2C
116 St John St, EC1   7253 3499   9–1A
82 City Rd, EC1   7253 1295   9–1C
"Why aren't there more of these places?" – this "smart"
sandwiches-and-so-on chain is "a cut above the rest"; they do
"great" coffee too. / www.benugo.com; L & afternoon tea only; W1 & EC1
branches closed Sat & Sun; W1 & EC1 branches, no credit cards.

Beotys WC2   £46   ④❷❸
79 St Martin's Ln   7836 8768   4–3B
*For its devoted clientèle, the Frangos family's Theatreland stalwart –
with its quirky Franco/Greek fare, its "consistent" service and its
quiet and civilised interior – is an "ideal fall back"; in fact,
"the place is practically a private club… and the food is just
as bad". / 11.30 pm; closed Sun.*

Berkeley Square W1   £64
7 Davies St   7629 6993   3–3B
*This ambitious but rather unatmospheric Mayfair restaurant
changed hands towards the end of our survey period; although the
chef remains, we've left it unrated pending a proper appraisal
of the new régime next year. / www.theberkeleysquare.com; 10 pm; closed
Sat & Sun; set weekday L £40 (FP).*

Bermondsey Kitchen SE1   £34   ④④❸
194 Bermondsey St   7407 5719   9–4D
*This "nice", "bright" and "happy" eatery has won a name locally
for its "quality brunches" and "great-value", "Spanish-influenced"
food; critics, though, say it's "gone off the boil", and is now
"very ordinary". / www.bermondseykitchen.co.uk; 10.30 pm; closed Sun D.*

Bertorelli's   £42   ⑤④④
11-13 Frith St, W1   7494 3491   4–2A
19-23 Charlotte St, W1   7636 4174   2–1C
44a Floral St, WC2   7836 3969   4–2D
15 Mincing Ln, EC3   7283 3028   9–3D
1 Plough Pl, EC4   7842 0510   9–2A
*An "anodyne" Italian chain that "has really lost its way" – it offers
"bland" cuisine, and its staff sometimes "chat rather than serve".
/ www.santeonline.co.uk; 9.30 pm-midnight; WC2 & Charlotte St closed Sun,
EC4 closed Sat & Sun.*

Best Mangal W14   £24   ❷❸④
104 North End Rd   7610 1050   7–2D
*"Hidden behind a take-away" near West Kensington tube,
this Turkish joint offers "simple" and "unbelievably cheap" kebabs
cooked "at a BBQ in the centre of the room"; ("there's an almost
indistinguishable sister branch 100 yards away"). / midnight.*

Bevis Marks EC3   £47   ❷①❷
4 Heneage Ln   7283 2220   9–2D
*"London's best kosher restaurant" occupies an "original" setting –
an intriguing annexe built onto an historic City synagogue;
its "varied" modern cuisine is realised to a "consistently high
standard", and service is very professional.
/ www.bevismarkstherestaurant.com; 7.30 pm; closed Fri D, Sat & Sun.*

Bibendum SW3   £67   ❸❷❷
81 Fulham Rd   7581 5817   5–2C
*With its "beautiful, relaxed and calm" '80s design (seen at its best
on a sunny lunchtime) and its "simply amazing" wine list,
this Brompton Cross landmark is still a "lovely" place to eat;
its "pricey" food is generally rated somewhere between "very good"
and "not outstanding". / www.bibendum.co.uk; 11.30 pm; booking:
max 12; set weekday L £47 (FP).*

Bibendum Oyster Bar SW3 £38 ❸❸❸
81 Fulham Rd 7589 1480 5–2C
*"For fresh crustacea" – not least "beautiful oysters" – the "lively"
bar at the entrance to the Chelsea Conran Shop remains
a "safe bet". / www.bibendum.co.uk; 10.30 pm.*

Big Easy SW3 £44 ❸❸❸
332-334 King's Rd 7352 4071 5–3C
*"It's a bit themey" and you have to be prepared to pay "Chelsea
prices", but this "pretty authentic American all-rounder" can offer
"a fun night out" – you get "filling" fodder to the accompaniment
of a live band (downstairs). / www.bigeasy.uk.com; 11.20 pm, Fri & Sat
12.20 am.*

Bistro 1 £18 ❹❷❸
27 Frith St, W1 7734 6204 4–3A **NEW**
75 Beak St, W1 7287 1840 3–2D
33 Southampton St, WC2 7379 7585 4–3D
*For "three courses for under a tenner", you "can't go wrong" at this
"cheap and cheerful" bistro chain. / www.bistro1.co.uk; 11.30 pm.*

Bistro Aix N8 £39 ❸❸❹
54 Topsfield Pde, Tottenham Ln 8340 6346 8–1C
*Fans say this popular Crouch End local offers "everything you would
expect from a French bistro"; at the à la carte prices, though, it can
seem "pricey" for what it is. / www.bistroaix.co.uk; 11 pm; closed Mon;
set always available £26 (FP).*

Bistrot 190 SW7 £39 ❺❺❹
190 Queen's Gate 7584 6601 5–1B
*"For a pre-Proms dinner", this once well-known brasserie, near the
Albert Hall, may be worth knowing about; feedback has shrunk
almost to nothing, though, and some reporters have found
standards "shockingly poor". / www.gorehotel.com; 11 pm.*

Bistrothèque E2 £38 ❹❸❸
23-27 Wadeson St 8983 7900 1–2D
*This "cool and funky factory-conversion" has the potential to be
"a real Bethnal Green gem"; its menu is "sloppily executed",
though, and "ordinary for the price". / www.bistrotheque.com; 10.30 pm;
closed weekday L.*

Black & Blue £41 ❸❸❹
90-92 Wigmore St, W1 7486 1912 3–1A
105 Gloucester Rd, SW7 7244 7666 5–2B
215-217 Kensington Church St, W8 7727 0004 6–2B
205-207 Haverstock Hill, NW3 7443 7744 8–2A
1-2 Rochester Walk, SE1 7357 9922 9–4C
*"If you love beef", this moderately "stylish" chain is of note for its
"upmarket" burgers and its very "decent" steak and chips. / 11 pm,
Fri & Sat 11.30 pm; no booking.*

Blah! Blah! Blah! W12 £25 ❸❸❸
78 Goldhawk Rd 8746 1337 7–1C
*"Crayons on tables bring out your inner artist", at this stalwart BYO
veggie in Shepherd's Bush; the year which saw a new owner
establish himself has been a bit "hit-and-miss", but its "wholesome"
and "creative" cooking generally seems to have held up.
/ www.gonumber.com/2524; 11 pm; closed Sun; no credit cards.*

Blakes
Blakes Hotel SW7 £101 ④❸❶
33 Roland Gdns 7370 6701 5–2B
Much "hand-holding under the table" goes on at this datedly
"romantic" South Kensington basement (which is best "if you can
stay the night too"); its "light" fusion cuisine evoked "the mystery
of the orient" for one reporter, but the real mystery here is how
they get away with the prices... / www.blakeshotel.com; 11 pm.

Blandford Street W1 £43 ④❸④
5-7 Blandford St 7486 9696 2–1A
"Despite at least two make-overs since its Stephen Bull days",
this "awkward" Marylebone venture still strikes many reporters
as "dull" – a shame, as fans continue to plug its "interesting"
English cooking. / www.blandford-street.co.uk; 10.30 pm; closed Sat L & Sun.

BLEEDING HEART EC1 £46 ❷❷❷
Bleeding Heart Yd, Greville St 7242 8238 9–2A
"For business, romance or pleasure", this "quirky" but "brilliant"
Gallic all-rounder – a rambling bar, bistro and basement restaurant,
"tucked-away in a Holborn courtyard" – is a true "perennial
favourite"; the food is "remarkably consistent" too, and the wine list
"outstanding". / www.bleedingheart.co.uk; 10 pm; closed Sat & Sun.

Blue Elephant SW6 £47 ❸❷❶
3-6 Fulham Broadway 7385 6595 5–4A
"OTT", "virtual jungle" décor – complete with "flowing streams and
real fish" – has long made this "unexpected" fixture in deepest
Fulham quite a "wow" destination, especially for romance; perhaps
surprisingly, the food can be "stunning" too (but it's also sometimes
rather "standard" nowadays). / www.blueelephant.com; midnight; closed
Sat L; set weekday L £29 (FP).

Blue Jade SW1 £28 ④❷④
44 Hugh St 7828 0321 2–4B
"Old-fashioned but still enjoyable", this Thai local in the Pimlico
backstreets is a "friendly" destination, if sometimes "lacking buzz".
/ 11 pm; closed Sat L & Sun.

Blue Kangaroo SW6 £29 ④④④
555 King's Rd 7371 7622 5–4B
"Kids love" this Chelsea hang-out, which has a soft-play zone in the
basement; the adult fare isn't too bad but "at the prices, could
be better". / www.thebluekangaroo.co.uk; 6.30 pm.

The Blue Pumpkin SW17 £29 ④❸❸
16-18 Ritherdon Rd 8767 2660 10–2C
"For a standard bistro supper", this "consistently good" Tooting
local is worth bearing in mind. / www.bluepumpkin.co.uk; 10.30 pm.

Bluebird SW3 £51 ⑤⑤⑤
350 King's Rd 7559 1000 5–3C
"Dreary" food, "very plain" décor and "awful" service – Conran
Restaurants deserves some sort of special award for its consistently
criminal mismanagement of this Chelsea landmark.
/ www.conran.com/eat; 10.30 pm; set weekday L £29 (FP).

Bluebird Café SW3 £33 ⑤⑤④
350 King's Rd 7559 1000 5–3C
"It's always busy, why?", say those who've encountered "some of London's worst-ever food and service" at Conran's Chelsea café; must have something to do with the "good people-watching" and the "lovely terrace for a sunny day". / www.conran.com/eat; 10 pm, Sun 6 pm; no booking.

Bluebird Club & Dining Rooms SW3 £48 ④④④
Beaufort St 7559 1129 5–3C
Tom Conran's year-old partnership with his dad at this Chelsea club dining room (now open to the public) risks coming off the rails – a few fans do laud its "sophisticated" style and "top-notch British classics", but critics complain of "murdered" food in a "sparse" environment. / www.conran.com/eat; 10.30 pm; D only, closed Sun.

Blueprint Café
Design Museum SE1 £48 ④④❸
28 Shad Thames, Butler's Wharf 7378 7031 9–4D
"Marvellous views" (of Tower Bridge and the Thames) reward visitors to this "light and sunny" first-floor dining room; unfortunately, they are "better than the food", which suffers from "rather OTT pricing". / www.conran.com/eat; 10.45 pm.

Bodean's £32 ❸❸❸
10 Poland St, W1 7287 7575 3–1D
Fulham Broadway, SW6 7610 0440 5–4A **NEW**
169 Clapham High St, SW4 7622 4248 10–2D
For "a pretty authentic American BBQ" ("be prepared to get messy"), this US-inspired mini-chain offers a total "meat-fest" at "decent prices", plus "American sports on the TV". / www.bodeansbbq.com; 11 pm.

Bohème Kitchen & Bar W1 £38 ❸④❸
19 Old Compton St 7734 5656 4–2A
This "trendy but relaxed" Soho bar/bistro is less frenetic than its neighbour, Café Bohème; culinary highlights include "great burgers", and – more surprisingly – a "tender and delicious" Chateaubriand. / www.bohemekitchen.co.uk; midnight.

Boiled Egg & Soldiers SW11 £20 ❸④④
63 Northcote Rd 7223 4894 10–2C
"Always a good cure for a hangover" – "if you can get in, that is"; this Battersea caff – unofficial rallying point for the nannies of the neighbouring Nappy Valley – has quite a name for its "fantastic" full English breakfasts. / 6.30 pm, Sun 4 pm; L & afternoon tea only; no Mastercard or Amex; no booking.

Boisdale SW1 £51 ❸❷❶
13-15 Eccleston St 7730 6922 2–4B
"The atmosphere's so good, you can forgive the loud tartan and stag horns" at this "hard-to-classify" but "very clubbable" Scottish fixture in Belgravia; live jazz spices up an essentially "old school" formula of "excellent" meat and game, plus a "comprehensive" choice of wine, whisky and cigars. / www.boisdale.co.uk; 11.15 pm; closed Sat L & Sun; set weekday L £35 (FP).

Boisdale of Bishopsgate EC2   £45   ④④④
202 Bishopsgate, Swedeland Ct   7283 1763   9–2D
"Unimaginative" food and sometimes "abysmal" service make this
"Scottish-themed" City bar/restaurant a pale shadow of the
Belgravia original; the main basement restaurant can seem "dingy",
but it is at least "well-spaced". / www.boisdale.co.uk; 9.30 pm; closed
Sat & Sun.

The Bollo House W4   £31   ④④❸
13-15 Bollo Ln   8994 6037   7–2A
This "light and airy" Chiswick-fringe gastropub still has its fans,
but sagging ratings support those who say it has "really
deteriorated" of late. / 10 pm; no Amex.

Bombay Bicycle Club   £35   ❷❸④
128 Holland Park Ave, W11   7727 7335   6–2A
3a Downshire Hill, NW3   7435 3544   8–2A
95 Nightingale Ln, SW12   8673 6217   10–2C
"Light", "fresh" and "well-crafted" curries are the cornerstone
of the success of this growing Indian chain; newer branches aren't
great shakes on the ambience front, but the Wandsworth original
is still seen as an "attractive" and "classy" destination.
/ www.thebombaybicycleclub.co.uk; 11 pm; D only ex NW3 & W11 Sun open
L & D.

Bombay Brasserie SW7   £55   ❸❸❸
Courtfield Close, Gloucester Rd   7370 4040   5–2B
"Faded colonial grandeur" lives on at this vast South Kensington
subcontinental (where the most prized seats are in the
conservatory); survey performance is middling, but for devotees this
is "still one of the best Indians" (and there's a "brilliant Sunday
buffet"). / www.bombaybrasserielondon.com; 11.30 pm.

Bombay Palace W2   £42   ❶❶❸
50 Connaught St   7723 8855   6–1D
"The dull room doesn't do justice" to this "hidden jewel in the
crown of Indian cuisine", north of Hyde Park; "even those who
aren't usually curry-aficionados" may fall for its "true" cuisine and
"fabulous and personable" service. / www.bombay-palace.co.uk;
11.30 pm.

Bonds
Threadneedles Hotel EC2   £60   ④④④
5 Threadneedle St   7657 8088   9–2C
An "airy" former City banking hall, which generally makes
"a reliable, if unexciting, business lunch haunt"; prices are "hefty",
though, and service can sometimes be "slow" or "arrogant".
/ www.theetoncollection.com; 10 pm; closed Sat & Sun.

Il Bordello E1   £39   ❶❶❷
75-81 Wapping High St   7481 9950   11–1A
The "pizzas are as big as bike wheels" and the staff are
"bonhomie personified", at this "cramped", "buzzing" and "family-
friendly" Wapping Italian. / 11 pm; closed Sat L.

La Bouchée SW7   £41   ❷❸❷
56 Old Brompton Rd   7589 1929   5–2B
For a "buzzy" and "romantic" atmosphere, this "cramped" and
"noisy" South Kensington bistro "always comes up trumps";
its "traditional" Gallic fare has had its ups-and-downs over the
years, but is currently "very much back on song". / 11 pm.

Le Bouchon Bordelais SW11 £42 ❷❷❷
5-9 Battersea Rise   7738 0307   10–2C
*Michel Roux's involvement was very much more in evidence this
year at this "atmospheric" Battersea bistro veteran, which achieved
all-round praise for its "authentic" Gallic cooking and its "fabulous"
("very French") service. / www.lebouchon.co.uk; 11 pm; set weekday L
£21 (FP).*

Boudin Blanc W1 £44 ❸❸❷
5 Trebeck St   7499 3292   3–4B
*This "reliable" and extremely popular old-favourite, in Shepherd
Market, is the epitome of a "cosy" and "romantic" bistro, serving
"hearty" French fare in a "buzzing" setting; "perfect" outside tables
for the summer. / www.boudinblanc.co.uk; 11 pm; set weekday L £28 (FP).*

Boulevard WC2 £37 ❹❸❹
40 Wellington St   7240 2992   4–3D
*"A useful little stop" that's "worth knowing about in Covent
Garden" – "crowded and fun", it serves food that's only "average",
but also "reliable" and "not too expensive".
/ www.boulevardbrasserie.co.uk; midnight.*

Boulevard Bar & Dining Room W1 NEW £37 ❸❹❸
55-59 Old Compton St   7287 0770   4–3A
*A "fantastic" heart-of-Soho location helps make this "lively" new
offshoot of the long-standing Covent Garden brasserie
a "wonderful" destination for younger-at-heart reporters; feedback,
though, is rather up-and-down. / www.boulevard-dining-room.co.uk;
10.50 pm; booking essential; set weekday L £23 (FP).*

Boxwood Café The Berkeley SW1 £57 ❹❸❹
Wilton Pl   7235 1010   5–1D
*It has its fans (especially for lunch), but feedback on Ramsay's
Knightsbridge basement brasserie is becoming very mixed;
"is Gordon spreading himself too thin?", asks one reporter – given
the high proportion of 'disappointing' meals recorded here, it might
begin to seem so. / www.gordonramsay.com; 11 pm; booking: max 8;
set weekday L £39 (FP).*

The Brackenbury W6 £37 ❷❷❷
129-131 Brackenbury Rd   8748 0107   7–1C
*This "snug" fixture in a "villagey" Hammersmith backwater is the
epitome of "an excellent local restaurant" (and boasts "a wonderful
al fresco terrace" too); "very competent" cooking and "a well-
priced wine list" are served without fanfare by "helpful" staff.
/ 10.45 pm; closed Sat L & Sun D.*

Bradley's NW3 £41 ❸❸❹
25 Winchester Rd   7722 3457   8–2A
*"The cooking's improved" again at this tucked-away Swiss Cottage
spot, whose ambience is somewhere between "stylish" and "dead";
even fans, though, concede "it's quite expensive" for what it is.
/ 11 pm; closed Mon, Sat L & Sun D; set weekday L £25 (FP).*

Brady's SW18 £22 ❸❷❸
513 Old York Rd   8877 9599   10–2B
*The Brady family's "basic, but always buzzing" fish-and-chip bistro
is an ever-popular Wandsworth destination; cooking standards this
year, though, were a bit more up-and-down than usual. / 10.30 pm;
D only, closed Sun; no Amex; no booking.*

La Brasserie SW3   £43   ④④❷
272 Brompton Rd   7581 3089   5–2C
The style of this '70s Brompton Cross veteran is "Parisian" in every respect (including staff "attitude"); it remains a "buzzy" spot – especially for weekend brunch – but at other times can just seem "old, tired and careless". / 11 pm; no booking, Sat L & Sun L.

La Brasserie
Ma Cuisine Bourgeoise TW1 NEW   £40
2 Whitton Rd   8744 9610   1–4A
Feedback is scant on the relaunch of this once-posh dining room (McClements, RIP) near Twickenham station (which we've therefore left unrated); a couple of early reports, though, hail its simpler, cheaper brasserie style as "a real return to form". / 10.30 pm; closed Sun.

Brasserie Roux
Sofitel St James SW1   £45   ❸❸❸
8 Pall Mall   7968 2900   2–3C
"For business lunches and pre-theatre suppers", this "formal" Gallic brasserie – in an "elegant" former banking hall, near Trafalgar Square – is well worth knowing about; for more convivial occasions, its attractions are a little less obvious. / www.sofitelstjames.com; 11.30 pm.

Brasserie St Quentin SW3   £43   ❸❷❸
243 Brompton Rd   7589 8005   5–2C
This "handsome" brasserie veteran lives in the shadow these days of its Knightsbridge neighbour, Racine; its "reassuring" charm and "well-priced" menu, however, still make it an ideal stand-by "for middle-class people who want to eat French food 'nicely'". / www.brasseriestquentin.co.uk; 10.30 pm.

Bread & Roses SW4   £25   ④④❸
68 Clapham Manor St   7498 1779   10–1D
The "very child-friendly" Sunday lunch is a particular feature at this "simple" but "welcoming" co-op-run boozer, near Clapham Common, which benefits from a "lovely garden". / 9.30 pm; no Amex; no booking.

Brew Wharf SE1   £30   ④⑤④
Brew Wharf Yd, 1 Stoney St   7378 6601   9–4C
It occupies "a great space" (in converted railway arches) and offers "good beers", but this large South Bank beer-hall/bistro otherwise "misses all round" – "staff lack interest" and prices seem "inflated". / www.brewwharf.com; 9.30 pm.

Brian Turner
Millennium Hotel W1   £61   ④④⑤
44 Grosvenor Sq   7596 3444   3–2A
Fans insist that TV-chef Turner – often present – "gives a feeling of real care" towards his guests at this "bland" Mayfair dining room; its never gathered much of following among reporters, though, and feedback is rather up-and-down. / 10.30 pm; closed Sat L & Sun.

Brick Lane Beigel Bake E1   £5   ❸④⑤
159 Brick Ln   7729 0616   1–2D
"The queue alone tells you that the beigels must be special" – particularly the "unbeatable salt-beef" ones – at this "amazingly cheap" East End institution; it's "always buzzing" ("even at 3am"). / www.beigelbakery.co.uk; open 24 hours; no credit cards; no booking.

The Bridge SW13 £35 ❸❸❸
204 Castelnau 8563 9811 7–2C
*Just south of Hammersmith Bridge, this "relaxed" gastropub
provides "pretty decent" cooking, and has a "great garden" too.
/ 10.30 pm.*

Brilliant UB2 £31 ❷❷❷
72-76 Western Rd 8574 1928 1–3A
*This "old-favourite" Punjabi, lost in the suburbs around Southall,
is still "hard to beat" – even a reporter who thought the food
"unmemorable" found a meal here "a fantastic experience"
("Bollywood movies included"). / www.brilliantrestaurant.com; 11.30 pm;
closed Mon, Sat L & Sun L; booking: weekends only.*

Brinkley's SW10 £34 ❹❸❷
47 Hollywood Rd 7351 1683 5–3B
*"A buzzing atmosphere every night of the week" shows that the
"fun" Chelsea flagship of John Brinkley's empire is a real "local
favourite"; "you don't really come here for the food", though –
it's more to do with the "dating scene" and the "fantastic-value"
wine list. / www.brinkleys.com; 11.30 pm; closed weekday L.*

Britannia W8 £35 ❸❷❸
1 Allen St 7937 6905 5–1A
*It's not often you find a "hidden masterpiece" in a "useful location";
this "wonderful new gastropub" has risen "from the ashes of a
venerable old boozer", in a Kensington side street, and serves
"serious" food at "reasonable prices". / www.britanniakensington.co.uk;
10.30 pm.*

**(The Court)
British Museum WC1** £36
Gt Russell St 7323 8990 2–1C
*Not before time, new caterers have been brought in at this
potentially splendid restaurant – in the glazed Great Court of the
museum – as our survey for the year was drawing to a close; let's
hope that they make a better fist of it than the last lot – it wouldn't
be difficult! / www.britishmuseum.co.uk; Thu & Fri 8.30 pm; L only, Thu-Fri
open L & D; no Amex.*

La Brocca NW6 £29 ❹❸❷
273 West End Ln 7433 1989 1–1B
*"A strong local following" supports this "homely" basement Italian,
lauding its "great pizza and pasta"; doubters, however, find it ever-
more "average". / 11 pm; booking: max 8.*

**The Grill
Brown's Hotel W1** NEW £75 ❹❷❹
Albemarle St 7493 6020 3–3C
*For fans, Rocco Forte's new Mayfair grill represents the "rebirth
of grand hotel dining", and its "old-fashioned" approach pleases
many reporters; only the service (led by ex-Savoy Grill supremo
Angelo Maresca) approaches "flawless", though – other aspects
of the operation often just seem "dull". / www.roccofortehotels.com;
10.30 pm; no booking at weekends; set weekday L £50 (FP).*

Browns £34 ⑤⑤④
47 Maddox St, W1 7491 4565 3–2C
82-84 St Martin's Ln, WC2 7497 5050 4–3B
Islington Grn, N1 7226 2555 8–3D
Butler's Wharf, Shad Thames, SE1 7378 1700 9–4D
3-5 Kew Grn, TW9 8948 4838 1–3A
Hertsmere Rd, E14 7987 9777 11–1C
8 Old Jewry, EC2 7606 6677 9–2C
"Once reliable, now just awful" – these "buzzy" English brasseries
too often deliver "dire" food, "slowly and painfully".
/ www.browns-restaurants.com; 10 pm-11 pm; EC2 closed Sat & Sun;
W1 L only.

Brula TW1 £38 ❷⓪❷
43 Crown Rd 8892 0602 1–4A
A "charming" and "crowded" St Margarets bistro (whose period
charms once commended it to the producers of 'Hercule Poirot');
its style is "simple and straightforward", and the short menu offers
"good value". / www.brulabistrot.com; 10.30 pm; no Amex; set weekday L
£25 (FP).

Brunello
Baglioni Hotel SW7 £75 ⑤⑤❸
60 Hyde Park Gate 7368 5700 5–1B
"Beautiful", "quirky" and "OTT" modern styling is the defining
feature of this "luxurious" (but "impersonal") boutique-hotel,
opposite Kensington Gardens; the Italian menu "looks good" and
the wine list is "amazing", but the whole experience often seems
"wildly overpriced". / www.baglionihotellondon.com; 10.30 pm; set always
available £41 (FP).

Buchan's SW11 £37 ④④④
62-64 Battersea Bridge Rd 7228 0888 5–4C
This Caledonian wine bar south of Battersea Bridge is "independent
of the usual chains" and "likeable" for it; its food is "decent,
if rather variable". / www.buchansrestaurant.co.uk; 10.45 pm.

The Builder's Arms SW3 £34 ❸❸⓪
13 Britten St 7349 9040 5–2C
"For a lazy long weekend lunch", this "tucked-away" pub off the
Kings Road offers "decent" food in a supremely "cosy" and
"relaxed" setting; "arrive early, or you'll not get a table". / 10.15 pm;
no Amex; no booking.

The Bull N6 £41 ④④❸
13 North Hill 0845 456 5033 1–1C
Like its sibling The House, this Highgate yearling can seem "unsure
as to whether it's a restaurant or a gastropub"; fans hail it as
a "good but pricey" destination, while critics insist it "needs
to improve to stay the course". / www.inthebull.biz; 10.30 pm; closed
Mon L; no Amex.

Buona Sera £30 ❸❷❷
289a King's Rd, SW3 7352 8827 5–3C
22 Northcote Rd, SW11 7228 9925 10–2C
"Good pizza" and "cheap bowls of pasta" maintain the popularity
of this "friendly", if "basic", duo; the café-style Clapham original
has a "real buzz" – the spin-off occupies a "quirky" Chelsea site,
where you "climb a ladder to some of the tables". / midnight;
SW3 closed Mon.

Busaba Eathai £27 ❷❸❷
106-110 Wardour St, W1   7255 8686   3–2D
8-13 Bird St, W1   7518 8080   3–1A
22 Store St, WC1   7299 7900   2–1C
The "omnipresent queue" (at Soho in particular) may
be "annoying", but it "bears testimony to the quality" of Alan Yau's
"Thai-meets-Wagamama" group, where "delicious and affordable"
dishes are served at communal tables in a "stylish" and "buzzy"
setting. / 11 pm, Fri & Sat 11.30 pm; W1 no booking; WC1 need 12+
to book .

Busabong SW10 £34 ❹❹❹
1a Langton St   7352 7414   5–3B
There were some disappointing reports this year on this Thai
stalwart near World's End; its loyal local fan club, however, again
hailed its "consistently excellent" food. / www.busabong.co.uk; 11.15 pm;
set weekday L £20 (FP).

Bush Bar & Grill W12 £39
45a Goldhawk Rd   8746 2111   7–1C
"Convenience for the Beeb" makes this hidden-away Shepherd's
Bush bar/restaurant something of a media canteen; it changed
hands and revamped in spring 2006, so we've left it unrated –
an early report suggests that, as of old, it has a "buzzy"
atmosphere and "variable" food. / www.bushbar.co.uk; 11 pm.

Bush Garden Café W12 £14 ❸❸❷
59 Goldhawk Rd   8743 6372   7–1C
"Hidden-away" next to Goldhawk Road tube, this "scuffed-but-
charming" café makes a "great place to hang out" (with a
"fabulous garden") for a "yummy breakfasts", "lovely cakes" and
"passable" snacks. / 7 pm; L only, closed Sun.

Butcher & Grill SW11 NEW £37 ❷❸❹
39 Parkgate Rd   7924 3999   5–4C
On a large former Café Rouge site, this Battersea newcomer offers
a meaty formula parallel to that of the Fishworks (fishmonger-cum-
restaurant) chain; the fare is pretty simple, but everything on our
first-week visit was of high quality. / Rated on Editors' visit;
www.thebutcherandgrill.com.

Butlers Wharf Chop House SE1 £52 ❹❸❸
36e Shad Thames   7403 3403   9–4D
This Thames-side Conran establishment boasts "a beautiful
location", with "great Tower Bridge views" and "outside tables
in summer"; though somewhat improved this year, the "traditional
British" cooking in the restaurant can still seem "below par" –
eating in the bar, however, can offer "excellent value".
/ www.conran.com/eat; 11 pm.

La Buvette TW9 £37 ❷❷❷
6 Church Walk   8940 6264   1–4A
This year-old sibling to St Margaret's Brula is a "very pleasant",
if slightly "old-fashioned", all-rounder, located just off a churchyard;
its "classic" bistro fare is served in a setting that's "cosy rather than
stylish". / www.la-buvette.com; 10.30 pm; no Amex.

The Cabin SW6 NEW £38 ❸❷❸
125 Dawes Rd 7385 8936 10–1B
"An excellent place for comfort food" – this *"reasonably-priced"* surf 'n' turf newcomer in Fulham (on the site of Hide, RIP) is praised by locals as a *"relaxed"* hang-out.
/ www.thecabinbarandgrill.co.uk; midnight; D only, ex Sun open L & D.

Cactus Blue SW3 £37 ⑤④④
86 Fulham Rd 7823 7858 5–2C
"The food has really gone downhill" – and it wasn't that hot in the first place – at this large Chelsea American; it's really *"more a bar than a restaurant"* (and, when there's a DJ, an *"ear-blastingly noisy"* one at that). / midnight; D only.

Café 209 SW6 £18 ❸❸❶
209 Munster Rd 7385 3625 10–1B
The *"extrovert"* owner Joy *"makes for good entertainment"* at this *"cheap and cheerful"* BYO Thai café in deepest Fulham; it's very *"noisy"* and *"crowded"* (*"get ready to rub elbows with your neighbours"*), but the scoff is *"consistently good"*. / 10.30 pm; D only, closed Sun, closed over December; no credit cards.

Café Bagatelle
Wallace Collection W1 £40 ⑤⑤❶
Manchester Sq 7563 9505 3–1A
"Must try harder", is the verdict at this *"airy"* Marylebone atrium-café, which seems to rely almost entirely on the attractions of its *"gracious"* setting. / www.wallacecollection.org; L only; no trainers.

Café Bohème W1 £37 ④❸❶
13 Old Compton St 7734 0623 4–2A
This *"very loud but fun"* bar/brasserie is a linchpin of (younger) Soho life, where the action goes on till late; despite its freewheeling style, the food is *"competent"* and service *"courteous"*.
/ www.cafeboheme.co.uk; 2.45 am, Sun 11.30 pm; booking: max 7.

Café Crêperie de Hampstead £20 ❷④④
2 Exhibition Rd, SW7 7589 8947 5–2C
77 Hampstead High St, NW3 no tel 8–2A
"It's squashed but the crêpes are delicious and filling, and there are lovely Breton salads and ciders", at the South Kensington branch (the better-known) of this mini-chain; take-away only at the Hampstead original. / www.hampsteadcreperie.com; 10.30 pm; NW3 no credit cards.

Café de Maya NW3 £25 ④❷④
38 Primrose Hill Rd 7209 0672 8–3B
"Primarily a locals' restaurant", this *"welcoming"* Primrose Hill fixture offers Thai/Malay fare that's *"so-so, but freshly cooked"*.
/ 11 pm; D only, closed Mon; no Amex.

Café des Amis du Vin WC2 £45 ④④④
11-14 Hanover Pl 7379 3444 4–2D
This *"pricey"* Gallic bistro – *"tucked-away"* near the ROH – falls far short of its potential; it can still be a handy destination, though, for a prix-fixe lunch or – best of all – for a glass of wine and some cheese in the *"bargain"* basement bar. / www.cafedesamis.co.uk; 11.30 pm; closed Sun; set weekday L £29 (FP).

Café du Jardin WC2 £40 ④❸④
28 Wellington St 7836 8769 4–3D
"Good-value, prix-fixe menus" are the star turn at this Covent Garden corner spot, which is a well-known and "reliable" lunch or pre-theatre venue; à la carte, however, it can seem "expensive for what it is". / www.lecafedujardin.com; midnight; set weekday L £23 (FP).

Café du Marché EC1 £42 ❷❷❶
22 Charterhouse Sq 7608 1609 9–1B
"A little bit of France, right in the heart of London" – that's the joy of this impeccably "consistent" and hugely popular Clerkenwell "stalwart", whose "warm" and "rustic" atmosphere suits both business and (especially) romance. / 10 pm; closed Sat L & Sun; no Amex.

Café Emm W1 £24 ④❸❸
17 Frith St 7437 0723 4–2A
"For decent food at decent prices" – "nothing spectacular", mind – this "buzzy" Soho stand-by delivers the goods. / www.cafeemm.com; 10.30 pm; no Amex; no booking after 6.30 pm.

Café Fish W1 £42 ❸④⑤
36-40 Rupert St 7287 8989 4–3A
The feel is "formulaic" and service "erratic", but this large West End canteen still serves some "dependable" fish dishes, and is "good pre- or post-theatre". / www.santeonline.co.uk; 11 pm, Sun 9 pm; set weekday L £27 (FP).

Café in the Crypt
St Martin's in the Fields WC2 £21 ⑤④❸
Duncannon St 7839 4342 2–2C
This large but "crowded" crypt-cafeteria, off Trafalgar Square, makes a "convenient" and atmospheric central stand-by; the food's "cheap" and comes in "big portions", but is "not that good". / www.stmartin-in-the-fields.org; 7.30 pm, Wed-Sat 11 pm; no Amex; no booking.

Café Japan NW11 £27 ❶❷⑤
626 Finchley Rd 8455 6854 1–1B
"Neon lights and cheap tables do little for the ambience, but add to the authenticity" of this "crowded" Golder's Green Japanese, opposite the station; its "excellent" sushi is some of "the best outside central London", and comes in "generous" portions too. / 10 pm; closed Mon, Tue, & Wed L - Fri L; no Amex.

Café Laville W2 £28 ④❸❷
453 Edgware Rd 7706 2620 8–4A
For the best view, "book the middle table by the glass wall", if you visit this "picturesque" café, above the canal at Maida Vale; its "lovely for breakfast", too; (licensed or you can BYO). / www.cafe-laville.co.uk; 11 pm; no Amex.

Café Lazeez £32 ❸❸❸
21 Dean St, W1 7434 9393 4–2A
93-95 Old Brompton Rd, SW7 7581 9993 5–2C
These "economical" but "quite stylish" modern Indians – which were among London's first 'new wave' subcontinentals – have never quite lived up to their promise; for a loyal fan club, though, they are "always enjoyable". / www.cafelazeez.com; W1 11.45 pm, SW7 12.30 am; W1 closed Sun.

Café Mamma TW9 NEW £38 ④❸❸
110 Kew Rd 8948 8330 1–4A
*Richmond's former 'Murano' has been re-launched without any
change of management; limited survey commentary confirms that
it remains "a good 'convenience' restaurant", offering "reasonably-
priced" Italian fare.*

Café Med NW8 £36 ④④❸
21 Loudon Rd 7625 1222 8–3A
*There's "a lovely terrace" and "ample room for families" at this
"spacious" Med-inspired hang-out in St John's Wood (the sole
remaining outlet of a former group); its "basic" food is somewhere
between "consistent" and "uninspiring". / 11 pm; booking essential.*

Café Mozart N6 £26 ④❸❸
17 Swains Ln 8348 1384 8–1B
*"Watching Highgate's intelligentsia at play" helps pass the time
at this Viennese café, which does "excellent coffee and cakes"
(and "great fry-ups"); there's also hearty mittel European fare.
/ 10 pm; closed Mon D; no Amex; no booking at L.*

Café Pacifico WC2 £34 ④④❷
5 Langley St 7379 7728 4–2C
*Standards are improving at this "loud" and "buzzing" "party"-
cantina, in Covent Garden; it's long been known for "some of
London's most authentic Mexican food", but now needs to up its
game considerably if it's to catch up with the newer Latinos on the
block. / www.cafepacifico-laperla.com; midnight.*

Café Portugal SW8 £24 ❷❷❸
5a-6a Victoria Hs, South Lambeth Rd 7587 1962 10–1D
*As with nearby Bar Estrella, it's "like stepping into a café
in Portugal", when you visit this "cheerful" Vauxhall spot that's best
liked for its "amazing cakes, pastries and coffee".
/ www.cafeportugal.com; 11 pm.*

Café Rouge £30 ⑤⑤④
Branches throughout London
*"They only do the basics, and don't even get those right" at this
"poor pastiche" of a Gallic brasserie; some of its branches are
"handy", though, especially for breakfast. / www.caferouge.co.uk; 11 pm,
City branches earlier; most City branches closed all or part of weekend.*

Café Spice Namaste E1 £40 ❶❷❸
16 Prescot St 7488 9242 11–1A
*You "leave the grey City streets behind you" when you enter this
"gaudy" and "welcoming" Indian, near Tower Bridge – Cyrus
Todiwala's is a "genius" and his Parsi cooking is "subtle, different
and delicious". / www.cafespicenamaste.com; 10.15 pm; closed Sat L & Sun.*

Caffè Caldesi W1 £47 ④④④
118 Marylebone Ln 7935 1144 2–1A
*"More friendly and less formal" than its parent Caldesi, this Italian
bistro in Marylebone is popular for lunch; given its "variable"
standards, though, dinner here can seem "overpriced".
/ www.caldesi.com; 10.30 pm.*

Caffè Nero   £10   ④❸❸
Branches throughout London
"The best strong aromatic coffee around" underpins acclaim for this chic Italian chain; many reporters feel that, post the smoking ban, "it will be even better". / 7 pm-11 pm, City branches earlier; most City branches closed all or part of weekend; no credit cards; no booking.

La Cage Imaginaire NW3   £34   ❸❷❷
16 Flask Walk 7794 6674 8–1A
"Quiet" and "intimate" – this "small" and "tucked-away" Hampstead fixture feels slightly dated, but offers "a very nice dining experience that will not break the bank". / 11 pm; closed Mon L.

Calabash
Africa Centre WC2   £20   ❸④⑤
38 King St 7836 1976 4–3C
Impressively dated décor adds to the experience of visiting this long-established Covent Garden basement, which offers some "novel", "filling" and "'well priced" pan-African fare; if you go in the right frame of mind, the overall experience is "totally trippy and great fun". / 10.30 pm; closed Sat L & Sun; no Amex.

Caldesi W1   £55   ❸④④
15-17 Marylebone Ln 7935 9226 3–1A
Views, as ever, divide on this "cramped" Marylebone Italian near the Wigmore Hall; to devotees its "real" Tuscan cooking is "under-estimated" – to doubters it's "sound but not inspiring". / www.caldesi.com; 11 pm; closed Sat L & Sun.

Cambio de Tercio SW5   £46   ❷❸❸
163 Old Brompton Rd 7244 8970 5–2B
"It's not typical Spanish food", but the "innovative" cooking of this "very buzzy" South Kensington-fringe fixture can be "magnificent" nonetheless; "abrupt" service can be a drawback. / www.cambiodetercio.co.uk; 11.30 pm.

Camden Brasserie NW1   £38   ④④④
9-11 Jamestown Rd 7482 2114 8–3B
"The steak and chips are as good as ever", say fans of this stalwart local institution; its "cavernous and echoey" modern premises (to which it moved two years ago) have "none of the worn charm" of its former site, however, and some old-timers fear it's "losing the plot". / www.camdenbrasserie.co.uk; 11 pm.

Camerino W1   £48   ❸❷④
16 Percy St 7637 9900 2–1C
With its "distinguished" cooking and "immensely charming" service, this "light and bright" Italian is potentially an "ace" Fitzrovia destination; it "lacks atmosphere", though, and some reporters find it "ever more expensive". / www.camerinorestaurant.com; 11 pm; closed Sat L & Sun.

Canteen E1 NEW   £32   ④④❷
Unit 2 Crispin Pl, Old Spitalfields Mkt 0845 686 1122 9–1D
"The great concept" – a "nostalgic" menu of "simple English fare" ("like you wish Mum had cooked") – has made an instant smash hit of this elegantly "Edward Hopper-esque" new diner, by Spitalfields; too often, however, the realisation of the cooking "doesn't live up". / www.canteen.co.uk; 10.30 pm.

Cantina del Ponte SE1 £41 ⑤⑤⑤
Butler's Wharf Building, 36c Shad Thames 7403 5403 9–4D
The food is "not good" and comes at "extraordinary" prices at this
Conran group pizzeria, which seems to trade exclusively on its
"great" Thames-side location. / www.conran.com/eat; 11 pm; set always
available £26 (FP).

Cantina Italia N1 £30 ❷❷❷
19 Canonbury Ln 7226 9791 8–2D
"The pizzas are very good, but it's the atmosphere which really
makes the place" – this is a "real neighbourhood Italian" and,
appropriately enough, it "attracts lots of Italians".
/ www.cantinaitalia.co.uk; 11 pm, Fri & Sat 11.30 pm; closed weekday L;
no Amex.

Cantina Vinopolis
Vinopolis SE1 £44 ④④④
1 Bank End 7940 8333 9–3C
The "astonishing" wine list is, increasingly, the sole reason to seek
out these potentially atmospheric vaults in the South Bank's
museum of wine – with its "could-be-anywhere" food and its
"indifferent" service, it seems ever more "depressing" and
"touristy". / www.cantinavinopolis.com; 10.30 pm; closed Sun D.

Il Cantuccio di Pulcinella SW11 £29 ❷0❷
143 St John's Hill 7924 5588 10–2C
"Everything a neighbourhood Italian should be" – this "casual"
Wandsworth two-year-old inspires a hymn of praise with its
"welcoming" service and "fantastic" food (including wood-fired
pizza). / www.ilcantucciodipulcinella.co.uk; 11.30 pm; closed Tue L; no Amex;
set weekday L £14 (FP).

Canyon TW10 £47 ⑤⑤❸
Riverside 8948 2944 1–4A
The "lovely riverside setting" and "pleasant brunch" are the only
real plusses nowadays at this California-style restaurant
in Richmond, which draws huge flak for its punishing prices,
its "sloppy" service and its "couldn't-care-less" fusion fare.
/ www.hertfordgroup.co.uk; 10.30 pm; set weekday L £28 (FP).

THE CAPITAL RESTAURANT
CAPITAL HOTEL SW3 £79 ❷❷❸
22-24 Basil St 7591 1202 5–1D
Eric Chavot's "meticulous" cuisine has long earned this "plush" and
quite "stuffy" Knightsbridge dining room a slot near the top
of London's premier league – this year's reports, however, were not
quite as consistent as usual. / www.capitalhotel.co.uk; 10.45 pm;
set weekday L £50 (FP).

LE CAPRICE SW1 £54 ❷00
Arlington Hs, Arlington St 7629 2239 3–4C
"Nothing changes" ("and that's just fine"), at this "perennially
winning" brasserie near the Ritz – with its "faultless" food and its
"slick" service, it simply "never misses a beat" (and there's often
a "sprinkling of celebs" too). / www.caprice-holdings.co.uk; midnight.

Caraffini SW1 £44 ❷0❷
61-63 Lower Sloane St 7259 0235 5–2D
"The best of the Belgravia 'neighbourhood' Italians", this "extremely
friendly" stand-by offers "nothing fancy" (but with "a touch
of Sloane Square glitz"); few reporters seem to mind that it's
"cramped" and often "noisy". / 11.30 pm; closed Sun.

Caramel SW1 NEW £27 ④❸❷
77 Wilton Rd 7233 8298 2–4B
"Decent food at decent prices" has quickly helped this new café/bistro gather quite a Pimlico following, not least for weekend brunching – "their breakfasts and smoothies are great for hangovers!" / 11 pm; closed Mon D & Sun D; no Amex.

Caravaggio EC3 £48 ④④⑤
107-112 Leadenhall St 7626 6206 9–2D
Reporters feel that "they take their customers for granted" at this "glitzy" City Italian, which serves "1970s food at 2020 prices". / www.estruscarestaurants.com; 10 pm; closed Sat & Sun.

Carluccio's Caffè £28 ④④❸
8 Market Pl, W1 7636 2228 3–1C
St Christopher's Pl, W1 7935 5927 3–1A
236 Fulham Road, SW10 7376 5960 5–3B
1-7 Old Brompton Rd, SW7 7581 8101 5–2C
5-6 The Grn, W5 8566 4458 1–3A
305-307 Upper St, N1 7359 8167 8–3D
32 Rosslyn Hill, NW3 7794 2184 8–2A
60 St John's Wood High St, NW8 7449 0404 8–3A
Putney Wharf, Brewhouse St, SW15 8789 0591 10–2B
Reuters Plaza, 2 Nash Court, E14 7719 1749 11–1C
12 West Smithfield, EC1 7329 5904 9–2A
This "buzzy" Italian deli-café chain has won a huge following as a "generally reliable" all-day stand-by; the year in which the business 'floated', though, saw a continuation of the long-term decline in culinary standards. / www.carluccios.com; 11 pm; no booking weekday L.

Carnevale EC1 £34 ❷❷❸
135 Whitecross St 7250 3452 9–1B
This "vegetarian haven" offers "very fresh and tasty food" in an unlikely backstreet site that's "handy for Barbican". / www.carnevalerestaurant.co.uk; 11 pm; closed Sat L & Sun; set weekday L £14 (FP).

Carpaccio's SW3 £51 ⑤⑤❸
4 Sydney St 7352 3433 5–2C
"The good ambience is all you get" at this "lively" Chelsea hang-out – the Italian cooking is too often "disappointing", and "service should be better", given the "hefty" prices. / www.carpaccio.com; 11.30 pm; closed Sun.

Casale Franco N1 £37 ④❸❸
rear of 134-137 Upper St 7226 8994 8–3D
For fans, this "atmospheric" Islington stalwart, hidden down an alleyway, is a "real local favourite" (or even "London's most underrated Italian"); doubters, though, just find it "very ordinary". / www.casalefranco.co.uk; 11 pm; closed Mon & weekday L; need 6+ to book.

The Castle SW11 £27 ❸④❸
115 Battersea High St 7228 8181 10–1C
"A standard Young's pub", notable for its pretty garden in an unlikely part of Battersea; on the food front, "good burgers" are a highlight. / 10 pm; no Amex.

Cat & Mutton E8 £34 ④④❸
76 Broadway Mkt 7254 5599 1–2D
"Good" ("if not exactly 'gastro-'") pub fare makes this "comfy" Hackney boozer a very popular local. / www.catandmutton.co.uk; 10 pm; closed Mon L & Sun D.

Cây Tre EC1 £26 ②④⑤
301 Old St 7729 8662 9–1B
*"Inspired" Vietnamese cooking at "bargain" prices has made a big
name for this small Hoxton two-year-old; both the service and the
"cheesy" décor, however, "leave something to be desired".
/ www.vietnamesekitchen.co.uk; 11 pm.*

Cecconi's W1 £60 ❸❸❷
5a Burlington Gdns 7434 1500 3–3C
*A "Eurotrashy crowd" drives the "buzzy" scene at this Venetian-
inspired Mayfair brasserie, which is now a more "relaxed and
inviting" place since Nick (Soho House) Jones's "brilliant facelift"
last year; except for the "fantastic" breakfast, though, the cooking
is no more than "competent". / www.cecconis.co.uk; midnight.*

Cellar Gascon EC1 £35 ❶❸❸
59 West Smithfield Rd 7796 0600 9–2B
*The neighbouring spin-off to Club Gascon serves "fabulous",
"rustic" French dishes in "miniscule" tapas-style portions;
"many good small producers" feature on its "excellent" SW France
wine list. / 10 pm; closed Sat L & Sun.*

Le Cercle SW1 £38 ❶❷❷
1 Wilbraham Pl 7901 9999 5–2D
*This "secret cellar" on the fringe of Belgravia – a two-year-old
sibling to the fabled Club Gascon – gets an "all round thumbs-up"
for its "knowledgeable" staff, "interesting" design and its
"consistently superb" tapas dishes. / 11 pm; closed Mon & Sun;
set weekday L £25 (FP).*

Chakalaka SW15 £40 ❸❷❸
136 Upper Richmond Rd 8789 5696 10–2B
*"For anyone wanting to sample South African cuisine", this Putney
yearling makes an "interesting" destination, majoring in "hearty"
game dishes (using springbok, kudu, ostrich, etc); the ambience
is "appealing", but can be "loud". / www.chakalakarestaurant.co.uk;
10.45 pm; closed weekday L; no Amex; set always available £24 (FP).*

Chamberlain's EC3 £55 ④④④
23-25 Leadenhall Mkt 7648 8690 9–2D
*"Good grub with which to impress business associates" makes this
"closely-packed" City fish restaurant popular with some reporters;
even fans acknowledge it's "unnecessarily expensive", though,
and critics find "no redeeming features whatsoever".
/ www.chamberlains.org; 9.30 pm; closed Sat & Sun; set dinner £21 (FP).*

Chamomile NW3 £19 ❸❷④
45 England's Ln 7586 4580 8–2B
*"A fabulous breakfast selection" is the headline attraction at this
"helpful" Belsize Park café/pâtisserie. / 5.45 pm; L only; no Amex.*

Champor-Champor SE1 £41 ❷❷❶
62 Weston St 7403 4600 9–4C
*"Genuinely different" and "wonderfully-presented" Malay/fusion
food – not to mention the "bizarre" but "beautiful" décor –
has long won acclaim for this "psychedelic" Borough "jewel";
this year, however, saw some uncharacteristically "variable" reports.
/ www.champor-champor.com; 10.15 pm; closed L, closed Sun; booking:
max 12.*

The Chancery EC4 £44 ❷❶❸
9 Cursitor St   7831 4000   9–2A
*"Perfect for business" – this "hidden gem" off Holborn is almost
unanimously praised by reporters for its "accomplished" cooking,
its "pleasant" ambience and its "excellent" service.*
/ www.thechancery.co.uk; 10 pm; closed Sat & Sun.

The Chapel NW1 £32 ❹❸❸
48 Chapel St   7402 9220   6–1D
*One of the "original" gastropubs (1995), this "relaxed" place near
Edgware Road tube is still a favourite for some reporters. / 10 pm.*

Chapter Two SE3 £41 ❷❷❸
43-45 Montpelier Vale   8333 2666   1–4D
*Thanks to its "high-quality" fare and "reasonable" prices,
this "solid" brasserie – a spin-off from Kent's famous Chapter 1 –
is often hailed as the "best place in Blackheath by a country mile".*
/ www.chaptersrestaurants.co.uk; 10.30 pm.

Le Chardon SE22 £32 ❷❸❷
65 Lordship Ln   8299 1921   1–4D
*A tiny East Dulwich fixture – with the interior of a tiled Victorian
shop – where "wonderful", if "old-fashioned", Gallic dishes are
served "in semi-darkness"; it makes an ideal setting "for whispering
sweet nothings and drinking gallons of vin rouge".*
/ www.greenbar.co.uk; 11 pm; set weekday L £21 (FP).

Charlotte's Place W5 £43 ❸❸❹
16 St Matthew's Rd   8567 7541   1–3A
*This neighbourhood spot by Ealing Common takes different
reporters different ways – fans says it offers "delicious" food and
"great" service, but doubters just find it "woefully overpriced".*
/ www.charlottes.co.uk; 10.30 pm; closed weekday L & Sun D; no Amex.

Chelsea Bun Diner SW10 £23 ❸❷❸
9a Lamont Rd   7352 3635   5–3B
*"A great cosmopolitan menu selection – from a San Francisco
brunch to a full English breakfast" – in "huge portions" too –
makes this World's End "institution" a classic start-the-day
destination; (licensed or you can BYO). / 11 pm; no Amex; no booking,
Sat & Sun.*

Chelsea Kitchen SW3 £17 ❹❸❹
98 King's Rd   7589 1330   5–2D
*"Young, old, rich and poor alike" all huddle together at this "time-
warped", '50s King's Road "pit stop"; the basic fodder "won't rock
your world", but it is "amazing value"; (licensed or you can BYO).*
/ 11.45 pm.

Cheyne Walk Brasserie SW3 £57 ❸❸❶
50 Cheyne Walk   7376 8787   5–3C
*"The great décor"... "the central open grill"... "the lush upstairs
bar" – all contribute to the "enticing" ambience at this "fun"
Chelsea three-year-old; prices may be "exorbitant", but the "lovely,
simple" food was better rated this year, as was the service.*
/ www.cheynewalkbrasserie.com; 10.30 pm; closed Mon L & Sun D; booking
essential; set weekday L £29 (FP).

CHEZ BRUCE SW17 £55 **❶❷❷**
2 Bellevue Rd 8672 0114 10–2C
Bruce Poole may keep a low media profile, but he is a "real culinary star", and the acclaim for his "unpretentious" and "relatively affordable" cuisine is such that – for the second year – this "neighbourhood" spot, by Wandsworth Common, is the survey's overall favourite; service is "thoughtful", too, and the wine list "phenomenal". / www.chezbruce.co.uk; 10.30 pm, Sun 10 pm; booking: max 6 at D.

Chez Gérard £40 ⑤④④
Thistle Hotel, 101 Buck' Palace Rd, SW1 7868 6249 2–4B
31 Dover St, W1 7499 8171 3–3C
8 Charlotte St, W1 7636 4975 2–1C
119 Chancery Ln, WC2 7405 0290 2–2D
45 East Ter, Covent Garden, WC2 7379 0666 4–3D
9 Belvedere Rd, SE1 7202 8470 2–3D
64 Bishopsgate, EC2 7588 1200 9–2D
14 Trinity Sq, EC3 7480 5500 9–3D
1 Watling St, EC4 7213 0540 9–2B
"Dull" food and "dire" service are too often the themes of reports on this once-popular steak-frites chain; it receives most support as "a good formula for a business lunch". / www.santeonline.co.uk; 10 pm-11.30 pm; City branches closed all or part of weekend.

Chez Kristof W6 £39 **❸❸❷**
111-115 Hammersmith Grove 8741 1177 7–1C
This "chic" (for Hammersmith) yearling is "a great local venue", with generally "comforting" bistro cuisine and a "beautiful" outside terrace; the interior is "closely-packed" and "noisy", though, and service "can be erratic". / www.chezkristof.co.uk; 11 pm; set always available £20 (FP).

Chez Kristof (Deli) W6 £20 **❸④❸**
111 Hammersmith Grove 8741 1177 7–1C
"Total chaos at the weekend" is a defining feature of this trendy deli, dominated by a single communal table; fans say it's "just what you want" for a casual snack or breakfast, but there was also the odd "let-down" this year. / www.chezkristof.co.uk; 8 pm, Sun 6 pm.

Chez Liline N4 £39 **❶❸⑤**
101 Stroud Green Rd 7263 6550 8–1D
It has "a very odd location" and "no atmosphere" ("despite the recent revamp"), but this 20-year-old Finsbury Park institution continues to serve "sublime" fish, "with a Mauritian twist". / 10.30 pm; closed Sun L; set weekday L £26 (FP).

Chez Lindsay TW10 £37 **❸❷❷**
11 Hill Rise 8948 7473 1–4A
"Fine" crêpes (plus tasty seafood and ciders) at "good-value" prices win praise for this "delightful" Breton bistro, near Richmond Bridge. / 10.45 pm; no Amex.

Chez Marcelle W14 £25 **❶④⑤**
34 Blythe Rd 7603 3241 7–1D
Marcelle is an Olympia institution, and fans say her Lebanese food is simply "unbeatable"; décor is "non-existent", though, and service can be "slow". / 10 pm; closed Mon, Tue-Thu D only; no credit cards.

Chiang Mai W1 £30 ❷④④
48 Frith St 7437 7444 4–2A
"It's a bit cramped, and ambience is lacking", but this long-established Soho fixture continues to serve some "excellent" Thai fare (including from a "great veggie menu"). / 11 pm; closed Sun L; set dinner £20 (FP).

Chimes SW1 £28 ⑤④④
26 Churton St 7821 7456 2–4B
This "plain" old Pimlico pie-house wins praise for its "traditional English" charms (and "good cider") – doubters, however, insist you should save it "for when very drunk". / www.chimes-of-pimlico.co.uk; 10.15 pm.

China Tang
Dorchester Hotel W1 £60 ④④❸
53 Park Ln 7629 9988 3–3A
"Crazy" prices sour reports on star designer David Tang's "glamorous" but "cold" Cantonese newcomer, in the Mayfair basement formerly occupied by the Dorchester Club; it also suffers from "shambolic" service. / midnight.

The Chinese Experience W1 £30 ❷❶❸
118-120 Shaftesbury Ave 7437 0377 4–3A
"Don't worry that it sounds like a theme park"; this "efficient" yearling ("highly popular with Chinese customers") is ideal "for a quick and quality experience", with "terrific dim sum" a highlight; "unusually for Chinatown, staff treat you like old friends". / www.chineseexperience.com; 11 pm.

Chisou W1 £50 ❷❸④
4 Princes St 7629 3931 3–1C
"Exceptional" sushi at "reasonable" prices makes this Japanese café near Oxford Circus something of a "hidden oasis" for many reporters; the word is out, though – "it's packed at lunchtime". / 10.15 pm; closed Sun; set weekday L £28 (FP).

Chor Bizarre W1 £44 ❷❸❸
16 Albemarle St 7629 9802 3–3C
This "interesting" Mayfair Indian – with its "sumptuous", if "slightly cheesy", interior – has never won a particularly impressive following among reporters; fans, though, insist it's "a cut above the norm". / www.chorbizarre.com; 11 pm; closed Sun L.

Chowki W1 £25 ❸④④
2-3 Denman St 7439 1330 3–2D
It's still "cheap, tasty and by Piccadilly Circus", but this budget Indian bistro – featuring ever-changing, themed regional menus – struck some reporters as being "all over the place" this year. / www.chowki.com; 11.30 pm.

Choys SW3 £34 ④❸④
172 King's Rd 7352 9085 5–3C
A Chelsea Chinese "throwback" that's "been around forever"; regulars say the cooking is "reliable" and "decent enough" – sceptics that it's "very, very ordinary". / 11 pm.

Christopher's American Bar & Grill WC2 £54 ⑤⑤④
18 Wellington St 7240 4222 4–3D
A sense of 'decline and fall' permeates feedback on this grand surf 'n' turf American, in Covent Garden; it retains a business (and brunch) following, but – with its "bland" cuisine, its "charmless" service and its "excessive" bills – it now often seems "decidedly uninspiring". / www.christophersgrill.com; 11.30 pm; booking: max 12; set pre theatre £30 (FP).

Christopher's In The City EC3 £45 ④❸⑤
18 Creechurch Ln 7623 3999 9–2D
This oddly-decorated newcomer in a City backstreet seems to have made hardly any impact on reporters – this would be consistent with our own visit, which, apart from the hideous lighting, was totally unmemorable. / Rated on Editors' visit; www.christophersgrill.com; 11 pm; closed Sat & Sun.

Chuen Cheng Ku W1 £27 ❸④④
17 Wardour St 7437 1398 4–3A
"A fantastic selection of dim sum" comes "Hong Kong-style" (ie "thick and fast on trolleys") at this vast and "bustling" Chinatown landmark – "at other times the food is standard". / 11.45 pm.

Churchill Arms W8 £17 ❷④❸
119 Kensington Church St 7792 1246 6–2B
"Book ahead", if you want to be sure of enjoying the "fantastic cheap Thai food" on offer in the annexe of this "perennial favourite" Kensington boozer – it's "always packed". / 10 pm; closed Sun D.

Chutney SW18 £27 ❷0❸
11 Alma Rd 8870 4588 10–2B
"Great food, lovely service and good fun generally" win strong local praise for this "cheap and cheerful" Wandsworth Indian. / 11 pm; D only.

Chutney Mary SW10 £52 ❷❷❷
535 King's Rd 7351 3113 5–4B
"Magnificent" cooking over many years has made this Chelsea/Fulham border Indian a true contemporary "benchmark"; with its "elegant" setting and "attentive" service, it's quite "an oasis of calm" too. / www.realindianfood.com; 10.30 pm; closed weekday L; booking: max 12; set Sun L £31 (FP).

Chutneys NW1 £23 ❸④④
124 Drummond St 7388 0604 8–4C
This "crowded" and "scruffy" vegetarian in 'Little India' remains of most note for its "great-value" buffets. / 10.45 pm; no Amex; need 5+ to book; set weekday L £13 (FP).

Ciao Bella WC1 £31 ❸0❷
90 Lamb's Conduit St 7242 4119 2–1D
"Cheery staff" help create an "irresistible" atmosphere at this bustling Bloomsbury "institution"; it serves "cheap and cheerful", "'70s-style Italian cooking", including pizza and pasta – "the great daily specials" are the best bet. / www.ciaobellarestaurant.co.uk; 11.30 pm.

sign up for the survey at www.hardens.com

Cibo W14 £43 ❸❷④
3 Russell Gdns 7371 6271 7–1D
*"Still a favourite after all these years" – this once-celebrated
modern Italian near Olympia still enthuses its loyal fan club with
"terrific, seasonal cooking" and "delightful" service; the décor
is "bland", though, and not all reporters are wowed by the food.
/ www.ciborestaurant.com; 11 pm; closed Sat L & Sun D.*

Cicada EC1 £38 ❶❷❷
132-136 St John St 7608 1550 9–1B
*Will Ricker's "chilled" Clerkenwell hang-out has "remarkable
staying power for such a fashionable place" – his "patient" staff
serve up "top-notch" fusion fodder to a "beautiful" crowd.
/ www.cicada.nu; 10.45 pm; closed Sat L & Sun.*

Cigala WC1 £43 ④❸④
54 Lamb's Conduit St 7405 1717 2–1D
*Fans insist you get "cooking better than Moro" at this "Spartan"
("almost greasy spoon-like") Hispanic venture in Bloomsbury;
overall, however, feedback supports those who say it "can be
patchy". / www.cigala.co.uk; 10.45 pm.*

Cinnamon Cay SW11 £36 ❷❷❷
87 Lavender Hill 7801 0932 10–1C
*On a good day, you get "the best fusion food south of the river"
at this "different and interesting" Battersea Antipodean – the past
year, however, has seen the "occasional lapse".
/ www.cinnamoncay.co.uk; 10.30 pm; D only, closed Sun.*

THE CINNAMON CLUB SW1 £55 ❷❸❷
Old Westminster Library, Great Smith St 7222 2555 2–4C
*With its "subtle and beguiling" modern cuisine and its "classy" and
"airy" setting, this former library (with some books still in situ),
near Westminster Abbey, has become London's best-known Indian;
it's a consistent, if pricey, all-rounder, but service can sometimes
be "unsmiling". / www.cinnamonclub.com; 10.45 pm; closed Sat L & Sun.*

Cipriani W1 £70 ⑤⑤④
25 Davies Street 7399 0500 3–2B
*"A vulgar Eurotrash trattoria with rip-off prices and surly service" –
if you go "for the eye-candy", though, a visit to this Mayfair spin-off
from Venice's Harry's Bar can still be "amusing". / www.cipriani.com;
11.45 pm.*

Circus W1 £46
1 Upper James St 7534 4000 3–2D
*Approaching its tenth birthday, this once-minimalist Soho stand-by
was totally refurbished in more traditional and Gallic style in the
summer of 2006, so we've left it un-rated. / www.egami.co.uk; 11 pm;
closed Sat L & Sun; set weekday L £27 (FP).*

City Café
City Inn Westminster SW1 £36 ④❷❸
30 John Islip St 7932 4600 2–4C
*"Reliable" cooking and "slick" service help make this bistro of a
large hotel, near Tate Britain, a "hidden gem" for some reporters
(including veggies); Sunday brunch is "particularly good".
/ www.citycafe.co.uk; 11.30 pm.*

City Miyama EC4 £45 ❷❸⑤

17 Godliman St 7489 1937 9–3B

A "clinical and unwelcoming" City oriental, which "doesn't exactly aim to attract anyone other than Japanese bankers on expenses"; it serves "some really outstanding dishes", though, "particularly sushi". / 9.30 pm; closed Sat D & Sun.

Clarke's W8 £50 ❶❶❸

124 Kensington Church St 7221 9225 6–2B

Hold the front page; after 22 years Sally Clarke has introduced a new concept – choice – into the dinner menus at her Kensington HQ; let's hope it does nothing to disrupt her "eternally superb" cooking (founded on a California-style philosophy of "the best ingredients, carefully prepared"). / www.sallyclarke.com; 10 pm; closed Mon D & Sun; booking: max 14.

The Clerkenwell Dining Room EC1 £48 ❸❷

69-73 St John St 7253 9000 9–1B

"Straightforward quality" wins praise for this "plain"-looking Farringdon restaurant – which "bustles" with business lunches during the week, but is very chilled on Sundays; some reporters, though, find standards "variable". / www.theclerkenwell.com; 10.30 pm; closed Sat L & Sun D.

Clos Maggiore WC2 £53 ❸❷❶

33 King St 7379 9696 4–3C

With its "enchanting" ("fairy grotto") courtyard and its truly "incredible" wine list, this "very romantic" fixture (formerly called just 'Maggiore's') is a "real jewel among the Covent Garden tourist traps"; the cooking plays rather a supporting rôle, but it's sometimes "excellent". / www.maggiores.uk.com; 10.45 pm; closed Sat L & Sun; set weekday L £37 (FP).

The Club Bar & Dining W1 NEW

21 Warwick St 7734 1002 3–2D

Opening in autumn 2006, this newcomer just off Regent Street is the latest occupant of the site first made famous by the Sugar Club, and inhabited in more recent times by the Grocer on Warwick (RIP); in addition to 'all-day dining in brasserie style', there will also be a large basement bar. / www.theclubbaranddining.co.uk; midnight.

Club Gascon EC1 £65 ❶❷❷

57 West Smithfield 7796 0600 9–2B

"A foie gras frenzy!"; this "closely-packed" Smithfield phenomenon is famed for its "rich" and "luxurious" regional French cuisine – served in a "novel tapas style" – and its "imaginative" list of SW France wines; the dégustation menu is a "tour de force". / 10 pm; closed Sat L & Sun.

Club Mangia
The Punch Tavern EC4 £19 ❸❸❷

99 Fleet St 7353 6658 9–2A

The "good-quality buffet" at this "beautiful" old inn is "a great concept for busy people who want a decent meal", "without the usual City rip-off"; it's also good for breakfast, or afternoon tea. / 11.45 pm; closed Sat & Sun.

Coach & Horses EC1 £35 ❷❸

26-28 Ray St 7278 8990 9–1A

A "no-frills" boozer, behind 'The Guardian', where – on most accounts – the "regularly-changing" menu is "always inspiring". / www.thecoachandhorses.com; 10 pm; closed Sat L & Sun D.

Cocoon W1 £60 ❸④❷
65 Regent St 7494 7600 3–3D

"Lots of beautiful people" inhabit this "posey" West End "hot spot", which "looks like a set from Blade Runner"; the oriental food is "better than you might expect for such a trendy place", and served till late. / www.cocoon-restaurants.com; 11.45 pm; closed Sat L & Sun; set weekday L £42 (FP).

The Collection SW3 £60 ④⑤❸
264 Brompton Rd 7225 1212 5–2C

"Staff who are haughty for no particular reason almost add to the brilliant ambience", gushes one fan of this ritzy South Kensington hang-out; to its critics, though, it's merely "flash", "pretentious" and "very overpriced". / www.the-collection.co.uk; 11.30 pm; D only, closed Sun.

La Collina NW1 NEW £35 ❸❸❸
17 Princess Rd 7483 0192 8–3B

This notably "well-priced" – if "cramped" and "noisy" – Primrose Hill newcomer is clearly "trying very hard"; most reporters praise its "fresh" Italian cooking, but a minority (with whom we count ourselves) is unconvinced. / 11 pm; no Amex.

Le Colombier SW3 £44 ❸❷❷
145 Dovehouse St 7351 1155 5–2C

Didier Garnier's "tucked-away" Gallic fixture is particularly notable for its "delightful" terrace, and – especially for an "older" Chelsea clientèle – is a "perennial favourite"; its "classic" brasserie fare is "always reliable". / 10.30 pm.

Como Lario SW1 £37 ④④④
22 Holbein Pl 7730 2954 5–2D

Thanks to its "friendly" charms, this age-old trattoria near Sloane Square is "always heaving" – as ever, though, some reporters are mystified by its popularity, declaring it "really average" all-round. / www.comolario.uk.com; 11.30 pm; closed Sun.

Comptoir Gascon EC1 £34 ❶❷❶
61-63 Charterhouse St 7608 0851 9–1A

A "bijou" but "casual" Clerkenwell offshoot of the much fancier Club Gascon, which offers "perfect", "fantastically simple" rustic cuisine and "wonderful wines" – and all at prices so reasonable they are "a wonder to behold". / 10 pm; closed Mon & Sun; booking essential.

(ANGELA HARTNETT) THE CONNAUGHT W1 £78 ❸❸❸
Carlos Pl 7592 1222 3–3B

Fans say Angela Hartnett cooks up some "superb" dishes for this "discreet" Mayfair hotel's panelled dining room (and grill); doubters – who complain of "no wow-factor" – are pretty numerous, though, especially if they recall the "great" ancien-régime institution this used to be, pre-Ramsay; NB major refurb scheduled for 2007. / www.angelahartnett.com; 11 pm; jacket; booking: max 8; set weekday L £50 (FP).

The Contented Vine SW1 £35 ④④④
17 Sussex St 7834 0044 5–3D

"No one would travel" to this ordinary-looking wine bar – "in the Pimlico desert, however, it is something of an oasis". / www.contentedvine.com; 10.30 pm, 9.30 pm Sun.

Il Convivio SW1 £46 ❷⓿❸
143 Ebury St 7730 4099 2–4A
The chef at this "pretty" Belgravia Italian has "genuine flair",
and the service is "absolutely first-class", so it's mystifying that the
place is sometimes "a bit quiet"; the setting, with its glass roof,
is "particularly nice on a sunny day". / www.etruscarestaurants.com;
10.45 pm; closed Sun.

Coopers Arms SW3 £28 ④④④
87 Flood St 7376 3120 5–3C
There are still reports of "simple food done well" at this Chelsea
backstreet boozer; since the new régime, however, complaints
of "dreary" meals are on the up. / 9.30 pm; no booking, Sun.

La Copita W12 £23 ❸❸④
63 Askew Rd 8743 1289 7–1B
This "friendly" but "very cramped" shop-conversion in deepest
Shepherd's Bush offers tapas that are "surprisingly good" given the
bargain prices. / www.lacopita.co.uk; 10 pm; closed Mon & Sun L.

Coq d'Argent EC3 £56 ④④❸
1 Poultry 7395 5000 9–2C
The "unparalleled" 6th-floor setting of this Conran eyrie by Bank –
with an "unbeatable" garden and views – "never fail to impress for
business lunching"; prices are far too "steep", however, for food
that can seem "formulaic" and "pretentious". / www.conran.com/eat;
10 pm; closed Sat L.

Cork & Bottle WC2 £33 ⑤④⓿
44-46 Cranbourn St 7734 7807 4–3B
"A treasure amidst the tourist traps and flesh-pots of Leicester
Square" – this age-old basement remains a much-loved West End
rendezvous; "don't bother" with the "uninspired", "'80s-style" food,
though – just "head straight for the extraordinary wine list, and be
adventurous!" / www.donhewitson.com; 11 pm; no booking after 6.30 pm.

Corney & Barrow £32 ④④❸
Branches throughout London
"Perfect after-work venues" – thanks to their excellent locations
(now including Paternoster Square) and good styling;
the "predictable" bar snacks are "expensive", though and
sometimes "poor". / www.corney-barrow.co.uk; 10.30 pm; closed Sat & Sun.

Costa's Grill W8 £18 ④❷❸
12-14 Hillgate St 7229 3794 6–2B
"Not so much a taverna, more a way of life" – this "very friendly"
and "old-fashioned" Greek veteran, near Notting Hill Gate,
has kept some fans coming back "for nearly 40 years". / 10.30 pm;
closed Sun (closed 2 weeks in Aug); no credit cards.

Cottons £37 ④④❷
55 Chalk Farm Rd, NW1 7485 8388 8–2B
70 Exmouth Mkt, EC1 7833 3332 9–1A
"Good drinks and a lively atmosphere" fuel the "fun" at these
'Rhum Shops' in Camden Town and now also in Exmouth Market
on the former site of Coco, RIP; on a modest number of reports,
food quality varies from "spicy and well-prepared" to "dismal".
/ www.cottons-restaurant.co.uk; EC1 10 pm, Sun midnight; NW1 11 pm
; NW1 Mon-Fri L; EC1 Sat L; EC1 no Amex; EC1 no shorts; set always
available £35 (FP).

Les Coulisses EC2 NEW £48 ❸❷❸
33 Broadgate Circle   7628 1592   9–2D
It feels more like a clubby bar than a restaurant, but this Broadgate newcomer – whose parent establishment is in Toulouse – offers surprisingly decent food (as well as some interesting French regional wines). / Rated on Editors' visit; 10 pm; closed Sat & Sun; set weekday L £30 (FP).

The Cow W2 £39 ❷❹❷
89 Westbourne Park Rd   7221 0021   6–1B
"Oysters and Guinness is always a winner", in the "packed" ground-floor bar of Tom Conran's Irish boozer on the Bayswater/Notting Hill border; for those in search of more "hearty" fare, there's also an "agreeable" (if rather "pricey") dining room upstairs. / 10.30 pm; no Amex.

Cowshed W11 NEW £25 ❸❸❸
119 Portland Rd   7078 1944   6–2A
"Delicious toasties", "lovely cakes" and "good smoothies" are the sorts of dishes taken at the communal table of this new Holland Park beauty parlour café (part of the site that was once Orisini, RIP); only truly metrosexual men, however, are likely to feel at home here. / www.cowshedclarendoncross.com; L only.

Crazy Bear W1 £45 ❷❷❶
26 Whitfield St   7631 0088   2–1C
"A terrific experience" combining "both style and substance"; not only does this "sexy" Fitzrovia Thai have "amazing" décor – including a "funky" bar and "wild" loos – but the food is "fresh and fabulous" too. / www.crazybeargroup.co.uk; 10.30 pm; closed Sat L & Sun.

Crazy Homies W2 £35 ❸❺❷
127 Westbourne Park Rd   7727 6771   6–1B
"Piles of tacos and copious Margaritas" make for "gregarious" evenings at this "kitsch" Bayswater hang-out, which offers some of "the only decent Mexican fare in town"; service, however, "can be a little 'mañana'". / 10.30 pm; closed weekday L; no Amex.

Cristini £36 ❸❸④
13 Seymour Pl, W2   7724 3446   2–2A
28 Sussex Pl, W2   7706 7900   6–1D
"Very personal service" adds to the attractions of this Italian duo, which serve "honest" fare at "reasonable prices"; the Lancaster Gate branch is generally thought the nicer of the two. / www.cristini.co.uk; 10 pm; Seymour Pl, Sat-Mon D only; Sussex Pl closed Sun.

Cross Keys SW3 £40 ④④❸
1 Lawrence St   7349 9111   5–3C
Fans say the "lovely" conservatory dining room of this "hidden" Chelsea hostelry offers food that's "exciting, by pub standards" – overall, however, reporters rate it somewhere around "OK". / www.thexkeys.co.uk; 10.30 pm; set weekday L £24 (FP).

Crown & Goose NW1 £27 ❸❸❷
100 Arlington Rd   7485 8008   8–3B
This "lived-in" and "buzzy" Camden Town gastropub (in fact one of London's first) still serves "hearty plates of scoff" at "reasonable prices". / www.crownandgoose.com; 10 pm; no Amex.

The Crown & Sceptre W12 £29 ❸④❸
57 Melina Rd 8746 0060 7–1B
*In the backstreets of Shepherd's Bush, this "friendly" and modestly
trendified pub offers a short menu of "competently-prepared"
staples. / www.fullers.co.uk; 9.30 pm; no Amex.*

Cru N1 £44 ④④❷
2-4 Rufus St 7729 5252 9–1C
*"The wine is what counts" – the list is "fabulous" – at this "dark"
and "relaxed" Hoxton three-year-old (which is constructed around
a wine cage); the food, though, is "average, and not cheap".
/ www.cru.uk.com; 11 pm; closed Mon; set weekday L £26 (FP).*

Crussh £10 ❷❷④
1 Curzon St, W1 7629 2554 3–3B
BBC Media Village, Wood Ln, W12 8746 7916 6–2A
27 Kensington High St, W8 7376 9786 5–1A
One Canada Sq, E14 7513 0076 11–1C
Unit 21 Jubilee Pl, E14 7519 6427 11–1C
48 Cornhill, EC3 7626 2175 9–2C
6 Farringdon St, EC4 7489 5916 9–2A **NEW**
*"Heaven-sent smoothies" and "amazing soups" are the star turns
amongst the "healthy grub" served at this fast-growing chain; it's a
"clinical" operation, though – "just dine and dash". / www.crussh.com;
4.30 pm-7 pm; some branches closed all or part of weekend; no credit cards.*

Cuba Libre N1 £31 ④④❸
72 Upper St 7354 9998 8–3D
*"The food's nothing special" at this long-established Cuban-themed
joint by Islington Green; it's a "fun" place, though, whose "cocktails
make it worth a visit". / 10 pm; no Amex; booking: max 12.*

The Cuckoo Club W1 **NEW** £67 ❺④❸
99-101 Regent St, Victory Hs 7287 4300 3–3D
*This "busy and cool" new Mayfair supper club offers a "great night
out" – if you don't mind being "deafened", that is – but its
"forgettable" fare comes at "huge" prices. / www.thecuckooclub.com;
10 pm; D only, closed Sun-Tue.*

Curve
London Marriott
West India Quay E14 **NEW** £45 ④❷④
52 Hertsmere Rd 7093 1000, ext 2622 11–1C
*"Superb Canary Wharf views" add interest to the large ground-
floor restaurant of this new Isle of Dogs hotel; early reports – rather
in keeping with our own experience – are good-to-mixed. / 10.30 pm.*

CVO Firevault W1 £45 ❸❸❶
36 Gt Titchfield St 7636 2091 3–1C
*"Your date will be putty in your hands", say fans – practically all
thirtysomethings – of this very "different" candlelit cellar, entered
via a high-tech fireplace shop; the food is fine, but not the point.
/ www.cvo.co.uk; 10.30 pm; closed Sat L & Sun.*

Cyprus Mangal SW1 £24 ❶❸④
45 Warwick Way 7828 5940 2–4B
*Offering some of "the best freshly-cooked kebabs" in town,
this unassuming-looking Pimlico take-away – with a "pleasant"
restaurant behind – has, after a year in business, already won quite
a following. / midnight; no Amex.*

Da Mario SW7 £30 ❸❸❸
15 Gloucester Rd   7584 9078   5–1B
A "solid neighbourhood Italian" with an "amusing" style and offering scoff that's "always consistent" (especially "good, traditional pizza"); it's a "family-friendly" choice, and a handy stand-by in the thinly-provided purlieus of the Royal Albert Hall. / www.damario.co.uk; 11.30 pm.

Dalchini SW19 £30 ❷❷❸
147 Arthur Rd   8947 5966   10–2B
"Is it Indo-Chinese or Sino-Indian?"; whatever you call it, Mrs Sarkhel's "friendly" Wimbledon Town spot is widely – if not quite universally – praised for its "fascinating" 'Haka' cuisine. / www.dalchini.co.uk; 10.30 pm, Fri & Sat 11 pm; closed Mon; no Amex.

Dans le Noir EC1 £45 ⑤❶❷
29 Clerkenwell Grn   7253 1100   9–1A
"An interesting concept but they've forgotten about the food!"; you eat in the dark at this zany Clerkenwell newcomer, served by "amazing" partially-sighted and blind staff – it's a "fun and interesting" experience, but the dishes are "poor, and poor value". / www.danslenoir.com; 9.30 pm; no Amex.

Daphne NW1 £27 ❸❷❷
83 Bayham St   7267 7322   8–3C
This "charming", family-run taverna has long been a "cosy" and "comforting" feature of Camden Town; "you never get a great meal" from the "extensive" menu – "but always a good one". / 11.30 pm; closed Sun; no Amex.

Daphne's SW3 £50 ❸❸❷
110-112 Draycott Ave   7589 4257   5–2C
It's no longer in the spotlight, but "for a romantic date, or a lunch with the girls", this "cosy" and "upscale" Chelsea Italian is "a safe bet, even if it is a bit pricey". / www.daphnes-restaurant.co.uk; 11.30 pm; booking: max 12.

Daquise SW7 £25 ④④❸
20 Thurloe St   7589 6117   5–2C
"A post-fire refurb has left the old-fashioned character untouched" at this age-old haunt of Polish émigrés, by South Kensington tube; it serves "solid" food at "very reasonable prices". / 11 pm; no Amex.

The Dartmouth Arms SE23 £30 ❸❷❷
7 Dartmouth Rd   8488 3117   1–4D
This "extremely well-run" gastropub makes an "unexpected" find in Forest Hill; it delivers an "interesting seasonal menu" that's "strong on English classic dishes". / www.thedartmoutharms.com; 10 pm.

De Cecco SW6 £35 ❸❷❸
189 New King's Rd   7736 1145   10–1B
"Year-in year-out" this "cheerful" local "favourite", near Parson's Green, offers "good" Italian scoff and "friendly" service. / www.dececcorestaurant.com; 11 pm; closed Sun D.

Deep SW6 £50

The Boulevard, Imperial Wharf 7736 3337 5–4B

This ambitious, ultra-minimalist yearling – in a swanky but sterile development by Chelsea Harbour – was closed for much of 2006 for the filming of 'The f-word'; hopefully post-relaunch it will still offer "outstanding" Scandinavian seafood, but won't so often be "empty". / www.deeplondon.co.uk; 11 pm; closed Mon, Sat L & Sun D; set weekday L £33 (FP).

Defune W1 £62 ❷④⑤

34 George St 7935 8311 3–1A

This Japanese Marylebone veteran has a devoted fan club, for whom its sushi and teppan-yaki are "a culinary masterpiece" – but even they concede: "wow, they charge for it". / 10.45 pm; set brunch £40 (FP).

Delfina Studio Café SE1 £36 ❷⓪❷

50 Bermondsey St 7357 0244 9–4D

"An interesting concept that works" – this Bermondsey gallery is a "fabulous bright space", whose "inventive", "good-value" (and sometimes "fantastic") cuisine attracts "arty and City types" alike to its "widely-spaced" tables. / www.delfina.org.uk; 10 pm; L only, except Fri when open L&D, closed Sat & Sun.

Delfino W1 £32 ❷❷❸

121a Mount St 7499 1256 3–3B

"Excellent crispy pizzas" are the mainstay of this "bustling" Mayfair pizzeria; it has a "great location" too, opposite the Connaught. / www.finos.co.uk; 11 pm; closed Sat L & Sun.

La Delizia SW3 £23 ❸④④

63-65 Chelsea Manor St 7376 4111 5–3C

"It helps to speak Italian" to overcome the "lackadaisical" service at this "secret" Chelsea backstreet local; "fresh and delicious pizza" makes it worth braving the "cramped" conditions. / 11 pm; no Amex.

The Depot SW14 £37 ⑤④❷

Tideway Yd, Mortlake High St 8878 9462 10–1A

"A stunning location and views" are the "saving graces" of this Thames-side fixture, near Barnes Bridge – service is so-so, and the food is "highly formulaic". / www.depotbrasserie.co.uk; 11 pm.

Le Deuxième WC2 £42 ❸❸④

65a Long Acre 7379 0033 4–2D

"A good address to know in Covent Garden" – this "stylish", if slightly "stark" spot offers "simple" and "well-cooked" fare; it's "reliable pre- and post-theatre", and "an efficient choice for a straightforward business lunch". / www.ledeuxieme.com; midnight; set always available £23 (FP).

Devonshire House W4 £39 ④❸④

126 Devonshire Rd 8987 2626 7–2A

This Chiswick-fringe gastropub – which "tries to be a restaurant" – boasts a menu that supporters find "interesting without being too clever"; doubters, though, just find it "mediocre". / www.thedevonshirehouse.co.uk; 10.30 pm; closed Mon.

sign up for the survey at www.hardens.com 73

Dexter's Grill SW17 £30 ❸❷④
20 Bellevue Rd   8767 1858   10–2C
"It won't revolutionise your existence", but "for a juicy, meaty burger" this "relaxed", "family-friendly" neighbourhood spot has much to recommend it. / www.tootsies.co.uk; 11 pm, Sun 10.30 pm.

Deya W1 £45 ❷❷④
34 Portman Sq   7224 0028   2–2A
It's a shame about the "lighting, spacing and general ambience" of this "modern" dining room, adjacent to a hotel just north of Oxford Street – its "lively interpretation" of Indian cuisine is "very impressive". / www.deya-restaurant.co.uk; 10.45 pm; closed Sat L & Sun.

dim T £26 ④④❸
32 Charlotte St, W1   7637 1122   2–1C
3 Heath St, NW3   7435 0024   8–2A
"Funky" décor creates a "fun and buzzy" atmosphere at these "busy" oriental cafés, which serve "reasonable" dim sum and "self-select" noodle dishes. / 11 pm, NW3 Sat 11.30 pm; no Amex; NW3 no booking 7.30 pm - 9.30 pm.

Dine EC4 NEW £46 ❸④④
17-18 Tooks Ct   7404 1818   2–2D
The "inexpensive excellence" of the Gallic cuisine wins many fans for this "unpretentious" newcomer, "hidden-away behind the Royal Courts"; ratings are undercut, though, by those who find the whole operation too "rough around the edges". / www.dine-restaurant.co.uk; 9.30 pm; closed Sat & Sun; booking: max 6.

The Diner EC2 NEW £27 ❸❷❷
128 Curtain Rd   7729 4452   9–1D
"Comfortable and easy", this "first-class" diner, on the former Shoreditch site of South (RIP), makes a decent job of all the American classics – including some "fabulous" waffles and pancakes. / 11.30 pm; no Amex.

Dish Dash SW12 £29 ④④❸
11-13 Bedford Hill   8673 5555   10–2C
A "buzzing" Balham scene, which offers "an enjoyable evening at a reasonable price"; the "north African/Middle Eastern" fare is incidental. / www.dish-dash.com; 11 pm.

Ditto SW18 £38 ❷❸❷
55-57 East Hill   8877 0110   10–2B
This "great local", in Wandsworth, has gone from strength to strength since changing hands two years ago – only problem is that it's now "sometimes too popular for its own good". / www.doditto.co.uk; 10.30 pm.

Diverso W1 £46 ④④⑤
85 Piccadilly   7491 2222   3–4C
This rustically-styled but grand Italian, opposite the Ritz, offers food that's "well up to scratch" – unfortunately, it can also seem "overpriced", which is presumably why the place is often "not very busy". / www.diverso-restaurant.co.uk; 11.30 pm; closed Sun L.

Diwana Bhel-Poori House NW1 £20 ❸④⑤
121-123 Drummond St   7387 5556   8–4C
*"London's original south Indian vegetarian restaurant" –
a characterfully-dated BYO canteen near Euston – remains a very
popular destination, not least for the "wonderful" lunchtime buffet;
for those with long memories, however, it's "not a patch on what
it was". / 11.30 pm; set always available £10 (FP).*

$ EC1 £31 ④④❸
2 Exmouth Mkt   7278 0077   9–1B
*For some reporters, "tempting" burgers justify a visit to this
"cramped" and "busy" Clerkenwell pub-conversion; others, though,
say the only real draw is the "great cocktail bar, downstairs".
/ midnight.*

The Don EC4 £49 ❷❷❷
20 St Swithin's Ln   7626 2606   9–3C
*"A rare find" – this "discreet City institution" comprises not only
"the Square Mile's most pleasant formal restaurant" but also
a "very atmospheric" cellar brasserie; "impressive" wines
throughout help make this one of the survey's top business
destinations. / www.thedonrestaurant.com; 10 pm; closed Sat & Sun.*

don Fernando's TW9 £33 ❸❷❸
27f The Quadrant   8948 6447   1–4A
*Right by Richmond Station, this large and "lively", family-run outfit
is "the place for tapas" locally; "good fun" too.
/ www.donfernandos.co.uk; 11 pm; no Amex; no booking.*

Don Pepe NW8 £29 ❷❷❸
99 Frampton St   7262 3834   8–4A
*"You feel like you've stumbled into a family-run place somewhere
in Galicia", when you visit London's oldest tapas bar, near Lord's;
"the waiters can be a bit preoccupied with the football, but it offers
exceptional value". / 11.45 pm; closed Sun; set weekday L £13 (FP).*

Dorchester Grill
Dorchester Hotel W1 £80 ④④④
53 Park Ln   7629 8888   3–3A
*"It's bloody Brigadoon!" – revamping this once-excellent bastion
of old Mayfair has proved a "big mistake"; its new "Scots-bling"
décor is "absolutely appalling", and the food is "pretty dreadful"
too – the chef headed for the exit a few months after the re-
opening. / www.thedorchester.com; 11 pm; set weekday L £49 (FP).*

The Dove W6 £27 ④④❷
19 Upper Mall   8748 5405   7–2B
*This ancient Hammersmith tavern makes a "great riverside spot for
a lazy afternoon", even if its pub grub is totally incidental; no kids.
/ www.fullers.co.uk; 9 pm; closed Sun D; no booking.*

Dover Street Restaurant & Bar W1 £55 ⑤⑤❸
8-10 Dover St   7491 7509   3–3C
*"To be honest you go for the music, which can be great, not the
food" – which is "average and disappointing" – to this long-
established Mayfair dive; lunch, though, is "good value".
/ www.doverstreet.co.uk; 3 am; closed Sat L & Sun; no jeans or trainers.*

sign up for the survey at www.hardens.com

Dragon Castle SE17 NEW £28 ②②④
114 Walworth Rd 7277 3388 1–3C
Improbably located just south of Elephant & Castle, this large, bright and lofty Chinese newcomer has been hailed by early reporters as a "fantastic" all-rounder; from our early-days visit, it's easy to see it becoming a benchmark, and not just for south-Londoners. / 11 pm.

The Drapers Arms N1 £39 ❸④❸
44 Barnsbury St 7619 0348 8–3D
An upstairs dining room "of beautiful proportions" helps create an "upscale" tone at this popular Georgian tavern in Barnsbury; the food "is at the good end of average". / www.thedrapersarms.co.uk; 10 pm; D only, ex Sun L only; booking: max 8.

Drones SW1 £48 ④④④
1 Pont St 7235 9555 5–1D
Most of the better reviews of MPW's Belgravia outpost relate to its good-value set menus (and in particular Sunday lunch) – otherwise, it's generally rated somewhere between "pleasant enough" and "nothing special". / www.whitestarline.org.uk; 11 pm; closed Sat L & Sun D.

The Drunken Monkey E1 £22 ❸④❷
222 Shoreditch High St 7392 9606 9–1D
"Authentic" dim sum in a "buzzy" atmosphere – the pretty much invariable theme of commentary on this Clerkenwell boozer; thanks to the regular DJ, "it gets noisier as the night goes on". / www.thedrunkenmonkey.co.uk; 11.45 pm; closed Sat L.

Duke of Cambridge SW11 £36 ④④❶
228 Battersea Bridge Rd 7223 5662 10–1C
A "spacious" Battersea boozer with an "ever-changing" bar menu; it makes "a good drop-in destination". / www.geronimo-inns.co.uk; 10 pm, Sun 8 pm; no Amex.

The Duke of Cambridge N1 £39 ❸④❸
30 St Peter's St 7359 3066 1–2C
An "incredibly noisy" Islington gastropub which is "always full of young locals having a great time"; prices for its organic fare are "high", though, and it took more flak this year for "disinterested" service and "less interesting" food. / www.sloeberry.co.uk; 10.30 pm.

Duke on the Green SW6 NEW £37 ❸④❸
235 New King's Rd 7736 2777 10–1B
"At last, a competitor for the Sloaney Pony" – this newly souped-up boozer, on the other side of Parson's Green, is widely welcomed, not least for its "really good" food and "lovely" roof terrace. / www.dukeonthegreen.co.uk; 10.30 pm.

E&O W11 £43 ❶❷❶
14 Blenheim Cr 7229 5454 6–1A
Will Ricker's "über-cool", "fashionista favourite" in Notting Hill remains "an all-time winner" (and is "not as trendy and elitist as you might think"); not only do you get "brilliant fusion" tapas, but the "great buzzy bar" makes the place feel truly "alive". / www.eando.nu; 11 pm; booking: max 6.

The Eagle EC1 £25 ❸④❷
159 Farringdon Rd 7837 1353 9–1A
"The stress of finding a table is worth it", say the many fans of London's "original gastropub" (Clerkenwell, 1992), which still delivers its trademark "hearty" Mediterranean fare; nowadays "it's something of an institution, ie resting a bit on its laurels". / 11 pm, Sun 5 pm; closed Sun D; no Amex; no booking.

Eagle Bar Diner W1 £26 ❸④❷
3-5 Rathbone Pl 7637 1418 4–1A
You get "a great, really authentic diner experience" at this funky, boothed hang-out near Oxford Street, which delivers "splendid burgers" and "great NY-style breakfasts" (plus "tempting cocktails" and "top milkshakes"). / www.eaglebardiner.com; Mon-Wed 11 pm, Thu-Sat 1 am, Sun 6 pm; closed Sun D; no Amex; need 6+ to book.

Ealing Park Tavern W5 £35 ❸❷❷
222 South Ealing Rd 8758 1879 1–3A
"A great local hit" – thanks not least to its "fresh" and "consistent" cuisine, this "convivial" and "unpretentious" South Ealing gastropub goes from strength to strength; it's "always busy". / 10.30 pm; closed Mon L; booking: max 10.

Earl Spencer SW18 £32 ❷❸❷
260-262 Merton Rd 8870 9244 10–2B
It has an "unprepossessing" location, but fans of this "great" Southfields gastropub say it "can't be beaten in SW London"; the "daily-changing" and "adventurous" fare isn't quite up to its sibling (the Havelock) but often "excellent" all the same. / www.theearlspencer.co.uk; 10 pm; no booking.

The Easton WC1 £28 ❷④❷
22 Easton St 7278 7608 9–1A
A "wonderfully spacious" and "lively" pub, near trendy Exmouth Market; its "short" and "simple" menu ("no starters, one pud") delivers food that's "imaginative, varied and very tasty". / www.easton.co.uk; 10 pm; closed Sat L; no Amex.

Eat £11 ❸❸⑤
Branches throughout London
"Inventive and delicious soups" are a major plus at this popular sandwich chain; fans insist it "out-Prets Pret", but its ratings continue to trail its rival's. / www.eatcafe.co.uk; 5 pm-6 pm; most City branches closed all or part of weekend; no credit cards; no booking.

Eat & Two Veg W1 £33 ⑤⑤④
50 Marylebone High St 7258 8595 2–1A
"High expectations have plummeted" at this once-promising Marylebone veggie; service can be "very, very poor" and the cooking – which emulates meat dishes – is too often "insipid". / www.eatandtwoveg.com; 11 pm.

The Ebury SW1 £40 ④④❸
11 Pimlico Rd 7730 6784 5–2D
It's quite "cool" (for the area), and this large "Pimlico hinterland" bar/brasserie/restaurant has a "one-size-fits-all" charm which makes it especially useful given the lack of local alternatives; standards can vary, though, and prices strike some reporters as "too high". / www.theebury.co.uk; 10.30 pm.

Ebury Wine Bar SW1 £41 ❸❸❷
139 Ebury St 7730 5447 2–4A
The food at this Belgravia stalwart "has improved of late" (thanks, it seems, to the efforts of a new chef); it's a "welcoming" place too, with "good wine". / www.eburywinebar.co.uk; 10 pm; May-Aug closed Sun L.

Eco £26 ❸❸❸
162 Clapham High St, SW4 7978 1108 10–2D
4 Market Row, Brixton Mkt, SW9 7738 3021 10–2D
"Lovely fresh and crispy pizzas" have made this "buzzy" Clapham pizzeria a real local institution; the quirky branch in Brixton Market is less well known but "absolutely brilliant". / SW4 11 pm, SW9 5 pm; SW9 L only, closed Wed & Sun; SW9 no booking.

Ed's Easy Diner £23 ④❸❷
12 Moor St, W1 7439 1955 4–2A
Trocadero, 19 Rupert St, W1 7434 4439 3–3D
15 Gt Newport St, WC2 7836 0271 4–3B
362 King's Rd, SW3 7352 1956 5–3B
"The vividness of the décor" – "true '50s America in the heart of London" – is the special feature of this "kitsch" diner chain; the burgers are only "perfectly OK", but the milkshakes are "superb". / 10.30 pm-1 am; no Amex; no booking.

Eddalino W1 £50 ❸❸④
10 Wigmore St 7637 0789 3–1B
"It's under-reviewed and under-used", say fans of this "quiet" Italian, who hail it as "a nice find" in the thin area near the Wigmore Hall; doubters just find it "pricey" and "atmosphere-free". / www.eddalino.co.uk; 10.30 pm; closed Sat L & Sun.

Edera W11 £46 ④❸④
148 Holland Park Ave 7221 6090 6–2A
Some west Londoners do tip this Holland Park Italian as a notably "elegant" local, with "splendid" cooking; it also attracts flak, though, for being "very expensive and not very good". / 11 pm.

Edokko WC1 £33 ❶❶❸
50 Red Lion St 7242 3490 2–1D
"Ask to sit upstairs for the full traditional experience", if you visit this "incredibly authentic" Japanese, by Gray's Inn; "top-quality" sushi is the high-point of an "amazing-value" menu. / 10 pm; closed Sat & Sun; no Amex.

Efes £27 ④④❸
1) 80 Gt Titchfield St, W1 7636 1953 2–1B
2) 175-177 Gt Portland St, W1 7436 0600 2–1B
"Faded glory" nowadays defines these "tacky", once-quite-famous Turkish "time warps" in Marylebone; sometimes "grumpy" staff serve "filling" mezze and so on. / Gt Titchfield St 11.30 pm, Gt Portland St midnight; Gt Titchfield St closed Sun.

Eight Over Eight SW3 £45 ❶❷❷
392 King's Rd 7349 9934 5–3B
"Fun, if not as cool as E&O" – Will Ricker's nevertheless "ultra-trendy" Chelsea outpost delivers a similarly potent combination of "delicious and witty" Pan-Asian tapas "cooked exceptional well", in a "chic" and "buzzy" setting. / www.eightovereight.nu; 10.45 pm; closed Sun L; set weekday L £26 (FP).

1880
The Bentley Hotel SW7 £76 ❸❸❷
27-33 Harrington Gdns   7244 5555   5–2B
"Surroundings of opulent decadence" remain a key attraction at this "OTT" South Kensington basement; since Andrew Turner left, however, realisation of its grazing-menu concept – though "generally good" – "has declined", and service has sometimes seemed "incompetent". / www.thebentley-hotel.com; 10 pm; D only, closed Mon & Sun; booking: max 8.

Ekachai EC2 £25 ❷❷❸
9-10 The Arcade, Liverpool St   7626 1155   9–2D
If you can avoid the queue, this "reliable" and "value-for-money" Malaysian/Thai spot, near Liverpool Street, makes a "handy stand-by for swift City lunching". / www.silksandspice.net; 10 pm; closed Sat & Sun; no bookings.

Electric Brasserie W11 £42 ❹❹❷
191 Portobello Rd   7908 9696   6–1A
"Join the cool crowd", at this "packed" Notting Hill brasserie, which is the sort of "great people-watching" destination where Sunday brunch is a "must-book"; "exceptional burgers" are the menu high-point – otherwise, the food is often "not up to the prices". / www.the-electric.co.uk; 10.45 pm; set weekday L £27 (FP).

Elena's L'Etoile W1 £49 ❹❸❷
30 Charlotte St   7636 7189   2–1C
"May it never change", say fans of this "elegant" Fitzrovia "old faithful", where the "cosseting and smiling" staff are overseen by the octogenarian Elena Salvoni; even supporters may concede that it's "a tad pricey", though, and that the Gallic cuisine is "dependable rather than exciting". / www.elenasletoile.co.uk; 10.30 pm; closed Sat L & Sun.

Elephant Royale
Locke's Wharf E14 £39 ❹❷❷
Westferry Rd   7987 7999   11–2C
With its "lovely view across to Greenwich", this "pricey" Isle of Dogs river-side Thai (which has a "great" riverside terrace) makes a "fun" and "vibrant" destination; "good" cocktails, though, may eclipse the "OK" food. / www.elephantroyale.com; 11 pm; set weekday L £23 (FP).

11 Abingdon Road W8 £40 ❹❸❹
11-13 Abingdon Rd   7937 0120   5–1A
Although many reporters perceive this new Kensington restaurant – a sibling to Barnes's Sonny's, on the site that was Phoenicia (RIP) – as a "promising newcomer", the overall verdict is that's it's a pretty "soulless" place, with "uninventive" cooking. / 11 pm.

Elistano SW3 £37 ❹❹❹
25-27 Elystan St   7584 5248   5–2C
"What went wrong?"; this "noisy" backstreet Chelsea spot still strikes some reporters as a "perfect Italian local", but too many former fans say its standards have "gone off a cliff in the last two years". / 10.45 pm.

The Elk in the Woods N1 £38 ❸❸❶
39 Camden Pas 7226 3535 8–3D
*"Hidden amongst the antique shops off Upper Street",
this "very funky" Islington bar is more than just a deliciously "cosy"
drinking den – it serves "well-prepared light bites as well as more
substantial Mediterranean fare". / www.theelkinthewoods.co.uk; 11 pm;
no Amex.*

Embassy W1 £51 ④④⑤
29 Old Burlington St 7851 0956 3–3C
*Glitzy Mayfair nightclub, whose kitchen is overseen by 'name' chef
Gary Hollihead; for some reporters, it's a "favourite" venue with
"beautiful food" – to others, though, it's an "overpriced" and
"sterile" place to eat. / www.embassylondon.com; 11.30 pm; D only, closed
Mon & Sun.*

Emile's SW15 £30 ❸❷❷
96-98 Felsham Rd 8789 3323 10–2B
*"Hidden in the backstreets of Putney", this "secret" bistro is well-
known to locals for its "good-value, traditional fare" and its
"personal" service; the cooking, however, has seemed more
"amateurish" of late. / www.emilesrestaurant.co.uk; 11 pm; D only, closed
Sun; no Amex.*

The Endurance W1 £33 ④④❸
90 Berwick St 7437 2944 3–2D
*Soho is short on gastropubs, making this sleazily-situated boozer
one worth remembering; it serves "good, basic pub food", and is
"a great place for Sunday lunch". / L only.*

The Engineer NW1 £40 ❷④❷
65 Gloucester Ave 7722 0950 8–3B
*This "so-hip-it-hurts" Primrose Hill gastropub (which has
a "fantastic garden") was "back on form" this year; service which
was too "casual" still inspired complaints, but the "quality" food –
the "fabulous brunch", in particular – won renewed praise.
/ www.the-engineer.com; 11 pm; no Amex.*

Enoteca Turi SW15 £44 ❷❶❷
28 Putney High St 8785 4449 10–2B
*The "mesmerising" wine list – which offers an Italian "magic tour"
– has traditionally inspired most feedback on this "welcoming"
family-run Italian, near Putney Bridge; its "passionate" and
"innovative" cooking, however, is increasingly an attraction in its
own right. / www.enotecaturi.com; 11 pm; closed Sun; set weekday L
£29 (FP).*

The Enterprise SW3 £41 ④❷❷
35 Walton St 7584 3148 5–2C
*This "favourite" Knightsbridge hang-out may serve "unexceptional"
cuisine, but it's "always lively and cheerful", thanks to everyone
"drinking and gassing" as they wait for a table.
/ www.christophersgrill.com; 10.30 pm; no booking, except weekday L.*

L'Entrecôte Café de Paris W1 NEW £33 ④④④
3a/3b Baker St 7935 3030 3–1A
*A really dull new outpost of an international steak/frites chain,
five minutes' walk from Selfridges – perhaps they don't
do everything better abroad after all! / Rated on Editors' visit;
www.entrecote.co.uk; 11 pm.*

Epicurean Pizza Lounge EC1 £36 ❸④⑤
10 Clerkenwell Grn 7490 5577 9–1A
Fans say it "puts the pizzazz into pizza", but this year-old
Clerkenwell joint has had a very mixed reception, not least for its
"unbelievably uncomfortable" setting – we understand that
expansion may be planned. / www.eplounge.com; 11 pm; closed Mon L,
Tue L & Sun.

Eriki NW3 £34 ❶❶❷
4-6 Northways Pde, Finchley Rd 7722 0606 8–2A
Thanks to its "fantastic modern Indian food" (with "unusual
regional dishes"), its "extremely helpful" service and its "delightful"
décor, this "innovative" Swiss Cottage subcontinental attracts
nothing but praise. / www.eriki.co.uk; 11 pm; closed Sat L.

Esarn Kheaw W12 £25 ❶❷⑤
314 Uxbridge Rd 8743 8930 7–1B
For its fans, the "home-cooked north Thai food" at the Puntar
family's Shepherd's Bush fixture is some of "the best in London",
and "excellent value" too; pity about the "poor" décor.
/ www.esarnkheaw.co.uk; 11 pm; closed Sat L & Sun L.

L'Escargot W1 £45 ❷❷❷
48 Greek St 7437 2679 4–2A
This "sophisticated" Gallic "all-rounder" – long a linchpin of the
Soho scene – provides an "oasis of civility" in the West End;
its "classic" cuisine jumped up a gear in the year which saw a new
chef take charge – unfortunately, he, in turn, has also now moved
on. / www.whitestarline.org.uk; 11.30 pm; closed Sat L & Sun.

L'Escargot (Picasso Room) W1 £60 ❸❷❶
48 Greek St 7437 2679 4–2A
"A great place for a small celebration" or "romantic" assignation –
this "heavenly" little room (up a staircase from the main brasserie)
provides an "elegant" setting with "excellent and attentive" service;
most, if not quite all, reporters say the cuisine is "superb" too.
/ www.whitestarline.org.uk; 11.30 pm; closed Mon, Sat L & Sun.

Esenza W11 £43 ❸❷❸
210 Kensington Park Rd 7792 1066 6–1A
"Generous portions of well-executed dishes" make this "buzzy"
Notting Hill Italian popular with all who comment on it; feedback,
however, is surprisingly sparse. / www.esenza.co.uk; 11.30 pm;
set weekday L £27 (FP).

Est Est Est £36
29 Chiswick High Rd, W4 8747 8777 7–2B
27-29 Bellevue Rd, SW17 8672 3122 10–2C
38 High St, SW19 8947 7700 1–4A
This shiny Italian chain (majoring in pizza) changed hands in the
period of our survey; reports were very mixed, so we've left
a proper assessment till next year. / 11 pm.

L'Estaminet WC2 £43 ❸❸❸
14 Garrick St 7379 1432 4–3C
For its fans, this "slightly dated" Covent Garden "oasis" is the
epitome of "classic French cuisine" (and has a cheeseboard that's
"the stuff of dreams"); as ever, though, its detractors just find
it plain "unexceptional". / 10.30 pm; closed Sat L & Sun; set pre theatre
£26 (FP).

sign up for the survey at www.hardens.com 81

L'Etranger SW7　　　　　　　£50　❷❷❸
36 Gloucester Rd　7584 1118　5–1B
*"Interesting" Japanese/French fare, an "amazing" wine list and
"impeccable" service are winning a growing reputation for this
"small" and "trendy" South Kensington three-year-old.*
/ www.etranger.co.uk; 11 pm; closed Sat L & Sun; set weekday L £30 (FP).

The Evangelist EC4　　　　　　£30　❸❸❸
33 Black Friars Ln　7213 0740　9–3A
*"It was trendier a couple of years ago", but this bar in a City back-
lane – serving a "fairly routine" snacky menu – still makes a handy
place for a quick bite. / www.massivepub.com; 9 pm; closed Sat & Sun.*

Everest Inn SE3 NEW　　　　　£24　❷❷❸
39 Tranquil Vale　8852 7872　1–3D
*"Beautifully spiced and perfectly cooked Nepalese dishes at very
reasonable prices" win nothing but praise for this "charming" and
"unpretentious" Blackheath newcomer. / www.everestinn.co.uk;
11.30 pm.*

Exotika WC2　　　　　　　　£22　❷❷④
7 Villiers St　7930 6133　4–4D
*A pit stop well worth knowing about – this funny little café,
by Charing Cross station, wins consistent praise for its "slightly
zany" selection of "cheap and healthy fare"; BYO. / www.exotika.co.uk;
11 pm; closed Sun.*

Eyre Brothers EC2　　　　　　£47　❸❸❸
70 Leonard St　7613 5346　9–1D
*Slightly "off the beaten track", this "relaxed" and "clubby"
Shoreditch five-year-old serves "interesting" and "unusual" Iberian
cuisine (and makes a "good alternative business venue").
/ www.eyrebrothers.co.uk; 10.45 pm; closed Sat L & Sun.*

Fairuz　　　　　　　　　　£40　❷❸④
3 Blandford St, W1　7486 8108　2–1A
27 Westbourne Grove, W2　7243 8444　6–1C
*"Terrific" meze and other "really fresh and tasty" food is making
quite a name for this Lebanese mini-group – "they give Maroush
a run for their money, and the service is much better". / W2
11.30 pm, W1 11 pm.*

Fakhreldine W1　　　　　　　£50　❸❸❸
85 Piccadilly　7493 3424　3–4C
*"Book a window table for a Green Park view", when you visit this
first-floor Lebanese fixture (which benefited from a "loungey" refit
a couple of years ago); it's not inexpensive, but the food is usually
"delicious". / www.fakhreldine.co.uk; midnight.*

Il Falconiere SW7　　　　　　£35　④❸④
84 Old Brompton Rd　7589 2401　5–2B
*"Go for the excellent-value, set-priced menus" – they're what
makes it worth seeking out this long-established South Kensington
trattoria. / www.ilfalconiere.co.uk; 11.30 pm; closed Sun; set weekday L
£20 (FP).*

La Famiglia SW10 £45 ④④❸
7 Langton St 7351 0761 5–3B
To its fans, this World's End trattoria (with garden) is "a golden oldie", where "loyal" staff serve "Italian comfort food" in an ever-"bubbling" atmosphere; it can seem "complacent", though, and some experiences this year were "drab". / www.lafamiglia.co.uk; 11.45 pm.

The Farm SW6 £36
18 Farm Ln 7381 3331 5–3A
"Tucked-away" near Fulham Broadway, this potentially stylish, gastropub changed hands in early 2006; an early report suggests that "having at last dropped its pretentious prices" it may be feeling less "lifeless" – we've left it un-rated pending a proper assessment next year. / www.thefarmfulham.co.uk; 11 pm.

El Faro E14 NEW £45 ❸④❸
3 Turnberry Quay 7987 5511 1–3D
A true rarity – a recommendable newcomer on the Isle of Dogs; this tapas bar/restaurant may have no great aspirations, but its food was enjoyable and good value on our early-days visit, and the spacious waterside premises even have a touch of character. / Rated on Editors' visit; www.el-faro.co.uk; 11 pm; closed Sun; set weekday L £24 (FP).

Fat Boy's £29 ❸❸❸
33 Haven Grn, W5 8998 5868 1–2A
431-433 Richmond Rd, TW1 8892 7657 1–4A
68 High St, TW8 8569 8481 1–3A
10a-10b Edensor Rd, W4 8994 8089 10–1A
"Cheap and tasty" Thai cuisine wins popularity for these West London greasy spoons; they're also "great for breakfast or brunch" (of the British variety); at Chiswick, you can BYO. / 11 pm.

Faulkner's E8 £28 ❷❸④
424-426 Kingsland Rd 7254 6152 1–1D
"If fish 'n' chips is what you're after, this is worth the detour" – this veteran Dalston Market chippie serves "excellently battered" fish and "terrific" chips in "huge" portions. / 10 pm; need 8+ to book.

Feng Sushi £28 ❸❸❸
26 Elizabeth St, SW1 7730 0033 2–4A
218 Fulham Rd, SW10 7795 1900 5–3B
101 Notting Hill Gate, W11 7727 1123 6–2B
21 Kensington Church St, W8 7937 7927 5–1A
1 Adelaide St, NW3 7483 2929 8–2B NEW
13 Stoney St, SE1 7407 8744 9–4C
This "efficient" chain wins many fans with its "buzzy" branches and its "healthy" range of Japanese dishes (not least "good, fresh sushi"); it can, however, sometimes seem "overpriced". / www.fengsushi.co.uk; 11 pm, Sun-Wed 10 pm, SE1 Thu-Sat 10.30 pm; SW1 & SE1 closed Sun; SW1 need 5+ to book.

The Fentiman Arms SW8 £34 ④❷❷
64 Fentiman Rd 7793 9796 10–1D
"A very pretty garden" adds lustre to this "atmospheric" Kennington gastropub; its "tasty" scoff, however, can sometimes seem a mite "overpriced". / www.geronimo-inns.co.uk; 9.45 pm; no Amex.

Ferrari's SW17 £28 ④❸④
225 Balham High Rd 8682 3553 10–2C
This large Balham "neighbourhood" Italian incites mixed views – fans feel "every area should have one", but critics find it just "mediocre". / www.ferrarisrestaurants.co.uk; 11 pm.

Ffiona's W8 £38 ④❶❶
51 Kensington Church St 7937 4152 5–1A
"Some people find Ffiona rather full-on", but her "tireless and friendly" attentions generally make for "a great night out" at this quirky Kensington fixture; arguably the "earthy" home cooking and "womb-like" atmosphere make it "more of a winter place". / www.ffionas.com; 11 pm; D only, closed Mon.

Fifteen Restaurant N1 £81 ⑤④④
15 Westland Pl 0871 330 1515 9–1C
However "worthy" the cause, the basement dining room of Jamie Oliver's "funky" Hoxton project still leaves many critics feeling "robbed" by the "insane" prices demanded for its "ordinary" Italianate food; supporters say it has "improved", though, and its average survey ratings have now scraped off rock-bottom. / www.fifteenrestaurant.com; 9.30 pm; booking: max 6.

Fifteen Trattoria N1 £42 ❸❷❷
15 Westland Pl 0871 330 1515 9–1C
The upstairs at Jamie Oliver's Hoxton HQ is actually "a much nicer space than the restaurant" (despite charging about half the price); with its "helpful" trainees, "simple and fresh" Italian food and "fun" ambience, it's a much better advertisement for the Fifteen concept than down below. / www.fifteenrestaurant.com; 10 pm; booking: max 12.

The Fifth Floor Café
Harvey Nichols SW1 £38 ⑤⑤④
109-125 Knightsbridge 7823 1839 5–1D
"I have always been a fan of this airy café, but over the last three years standards have dropped every visit" – one reporter speaks for many about the sad decline of this once-notable rendezvous, which some still tip as "a place to meet girlfriends for a leisurely bite". / www.harveynichols.com; 10.30 pm, Sun 6 pm; closed Sun D; no booking at L.

The Fifth Floor Restaurant
Harvey Nichols SW1 £56 ④④⑤
109-125 Knightsbridge 7235 5250 5–1D
"You plough through an over-popular bar" to reach this "over-pricey" Knightsbridge dining room, which attracts ever less interest from reporters – the "incredible" wine list is the only feature generating anything approaching excitement. / www.harveynichols.com; 11 pm; closed Sun D.

Fig N1 £35 ❸❷❸
169 Hemingford Rd 7609 3009 8–3D
This "sweet" neighbourhood spot makes a "surprising find in a residential Islington backstreet", serving "imaginative" food in a "cramped", "front-room-style" setting. / www.figrestaurant.co.uk; 10 pm; closed Mon, Tue L, Wed L, Thu L, Fri L & Sun D; no Amex.

La Figa E14 £34 ❸❷❸
45 Narrow St 7790 0077 11–1B
This "very buzzy and lively" Docklands Italian – sibling
to Wapping's Il Bordello – is consistently praised for its "hearty and
tasty" grub, including "excellent" pizza and other "authentic"
dishes. / www.lafiga.co.uk; 11 pm.

Fina Estampa SE1 £35 ④❸❷
150 Tooley St 7403 1342 9–4D
"Great Pisco sours" have long been a high-point at this welcoming
Peruvian, near Tower Bridge; it offers a "reasonably-priced" and
"interesting" menu (though some dishes can be a bit "tasteless").
/ 10.30 pm; closed Sat L & Sun.

Fine Burger Company £24 ❸❸④
50 James St, W1 7224 1890 3–1A
256 Muswell Hill Broadway, N10 8815 9292 8–1C
330 Upper St, N1 7359 3026 8–3D
O2 Centre, Finchley Rd, NW3 7433 0700 8–2A **NEW**
37 Bedford Hill, SW12 8772 0266 10–2C
With its "solid and wholesome" burgers and "reasonable prices",
this "no-frills" chain "does what it says on the tin"; some claim
it "gives GBK a run for its money", but it doesn't match its rival's
food rating overall. / www.homebar.co.uk/fbc; 11 pm.

Fino W1 £44 ❷⓪❷
33 Charlotte St 7813 8010 2–1C
"Fabulous tapas with savoir faire", "slick" service and a "classy" but
"relaxed" style have won huge popularity for this "mega-cool"
Spanish basement, in Fitzrovia. / www.finorestaurant.com; 10.30 pm;
closed Sun; booking: max 12; set weekday L £30 (FP).

Fiore SW1 £46 ❸❷④
33 St James's St 7930 7100 3–4C
"Exceptional" service and "very good" food win praise for this
prominently-sited St James's Italian; what's most striking, though,
is how few reports it attracts – perhaps because the room is so
"dull". / www.fiore-restaurant.co.uk; 10.30 pm; closed Sat L & Sun L.

Fire & Stone WC2 £30 ❸❸❷
31-32 Maiden Ln 0845 330 0139 4–3D
"The aircraft-hangar-sized setting" creates a surprisingly "cool"
ambience at this offbeat Covent Garden venue; its "weird pizzas" –
featuring "themes from around the world" – can be "hit-and-miss",
but "generally beat chain-pizza hands-down". / www.fireandstone.com;
11 pm.

The Fire Stables SW19 £38 ④④❸
27-29 Church Rd 8946 3197 10–2B
This stylish but "noisy" gastropub offers "reliable if unexciting"
cooking – "Wimbledon lacks decent places, and it's OK".
/ www.thefirestables.co.uk; 10.30 pm; no Amex; booking: max 8, Sat & Sun;
set weekday L £22 (FP).

Firezza £24 ❷❷❸

12 All Saints Rd, W11 7221 0020 6–1B
48 Chiswick High Rd, W4 8994 9494 7–2B
276 St Paul's Rd, N1 7359 7400 8–2B
40 Lavender Hill, SW11 7223 5535 10–1C
205 Garrett Ln, SW18 8870 7070 10–2B
"Delicious", very "real" pizza, sold be the 1/2 metre, makes this
small – primarily take-way – chain a favourite option for many
reporters. / www.firezza.com; 11pm.

First Edition E14 £40 ❹❹❸

25 Cabot Sq, Canary Wharf 7513 0300 11–1C
One of the few non-group operations in Canary Wharf, this handily-
sited bar/restaurant is a hit with some of the local worker-bees
(mainly because it "doesn't feel as if you're in a financial centre");
standards, however, "vary". / 10 pm; closed Sat & Sun.

First Floor W11 £36 ❹❷⓿

186 Portobello Rd 7243 0072 6–1A
The "beautiful shabby-chic décor" remains the special feature
of this "stunning" dining room, overlooking Portobello Market;
the food, however, is "run-of-the-mill". / www.firstfloorportobello.co.uk;
10.30 pm; closed Mon & Sun D; no Amex.

Fish Central EC1 £21 ❸❹❹

149 Central St 7253 0229 9–1B
This Clerkenwell pit stop underwent a "bright" and "contemporary"
revamp a couple of years ago; under the bonnet, though, it remains
a "good", "honest" and "wholesome" chippie. / www.fishcentral.co.uk;
10.30 pm; closed Sun.

Fish Club SW11 £30 ⓿⓿❹

189 St John's Hill 7978 7115 10–2C
A great "new spin on fish 'n' chips" is hailed by fans of this
"friendly" Battersea yearling – true, it does feel like "eating in a
fishmongers", but you do get "wonderful fresh fish", "moreish"
chips and "a good array of sides"; (licensed or you can BYO).
/ www.thefishclub.com; 10 pm, Sun 9 pm; closed Mon; no Amex.

Fish Hook W4 NEW £42 ❷❸❹

6-8 Elliott Rd 8742 0766 7–2A
An ex-Trompette chef delivers "superb" cuisine (principally fish)
at this re-incarnated Chiswick local ("which has lost its South
African spelling and specialities"); its "snug" setting gets very
"noisy" and "crowded", though, and those "spoilt" by its
adventurous predecessor can find it a bit of a disappointment.
/ www.fishhook.co.uk; 10.30 pm; closed Mon.

Fish in a Tie SW11 £21 ❸❸❷

105 Falcon Rd 7924 1913 10–1C
This "very cheap" and "very cheerful" bistro near Clapham
Junction is a "wonderful" local; it's "claustrophobic", though –
"presumably they only manage such unbelievable prices because it's
rammed full every night". / 11.45 pm; no Amex; set weekday L £14 (FP).

Fish Shop EC1 £40 ❸❸❸

360-362 St John's St 7837 1199 8–3D
"They know exactly what to do with a fish" at this "light" and
"airy" bistro, which is consistently popular with Islington folk;
its location is especially handy "pre-Sadler's Wells".
/ www.thefishshop.net; 11 pm, Sun 8 pm; closed Mon.

fish! SE1 £39 ❸④④
Cathedral St 7407 3803 9–4C
"Simple" and "very fresh" fish dishes – albeit at "high" prices –
make this Borough Market fixture very popular; service can
struggle, but the setting – in a glass shed – is "interesting".
/ www.fishdiner.co.uk; 10.30 pm.

Fishmarket
Great Eastern Hotel EC2 £51
40 Liverpool St 7618 7200 9–2D
As our survey year was drawing to a close, this City seafood
restaurant (traditionally one of the less-unsatisfactory Conran
operations) changed hands – ratings, therefore,
seem inappropriate. / www.great-eastern-hotel.co.uk; 10.30 pm; closed
Sat & Sun.

Fishworks £46 ❷④④
89 Marylebone High St, W1 7935 9796 2–1A
6 Turnham Green Ter, W4 8994 0086 7–2A
134 Upper St, N1 7354 1279 8–3D
57 Regent's Park Rd, NW1 7586 9760 8–3B **NEW**
13/19 The Sq, Old Mkt, TW9 8948 5965 1–4A **NEW**
"The freshest fish, perfectly and simply cooked with no fuss or frills"
has won huge success for this "high-grade" fishmonger-cum-café
chain; the ambience is often "hectic", though, service can
be "slow", and prices can seem "high". / www.fishworks.co.uk;
10.30 pm; closed Mon; W4 closed Sun D.

5 Cavendish Square W1 £63 ④④❸
5 Cavendish Sq 7079 5000 3–1C
Given the "beautifully ornate" décor, the food at this palatial West
End bar/club/dining room "should be fabulous" – it's only
"average", though, and service can be "very slow". / www.no5ltd.com;
10.30 pm; closed Sat L & Sun D; no booking, Fri & Sat; set Sun L £41 (FP).

Five Hot Chillies HA0 £23 ❶❶❸
875 Harrow Rd 8908 5900 1–1A
Adulatory reviews continue to roll in for the "simple" and
"delicious" Indian food at this "authentic" BYO Sudbury canteen –
it's "well worth a journey". / 11.30 pm; no Amex.

Flâneur EC1 £42 ❸④❷
41 Farringdon Rd 7404 4422 9–1A
A "stunning" setting (even if it's "a bit clattery & shop-ish")
contributes to the "cool" but "odd" experience of "eating among
the groceries" at this Farringdon deli; brunch is a forte, but despite
"wonderful, fresh ingredients", results can be "hit-and-miss",
and service is "wobbly". / www.flaneur.com; 10 pm; closed Sun D.

Flat White W1 **NEW** £9 ❷❷❷
17 Berwick St 7734 4384 3–2D
"Starbucks eat your heart out"; fans insist that this Kiwi café
in Soho – named after one of its Antipodean-style brews – offers
"without a doubt the best coffee in London". / www.flat-white.co.uk;
no credit cards.

Florians N8 £34 ④❷❸
4 Topsfield Pde   8348 8348   1–1C
"There's always a buzz, and staff are unfailingly friendly" at this
"convivial Italian local" – long a linchpin of Crouch End; the food
is mostly "well-prepared" but it can also be "average".
/ www.floriansrestaurant.co.uk; 11 pm; no Amex; set weekday L £21 (FP).

Floridita W1 £55 ⑤⑤❸
100 Wardour St   7314 4000   3–2D
For "large parties who want to get hammered", this "noisy" and
"amazingly overpriced" Conran-backed Soho Cuban has its uses;
the food can be "terrible", though, and some of the staff seem
to find customers "rather a bind". / www.floriditalondon.com; 2 am;
D only, closed Sun.

Foliage
Mandarin Oriental SW1 £72 ❷❷❸
66 Knightsbridge   7201 3723   5–1D
With its "vibrant" cooking and "professional" service,
this Knightsbridge dining room can seem "strangely under-rated
and under-publicised"; at lunch, "the superb park view" helps make
it an "idyllic" venue – by night, however, the ambience seems more
"bland" (not helped by a "noisy" adjacent bar).
/ www.mandarinoriental.com; 10 pm; booking: max 6.

Food for Thought WC2 £16 ❷④④
31 Neal St   7836 0239   4–2C
This "old-faithful veggie", north of Covent Garden, retains quite
a fan club; it's not the "very crowded" (if "buzzing") basement
setting that does it, but the "unusually flavoursome" food
at "satisfyingly low prices"; BYO. / 8 pm; closed Sun D; no credit cards;
no booking.

The Food Room SW8 £37 ❶❷❸
123 Queenstown Rd   7622 0555   10–1C
"Excellent and imaginative" cooking makes this Battersea yearling
– sibling to Surbiton's French Table – something of a "hidden gem";
reporters have sometimes found it "empty", but – as the word gets
out – its "bright and airy" quarters seem to be warming up a bit.
/ www.thefoodroom.com; 10.30 pm; closed Mon, Tue L, Sat L & Sun D.

Footstool
St Johns SW1 £35 ⑤⑤④
St John's, Smith Sq   7222 2779   2–4C
"Never failing to disappoint" some reporters – this café in a
"potentially splendid" Westminster crypt is a safe tip only before
a concert in the hall above. / www.digbytrout.co.uk; L only, closed
Sat & Sun.

Formosa Dining Room
The Prince Alfred W9 £37 ❸❸❸
5a Formosa St   7286 3287   6–1C
A "relaxed" modern annexe to a beautiful Victorian pub in Maida
Value; it makes a pretty "reliable" destination for "good gastropub-
type fare". / 10.45 pm; no Amex.

**(The Fountain)
Fortnum & Mason W1** £38 ④❸❸
181 Piccadilly 7734 8040 3–3D
*"Always a treat" for traditional types – this "classic English-style"
St James's buttery offers "perfect nursery fare" all day long
(with "very good" breakfasts a highlight); it will probably
be redeveloped at some point in 2007, so hurry, hurry...!
/ www.fortnumandmason.co.uk; 7.30 pm; closed Sun; no booking at L.*

Four Regions TW9 £35 ❸❸④
102-104 Kew Rd 8940 9044 1–4A
*"Year after year, this Richmond haunt continues to keep its clients
happy"; "courteous" staff deliver a menu of "above-average"
Chinese "old favourites" (and now also with some Thai options).
/ 11.30 pm.*

The Four Seasons W2 £25 ❷⑤⑤
84 Queensway 7229 4320 6–1C
*"The food is worth the queue", say fans of this "authentic"
Bayswater Chinese institution, where "the tastiest roast duck
in town" – plus many other "terrific" dishes – bring many reporters
back time and again. / 11 pm.*

1492 SW6 £35 ❸④❸
404 North End Rd 7381 3810 5–4A
*This "lively" South American hang-out, near Fulham Broadway,
wins general (if not unanimous) praise for its "interesting Latin
food" and "excellent cocktails". / www.1492restaurant.com; 10.30 pm;
D only.*

The Fox EC2 £32 ❸④❷
28 Paul St 7729 5708 9–1C
*A "well-cooked", traditional-ish menu can justify a visit to this
"atmospheric" old boozer, south of Shoreditch; especially given the
backing of Eagle-founder Michael Belben, though, some reporters
see "room for improvement". / 10 pm; closed Sat & Sun; no Amex.*

Fox & Anchor EC1 £26 ❸❷❷
115 Charterhouse St 7253 5075 9–1B
*"A better way to start the day has not been invented" than the
"wicked" pleasure of "the ultimate full-fry" breakfasts served with
a pint of bitter (or Guinness) at this "old worlde" Smithfield pub.
/ www.foxandanchor.com; 10 pm; closed Sat & Sun.*

The Fox & Hounds SW11 £33 ❷❸❷
66 Latchmere Rd 7924 5483 10–1C
*"From the outside, it looks like an old man's pub", but this "laid-
back" Battersea boozer has a major under-40 following for its
"delicious" Mediterranean cuisine – locals insist it's "better than
most restaurants in the West End"! / 11 pm; Mon-Thu D only, Fri-Sun
open L & D; no Amex.*

The Fox Reformed N16 £32 ④❸❷
176 Stoke Newington Church St 7254 5975 1–1C
*A quirky, small wine bar – the sort of place to hang out over
a game of backgammon – whose "reliable" menu and friendly
service have long made it a feature of the area.
/ www.fox-reformed.co.uk; 10.30 pm, Sat & Sun midnight; closed weekday L.*

Foxtrot Oscar SW3   £38   ⑤⑤④
79 Royal Hospital Rd   7352 7179   5–3D
*Michael Proudlock's "entertaining" and "cliquey" Chelsea bistro has
changed little since its inclusion in that '80s style bible, the Sloane
Ranger Handbook; nowadays, though, its cooking can seem to be
of "school dinners" quality at best – "he needs to bring in Jamie
to sort it out!" / 11 pm; closed Sun D; no Amex.*

Franco's SW1 NEW   £48   ④④④
61-63 Jermyn St   7499 2211   3–3C
*For its fans, the Hambro family's relaunch of this St James's veteran
(est 1946) has created a "great, new modern Italian"; as voluble,
however, are critics who find the cooking "average", the portions
"small" and the evening ambience "dead" – and all at prices which
are "taking the p***"! / www.francoslondon.com; 10.45 pm; closed Sun.*

Frankie's Italian Bar & Grill   £40   ⑤⑤④
Criterion, 224 Piccadilly, W1   7930 0488   3–3D NEW
3 Yeomans Row, SW3   7590 9999   5–2C
68 Chiswick High Rd, W4   8987 9988   7–2B NEW
263 Putney Bridge Rd, SW15   8780 3366   10–2B NEW
*"A huge let-down"; Franco Dettori and MPW's fast-growing posh
pizza chain – with its oddball "Las Vegas casino" décor –
just seems "incompetent" to many reporters; as to the new branch
in the former Criterion Grill (RIP) – "it does not deserve this
splendid space". / 11 pm; W4 Mon-Fri L.*

Franklins SE22   £40   ❷❷❸
157 Lordship Ln   8299 9598   1–4D
*For its East Dulwich fan club, this "friendly" and "buzzy"
neighbourhood spot is "the best place for miles around"; it serves
a "short" but "interesting" menu of "traditional English" food.
/ www.franklinsrestaurant.com; 10.30 pm; set weekday L £22 (FP).*

Frantoio SW10   £37   ❸❷❷
397 King's Rd   7352 4146   5–3B
*This "very friendly" World's End Italian "goes from strength
to strength", even if the food is "fairly standard". / 11.15 pm.*

Fratelli la Bufala NW3   £32   ④❸❸
45a South End Rd   7435 7814   8–2A
*"Great pizza and good-value lunches" make this "very friendly"
and "enthusiastic" Hampstead Italian a "real find", for most
reporters; the minority who complain of "insipid" cooking and
"clueless" service, however, are bemused by its popularity. / 11 pm.*

Frederick's N1   £47   ❸❸❷
106 Camden Pas   7359 2888   8–3D
*This "lovely" Islington "old-stager" – which benefits from an "airy"
conservatory and garden – continues to 'coast'; on most accounts,
it still provides "enjoyable" cooking, but the menu's "lack of
ambition" features in ever more reports. / www.fredericks.co.uk; 11 pm;
closed Sun; no Amex; set pre theatre £28 (FP).*

The Freemasons SW18   £32   ❸❷❷
2 Wandsworth Common Northside   7326 8580   10–2C
*"A good vibe and consistently good food" ("in an area that lacks
gastropubs") ensures that this Wandsworth yearling is "always
packed", and "deservedly so". / www.freemasonspub.com; 10 pm,
Sun 9.30 pm.*

Freemasons Arms NW3 £37 ④④❸
32 Downshire Hill   7433 6811   8–2A
A "fantastic beer garden" has helped make this year-old gastropub
a notable Hampstead destination; some reporters find the food
"excellent" – there are doubters, too, though, who say: "don't buy
the hype". / www.freemasonsarms.co.uk; 10 pm.

French House W1 £45 ❸❸❷
49 Dean St   7437 2477   4–3A
With its "cosy" and "intimate" setting, this small first-floor dining
room, above a famous Soho pub, is a "jewel" for most reporters;
the "authentic" Gallic fare is not the main point, but it
is "good value". / 11 pm; closed Sun; booking: max 8.

Fresco W2 £18 ❷❶❸
25 Westbourne Grove   7221 2355   6–1C
"Brilliant fresh fruit juices and smoothies" – plus "a great range
of Middle Eastern snacks at reasonable prices" – make it well
worth knowing about this "cramped" Bayswater pit stop. / 11 pm;
set weekday L £10 (FP).

Friends SW10 £34 ④❷❸
6 Hollywood Rd   7376 3890   5–3B
For a "casual" bite, locals recommend this "friendly and personal"
Chelsea Italian, and in particular its "good pizza". / 11 pm; closed
weekday L, Sat D & Sun D; no Amex.

Frocks E9 £37 ④④④
95 Lauriston Rd   8986 3161   1–2D
This "cosy and homely" bistro has become a fixture of the area
round Victoria Park; fans praise it for its "unpretentious" style and
"imaginative food" – doubters just find it "distinctly average".
/ 10.30 pm, Sun 9 pm; closed weekday L.

La Fromagerie Café W1 £33 ❶❷❷
2-4 Moxon St   7935 0341   3–1A
"There are less than 20 seats (in fact stools)" around the
communal table of this celebrated and "wonderfully atmospheric"
Marylebone shop; the quality of its cheese, charcuterie and so on
is "second to none". / www.lafromagerie.co.uk; 7 pm; L only; no booking.

The Frontline Club W2 £42 ④❷❷
13 Norfolk Pl   7479 8960   6–1D
"The pictures on the wall are more interesting than the food",
at this "mix of photo-journalists' club and restaurant"; it has
a "lovely" feel, though, and "in the gastro-desert that is Paddington,
draws diners like a village pump draws the thirsty".
/ www.thefrontlineclub.com; 10.30 pm; closed Sat L & Sun D.

Fryer's Delight WC1 £9 ❸❸⑤
19 Theobald's Rd   7405 4114   2–1D
For "proper cabbies' fish 'n' chips", it's hard to beat this decidedly
"no-frills" Holborn institution; if you wish, you can BYO. / 10 pm;
closed Sun; no credit cards; no booking.

Fuego Pizzeria SW8 NEW £19 ❸❷⑤
388 Wandsworth Rd   7622 7999   10–1D
This unpretentious new Lambeth pizzeria is already establishing
itself as a 'value' destination in a decidedly thin area; perhaps
it helps that its owners previously held senior posts at 'name'
restaurants in the West End. / Rated on Editors' visit; 11 pm.

Fujiyama SW9 £19 ❷④❸
7 Vining St   7737 2369   10–2D
The setting is "cramped" and service "can be random", but this "friendly" Brixton Japanese outfit knocks out "delicious" grub (now including sushi) at "cheap" prices. / www.newfujiyama.com; midnight; no Amex.

Fung Shing WC2 £34 ❷❸④
15 Lisle St   7437 1539   4–3A
"Seasonal specials" and "wonderful seafood" ("lobster noodles is a must-have") are the way to go at this Chinese stalwart, which – until quite recently – was rated Chinatown's best destination; staff are "usually friendly" too, but "please, please redecorate". / www.fungshing.co.uk; 11.15 pm.

Furnace N1 £30 ❸④❸
1 Rufus St   7613 0598   9–1D
A "Hoxton hot spot" – since its opening in 2002 – serving "good" pizzas with "tasty" toppings. / 11 pm; closed Sat L & Sun; no Amex.

Fuzzy's Grub £9 ❶❶❸
6 Crown Pas, SW1   7925 2791   3–4D
10 Well Ct, EC4   7236 8400   9–2B
62 Fleet St, EC4   7583 6060   9–2A
"Quite outstanding roasts" – served with salads and "incredible roast potatoes", or as "the best bap you will ever taste!" – win fervent praise for these doggedly British "upmarket greasy spoons"; they are also hailed for "amazing" breakfasts and "fabulous" pies. / www.fuzzysgrub.com; EC4 3 pm, SW1 4 pm; closed Sat & Sun; no credit cards; no booking.

Gabrielles W1 £46 ④⑤④
14 Heddon St   7494 2234   3–2C
Too many gripes of "slow" service and "mediocre" food have made this a far-from-classic year for this Mediterranean corner spot, just off Regent Street; perhaps the new chef can shake things up. / www.gabrielles.com; 11 pm; closed Sun.

Gaby's WC2 £25 ❸❷⑤
30 Charing Cross Rd   7836 4233   4–3B
"Great for a bite before the flicks or theatre" – this age-old Israeli café, near Leicester Square tube, is known for its "trademark salt beef" and "super falafel pittas". / midnight; no credit cards.

Gail's Bread NW3 NEW £14 ❸❷④
64 Hampstead High St   7794 5700   8–1A
Shame about the "steep prices" – otherwise reports on this new Hampstead café/bakery are largely a hymn of praise to its "simply delicious selection of breads, cakes and savouries" and "friendly" staff; "they make a mean coffee too". / www.gailsbread.co.uk; 9 pm; no Amex.

Galicia W10 £29 ❸❷❷
323 Portobello Rd   8969 3539   6–1A
"Formica tables and strip lighting" – not to mention "many Spanish customers" and "brusque" service – add to the "very authentic" credentials of this "squashed" Portobello veteran. / 11.30 pm; closed Mon; set Sun L £15 (FP).

Gallipoli £24 ❸❸❷
102 Upper St, N1   7359 0630   8–3D
107 Upper St, N1   7226 5333   8–3D
120 Upper St, N1   7359 1578   8–3D
You get "great fun and good value" at this trio of Turkish bistros
in Islington; that they're "cramped" and usually "crowded" is all
part of their charm. / www.gallipolicafes.com; 11 pm, Fri & Sat midnight;
107 Upper St closed Mon.

Galvin at Windows
Park Lane Hilton Hotel W1 NEW £65 ❷❷❸
22 Park Ln, 28th Floor   7208 4021   3–4A
"The most incredible views" have long been a feature of this 28th-
floor dining room, which underwent a major revamp this year; Chris
Galvin now oversees André Garrett at the stoves, and the
"consistent and well-grounded" cooking now better "lives up to the
spectacle". / www.hilton.co.uk/londonparklane; 10.30 pm; closed
Sat L & Sun D.

Galvin Bistrot de Luxe W1 £40 ❷❷❷
66 Baker St   7935 4007   2–1A
"Hats off!"; Chris & Jeff Galvin's new 'Bistrot de luxe' – the most-
mentioned newcomer of the year – "does exactly what it says
on the tin", offering "honest" and "sensibly-priced" Gallic cuisine
and "discreet" service in a "smart" (if slightly "corporate") setting.
/ www.galvinbistrotdeluxe.co.uk; 11 pm; set weekday L £28 (FP).

Ganapati SE15 £26 ❸❷④
38 Holly Grove   7277 2928   1–4C
"An exciting but simple" menu of "great" south Indian dishes and
"knowledgeable" service win praise for this "unpretentious",
"refectory-style" yearling, in Peckham Rye. / 10.45 pm; closed Mon.

Garbo's W1 £36 ④❸⑤
42 Crawford St   7262 6582   2–1A
This "old-fashioned" Swedish twenty-year-old, in Marylebone, offers
fare that's "not outstanding but pleasant"; many people know it for
its "tremendous" lunchtime smorgasbord (which is "great for the
greedy"). / 10.30 pm; closed Sat L & Sun D; no Maestro; set weekday L
£23 (FP).

The Garden Café NW1 £29 ④④❶
Inner Circle, Regent's Pk   7935 5729   8–4B
The setting "amidst the shrubs and rose blooms" may be "idyllic",
but this characterfully '70s park café (relaunched a year ago) risks
becoming "a wasted opportunity" – "prices are way too high for
the quality of the food". / www.thegardencafe.co.uk; L only; no Amex.

Garlic & Shots W1 £30 ④④④
14 Frith St   7734 9505   4–2A
How come this 'shooters bar' in prime Soho – where all drinks
(including the beer) and all food (including the ice cream) are laced
with garlic – attracts such little feedback?; come to think of it…
/ Rated on Editors' visit; www.garlicandshots.com; 11.15 pm; D only; no Amex;
no booking.

Garrison SE1 £37 ❸❸❶
99-101 Bermondsey St   7089 9355   9–4D
"The wonderfully homely, if squashed, interior is packed to capacity
almost every night", at this "hip" gastropub "jewel";
near Bermondsey Market; the food is "generous" (if a bit "hit and
miss") and service "lovely" (if a bit "on-off"). / 10 pm.

sign up for the survey at www.hardens.com

Gastro SW4 £42 ④⑤❷
67 Venn St 7627 0222 10–2D
*A "shabby" bistro "classic" in "the heart of Clapham"; it still has
a "lovely" ambience, but its "pricey" and "hit-and-miss" cuisine and
its "moody" and "disdainful" service win it few new friends.
/ midnight; no credit cards; set weekday L £22 (FP).*

The Gate W6 £35 ❷❸④
51 Queen Caroline St 8748 6932 7–2C
*"A perennial veggie favourite" – "hidden down a Hammersmith
backstreet" – where fans say "even carnivores can't help but
be impressed"; ratings – particularly for service and ambience –
slipped this year, though, and there were gripes about "high prices".
/ www.thegate.tv; 10.45 pm; closed Sat L & Sun.*

Gaucho £35 ❷④④
Chelsea Farmers' Mkt, Sydney St, SW3 7376 8514 5–3C
30 Old Brompton Rd, SW7 7584 8999 5–2B
*"Chalet-style" décor (and a great outside terrace at the Chelsea
Farmers' Market branch) sets the rustic scene at these "haphazard
but willing" Argentine grills; "fantastic steak and chips" is the star
menu attraction. / www.elgaucho.co.uk; SW3 6.30 pm, SW7 11.30 pm;
SW3 L only, SW7 D only; SW3 no credit cards; SW3 no booking in summer,
SW7 no bookings before 7 pm.*

Gaucho Grill £45 ❸④④
25 Swallow St, W1 7734 4040 3–3D **NEW**
125 Chancery Ln, WC2 7242 7727 2–1D
89 Sloane Ave, SW3 7584 9901 5–2C
64 Heath St, NW3 7431 8222 8–1A
29 Westferry Circus, E14 7987 9494 11–1B
5 Finsbury Ave, Broadgate, EC2 7256 6877 9–1C **NEW**
1 Bell Inn Yd, EC3 7626 5180 9–2C
*With its "succulent" steaks and "extensive" wine list, this Latin
American steak-house chain is a "carnivore heaven" for many
reporters (and notable as "a good safe choice for a business
occasion"); its Swallow Street branch now occupies the amazing
tiled premises that were previously Destino (RIP).
/ www.gauchosgrill.com; 11 pm; EC3 & WC2 closed Sat & Sun.*

LE GAVROCHE W1 £120 ❷❶❷
43 Upper Brook St 7408 0881 3–2A
*To those of an "old-fashioned" disposition, Michel Roux Jr's slightly
"stuffy" Mayfair basement – with its "sumptuous" Gallic cuisine,
its "overwhelming" wine list and its "wonderful" service – is simply
"the epitome of classic fine dining"; "make sure you take a big fat
credit card!" / www.le-gavroche.co.uk; 10.45 pm; closed Sat L & Sun; jacket
required; set weekday L £52 (FP).*

Gay Hussar W1 £39 ④❸❷
2 Greek St 7437 0973 4–2A
*This Soho classic is still a "timeless" favourite for those enamoured
of its "jolly" and "comfortable" atmosphere and its "old-fashioned,
hearty Hungarian food"; its ratings are slipping though, and critics
say its style "just feels dated". / www.gayhussar.co.uk; 10.45 pm;
closed Sun.*

The Gaylord E14 £20 ❷④④
141 Manchester Rd   7538 0393   2–1B
*"Don't let the location put you off!" – this "local gem", in an Isle
of Dogs shopping-parade, offers a "rich and varied" Indian menu
that's cooked "with a little more care than usual"; service, though,
can be "off-hand". / 11.45 pm.*

Geale's W8 £29 ④❸④
2 Farmer St   7727 7528   6–2B
*For those with long memories, this "old-fashioned" fish 'n' chip
veteran, off Notting Hill Gate, "has gone downhill"; it still wins
praise, however, for its "helpful" staff and "generous portions
of fresh fish" – perhaps a major refurb' (scheduled for late-2006)
will prove a turning point. / 11 pm; closed Sun L.*

Geeta NW6 £16 ❷❷⑤
57-59 Willesden Ln   7624 1713   1–1B
*Awful décor/awesome food has long been the equation at this
"lovely, family-run South Indian restaurant" in Kilburn; its ratings
have come of the boil, though, and the odd "disastrous" meal has
been reported of late; (licensed or you can BYO). / 10.30 pm, Fri &
Sat 11.30 pm; no Amex.*

George & Vulture EC3 £40 ⑤❸❷
3 Castle Ct   7626 9710   9–3C
*Fans insist that this Dickensian City chop house (featured
in 'Pickwick Papers') serves "historic" food; those of a more
contemporary mindset, however, find it "so bad it's amazing it still
exists". / L only, closed Sat & Sun.*

Getti £41 ⑤④⑤
16-17 Jermyn St, SW1   7734 7334   3–3D
42 Marylebone High St, W1   7486 3753   2–1A
*There "little to recommend" this West End Italian duo, which offer
"very average food at above-average prices". / 10.45 pm.*

Ghillies £38 ④④❸
271 New King's Rd, SW6   7371 0434   10–1B
94 Point Pleasant, SW18   8871 9267   10–2B
*Mixed reviews have greeted this west London mini-chain's adoption
of a "fusion tapas" formula, but, on balance, reporters feel the food
has "gone downhill since they stopped specialising in fish"; SW18,
however, still benefits from a "lovely" riverside setting,
with "superb" views. / 10 pm; no Amex.*

Giardinetto W1 £58 ❸❷⑤
39-40 Albemarle St   7493 7091   3–3C
*Given Maurizio Vilona's "inventive" cooking, the "friendly" staff and
the "fantastic" wine list, this Mayfair Italian should have become
the talk of the town when it moved from its former Fitzrovia site;
more's the pity, then, that these expensive new premises have
"no ambience whatsoever". / www.giardinetto.co.uk; 11 pm; closed
Sat L & Sun; set weekday L £37 (FP).*

sign up for the survey at www.hardens.com   95

Gilgamesh NW1 NEW £47 ④❷❶
The Stables, Camden Mkt, Chalk Farm Rd 7482 5757 8–2B
Mega-lavish in style, this £12m 800-seat newcomer is arguably London's most dramatic restaurant opening ever; there's nothing wrong with Ian Pengelley's pan-Asian fare, but it's pricey for what it is, and there must be some doubt whether Camden Town can sustain such a behemoth. / Rated on Editors' visit; www.gilgameshbar.com; 11.45 pm.

Gili Gulu WC2 £20 ④⑤⑤
50-52 Monmouth St 7379 6888 4–2B
"If you're very hungry and not too fussy", consider a visit to these "cheap conveyor-belt sushi" joints near Covent Garden – "the service and ambience are pretty poor, but the prices are amazing!" / 11 pm; no Amex; no booking.

Ginger W2 £32 ❸❸④
115 Westbourne Grove 7908 1990 6–1B
A "modern and innovative" Bayswater Bangladeshi; it's a "shame" about the "rather muted and soulless" atmosphere, as the cuisine is rather "interesting". / www.gingerrestaurant.co.uk; 10.30 pm; closed weekday L; set pre theatre £20 (FP).

Giraffe £30 ④❸❸
6-8 Blandford St, W1 7935 2333 2–1A
270 Chiswick High Rd, W4 8995 2100 7–2A
7 Kensington High St, W8 7938 1221 5–1A
29-31 Essex Rd, N1 7359 5999 8–3D
46 Rosslyn Hill, NW3 7435 0343 8–2A
Royal Festival Hall, Riverside, SE1 7928 2004 2–3D
27 Battersea Rise, SW11 7223 0933 10–2C
"They're always packed", so they must be doing something right at this "upbeat" chain, whose "wonderful array of brunch treats" and "yummy burgers" are highlights of a sometimes "confused" 'world food' offering; avoid at weekends if you don't like "kid mayhem". / www.giraffe.net; 11 pm; no booking at weekends.

Glaisters SW10 £34 ④④❷
4 Hollywood Rd 7352 0352 5–3B
A "reasonably-priced" brasserie on the fringe of Chelsea, where "the great atmosphere in the garden room" is its raison d'être. / www.glaisters.co.uk; 10.45 pm; set always available £21 (FP).

Glas SE1 £42 ❷❷④
3 Park St 7357 6060 9–4C
"A Swedish take on the vogue for tapas-style portions" – featuring "unbeatable herring" and "a great range of aquavits" – goes down well at this offbeat Borough Market yearling; the small and percussive "IKEA-inspired" setting, however, is no great shakes. / www.glasrestaurants.com; 10 pm; closed Sun.

The Glasshouse TW9 £52 ❶❶❸
14 Station Pde 8940 6777 1–3A
It may be "stuck away in a parade of shops, by Kew Station", but the western outpost of the Nigel Platts-Martin empire is "just about flawless in every respect", thanks not least to its "pitch-perfect" service and its "cracking" cuisine; it is, however, somewhat "cramped and noisy". / www.glasshouserestaurant.co.uk; 10.30 pm.

Globe Restaurant NW3 £40 ❸②④
100 Avenue Rd 7722 7200 8–2A
It's not just the "smiley" service and "very good-value pre-theatre
menu" (Hampstead Theatre, that is) which makes this "slightly
drab" spot of note – its "breathtaking" Thursday evening drag
cabaret offers "the best night out in London".
/ www.globerestaurant.co.uk; 11 pm; closed Sat L & Sun.

Golden Dragon W1 £27 ❸④④
28-29 Gerrard St 7734 2763 4–3A
For "top dim sum" some reporters would tip this as an "above-
average" Chinatown fixture. / midnight.

Golden Hind W1 £18 ❶②❸
73 Marylebone Ln 7486 3644 2–1A
You get some of "the best fish and chips in London" – served by
"people who know their stuff" – at this "cramped" and "old-
fashioned" Marylebone chippie; new owners have greatly improved
its standards in recent times; BYO. / 10 pm; closed Sat L & Sun.

Good Earth £40 ❷②❸
233 Brompton Rd, SW3 7584 3658 5–2C
143-145 The Broadway, NW7 8959 7011 1–1B
"Still a safe pair of hands"; this "smart and traditional" small
Chinese chain benefits from "attentive" service, and serves food
that's "not cheap but almost invariably excellent". / 10.45 pm.

Gopal's of Soho W1 £27 ❸❸④
12 Bateman St 7434 1621 4–2A
One of Soho's few 'traditional' curry houses of any note; it continues
to attract modest but consistently positive reports. / 11.30 pm; closed
Sun.

GORDON RAMSAY SW3 £91 ❶❶❷
68-69 Royal Hospital Rd 7352 4441 5–3D
His face may never be off the TV, but Gordon Ramsay's
"unbelievable" Chelsea flagship – again the survey's
No. 1 restaurant – is "impossible to fault"; chef Mark Askew's
cuisine is "sublime and memorable", and staff (overseen by
Jean-Claude) "couldn't be more attentive and charming"; (NB
around the publication date of this guide, the restaurant emerges
from a major revamp). / www.gordonramsay.com; 11 pm; closed
Sat & Sun; no jeans or trainers; booking: max 8; set weekday L £58 (FP).

GORDON RAMSAY AT CLARIDGE'S
CLARIDGE'S HOTEL W1 £83 ❸❷❷
55 Brook St 7499 0099 3–2B
For many fans, it's "a rare treat" to feast on Mark Sargeant's
"sumptuous" cuisine in this "beautiful" Art Deco chamber in
Mayfair; it also has many critics, though, for whom – despite the
"Everest-like" prices – it remains a "poor relation" of Ramsay's
Chelsea flagship. / www.gordonramsay.com; 11 pm; no jeans or trainers;
booking: max 8; set weekday L £50 (FP).

Gordon's Wine Bar WC2 £22 ⑤❸❶
47 Villiers St 7930 1408 4–4D
"Dark, dank and wonderful" – this ancient "dive" of a wine bar
features a "superb and cheap wine list" best enjoyed at a table in
its "cave-like" vault (or on the huge summer terrace); as for food,
"forget it!" – if you must, go for the cheese. / www.gordonswinebar.com;
11 pm; no booking.

sign up for the survey at www.hardens.com

The Goring Hotel SW1 £67 €00
15 Beeston Pl 7396 9000 2–4B
"Stylishly refurbished" (by David Linley), the "comfortable" and
"elegant" dining room of this family-owned Victoria hotel goes from
strength to strength; "well-spaced" tables and "unfussy" service
make it a particular business favourite – it's also popular for
"a classic English breakfast". / www.goringhotel.co.uk; 10 pm; closed
Sat L; booking: max 12.

Gourmet Burger Kitchen £20 ❷
49 Fulham Broadway, SW6 7381 4242 5–4A
50 Westbourne Grove, W2 7243 4344 6–1B
131 Chiswick High Rd, W4 8995 4548 7–2A
200 Haverstock Hill, NW3 7443 5335 8–2A
331 West End Ln, NW6 7794 5455 1–1B
44 Northcote Rd, SW11 7228 3309 10–2C
333 Putney Bridge Rd, SW15 8789 1199 10–2B
"The best burgers outside the US!" – in "huge" portions and with
"imaginative" toppings – again made these booming self-service
"feeding stations" the survey's most-mentioned group; well, it can't
be the service or the décor. / www.gbkinfo.co.uk; 11 pm; no Amex;
no booking.

Gourmet Pizza Company £21
7-9 Swallow St, W1 7734 5182 3–3D
Gabriels Wharf, 56 Upper Ground, SE1 7928 3188 9–3A
18 Mackenzie Walk, E14 7345 9192 11–1C
"A great location by the Thames" (at the "crowded" SE1 branch)
risks becoming the sole point of interest of this once-innovative
chain – its "eclectic" pizzas seem ever more "unremarkable".
/ www.gourmetpizzacompany.co.uk; 11.30 pm, E14 10.30 pm; E14 closed
Sat & Sun; W1, need 8+ to book.

Gow's EC2 £48 ❸❷❷
81-82 Old Broad St 7920 9645 9–2C
"Traditional and consistent", this refurbished fish restaurant,
near Liverpool Street, is establishing itself as "a perfect all-rounder
for a long City lunch"; it also does a "good-value set dinner" ("if you
don't mind eating alone!"). / www.ballsbrothers.co.uk; 9.30 pm; closed
Sat & Sun; booking: max 10; set dinner £32 (FP).

The Gowlett SE15 £24 ❸ ❷
62 Gowlett Rd 7635 7048 1–4C
"It may look "intimidating", but this Peckham boozer is universally
hailed by the locals for its "magnificent" stone-bake pizzas and its
"even better" real ale; "worth a detour, if you're in the area".
/ www.thegowlett.com; midnight.

Goya SW1 £32 ❷❸
2 Ecclestone Pl 7730 4299 2–4B
"If you're stuck in Victoria", this "buzzy" bar (no longer part of a
chain) is a "cheap but fun" venue with "OK tapas".

Grafton House SW4 NEW £39 ❸
13-19 Old Town 7498 5559 10–2D
This large new bar/restaurant in Clapham has inspired limited
reports – it's as a "great weekend destination for brunch, roasts
or cocktails" that it's of most interest. / www.graftonhouseuk.com;
10.30 pm, Sun 8.30 pm; D only, ex Sun open L & D; booking essential.

The Grapes E14 £45 ❷❸❷
76 Narrow St 7987 4396 11–1B
Fans of this "quaint" dining room over a riverside pub in the depths
of Docklands say it offers an "awesome" combination of "historic"
ambience and "honest" cooking (not least "the freshest fish").
/ 9 pm; closed Sun D.

Gravy W4 £38 ④④④
142 Chiswick High Rd 8994 6816 7–2B
Opinion on this somewhat "stark" Chiswick brasserie remains a bit
divided; to fans, it's a "great, friendly local" – to detractors,
"pleasant enough, but nothing special and not that cheap".
/ www.gravyrestaurant.co.uk; 10.45 pm; closed Sun D.

Great Eastern Dining Room EC2 £40 ❷❷❸
54 Gt Eastern St 7613 4545 9–1D
"Nobu-esque food for a fraction of the price" helps make a visit
to Will Ricker's "lively" and "laid-back" Shoreditch hang-out a "truly
enjoyable" experience, if quite a "loud" one.
/ www.greateasterndining.co.uk; 11 pm; closed Sat L & Sun.

Great Nepalese NW1 £25 ❷❷⑤
48 Eversholt St 7388 6737 8–3C
"Not many restaurants are as consistent" (or "have had such sweet
service over 20 years") as this "courteous" subcontinental, beside
Euston Station; the "taste-bud titillating" Nepalese specials are
best. / 11.30 pm.

The Green NW2 £33 ❸❸❸
110 Walm Ln 8452 0171 1–1A
Reports are up-and-down, but – on balance – this large gastropub
(which puts a Caribbean spin on some dishes) is "great for
Willesden Green locals", or anyone else finding themselves
thereabouts. / www.thegreennw2.co.uk; 11 pm; no Amex.

Green & Red Bar & Cantina E1 NEW £38 ❷❷❷
51 Bethnal Green Rd 7749 9670 1–2D
"Excellent real (not Tex-Mex)" food – using the "freshest
ingredients" in "hearty" dishes – makes this "very lively" new bar
and cantina, near Brick Lane, "the most authentic Mexican
in London"; its tequila cocktails pack quite a "punch" too.
/ www.greenred.co.uk; 11 pm; closed Mon L, Tue L, Wed L, Thu L, Fri L,
Sat D & Sun D.

The Green Olive W9 £37 ❸❸❸
5 Warwick Pl 7289 2469 8–4A
This Italian venture has long been a fixture of Little Venice; fans say
that – with its "delicious" food and its "intimate" atmosphere –
it's "back on form"; for doubters, though, it's just "not a bad local".
/ 11 pm; booking: max 20.

Green's SW1 £55 ❸❷❸
36 Duke St 7930 4566 3–3D
Simon Parker-Bowles's "very discreet" and "club-like" bastion (in the
heart of St James's) is a "staple" for those of a "traditional" bent,
serving "simple", "classic" British fare – predominantly fish.
/ www.greens.org.uk; 11 pm; closed Sun, May-Sep.

sign up for the survey at www.hardens.com

The Greenhouse W1 £84 ③❷④
27a Hays Mews   7499 3331   3–3B
It may have a "wonderful secluded mews location", but Marlon Abela's "muted" refit of this Mayfair stalwart has robbed it of the romantic appeal it once had – it's now very much a business destination; the "90-odd page" wine list is "a wow", and the food is often "fantastic", but prices are "frightening".
/ www.greenhouserestaurant.co.uk; 11 pm; closed Sat L & Sun; booking: max 6-10; set weekday L £52 (FP).

Greenwich Park Bar & Grill SE10 £38 ⑤④④
King William Wk   8853 7860   1–3D
It may have "a great location" (right by the entrance to the park), but the décor of this year-old pub-conversion is "irritating", and the food can be simply "appalling". / www.thegreenwichpark.com; 11 pm; no Amex; set always available £25 (FP).

Greig's W1 £46 ④④④
26 Bruton Pl   7629 5613   3–2B
Fans say the "steaks are still excellent" at this "old-school" Mayfair grill-house (recently revamped in, er, old-school style); critics are in the majority, however, and they consider it very "expensive" and "unexciting". / www.greigs.com; midnight; set weekday L £27 (FP).

Grenadier SW1 £37 ④④❷
18 Wilton Row   7235 3074   5–1D
This ultra-"cute" pub, in a picturebook Belgravia mews is "a hidden jewel" (or would be, if it weren't in every tourist guide); the "stodgy" traditional fodder in the "cosy" dining room is no great shakes – opt instead for a sausage and a Bloody Mary at the bar. / 11 pm.

The Greyhound NW10 £33 ④❸❸
64-66 Chamberlayne Rd   8969 8080   1–2B
A "friendly" Queen's Park gastropub (and garden), where the food is invariably rated somewhere between "good" and "average". / www.breadandhoney.net; 10.30 pm; closed Mon L.

The Greyhound at Battersea SW11 £45 ❸❸❸
136 Battersea High St   7978 7021   10–1C
The "mammoth" wine lists – there are two – have helped make quite a name for Mark van der Goot's Battersea gastropub, and the cuisine is "a cut above" too; it's quite a "pricey" place, though, and its approach can sometimes seem a bit "precious". / www.thegreyhoundatbattersea.co.uk; 10 pm; closed Mon & Sun D; set Sun L £30 (FP).

The Grove W6 £35 ④④❸
83 Hammersmith Grove   8748 2966   7–1C
This "relaxed" Hammersmith hang-out wins praise for its "decent" (largely organic) food; it is not without critics, though, and can seem "on the expensive side for a pretty pub-like gastropub". / www.groverestaurants.co.uk; midnight; no Amex.

Grumbles SW1 £35 ❸❷❸
35 Churton St   7834 0149   2–4B
A "no-frills", very '60s bistro in Pimlico, which – with particular help from its "friendly" staff – lived up better this year to its reputation as a "great local eatery". / www.grumblesrestaurant.co.uk; 11.15 pm; no Amex; set weekday L £22 (FP).

The Guinea Grill W1 £52 ❷❸❷
30 Bruton Pl 7409 1728 3–3B
Attached to a "cosy pub in the heart of Mayfair", this "true old-fashioned grill" offers a "dated but good" formula featuring "wonderful" steaks and "pies that couldn't come bigger or better"; it's "always a hit with visiting Americans". / www.theguinea.co.uk; 10.30 pm; closed Sat L & Sun; booking: max 8.

The Gun E14 £25 ❸❹❸
27 Coldharbour Ln 7515 5222 11–1C
With its "wonderful Thames-side location across from the Dome", this "smarter than usual" Isle of Dogs gastropub is hailed by fans as a "rare jewel" in a "desolate area"; "service can struggle", though, and the "cheaper, more cheerful bar" wins more praise than the "pricier" dining room (£46). / www.thegundocklands.com; 10.30 pm.

Gung-Ho NW6 £33 ❷❷❷
328-332 West End Ln 7794 1444 1–1B
A West Hampstead fixture long acclaimed as "the best Chinese restaurant in NW London", thanks to its "fresh-tasting" food, its "top notch" service and its "crisp but informal" décor. / 11.30 pm; no Amex.

The Gunmakers EC1 £32 ❹❸❸
13 Eyre Street Hill 7278 1022 9–1A
Those who've discovered this "tucked-away pub" praise it as "a hidden Clerkenwell find", with a "lovely" atmosphere and "quite acceptable" food. / www.thegunmakers.co.uk; 10 pm; closed Sat & Sun D; no Amex; no booking Fri D.

Haandi SW7 £38 ❷❸❹
7 Cheval Pl 7823 7373 5–1C
This Knightsbridge basement is "one of the best Indians in central London" (of the fairly straightforward variety); NB it is still there, but you can't see it from Brompton Road any more. / www.haandi-restaurant.com; 11 pm.

Haché NW1 £20 ❷❷❷
24 Inverness St 7485 9100 8–3B
You get "amazing burgers", "delicious, fresh salads" and "good chips" at this "airy" and "very atmospheric" yearling, in Camden Town. / www.hacheburgers.co.uk; 10.30 pm.

Hadley House E11 £40 ❸❹❹
27 Wanstead High St 8989 8855 1–1D
This small and unpretentious Wanstead local offers food that's "exciting for the area" and generally "well-executed" too; "greater attention to décor and service", however, "might encourage more frequent visits". / 10 pm; no Amex.

HAKKASAN W1 £75 ❸❹❷
8 Hanway Pl 7927 7000 4–1A
A "Bond film" interior and "amazing" Chinese cuisine (not least "sublime" lunchtime dim sum) make Alan Yau's "sexy" and "electric" basement oriental, tucked-away off Tottenham Court Road, a "fabulous" destination; it can seem rather "full of itself", though, and evening prices are "appalling". / midnight, Mon & Sun 11 pm; no shorts; set weekday L £51 (FP).

Halepi W2 £36 ❸④❸
18 Leinster Ter 7262 1070 6–2C
Now bereft of its Belsize Park sibling, this "cosy", "veteran" Greek taverna in Bayswater is still hailed by its "loyal and cosmopolitan" regulars for being "as reliable as ever". / midnight; set always available £32 (FP).

Hamburger Union £21 ❸④④
22-25 Dean St, W1 7437 6004 4–2A
4-6 Garrick St, WC2 7379 0412 4–3C
"A huge upgrade from McDonalds" – these simple stand-bys serve up "proper" burgers and "excellent" chips; service, though, can be "none too enthusiastic". / www.hamburgerunion; 10.30 pm; no Amex; no booking.

Hammersmith Café W6 £15 ❸❷④
1a Studland St 8748 2839 7–2B
"For value-for-money, café-style Thai food", locals say you "can't beat" this café near the cinema (by day, a greasy spoon); BYO. / 10.30 pm; closed Sun L; no credit cards.

The Han of Nazz E2 NEW £30 ❸❸❷
4 Calvert Ave 7033 3936 1–2D
"Eccentric" Ottoman décor (by the same man as designed Theatreland's Sarastro) and "great Turkish food" win praise for this Shoreditch newcomer; it's "splendid for large groups". / www.hanofnazz.co.uk; 10.30 pm; no Amex; set weekday L £17 (FP).

Hara The Circle Bar SE1 NEW £47 ❷④④
Queen Elizabeth St 0845 226 9411 9–4D
It's a shame that this "chilled" new Indian bar/restaurant, hidden-away near Tower Bridge, is sometimes found "empty", as its ambitious dishes are sometimes "very good". / www.hararara.co.uk; midnight; set always available £26 (FP).

Harbour City W1 £25 ❸❸❸
46 Gerrard St 7439 7859 4–3B
"A huge number of Chinese customers" helps boost confidence in this "cheap and cheerful" Chinatown fixture, known for its "excellent" dim sum. / 12.30 am.

Hard Rock Café W1 £33 ④❸❷
150 Old Park Ln 7629 0382 3–4B
"Call me crazy... but this place never lets me down", say the (many) diehard fans of this ageing rocker by Green Park, who say it's "noisy, but worth it"; for critics, though, the food has become far too "run-of-the-mill". / www.hardrock.com; 1 am; need 10+ to book.

Hardy's W1 £42 ④❷❸
53 Dorset St 7935 5929 2–1A
This old-fashioned and unusually civilised Marylebone wine bar offers some good wine and decent, traditional British fare; it provoked a couple of "disappointing" reports this year, however. / www.hardys-w1.com; 10 pm; closed Sat L & Sun; no Amex.

Hare & Tortoise £21 ❸❸④
15-17 Brunswick Sq, WC1   7278 4945   2–1D
373 Kensington High St, W14   7603 8887   7–1D
38 Haven Grn, W5   8610 7066   1–2A
296-298 Upper Richmond Rd, SW15   8394 7666   10–2B
"Another good chain, in the Wagamama mould" – these no-frills
cafés are pretty much universally hailed as *"great stand-bys"*,
offering *"massive bowls of tasty noodles"*, as well as *"excellent-
value"* sushi and other oriental fare. / 10.30 pm.

Harlem £35 ⑤⑤④
78 Westbourne Grove, W2   7985 0900   6–1B
469 Brixton Rd, SW9   7326 4455   10–1D
At these *"packed"* and *"trendy"* American diners, it's too often the
case that *"the right arm doesn't know what the left arm is doing"*;
the food is *"run-of-the-mill"* too, but can sometimes rise to the
challenge of a *"good brunch"*. / www.harlemsoulfood.com; 2 am,
Sun midnight.

Harry Morgan's NW8 £30 ❸❸⑤
31 St John's Wood High St   7580 4849   8–3A
This St John's Wood deli-institution generally lives up to its name for
"the best salt-beef sandwiches" in town; this year, however,
the occasional reporter found it *"disappointing"*. / www.harryms.co.uk;
10 pm.

**Harry Ramsden's
Regent Palace Hotel W1** £26 ④④④
Sherwood St   7287 3148   3–3D
Reporters divide into two camps over this chain chippie,
near Piccadilly Circus; to fans it's *"not haute cuisine, but cheap"*,
and offers *"good quality fish 'n' chips"* – to foes its *"simply
disgusting"*. / 10 pm.

The Hartley SE1 £32 ④④❸
64 Tower Bridge Rd   7394 7023   1–3C
"In an area devoid of good restaurants" (a mile or so south
of Tower Bridge), this gastropub *"oasis"* is *"a dependable fish
finger-sandwich kind of place"*. / www.thehartley.com; 10 pm, Sun 7 pm;
closed Sun D.

Harwood Arms SW6 £30 ❸❷❷
29 Walham Grove   7386 1847   5–3A
This *"jolly pub"*, in a Fulham backstreet, is *"full of thirtysomethings
with dogs and babies in tow"*; it wins consistent praise, not least for
the *"delicious Sunday roast"*. / www.harwoodarms.co.uk; 11 pm; no Amex.

The Havelock Tavern W14 £35 ❶⑤❸
57 Masbro Rd   7603 5374   7–1C
"It's back!", and – after a fire – everything is thankfully *"just the
same as ever"* at this madly-popular Olympia backstreet gastropub;
its *"bally brilliant"* cooking is still *"the best of any pub in west
London"*, and the staff still *"act like you should be grateful they're
talking to you"*. / www.thehavelocktavern.co.uk; 10 pm; no credit cards;
no booking.

The Haven N20 — £34 ❷❷❷
1363 High Rd   8445 7419   1–1B
"A godsend in the area" – this Whetstone local offers "fairly
sophisticated" cuisine in "about the most unexpected location
imaginable", and it draws "a firm following" from many northerly
postcodes. / www.haven-bistro.co.uk; 11 pm.

Hawksmoor E1 NEW — £38
157 Commercial St   7456 1006   9–1D
From a young team with a couple of successes already behind 'em,
this new steakhouse-cum-cocktail bar opened, just north
of Spitalfields, as this guide was going to press; should be one
to watch. / 10.30 pm; closed Mon, Tue-Fri D only, Sat & Sun open L & D.

Haz E1 — £29 ❸❸❸
9 Cutler St   7929 7923   9–2D
"Great value for money" – especially by City standards – ensures
that this large but "tightly-packed" Turkish restaurant is always
"very buzzy". / www.hazrestaurant.com; 11.30 pm.

Hazuki WC2 — £32 ❸❷④
43 Chandos Pl   7240 2530   4–4C
This "friendly" and "useful" Theatreland restaurant, is especially
"convenient for the Coliseum" and serves "proper" Japanese
cuisine. / www.hazukilondon.co.uk; 10.30 pm, Sun 9 pm; closed Sun L.

Henry J Beans SW3 — £27 ④④❸
195-197 King's Rd   7352 9255   5–3C
A veteran burger-joint in Chelsea that "comes into its own
in summer" thanks to its surprisingly huge garden.
/ www.henryjbeans.com; midnight.

High Road Brasserie W4 NEW — £40
162-170 Chiswick High Rd   8742 7474   7–2A
The latest extension to Nick (Soho House) Jones's empire – on the
Chiswick site that was Foubert's Hotel, with the backing of Ant
& Dec – opens as this guide goes to press; expect it to be a smash-
hit with west London media-luvvies... but not necessarily
on account of the food.

The Hill NW3 — £37 ④④❸
94 Haverstock Hill   7267 0033   8–2B
"A zesty combination of funky design, good food, and an interesting
crowd" win praise for this eclectically-decorated Chalk Farm
gastropub; there's even the odd "celeb-spotting" opportunity.
/ www.geronimo-inns.co.uk; 11 pm; closed Mon L, Tue L & Wed L; no Amex.

Hilliard EC4 NEW — £19 ❶❶❷
26a Tudor St   7353 8150   9–3A
"Absolutely fabulous" sandwiches, soups, quiches, stews and coffee
– all made from "fantastic" ingredients – win consistent rave
reviews for this "light and airy" new café/take-away, by the Temple.
/ www.hilliardfood.co.uk; 8.45 pm; closed Sat & Sun.

Hole in the Wall W4 — £36 ❸❸❷
12 Sutton Lane North   8742 7185   7–2A
With its "reliable" cooking and "great garden", this "spacious"
Chiswick gastropub wins nothing but praise; "it attracts mainly
a local crowd, as it's so hidden away in the backstreets". / 10 pm.

Holly Bush NW3   £33   ❸❸❷
22 Holly Mount   7435 2892   8–1A
"Hidden-away in a country-like setting, but only 100 yards from Hampstead tube", this "lovely rustic-style" pub offers "a fantastic trip into a bygone era"; the "traditional" menu is "wholesome" but "doesn't try too hard". / www.hollybushpub.com; 10 pm; no Amex.

Homage
Waldorf Hilton WC2   £49   ❹❸❷
22 Aldwych   7759 4080   2–2D
In its first year of operation, this "gorgeous" former ballroom, on the fringe of Covent Garden, has incited only a small number of reports, and a fair number of these are in the "awful" category; time for a re-launch? / www.homagerestaurant.co.uk; 11 pm; closed Sat L & Sun L; booking: max 6.

Home EC2   £41   ❷❸❷
100-106 Leonard St   7684 8618   9–1D
It's probably better-known for its basement bar, but this "hip" and "buzzy" restaurant remains – after a decade in business – "one of the better bets in trendy Shoreditch", and its "wholesome" cooking is "much better than you might expect". / www.homebar.co.uk; 10.30 pm; closed Sat L & Sun.

Hope & Sir Loin EC1   £36   ❸❹❺
94 Cowcross St   7253 8525   9–1A
"Smithfield's secret place to gorge on sausage, black pudding and Guinness before 9am" – this dining room over an age-old pub is thought by some reporters to offer "London's best full English breakfast"; no one mentions its lunchtime grills. / breakfast & L only, closed Sat & Sun; no Amex.

Hosteria Del Pesce SW6 NEW   £95
84-86 Lillie Rd   7610 0037   5–3A
We couldn't quite persuade ourselves to invest the time in an early-days visit to this new Italian fish specialist, which opened in summer 2006; press reviews have invariably noted the disparity between its enormously high prices – apparently reflecting the cost of flying stuff in daily – and its grungy Fulham location. / 11.30 pm; D only, closed Mon.

Hot Stuff SW8   £20   ❶❶❸
19 Wilcox Rd   7720 1480   10–1D
"Service with a smile" and "great", "stupidly cheap" Indian/West African food makes this "rough and ready" South Lambeth café a much-prized "neighbourhood favourite"; BYO. / www.eathotstuff.com; 10 pm; closed Sun.

The House N1   £43   ❸❸❸
63-69 Canonbury Rd   7704 7410   8–2D
"You could take a date, your aged father, or your kids" to this "buzzing" Islington gastropub "all-rounder", which serves an "easy, hearty and appealing" Gallic menu; you pay "top whack", though. / www.inthehouse.biz; 10.30 pm; closed Mon L; no Amex.

Hoxton Apprentice N1   £36   ❹❹❸
16 Hoxton Sq   7739 6022   9–1D
This "trendy" and "buzzy" Hoxton 'training-restaurant' (for the disadvantaged and unemployed) is "a good cause" that often provides "good food" ("classic brunches", in particular); its performance, though, can seem "completely random". / www.hoxtonapprentice.com; 11 pm; closed Mon; no Amex.

Hoxton Square Bar & Kitchen N1 £32 ❸④❸
2-4 Hoxton Sq   7613 0709   9–1D
As bar grub goes, its "hard to fault" the "tasty" fare at this large, stylish bunker, where "from the outside tables, you can watch the wonders of Hoxton Square". / 10 pm; closed weekday L.

Hudson's SW15 £32 ❸❷❷
113 Lower Richmond Rd   8785 4522   10–1A
A "lovely" atmosphere is the highlight at this well-established Putney bistro; it's "a great place for brunch" – otherwise the "food is fine, but not stellar". / 10.30 pm.

Hugo's £33 ④④❷
51 Prince's Gate, SW7   7596 4006   5–1C
25 Lonsdale Rd, NW6   7372 1232   1–2B
"Tasty" (but "pricey") organic fare makes the "relaxed" arts-centre annexe (SW7) a useful "oasis" in the desert around the Albert Hall (and also a good brunch spot); it boasts a "lovely summer terrace"; (the NW6 branch inspired little feedback). / 10.30 pm.

Hummus Bros W1 NEW £14 ❸❷④
88 Wardour St   7734 1311   3–2D
"Very tasty hummus with various toppings" plus pita is the basic proposition of this "wholesome and healthy" concept; as a "swift refuelling stop" it has been a "welcome addition" to Soho. / www.hbros.co.uk; 11 pm; closed Sun.

Hunan SW1 £46 ❶❶④
51 Pimlico Rd   7730 5712   5–2D
"It looks shabby, but put yourself in the hands of the staff and the food is outstanding", is a typical verdict on this long-established Pimlico Chinese, where the hand-over from Mr Peng (senior) to Mr Peng (junior) "seems to be going well". / 11.30 pm; closed Sun.

Huong-Viet
An Viet House N1 £21 ❷⑤④
12-14 Englefield Rd   7249 0877   1–1C
"You get fantastic food every time" at this "great-value" Vietnamese canteen, which has an "unusual" setting (originally De Beauvoir Town's public baths); service is increasingly "erratic", though. / 11 pm; closed Sun; no Amex.

Hush W1 £55 ④④❸
8 Lancashire Ct   7659 1500   3–2B
A "happening" bar and "great outside dining" help draw reporters to this trendy joint, in a "secluded" yard just off Bond Street; the "solid" brasserie food is "expensive for what it is", though, and staff can give the impression they're "doing you a favour". / www.hush.co.uk; 11 pm; closed Sun; booking: max 12.

I Thai
The Hempel W2 £65 ⑤⑤④
31-35 Craven Hill Gdns   7298 9001   6–2C
Potentially "it's a gem hidden-away from the world", but this Zen-minimalist basement is too often let down by its "amateurish" service and its "uneventful" fusion cuisine. / www.the-hempel.co.uk; 10.30 pm; D only, closed Sun.

The Ifield SW10
£35   ④❸❸
59 Ifield Rd   7351 4900   5–3B
It's "a bit hit-and-miss" nowadays, but this louche Earl's Court-
fringe gastropub is still "generally good". / midnight; Mon-Thu D only.

Ikeda W1
£68   ❷❸⑤
30 Brook St   7629 2730   3–2B
"You get fabulously good sushi and sashimi, but it's rather expensive
and there's a poor atmosphere" at Mrs Ikeda's unchanging Mayfair
veteran; "if you actually care about Japanese food, rather than the
'scene' then you should give it a go". / 10.30 pm; closed Sat L & Sun.

Ikkyu W1
£29   ❸④④
67a Tottenham Court Rd   7636 9280   2–1C
This "totally unpretentious" basement, near Goodge Street tube
is an old favourite thanks to its "authentic" Japanese fare and its
"it-could-be-Tokyo" style; service can be "horrendous" though,
and "a lick of paint" wouldn't go amiss. / 10 pm; closed Sat & Sun L;
no Maestro.

Imli W1 NEW
£25   ❸❷❸
167-169 Wardour St   7287 4243   3–1D
"For a quick bite" in the West End, this "bright" and "functional"
newcomer provides "exceptionally friendly" service, and an
"interesting" take on "Mumbai street food". / www.imli.co.uk; 11 pm.

Imperial China WC2
£36   ❸❷❸
25a Lisle St   7734 3388   4–3B
This rather "upmarket" Chinatown "favourite" is hailed by some
reporters as an "oasis of sanity", thanks not least to its "completely
reliable" cooking. / 11.30 pm.

Imperial City EC3
£41   ❷❸❸
Royal Exchange, Cornhill   7626 3437   9–2C
"Surprisingly interesting food for the Square Mile" – plus an
"interesting basement location" – help make this well-established
oriental "a reliable and, by City standards, fairly-priced option".
/ www.orientalrestaurantgroup.co.uk; 10.30 pm; closed Sat & Sun.

Inaho W2
£30   ❶⑤⑤
4 Hereford Rd   7221 8495   6–1B
"Absolutely fantastic, and a complete bargain" – the sushi at this
"tiny" and "delightfully eccentric" Bayswater café contends for the
"best in London" title; service is "minimal", though, and the setting
"cramped". / 11 pm; closed Sat L & Sun; no Amex or Maestro.

INC Bar & Restaurant SE10
£39   ④④④
7 College Approach   8858 6721   1–3D
A "noisy" Greenwich bar/restaurant which "relies too much on its
great décor" (by designer Laurence Llewelyn-Bowen) – the food
is "not great" and service "not much better". / www.incbar.com; 10 pm;
closed Mon, Tue, Wed, Thu, Fri L, Sat L & Sun; no Amex.

Incognico WC2
£45   ❸❸❸
117 Shaftesbury Ave   7836 8866   4–2B
After a recent re-launch, this "sombre" Theatreland site looks set
to re-establish itself as a handy pre-show and business option,
thanks to its "dependable", "French-accented" cooking and its
"unfussy" service. / www.incognico.com; 11 pm; closed Sun L.

sign up for the survey at www.hardens.com

L'Incontro SW1 £55 ❸❸❸
87 Pimlico Rd 7730 6327 5–2D
"It could be a stylish restaurant in Milan", say fans of this "discreet" Pimlico stalwart; as ever, though, sceptics insist it's just "very expensive and uninspiring". / www.lincontro-restaurant.com; 11.30 pm; closed Sun; set weekday L £35 (FP).

India Club
Strand Continental Hotel WC2 £21 ④④④
143 Strand 7836 0650 2–2D
"The shoddy décor and slow service add to experience!", say fans of this "very New Delhi", "formica-tabled" canteen, which "hasn't changed in 20 years"; "love it or hate it", it serves "filling food" that "couldn't be much cheaper" (and you can BYO). / 10.45 pm; no credit cards; booking: max 6.

Indian Ocean SW17 £25 ❷❷❸
216 Trinity Rd 8672 7740 10–2C
"A good all-round local" – as ever, that's pretty much the whole story on this long-running Wandsworth curry house, where the food is "delicious". / 11.30 pm.

Indian Zing W6 NEW £28 ❷❶❸
236 King St 8748 5959 7–2B
With his "fresh, modern approach to Indian cooking", Manog Vasaikar's "elegant and contemporary" Hammersmith newcomer has impressed many reporters; service is notably "charming and attentive" too. / www.indianzing.co.uk; 11 pm.

Indigo
One Aldwych WC2 £53 ❸❷❷
1 Aldwych 7300 0400 2–2D
"The gentle buzz from the bar below" adds to the "casual yet sophisticated" ambience of this "comfortable" mezzanine restaurant, on the fringe of Covent Garden; its "very solid" cooking and handy location make it particularly popular for business. / 11.15 pm; set pre theatre £37 (FP).

The Inn at Kew Gardens
Kew Gardens Hotel TW9 NEW £32 ❸❸❷
292 Sandycombe Ln 8940 2220 1–4A
"A former dive that's been well renovated into a gastropub" – "it makes a perfect choice for a casual meal", and offers a menu that's "short and well-cooked". / www.theinnatkewgardens.com; 10 pm.

Inn the Park SW1 £45 ④⑤❸
St James's Pk 7451 9999 2–3C
"The Royal Parks should boot Oliver Peyton out" from this "unique" St James's Park venue; with its "memorable" setting and its "idyllic views", it "could be so good" – as it is, it's "a wasted opportunity", with "shambolic" service and "seriously average" British food. / 8.30 pm.

Inshoku SE1 £23 ❸❸❸
23-24 Lower Marsh 7928 2311 9–4A
"A useful address in the wastes around Waterloo Station" – this "no-fuss" café has a "welcoming" style and its "reasonably-priced" grub includes "fresh and well executed" sushi and sashimi; don't fancy Japanese? – fine, they just opened a chippie next door! / 10.30 pm; closed Sat L & Sun; set weekday L £13 (FP).

Inside SE10 £38 ❶❷④
19 Greenwich South St 8265 5060 1–3D
*Guy Awford's "interesting but not overly esoteric" cooking
is "London's best-kept secret", according to the many local fans
of this "tucked-away gem" – by quite a margin, "Greenwich's best
restaurant". / www.insiderestaurant.co.uk; 11 pm; closed Mon & Sun D.*

Isarn N1 £32 ❷❶❷
119 Upper St 7424 5153 8–3D
*With its "creative" cooking, "gentle" service and "clean cut" décor
– not to mention its "affordable" prices – this Thai yearling
is proving to be an "accomplished" addition to the Islington scene.
/ www.isarn.co.uk; 11.30 pm.*

Ishbilia SW1 £37 ❷❷④
9 William St 7235 7788 5–1D
*"Look around the room and you feel like you're dining in Beirut",
at this authentic Lebanese, by Harvey Nics, where "absolutely
delicious grills and mezze" are "served with a smile". / 11.30 pm.*

Ishtar W1 £29 ④④❸
10-12 Crawford St 7224 2446 2–1A
*In its first year, this Turkish venture in Marylebone has induced only
modest (and "inconsistent") feedback; an "intimate" ambience and
"cheap" prices make it a handy stand-by nonetheless.
/ www.ishtarrestaurant.com; midnight; no Amex.*

The Island NW10 NEW £34 ❷❸❸
123 College Rd 8960 0693 1–2B
*"New in Kensal Green", this "sophisticated" new gastropub
(connected with Chelsea's Pig's Ear) "shows great potential", thanks
not least to its "interesting menu of well-executed British
favourites". / www.islandpubco.com; 11 pm; closed Mon L; no Amex.*

Island
Royal Lancaster Hotel W2 £49 ❸❶❸
Lancaster Ter 7551 6070 6–2D
*Detractors say "it's in the middle of a roundabout, and not worth
crossing the road for", but this striking yearling mostly attracts
praise as a "classy" destination, with "acceptable" cooking and
good park views. / www.royallancaster.co.uk; 11 pm; booking: max 10;
set weekday L £29 (FP).*

Istanbul Iskembecisi N16 £23 ❸❸④
9 Stoke Newington Rd 7254 7291 1–1C
*This "old-established" fixture has traditionally been ranked in the
"first division" of Dalston's many Turkish eateries; fans still say it's
"always enjoyable" – sceptics, though, find they've "eaten better".
/ www.istanbuliskembecisi.co.uk; 5 am; no Amex.*

Italian Kitchen WC1 £36 ❸❷❸
43 New Oxford St 7836 1011 2–1C
*Now back on "solid" (if "not exciting") form, this Bloomsbury
Italian of long standing can be a "good-value" destination, especially
if you visit before 7pm. / www.italiankitchen.uk.com; 10.45 pm.*

Itsu £26 ❷❸❸
1 Hanover Sq, W1   7491 9799   3–2C
103 Wardour St, W1   7479 4790   3–2D
118 Draycott Ave, SW3   7590 2400   5–2C
28a Jubilee Pl, E14   7512 9650   11–1C **NEW**
Level 2, Cabot Place East, E14   7512 5790   11–1C
"I love this place, and I don't like sushi!" – these "funky" joints are "the best of the conveyor-belt chains" for those not too hung-up on authenticity; alongside familiar items, there are "new-style" creations (such as carpaccio sashimi). / www.itsu.co.uk; 11 pm, E14 10 pm; E14 closed Sat & Sun; no booking.

THE IVY WC2 £51 ❸❷❷
1 West St   7836 4751   4–3B
It's still a "place to be seen" – and still reporters' second-favourite overall – but Theatreland's "former fail-safe" is ever more at risk of slipping from "classic" to "cliché" status, and the cooking often seems "complacent" nowadays; you still need to book months ahead for peak-time tables. / www.the-ivy.co.uk; midnight; booking: max 6.

Izgara N3 £24 ❷❸❸
11 Hendon Lane   8371 8282   1–1B
The "very fresh, very tasty Turkish food" is "wonderful value" at this "always-busy" Finchley café/take-away. / www.izgararestaurant.com; midnight.

Jaan
The Howard WC2 £59 ❷❷④
12 Temple Pl   7300 1700   2–2D
"Much better than one would expect from a rather understated hotel" – this "sober"dining room, near Temple, offers "innovative" (but "unpretentious") Asian-fusion cuisine and "great service every time"; in summer, you can eat in the "lovely covered courtyard". / 10.30 pm; closed Sat L & Sun.

Jade Garden W1 £26 ❸④❸
15 Wardour St   7437 5065   4–3A
A long-standing Chinatown fixture that's occasionally hailed as a "hidden gem"; only for its "fantastic" dim sum, however, does it win significant support. / www.londonjadegarden.co.uk; 11.30 pm; set always available £17 (FP).

Jashan £21 ❶❶④
1-2 Coronet Pde, Ealing Rd, HA0   8900 9800   1–1A
19 Turnpike Ln, N8   8340 9880   1–1C
They can seem "unattractive from the street", but the food at this duo of south Indian curry houses is "delicious", and so "reasonably priced"; service is "pleasant and polite". / www.jashanrestaurants.co.uk; 10.30 pm; N8 D only, closed Mon; no Amex.

Jenny Lo's Tea House SW1 £23 ❶❷❸
14 Eccleston St   7259 0399   2–4B
"Fast, fresh and delicious" oriental fare – "the best black bean seafood noodles this side of HK", for example – attracts a devoted following to this "crowded and loud" Belgravia canteen. / 10 pm; closed Sat L & Sun; no credit cards; no booking.

Jim Thompson's £33 ⑤⑤❸
617 King's Rd, SW6   7731 0999   5–4A
889 Green Lanes, N21   8360 0005   1–1C
For a "fun, cheap and tasty" meal, some reporters still tip these Thai theme-palaces; increasingly, though, service is "off-hand", and the food can be "dreadful". / www.jimthompsons.com; 11 pm.

Jin Kichi NW3 £33 ❶②④
73 Heath St   7794 6158   8–1A
"You always have to book, even mid-week" for the "authentic" and "great-value" fare – not least "excellent sushi" and "great" yakitori – which is served at this "crushed" Japanese café in Hampstead. / www.jinkichi.com; 11 pm; closed Mon, Tue-Fri D only, Sat & Sun open L & D.

Jindalle SW1 NEW £25 ❸④④
6 Panton St   7930 8881   4–4A
This unpretentious new Korean, off Haymarket, makes a handy lunch or pre-theatre stand-by; on our early-days visit, however, service was slow – make sure you leave plenty of time before curtain-up. / Rated on Editors' visit; 10.45 pm.

Joanna's SE19 £33 ❸②❸
56 Westow Hill   8670 4052   1–4D
This fixture of Crystal Palace's main drag "has improved over the years and is getting quite sophisticated" nowadays; it serves "good, solid European fare", in an area dominated by curry houses and ethnic cafés. / www.joannas.uk.com; 11 pm.

Joe Allen WC2 £40 ④❸❶
13 Exeter St   7836 0651   4–3D
"Reliable, relaxed and fun", this long-established Covent Garden "dive" is of most note for its late-night "Theatreland buzz"; foodwise, stick to "burgers" (famously not on the menu) or "brunch" – "the rest is a little unexciting". / www.joeallenrestaurant.com; 12.45 am; set weekday L £28 (FP).

Joe's Brasserie SW6 £30 ❸❸②
130 Wandsworth Bridge Rd   7731 7835   10–1B
"Fantastic-value" wines fuel the buzz at John Brinkley's brasserie in the depths of Fulham; on the food front, burgers and "a great brunch" are the lead attractions. / www.brinkleys.com; 11 pm.

Joe's Café SW3 £41 ❸④④
126 Draycott Ave   7225 2217   5–2C
A chic Brompton Cross veteran, serving "pricey" salads and other nibbles to "ladies who lunch"; this year saw the addition of booths and banquette seating. / 11 pm; breakfast & L only; no booking at weekends.

Joy King Lau WC2 £23 ❸④④
3 Leicester St   7437 1132   4–3A
"Better than most in Chinatown", this "busy" and "down-at-heel" behemoth, just off Leicester Square, serves "good-value" grub, including some "first-class" dim sum. / 11.30 pm.

Julie's W11 £47 ④④❶
135 Portland Rd   7229 8331   6–2A
With its "fairy grotto" atmosphere ("unchanged since the '70s"), this labyrinthine Holland Park stalwart makes a "magical" romantic and party venue; prices are "steep", though, and the food "is never going to set the world on fire". / www.juliesrestaurant.com; 11 pm.

Julie's Wine Bar W11 £47 ④④❷
135 Portland Rd 7727 7985 6–2A
"The food now has the same poor-value prices as the next door restaurant", but this Holland Park wine bar – with its "naughty alcoves and discreet corners" – is still "a long-time favourite" for some reporters. / www.juliesrestaurant.com; 11.30 pm.

The Junction Tavern NW5 £34 ❸❷❷
101 Fortess Rd 7485 9400 8–2B
In Kentish Town, "an always-appealing trusty local" that's "convenient for both the tube and the Heath"; the food "has its ups and downs", but is "not overpriced". / www.junctiontavern.co.uk; 10.30 pm; no Amex; booking: max 12.

Just Gladwins EC3 £50 ❸④④
Minster Ct, 1 Mark Ln 7444 0004 9–3D
Peter Gladwin's City basement generally affords the "all-round standards expected by its business clientèle" (and, perhaps inevitably, can seem "overpriced"). / www.justgladwins.com; L only, closed Sat & Sun.

Just Oriental SW1 £33 ❸❷④
19 King St 7930 9292 3–4D
Quite "funky" by St James's standards, this basement bar offers a "good-quality" oriental snack menu at the sort of "reasonable" prices which are "hard to find in this part of town". / www.justoriental.com; midnight; closed Sat L & Sun.

Just St James SW1 £56 ❸④④
12 St James's St 7976 2222 3–4D
"Grand and spacious" or "cavernous" (to taste) – this former banking hall in St James's has some popularity as a business destination; given the "steep" prices, though, the food is sometimes only "passable", and service can be "lax". / www.juststjames.com; 11 pm; closed Sat L & Sun.

Just The Bridge EC4 £40 ④⑤④
1 Paul's Walk 7236 0000 9–3B
"It's a shame more is not made of this great location" (a bar/restaurant "tucked-away under the Millennium Bridge, with super views"); it's again criticised for its "tired" food and "poor" service. / www.justthebridge.com; 10 pm; closed Sat & Sun; booking: max 11.

K10 EC2 £28 ❷❸❸
20 Copthall Ave 7562 8510 9–2C
"A great lunch staple in the City" – this conveyor-sushi basement is consistently well rated for its "high-quality" food ("a mix of traditional and modern sushi and some hot dishes"). / www.k10.net; L only, closed Sat & Sun; no booking.

Kai Mayfair W1 £50 ❶❷❸
65 South Audley St 7493 8988 3–3A
The prices may be "hideous", but "the food really is exceptional" at this "quiet" and comfortable Chinese fixture in Mayfair; thanks not least to a wine list strong on first-growth clarets, it makes "an excellent venue for client entertaining". / www.kaimayfair.com; 10.45 pm.

Kaifeng NW4 £47 ❸②④
51 Church Rd 8203 7888 1–1B
This Harrow restaurant has long had a reputation for "very good
Kosher Chinese food"; critics, though, say its "quality is heading
downhill, whilst prices are on the way up". / 10.30 pm; closed Fri & Sat.

Kandoo W2 £24 ❸②❸
458 Edgware Rd 7724 2428 8–4A
"A useful BYO-spot at the top of the Edgware Road, serving tasty
Persian cooking"; "the garden is a pleasant surprise when the
weather holds out". / midnight; no Amex.

kare kare SW5 £35 ❷②④
152 Old Brompton Rd 7373 0024 5–2B
"Delicious new spins" on classic dishes win a devoted fan club for
this Earl's Court Indian; fans say it's "immeasurably better than the
Star" (next door), and "don't understand why it doesn't have
a bigger following". / www.karekare.co.uk; 11 pm.

Karma W14 £28 ❸②④
44 Blythe Rd 7602 9333 7–1D
"An inventive, fresh menu full of regional specialities" gives "an air
of authenticity" to this agreeable newcomer "tucked-away behind
Olympia" (on the former site of Cotto, RIP). / www.k-a-r-m-a.co.uk;
11.30 pm.

Kastoori SW17 £22 ❶❶❸
188 Upper Tooting Rd 8767 7027 10–2C
For a culinary "voyage of discovery", it's hard to beat this "happy"
(but "dreary"-looking) Tooting veteran; its "unique" and "heavenly"
Gujarati/East African cooking provides "a great argument for
vegetarianism". / 10.30 pm; closed Mon L & Tue L; no Amex or Maestro;
booking: max 12.

Kasturi EC3 £32 ❸②❸
57 Aldgate High St 7480 7402 9–2D
"Interesting" dishes and "pleasant" service combine to make this
Indian restaurant, near Aldwych, of some note by City standards.
/ www.kasturi-restaurant.co.uk; 11 pm, Sat 9.30 pm; closed Sun L.

Katana
The International WC2 £33 ④④④
116 St Martin's Ln 7655 9810 4–4B
An "excellent" Trafalgar Square location makes this "trendy" dining
room, above a bar, a handy stand-by; its "faux-fusion" fare,
however, incites very mixed reports. / www.theinternational.uk.com;
11 pm, Sun 9.30 pm.

Kaz Kreol NW1 NEW £25
35 Pratt St 7485 4747 8–3C
London's only Seychellois restaurant occupies the ground floor of a
former Camden Town pub; it opened just too late to catch any
survey commentary, but press reports are broadly encouraging.

Kazan SW1 £34 ❸②❸
93-94 Wilton Rd 7233 7100 2–4B
"High-quality" fare at "moderate" prices is winning a "growing local
following" for this "fun" Turkish restaurant – "there's not much
in Pimlico to beat it". / midnight; no Amex.

Ken Lo's Memories SW1 £46 ❷❷❷
67-69 Ebury St 7730 7734 2–4B
"An old favourite that still surprises", this "smart" Belgravia Chinese "deserves an award" for the "amazing consistency" of its cooking – it may be "expensive", but it's "tremendous". / 11 pm; closed Sun L.

Ken Lo's Memories of China W8 £48 ❷❷❸
353 Kensington High St 7603 6951 7–1D
The "memorable" food at this "top-notch" oriental, near Olympia, is "a step up from most other classy Chinese places"… "but, boy, do you pay for it". / 11 pm.

Kensington Arms W8 NEW £32 ❸❸④
41 Abingdon Rd 7938 3841 5–1A
This newly-revamped boozer (now more of a swish bar) has a handy location "just off Kensington High Street"; it serves "first-class" gastrofare, not to mention "a selection of fine Cornish ales". / 9.45 pm; no Amex.

Kensington Place W8 £52 ❸❸④
201-209 Kensington Church St 7727 3184 6–2B
For many "loyal local fans", this "noisy, stark and crowded" Kensington goldfish bowl is still a "reliable old favourite", serving "comfort food with a twist"; critics find the cooking ever more "tired", though, and there are calls for "a total revamp". / www.egami.co.uk; 10.45 pm; set weekday L £34 (FP).

(Brew House) Kenwood House NW3 £24 ④❸❷
Hampstead Heath 8341 5384 8–1A
For an "excellent afternoon tea", "perfect Sunday lunch" or "wonderful breakfast", combine "a healthy stroll on Hampstead Heath" with a trip to this posh cafeteria (which has a beautiful garden). / www.companyofcooks.com; 6 pm (summer), 4 pm (winter).

Kettners W1 £35 ④④❷
29 Romilly St 7734 6112 4–2A
For "pure nostalgia", this "historic" Soho "institution" (an upmarket PizzaExpress nowadays, complete with pianist and champagne bar) is hard to beat; too often, though, "poor" service and "overpriced" food take the edge off the experience. / www.kettners.com; midnight; need 7+ to book.

Kew Grill TW9 £43 ❷❸❸
10b Kew Grn 8948 4433 1–3A
"Not as good as the hype, but better than many people presume" – Wozza's "buzzy" Kew yearling is settling down as a good, if "pricey", all-rounder; highlights of the "unfussy" menu include "great steaks" and "brilliant burgers". / www.awtonline.co.uk; 10.30 pm; closed Mon L; set weekday L £27 (FP).

Khan's W2 £16 ❷④④
13-15 Westbourne Grove 7727 5420 6–1C
This "canteen-like" Bayswater veteran provides "Indian food like they serve in India", "astonishingly fast" and at "cheap" prices; "gorgeous lassis make up for the lack of alcohol". / www.khansrestaurant.com; 11.45 pm.

Khan's of Kensington SW7 £26 ❸❷④
3 Harrington Rd 7581 2900 5–2B
A "friendly" and "always reliable" curry house that's long been a firm favourite for some South Kensington locals. / 11 pm.

Khyber Pass SW7 £25 ❷❷④
21 Bute St   7589 7311   5–2B
This "cramped" South Kensington Indian has "smartened itself up" in recent times; "the food is still good", though, and "you can still get a table at short notice". / midnight; need 4+ to book.

Kisso SW5 £40 ❸④④
251 Old Brompton Rd   0871 426 3416   5–3A
This "unassuming" Earl's Court café serves a "varied" Japanese menu that's "good value"; it's "a handy neighbourhood spot, but not a destination". / 11 pm.

Koba W1 £40 ❷❶❷
11 Rathbone St   7580 8825   2–1C
This "cool Korean" yearling has proved "a really welcome addition" to Fitzrovia, but remains surprisingly little-known; staff "truly care that you enjoy yourself", and they serve an "interesting" menu (much of it barbecued at the table). / 11 pm; closed Sun L.

Kolossi Grill EC1 £24 ❸❶❷
56-60 Rosebery Ave   7278 5758   9–1A
"The best value in town for more than 25 years!" – fans are not reticent in their support for this "excellent local Greek restaurant", which offers "good" and "hearty" cooking, as well as "Clerkenwell's most friendly service". / www.kolossigrill.com; 11 pm; closed Sat L & Sun.

Konditor & Cook £19 ❶④④
Curzon Soho, 99 Shaftesbury Ave, W1   7292 1684   4–3A
46 Gray's Inn Rd, WC1   7404 6300   9–1A
10 Stoney St, SE1   7407 5100   9–4C
22 Cornwall Rd, SE1   7261 0456   9–4A
"Sensational cakes and brownies" are highlights of these "divine" café/take-aways, which also do "very good sarnies, salads and coffee". / www.konditorandcook.com; 11 pm; no booking.

Konstam at the Prince Albert WC1 NEW £37 ④❷❸
2 Acton St   7833 5040   8–3D
The 'concept' of this ambitious new gastropub near King's Cross – "sourcing all produce from within the M25" – is a "worthy" one, and some early reports are of "fine" cuisine; doubters, though (with whom, from our initial visit, we count ourselves) say "the gimmick is pointless if the food isn't nice". / www.konstam.co.uk; 10 pm; closed Sun; no Amex.

Kovalam NW6 £20 ❷❷⑤
12 Willesden Ln   7625 4761   1–2B
A Kilburn-fringe "local favourite" – "what it lacks in décor, it makes up for with charming service and great-value south Indian specialities". / www.kovalamrestaurant.co.uk; 11 pm.

Kulu Kulu £21 ❷④⑤
76 Brewer St, W1   7734 7316   3–2D
51-53 Shelton St, WC2   7240 5687   4–2C
39 Thurloe Pl, SW7   7589 2225   5–2C
With their "authentic" and "great-value" sushi, these "buzzing" (but "Spartan") Kaiten-Zushi outfits have made a name as "the best of the Japanese 'belt' operators"; sometimes, though, they've been a bit "dull" of late. / 10 pm, SW7 10.30 pm; closed Sun; no Amex; no booking.

FSA

Kurumaya EC4 £28 ②④④
76-77 Watling St 7236 0236 9–2B
"An excellent variety of fresh sushi" wins praise for this *"quality conveyor-sushi"* joint in the City; service, though, can be *"inattentive".* / www.kurumaya.co.uk; 9.30 pm; closed Sat & Sun.

Kwan Thai SE1 £37 ❸②④
Unit 1, Hay's Galleria 7403 7373 9–4D
With its *"boring '80s décor"* and *"familiar"* (if *"well-cooked"*) dishes this South Bank Thai is of interest mainly to local office workers; on a nice day, though, it's *"worth a trip if you can get a table on the river".* / www.kwanthairestaurant.co.uk; 10.30 pm; closed Sat L & Sun.

L-Restaurant & Bar W8 NEW £41 ❸②④
2 Abingdon Rd 7795 6969 5–1A
This Kensington newcomer – whose impressive dining room is mostly made of glass – has had a hard time from the press; we enjoyed both our early-days visits, however, once for a good-value set lunch, and the other time for a selection of tasty starters from the Spanish-influenced menu. / Rated on Editors' visit; www.l-restaurant.co.uk; 10.30 pm; closed Mon; set weekday L £26 (FP).

The Ladbroke Arms W11 £37 ②④②
54 Ladbroke Rd 7727 6648 6–2B
The main problems with this *"lovely"* Notting Hill pub – which offers *"consistently good"* food – are that it is both *"cramped"* and far *"too popular"*; grab an outside table on a sunny day, though, and eating here can be *"great".* / 9.45 pm; no booking after 7.30 pm.

Ladurée
Harrods SW1 NEW £50 ❸④❸
door 1b Hans Rd entrance 7730 1234 5–1D
"Paris's best croissants have finally made it to London" – bringing Ladurée's trademark *"perfect macaroons"* with them – and are now available at this impressive new Knightsbridge tea-room (which also does good-but-pricey salads and so on); in our experience, though, it's the people-watching that really makes the place! / www.laduree.fr; 9 pm, Sun 6 pm.

Lahore Kebab House E1 £20 ❶④⑤
2-4 Umberston St 7488 2551 11–1A
"Exactly how one would imagine eating in Karachi" – this *"chaotic"* and unbelievably popular East End institution is now *"much expanded"*, but *"still serves the best kebabs in town"*; BYO. / midnight; need 12+ to book.

Lamberts SW12 £40 ❶❶❷
2 Station Pde 8675 2233 10–2C
To say it's *"without peer in Balham"* doesn't do full justice to the *"impressive"* cooking and *"top hospitality"* on offer at this *"jewel"* behind the tube station – *"it's not Chez Bruce, but it's a fair second hereabouts".* / www.lambertsrestaurant.com; 10.30 pm; closed Mon, Tue-Fri D only, Sat & Sun open L & D; no Amex.

(Winter Garden)
The Landmark NW1 £50 ④❸❷
222 Marylebone Rd 7631 8000 8–4A
The "magnificent" atrium of this Marylebone hotel is of no great
interest as a serious dining destination; the Sunday buffet –
at which "the champagne flows" – has its fans, though,
and afternoon tea here can be "excellent".
/ www.landmarklondon.co.uk; 1 am; booking: max 12.

Lanes
East India House E1 £45 ❸❷④
109-117 Middlesex St 7247 5050 9–2D
"Very attentive staff" and "well-spaced tables" help overcome the
basement location of this City-fringe bar and restaurant; with its
"high-quality" food, it is very "well set up for a quick business
lunch". / www.lanesrestaurant.co.uk; 10 pm; closed Sat L & Sun.

The Lanesborough
The Lanesborough Hotel SW1 £78 ④❷⓿
Hyde Park Corner 7259 5599 5–1D
For a "superb" breakfast or an afternoon tea that's "a real treat",
the conservatory of this OTT-grand hotel has quite a few fans;
dinner, though, is "overpriced" and "under par".
/ www.lanesborough.com; 11.30 pm; set dinner £50 (FP).

Langan's Bistro W1 £34 ❸❷❷
26 Devonshire St 7935 4531 2–1A
This "closely-packed" bistro veteran in Marylebone retains a small,
but loyal fan club; service is "lovely" and the cooking – if "nothing
fancy" – is usually "well prepared". / www.langansrestaurants.co.uk;
11 pm; closed Sat L & Sun.

Langan's Brasserie W1 £48 ④❸❷
Stratton St 7491 8822 3–3C
The "glory days" of this "faded" Mayfair legend may have passed,
but, despite its "old-fashioned" food, it's "always buzzing" and –
for some reporters – "still a place to be seen".
/ www.langansrestaurants.co.uk; midnight; closed Sat L & Sun.

Langan's Coq d'Or Bar & Grill SW5 £37 ❸❷❸
254-260 Old Brompton Rd 7259 2599 5–3A
"Good, solid Gallic fare" and "conscientious old-school staff" make
this Parisian-style brasserie in Earl's Court a favourite for some
reporters (especially for brunch) – "why isn't it more popular"?
/ www.langansrestaurants.co.uk; 11 pm.

The Lansdowne NW1 £39 ❸④❷
90 Gloucester Ave 7483 0409 8–3B
"An attractive, relaxed crowd" frequents this "buzzy" and
"very Primrose Hill" gastropub, where the cuisine is "robust" and
"innovative", but where the service is "very variable" ("from surly
to superlative"). / 10.30 pm; no Amex.

La Lanterna SE1 £32 ❸⓿❷
6-8 Mill St 7252 2420 11–2A
"The owner greets you like an old friend" at this "reliable" Italian
near Butlers Wharf ("an area lacking that many alternatives");
its virtues include "good pizza", "fair prices" and
a "nice courtyard". / www.pizzeriadelanterna.co.uk; 11 pm; closed Sat L.

FSA

Latium W1 £42 ❶❷❸
21 Berners St 7323 9123 2–1C
"It's well worth seeking out" this "stimulating" but "still undiscovered" Italian, north of Oxford Street; the cooking is "superb", the setting "calm", there's a "fantastic" regional wine list and service is "truly professional". / www.latiumrestaurant.com; 10.30 pm; closed Sat L & Sun.

Latymers W6 £22 ❸④⑤
157 Hammersmith Rd 8741 2507 7–2C
You get "great-value" Thai food in this "reliable" dining room at the back of a Hammersmith gin palace; it gets very "busy", though, and service can be "autocratic". / 10 pm; closed Sun D; no Amex; no booking at L.

Laughing Gravy SE1 £39
154 Blackfriars Rd 7721 7055 9–4A
As a family-run venture, this "cosy and cool" Southwark bar/restaurant developed a happy reputation as "a surprise find in a dire location"; it changed hands in 2006 – so we've left it unrated – but the new management apparently plan no great changes. / www.laughinggravy.com; 10 pm; closed Sat & Sun.

Launceston Place W8 £50 ❸❸❷
1a Launceston Pl 7937 6912 5–1B
"Nestling" in a Kensington backstreet, this "intimate" haven has long been a top romantic destination; foodwise, though (judged by its high past standards) it's "gone off the boil" of late – perhaps the recent arrival of a new chef will herald a return to form. / www.egami.co.uk; 11 pm; closed Sat L & Sun D; set weekday L £33 (FP).

Laureate W1 £27 ④④④
64 Shaftesbury Ave 7437 5088 4–3A
After a year in business, this "nicely decorated" Chinatown corner spot doesn't quite seem to have maintained its early momentum; for "very good dim sum", though, it remains a popular choice. / 11.30 pm; no Amex.

Lavender £27 ④❸❷
112 Vauxhall Walk, SE11 7735 4440 2–4D
171 Lavender Hill, SW11 7978 5242 10–2C
24 Clapham Rd, SW9 7793 0770 10–1D
"Friendly", "comforting" and "reliable" – these south London pub-conversions make good spots "for a relaxing meal with friends". / 10 pm; SW9 & SW11 closed Mon L, SE11 closed Sat L & Sun.

The Ledbury W11 £65 ❶❶❷
127 Ledbury Rd 7792 9090 6–1B
Brett Graham's "stunningly good" (and "complex") cuisine is "amongst London's best", and, with the help of a "wonderful" wine list, it has helped make this "chic" (if somewhat "subdued") yearling a truly "grown-up" destination of the sort that's rare in Notting Hill; service is "impeccable" too. / www.theledbury.com; 10.30 pm.

Lemonia NW1 £31 ④❷❶
89 Regent's Park Rd 7586 7454 8–3B
"Take your earplugs" to this "big and noisy" Primrose Hill taverna – a "long-time" north London favourite, where the "wonderful staff" always "create a laugh"; the food is "acceptable, if rather standard". / 11.30 pm; closed Sat L & Sun D; no Amex.

Leon £25 ❷❸❸
35-36 Gt Marlborough St, W1   7437 5280   3–2C
136 Old Brompton Rd, SW3   7589 7330   5–1D **NEW**
3 Crispin Pl, E1   7247 4369   9–1D **NEW**
12 Ludgate Circus, EC4   7489 1580   9–2A **NEW**
*"Expertly filling a gaping hole in the market", this "great" organic
diner concept – where "simple" dishes "bursting with flavour" are
served "at the speed of McDonalds" – is fast establishing itself as a
major hit; "if there's any justice in the world, there will soon
be hundreds of 'em". / 10 pm; EC4 closed Sat & Sun; SW3 no Amex.*

Levant W1 £43 ❹❹❶
Jason Court, 76 Wigmore St   7224 1111   3–1A
*"Belly-dancing adds to the fun" of a visit to this "loud" and "exotic"
Lebanese "den", "tucked-away" behind St Christopher's Place
(and complete with romantic "hideaway" booths); the food
is "average", though, and can "take ages". / www.levant.co.uk;
11.30 pm.*

Levantine W2 £37 ❹❹❸
26 London St   7262 1111   6–1D
*Though hailed in some reports as "a good restaurant in an area
lacking competition", feedback on this "fun", souk-style operation,
near Paddington Station, remains very mixed. / www.levant.co.uk;
11.30 pm.*

The Light House SW19 £43 ❸❷❸
75-77 Ridgway   8944 6338   10–2B
*"Interesting" Italian/Asian fusion fare, and "delightful" staff help
make this "pleasant" (if slightly "canteen-y") restaurant an ongoing
Wimbledon "favourite". / 10.30 pm; closed Sun D; set weekday L
£28 (FP).*

Lightship E1 £43 ❹❷❶
5a Katharine's Way, St Kath's Dock   7481 3123   9–3D
*An "unforgettable" setting – a former lightship, now moored near
Tower Bridge – makes this "truly unique" venture a favourite for
romance; the Scandinavian food is "reasonably good", but rather
incidental. / www.lightshipx.com; 10 pm; closed Mon L, Sat L & Sun.*

Lillo e Franco W8 **NEW** £27 ❷❷❹
9 Kensington Square   7937 4898   5–1A
*"The best attempt anyone has had at this site in the 34 years
we've lived nearby" – this hidden-away new Kensington café
is eager to please, and serves "excellent pizza" and other simple
but high-quality Italian dishes. / Rated on Editors' visit; 11.30 pm.*

Lilly's E1 £34 ❸❸❷
75 Wapping High St   7702 2040   11–1A
*This upscale boothed "diner" in Wapping makes "an excellent
stand-by" for lunch or dinner; it's also a good destination for
"an impressive brunch". / www.lillysrestaurant.co.uk; 11 pm; set weekday L
£20 (FP).*

Lime E14 **NEW** £38 ❸❷❸
1 Regatta Point, Manilla St   7515 4500   11–2C
*A few minutes' walk from Canary Wharf, this comfortable new
Indian benefits from a pleasant interior, and friendly and efficient
service; on our early-days visit the food – if nothing remarkable –
was pretty good value too. / Rated on Editors' visit;
www.limerestaurant.co.uk; 11.30 pm; set weekday L £19 (FP).*

sign up for the survey at www.hardens.com

Lindsay House W1 £76 ❸❸❷
21 Romilly St   7439 0450   4–3A
*Irishman Richard Corrigan is "one of the finest chefs in London",
and a visit to this "quaint" and "utterly charming" Soho townhouse
is often "a joy"; the place suffers from "inconsistency", though –
perhaps the mid-2006 refurbishment will improve matters.*
/ www.lindsayhouse.co.uk; 11 pm; closed Sat L & Sun; set pre theatre £48 (FP).

Lisboa Pâtisserie W10 £5 ❷❸❸
57 Golborne Rd   8968 5242   6–1A
*"Crowded" and "authentic", this "buzzy" Portuguese coffee shop
has become a real Portobello "institution"; "terribly more-ish"
custard tarts and "superb" coffee are star features.* / 7.30 pm;
L & early evening only; no Amex; no booking.

Little Bay £24 ❸❷❷
140 Wandsworth Bridge Rd, SW6   7751 3133   10–1B
228 Belsize Rd, NW6   7372 4699   1–2B
228 York Rd, SW11   7223 4080   10–2B
171 Farringdon Rd, EC1   7278 1234   9–1A
*"Splitting the bill is always a pleasant surprise" at this "friendly",
"efficient" and "buzzing" small chain, where the "honest" scoff
is "incredible at the price"; look out for "jovial opera singers"
at SW11.* / www.little-bay.co.uk; 11.30 pm; NW6 no credit cards.

Little Earth Café
Triyoga NW3 £15 ❷❸④
6 Erskine Rd   7449 0700   8–3B
*You don't have to be a Raw Food zealot to seek out the small foyer
café at Madonna's favourite yoga centre – the zingy, ultra-healthy
veggie dishes and juices (from some of the team behind Camden's
Heartstone, RIP) are fabulous; remember to take your shoes off
as you go in.* / Rated on Editors' visit; 8 pm, Sat & Sun 6 pm; L & early
evening only.

Little Italy W1 £53 ④④❸
21 Frith St   7734 4737   4–2A
*"It turns into a dance party after 11 pm", at this late-night Soho
Italian; reporters who don't mind the premium prices praise the
"tasty" food and "fun" atmosphere.* / 4 am, Sun midnight.

The Little Square W1 £38 ④❸❷
3 Shepherd Mkt   7355 2101   3–4B
*The food's unremarkable, but this "friendly" little bistro
is reasonably-priced and benefits from a "romantic" Shepherd
Market location.* / 11 pm.

Livebait £41 ④④⑤
21 Wellington St, WC2   7836 7161   4–3D
43 The Cut, SE1   7928 7211   9–4A
*The "slide in standards" at this once-commendable fish and
seafood chain "has not been checked" – its "uninterested" staff,
serve "unexciting" fare in "cold" branches that are infamously
reminiscent of a "gents' loo".* / www.santeonline.co.uk; WC2 11.30 pm,
SE1 11 pm, Sun 9 pm; WC2 closed Sun.

Living Room £37

3-9 Heddon St, W1   0870 166 2225   3–2C **NEW**
18-26 Essex Rd, N1   0870 442 2712   8–3D
Now with a large new outpost in the West End – this national bar/restaurant chain is hailed by some reporters as a handy option "for a drink and a bite"; it's a bit "mundane", though.
/ www.thelivingroom.co.uk.

LMNT E8 £26 ❸❸❶

316 Queensbridge Rd   7249 6727   1–2D
"Crazy" and "extravagant" Egyptian-style décor has made this Hackney pub-conversion a real East End hit; perhaps surprisingly, the cooking is "tasty" too, and "reasonably-priced". / 11 pm; no Amex.

Lobster Pot SE11 £43 ❷❷❶

3 Kennington Ln   7582 5556   1–3C
"Bonkers" décor (with "piped seagulls and foghorns") wafts you on an "overwhelmingly Gallic" maritime fantasy, when you visit the Régent family's "surreal" Kennington fixture; the traditional Breton fish and seafood, though, is often "stunning".
/ www.lobsterpotrestaurant.co.uk; 10.30 pm; closed Mon & Sun; booking: max 8; set weekday L £25 (FP).

LOCANDA LOCATELLI
CHURCHILL INTERCONT'L W1 £56 ❷❷❷

8 Seymour St   7935 9088   2–2A
Giorgio Locatelli's "refreshingly simple" but "heavenly" cooking has won wide acclaim for this "glamorous" restaurant, just north of Oxford Street; doubters find its reputation "overblown", but, for most reporters, this remains one of London's top Italians.
/ www.locandalocatelli.com; 11 pm, Fri & Sat 11.30 pm; booking: max 8.

Locanda Ottoemezzo W8 £55 ❷

2-4 Thackeray St   7937 2200   5–1B
"Well hidden" off Kensington High Street, this "comfortable" Italian certainly offers "a sense of welcome"; it's "not bad food-wise", but as to the prices – "they have to be joking".
/ www.locandaottoemezzo.co.uk; 10.30 pm; closed Sat L & Sun; set weekday L £36 (FP).

Loch Fyne £35 ❸

2-4 Catherine St, WC2   7240 4999   2–2D
175 Hampton Rd, TW2   8255 6222   1–4A
This national fish 'n' seafood chain put in a better showing this year, winning more praise for its "decent" but "dull" formula.
/ www.lochfyne.com; 10 pm-11 pm; set pre theatre £24 (FP).

The Lock Dining Bar N17 **NEW** £37 ❷❷

Heron Hs, Hale Wharf, Ferry Ln   8885 2829   1–1C
"Stuck in the wastelands of Tottenham", this "cheap and cheerful" newcomer (on the site of Mosaica at the Lock, RIP) has so far only attracted a few reports; such as they are, however, suggest that – by local standards – the food is "astounding".
/ www.thelock-diningbar.com; 10 pm; closed Mon D, Sat L & Sun D; no Amex.

Loco £32 ④❸❸
222 Munster Rd, SW6   7381 6137   10–1B
3b Belvedere Rd, SE1   7401 6734   2–3D
1 Lawn Terrace, SE3   8852 0700   1–4D
A "lively" and "welcoming" atmosphere is the strong suit of this small Italian chain (whose Blackheath branch in particular has a "wonderful interior"); the food "can be tasty, but is variable in quality". / www.locorestaurants.com; 10.30 pm; SE3 closed Mon, Tue-Fri L & Sun D.

The Lord Palmerston NW5 £30 ❷❸❷
33 Dartmouth Park Hill   7485 1578   8–1B
New owners (Geronimo) have tinkered with – but not yet wrecked – the formula that had made this "busy" Dartmouth Park gastropub such a success; its cuisine offers "just the right combination of ambition and realism". / 10 pm; no Amex; no booking.

Lots Road SW10 £35
114 Lots Rd   7352 6645   5–4B
This "pleasing" hang-out, by the gates to Chelsea Harbour is a "real gastropub" serving "decent" scoff (not least "great burgers"); it was recently bought by Karen Jones (creator of Café Rouge), so change may be afoot. / 10 pm; no Amex.

**The Lotus Chinese
Floating Restaurant E14** £33 ❸④❸
38 Limeharbour   7515 6445   11–2C
This Chinese barge floating near the London Arena is sometimes dismissed as a gimmick; most reporters, though, praise its "value for money" (and "good dim sum" in particular).
/ www.lotusfloating.co.uk; 11 pm.

Lou Pescadou SW5 £41 ❷❷❸
241 Old Brompton Rd   7370 1057   5–3A
"Charming, very Gallic service" adds a personal element to a visit to this Earl's Court "old-timer"; with its "brilliant" fish and seafood, "it's just the sort of solid place it's easy to forget, but well worth a detour". / midnight; set always available £25 (FP).

Louvaine SW11 £33 ❸❷❷
110 St John's Hill   7223 8708   10–2C
This "intimate and charming" bistro is a smash hit with its tiny local fan club, who say its "friendly" service and "delicious" food make it "the best place in the cluster near Clapham Junction".
/ www.louvaine.co.uk; 10.30 pm; closed Mon, weekday L & Sat L.

Love India SW3 £36 ❷❷④
153 Fulham Rd   7589 7749   5–2C
Despite its "fine" cooking, this basement curry house used to be too-often empty; since last year's name-change, however (from Tandoori of Chelsea), the "lighter" décor and lower prices seem to be winning a wider following. / 11.30 pm.

**Lowiczanka
Polish Social & Cultural Assoc'n W6** £29 ④④⑤
238-246 King St   8741 3225   7–2B
"Go hungry", so as best to appreciate the "hearty" Polish fare at this bargain café, attached to a Hammersmith cultural centre.
/ 11.30 pm, Sat 1 am; set weekday L £17 (FP).

FSA

Luciano SW1 NEW   £49   ❸④❸
72-73 St James's St   7408 1440   3–4D
*MPW's large new art-filled Italian, near St James's Palace, divides
opinion – fans who praise its "straightforward classic dishes" and
"fabulous décor" are pretty evenly matched by critics complaining
of "uninspired" food or "abysmal" service.
/ www.lucianorestaurant.co.uk; 10.30 pm; closed Sun.*

Lucio SW3   £49   ❸❷❸
257 Fulham Rd   7823 3007   5–3B
*Fans say you get "first-class everything" at this "smart" Chelsea
Italian two-year-old; a growing band of sceptics, though, feel it's
"not quite as good as it thinks it is". / 10.45 pm; set weekday L £32 (FP).*

Lucky Seven W2   £32   ❷❸❷
127 Westbourne Park Rd   7727 6771   6–1B
*"There's no better place for junk-foodies" than Tom Conran's
"vibey" homage to '50s America, on the fringe of Notting Hill;
it serves "mouth-watering" burgers and "terrific" shakes, for which
you may need to "squish up" in the shared booths. / 11 pm; no Amex;
no booking.*

Luigi's WC2   £47   ⑤④④
15 Tavistock St   7240 1795   4–3D
*Its devotees still see this Covent Garden townhouse stalwart as an
"old-fashioned but honest" favourite; to doubters, though, it's just
"a boring old Italian, and there's nothing more to say".
/ www.luigisofcoventgarden.com; 11.30 pm; closed Sun; set pre theatre
£26 (FP).*

Luna Rossa W11   £35   ④⑤④
192 Kensington Park Rd   7229 0482   6–1A
*A year-old Notting Hill pizzeria that's "fun but rather chaotic";
some reporters were "disappointed" by the pizzas, but others find
them "good"... "when they arrive". / 11.30 pm; no Amex.*

Lundum's SW7   £46   ❷①①
119 Old Brompton Rd   7373 7774   5–2B
*An "elegant" setting (complete with "little booths" and a "library
bar") and "immaculate" service add to the "wonderful, romantic
atmosphere" of this "outstanding family-run restaurant" in South
Kensington; the "authentic" Danish fare is "fantastic" too –
not least the "great Sunday brunch buffet". / www.lundums.com;
11 pm; closed Sun D.*

Ma Cuisine   £36   ❸❸④
6 Whitton Rd, TW1   8607 9849   1–4A
9 Station Approach, TW9   8332 1923   1–3A
*"Even though they sometimes feels like a trip back to the '70s",
John McClement's "informal" and "cramped" local bistros –
in Twickenham and Kew – please most people most of the time
with their "rustic" fodder, which is served at "very reasonable
prices". / 10.30 pm; TW1 closed Sun; no Amex.*

Ma Goa £31 ❶❶❷

194 Wandsworth Bridge Rd, SW6 7384 2122 10–1B **NEW**
244 Upper Richmond Rd, SW15 8780 1767 10–2B
"Tongue-tingling" Goan cooking and "always-courteous" service
have long made the Kapoor family's "homely and down-to-earth"
Putney Indian a wonderful "find"; its new sibling in Fulham has
likewise won instant acclaim. / 11 pm; SW15 closed Mon-Sat D,
SW6 closed Mon; booking essential.

Made in China SW10 £35 ❷❷⑤

351 Fulham Rd 7351 2939 5–3B
"Although the room is pretty basic and overlit", this canteen-like
Chelsea Chinese is "generally a good experience", thanks to its
"fast" service and "imaginative and good-value" chow. / 11.30 pm.

Made in Italy SW3 £36 ❷⑤④

249 King's Rd 7352 1880 5–3C
"Extraordinarily good authentically Neapolitan pizza" (by the
metre) draws a dedicated following to this Chelsea institution;
"deplorable" service, though, can contribute to a "chaotic"
ambience. / 11.30 pm; closed weekday L; no Amex.

Madhu's UB1 £31 ❶❷❷

39 South Rd 8574 1897 1–3A
"Well beyond the standards of some of the Michelin-starred
Indians", this ordinary-looking Southall joint remains a Mecca for
curry-lovers, thanks to "absolutely authentic" cooking, which
is "often sublime". / www.madhusonline.com; 11.30 pm; closed Tue,
Sat L & Sun L.

Maggie Jones's W8 £40 ④❸❶

6 Old Court Pl 7937 6462 5–1A
As "a place to snuggle up to your better half", this "dark" and
"rustic" veteran near Kensington Palace still has many devotees;
even they would concede, however, its "calorie-laden" fodder
is "not exactly cutting-edge". / 11 pm.

Maison Bertaux W1 £9 ❷❷❷

28 Greek St 7437 6007 4–2A
"Pukka pâtisserie (including "the best croissants in the world")
underpins reporters' enduring love-affair with this "great Soho
hideaway" (est 1871); "its stolid refusal to redecorate has won
countless hearts". / 11 pm, Sun 9 pm; no credit cards; no booking.

Maison Blanc Vite £20 ❸④④

193 Piccadilly, W1 7287 6311 3–3D **NEW**
135 Fenchurch St, EC3 7929 6996 9–3D
From the well-known pâtisserie chain – a new duo of grand
café/take-aways in handy locations; they offer good-quality Gallic
snacks (including some "stunning" sandwiches), at good prices.
/ Rated on Editors' visit; W1 6 pm, EC3 4 pm; EC3 closed Sat & Sun;
no Amex.

Malabar W8 £31 ❷❷❸

27 Uxbridge St 7727 8800 6–2B
"A million miles ahead of generic Indians, but not trying to re-invent
the wheel" – year-in-year-out, this curry house favourite, off Notting
Hill Gate, is praised for its "inventive and hugely tasty" food and its
"delightful" service. / www.malabar-restaurant.co.uk; 11.30 pm.

Malabar Junction WC1   £38   ❸❸❷
107 Gt Russell St   7580 5230   2–1C
The "calm, spacious and elegant" conservatory creates an unusual
ambience at this vaguely "colonial"-feeling Bloomsbury ten-year-old,
which serves a "reliable" south Indian menu. / 11 pm.

The Mall Tavern W8   £36   ❸④❸
71-73 Palace Gardens Ter   7727 3805   6–2B
Just off Notting Hill Gate, this handily-located gastropub, offers
"interesting" and "well-executed" cooking; it also benefits from
a "small, quiet garden". / www.malltavernlondon.com; 10.30 pm.

Malmaison Brasserie EC1   £42   ❸❷❷
18-21 Charterhouse St   7012 3700   9–1B
"Much better than you might expect" – the "chic" dining room
of this Clerkenwell design-hotel is emerging as something of a
"hidden gem", and service, in particular, is "exemplary".
/ www.malmaison.com; 10.30 pm; set weekday L £26 (FP).

Mamounia W1   £59   ④❷❷
37a Curzon St   7629 2211   3–4B
This "colourful" and "comfortable" Mayfair Moroccan ("complete
with shisha pipes and belly dancing") is a "favourite for the younger
Arab crowd"; it seems a better bet for "tasty" nibbles in the bar
than for the more substantial (and heftily-priced) fare in the
restaurant below. / www.mamounialounge.com; 11.30 pm.

La Mancha SW15   £36   ④④❸
32 Putney High St   8780 1022   10–2B
The tapas are "nothing special", but this large Putney hang-out
is "fun" nevertheless, and "manic at weekends".
/ www.lamancha.co.uk; 11 pm; need 6+ to book.

Mandalay W2   £18   ❶❶④
444 Edgware Rd   7258 3696   8–4A
"Lovely staff go out of their way to make you feel at home", at this
family-run shop-conversion, near Edgware Road tube; it "looks a bit
like an old caff" but is "always packed", thanks to the "incredible
value" of its "marvellous and unusual" Burmese fare. / 11 pm;
closed Sun.

Mandarin Kitchen W2   £33   ❶④④
14-16 Queensway   7727 9012   6–2C
"Orgasmic" Chinese seafood dishes – this is "the best place in town
for lobster" – win the customary raves for this "scruffy old
Bayswater stalwart"; the place is "always packed" – you can book,
but it doesn't seem to make much difference. / 11.30 pm.

Mangal Ocakbasi E8   £16   ❶❷❸
10 Arcola St   7275 8981   1–1C
"Worth the trip out to Dalston"; this "brilliant", if basic, Turkish
café serves "fantastic" kebabs – some of "the best grilled meat
in London" – at "prices which defy economics"; BYO.
/ www.mangal1.com; midnight; no credit cards.

Mango Room NW1   £35   ❷❸❶
10-12 Kentish Town Rd   7482 5065   8–3B
"A great find in the heart of Camden Town" – this "always-
buzzing" joint, recently expanded, offers "fresh and delicious"
modern Caribbean cooking in a "laid-back" and "dimly-lit" setting.
/ www.mangoroom.co.uk; 11 pm.

Mango Tree SW1   £45   ❸❸④
46 Grosvenor Pl   7823 1888   2–4B
*The ambience may be a bit "sterile", but "fabulous" (if "pricey")
Thai cooking draws a big following to this large and airy venture, at
the foot of a Belgravia office block. / www.mangotree.org.uk; 11 pm;
closed Sat L.*

Manicomio SW3   £47   ❸④❸
85 Duke of York Sq   7730 3366   5–2D
*"A lovely terrace in a pedestrian area" is the prime draw to this
Italian three-year-old, near Sloane Square; on the downside, the
interior is "bland", service is "indifferent" and the "uncomplicated"
food is "pricey" for what it is – go instead for a "yummy panini in
the adjoining café". / www.manicomio.co.uk; 10.30 pm.*

Manna NW3   £34   ❸❷❸
4 Erskine Rd   7722 8028   8–3B
*This venerable Primrose Hill veggie – the UK's first – still offers
some "original" dishes; it's "fairly pricey", though, the food can be
"hit-and-miss", and the setting is "hardly luxurious".
/ www.manna-veg.com; 10.45 pm; closed weekday L; no Amex.*

Manzi's WC2
1 Leicester St
*STOP PRESS! As this guide was going to the printers, news reached
us of a landlord's repossession of the site of this Theatreland fish
veteran – a sad end, it seems, to nearly 80 years' trading.*

Mao Tai SW6   £42   ❷❷❸
58 New King's Rd   7731 2520   10–1B
*Now bereft of its Chelsea sibling, the original and better Fulham
half of this Chinese duo has undergone a refurb to make it
"trendier" (and "with a cool new bar"); it continues to serve food
that's "outstanding, if expensive". / www.maotai.co.uk; 11.30 pm.*

Marine Ices NW3   £26   ④❷❷
8 Haverstock Hill   7482 9003   8–2B
*"Fun for all the family" has kept the Mansi family's Chalk Farm
pizzeria and ice cream parlour in business for over 75 years; the
food generally is merely "solid", but the ice cream is "heaven".
/ 11 pm; no Amex.*

Maroush   £40   ❸④⑤
I) 21 Edgware Rd, W2   7723 0773   6–1D
II) 38 Beauchamp Pl, SW3   7581 5434   5–1C
III) 62 Seymour St, W1   7724 5024   2–2A
IV) 68 Edgware Rd, W2   7724 9339   6–1D
V) 3-4 Vere St, W1   7493 3030   3–1B
"Garden") 1 Connaught St, W2   7262 0222   6–1D
*"Branches vary" at this successful Lebanese chain (some of which –
I, II & V – have café-take-aways whose "tasty shawarmas" are
"great for late night snacks"); their ambience can be "a let-down",
but the "authentic" food is generally "fresh", "healthy" and "filling".
/ www.maroush.com; 12.30 am-5 am.*

The Marquess Tavern N1 NEW £36 ❸❸❷
32 Canonbury St 7354 2975 8–2D
An elegantly stripped-down Canonbury boozer, relaunched as a
gastropub in the summer of 2006; it serves a fairly short menu
of British dishes – of high quality on our early-days visit – plus a
good list of wines, beers and ciders. / Rated on Editors' visit; 10.30 pm;
closed Mon L, Tue L, Wed L, Thu L, Sat D & Sun D.

Masala Zone £23 ❸❸❸
9 Marshall St, W1 7287 9966 3–2D
147 Earl's Court Rd, SW5 7373 0220 5–2A
80 Upper St, N1 7359 3399 8–3D
A mega-popular "Indian fast-food" chain, offering "cheap" and
"authentic" street-food in a "welcoming" and "bustling" setting.
/ www.realindianfood.com; 11 pm; no Amex; no booking.

Mash W1 £41 ⑤⑤⑤
19-21 Gt Portland St 7637 5555 3–1C
A "once-cool" venue, near Oxford Circus, where the bar still
"buzzes" (and can be "incredibly noisy"); the dining room, though,
is a "let-down" – service can be "inexcusably slow" and the food
is "poor". / www.mashbarandrestaurant.co.uk; 10.30 pm; closed Sun.

The Mason's Arms SW8 £32 ❸④❸
169 Battersea Park Rd 7622 2007 10–1C
Sale to Fullers hasn't dented the charms of this "noisy" boozer,
by Battersea Park station, where "standard" gastropub fare
is served "in good portions". / 10 pm.

Matilda's SW11 £34 ④④④
74-76 Battersea Bridge Rd 7228 6482 5–4C
"Matilda is no longer present" at this Battersea gastropub, where
the cooking has lost its "Italian accent" and is now pretty
humdrum. / midnight; no Amex.

Matriciano SW6 £36 ❸❸❸
108-110 New King's Rd 7731 2142 10–1B
"Lively" and quite "chic" ("by Fulham standards"), this Parson's
Green Italian – which decamped a while ago from Brompton Cross
– appears to be settling in as a useful all-rounder. / 11.30 pm;
Mon-Thu D only, Fri-Sun open L & D.

Matsuri £60 ❷❷④
15 Bury St, SW1 7839 1101 3–3D
Mid City Place, 71 High Holborn, WC1 7430 1970 2–1D
"They may not be exciting or buzzy", but these "calm" Japanese
fixtures – in St James's and Holborn – win high praise for their
"polite and helpful" staff and for sushi that's "expensive, but worth
it"; in SW1, a "superb" teppan-yaki injects an element of theatre.
/ www.matsuri-restaurant.com; SW1 10.30 pm; WC1 10 pm; WC1 closed Sun;
set pre theatre £35 (FP).

Mawar W2 £23 ❸④⑤
175a Edgware Rd 7262 1663 6–1D
"Popularity with Indonesian/Malaysian locals and students" speaks
much for the authenticity of this grungy – but "friendly, cheap and
cheerful" – basement canteen, near Edgware Road Tube; BYO.
/ 11 pm.

sign up for the survey at www.hardens.com

Maxwell's £29 ④④❸
8-9 James St, WC2 7836 0303 4–2D
76 Heath St, NW3 7794 5450 8–1A
*On a good day you get "American classics at a fair price" at these
Covent Garden and Hampstead veterans; fans say they're
"dependable if predictable" – critics that they're "best avoided
unless drunk". / www.maxwells.co.uk; midnight; NW3 closed Mon L.*

MAZE W1 £50 ❷❸❸
10-13 Grosvenor Sq 7107 0000 3–2A
*"An exciting addition to the Ramsay stable"; Jason Atherton's
"thoughtful" tapas dishes come in an "incredible range of masterly
combinations" at this "upbeat" Mayfair yearling; portions are
"tiny", though, the setting is a tad "bland", and the prices can seem
"outrageous". / 11 pm.*

Medcalf EC1 £37 ❷❸❸
40 Exmouth Mkt 7833 3533 9–1A
*With its "real old-fashioned" British menu, and its "funky" setting
(a converted butcher's shop), this "buzzing" bar/restaurant
in Clerkenwell is quite a "neighbourhood" linchpin; there's a feeling,
though, that it's "slipped a bit" of late – a fact possibly not
unconnected with its recent expansion. / www.medcalfbar.co.uk; 10 pm;
closed Fri D & Sun D; no Amex.*

Mediterranean Kitchen £31 ⑤⑤④
50-51 St Martin's Ln, WC2 7836 8289 4–4C
25-35 Gloucester Rd, SW7 7589 1383 5–2B
184 Kensington Park Rd, W11 7221 1150 6–1A **NEW**
127 Kensington Church St, W8 7727 8142 6–2B
3-5 Campden Hill Rd, W8 7938 1830 5–1A
334 Upper St, N1 7226 7916 8–3D
*Fans find it "basic but useful", but reporters generally are very
down on this growing chain, where the service is "haphazard" and
the food can be "terrible". / 11 pm.*

Mediterraneo W11 £43 ❷❷❸
37 Kensington Park Rd 7792 3131 6–1A
*A "casual but grown-up" sibling to the better-known Osteria
Basilico, nearby, offering similarly "good Italian home-cooking" in a
"busy, buzzy, fun, bistro-type" Notting Hill setting. / 11.30 pm;
booking: max 10; set weekday L £27 (FP).*

Mekong SW1 £22 ❸❷❸
46 Churton St 7630 9568 2–4B
*As a "neighbourhood stand-by", this "basic" and "cramped" Pimlico
veteran has many admirers, not least for its "ever-reliable" cuisine
(mostly Vietnamese, with a few Thai and Chinese dishes).
/ 11.30 pm.*

Mela WC2 £32 ❸❸❸
152-156 Shaftesbury Ave 7836 8635 4–2B
*This "diner-like" café remains a "favourite everyday Indian" for
many reporters, thanks to its convenient Theatreland location,
its "different" and "changing" menu and its "reasonable" prices.
/ www.melarestaurant.co.uk; 11.15 pm; set pre theatre £20 (FP).*

Melati W1 £28 ④❸⑤
21 Gt Windmill St   7437 2745   3–2D
Especially "for a quick pre-theatre" bite, this "cheap"
Malay/Indonesian canteen hits the spot; the food is "solid", but the
"ambience could do with livening up"; see also Melati, Peter Street.
/ 11.30 pm.

Melati W1 £24 ❸❸⑤
30-31 Peter St   7437 2011   3–2D
Like its (unrelated) namesake on Windmill Street (see also),
this "gem" in the sleazy heart of Soho has a loyal fan club;
if anything, the "authentic" Malaysian food and "efficient" service
win stronger praise here. / www.melati-restaurant.co.uk; 11.30 pm;
no Amex or Maestro.

Memories of India SW7 £29 ❸❷❸
18 Gloucester Rd   7581 3734   5–1B
A "solid" and "friendly" South Kensington local, which – thanks
to its "tasty" subcontinental cooking – maintains a small but loyal
following. / 11.30 pm.

Memsaheb on Thames E14 NEW £29 ❷❷❸
65/67 Amsterdam Rd   7538 3008   11–2D
A "really great local Indian" hidden-away on the Isle of Dogs;
it offers "all the usual favourites plus some more unusual dishes".
/ www.memsahebuk.com; 11.30 pm; closed Sat L & Sun L.

Menier Chocolate Factory SE1 £33 ④❸❷
51-53 Southwark St   7378 1712   9–4B
This "individual" venture – a "buzzy" theatre-cum-dining room
in Southwark – is probably best enjoyed as a whole-evening
"combo", though some reporters do use it pre-/post- a show
elsewhere. / www.menierchocolatefactory.com; 11 pm; closed Mon D,
Sat L & Sun.

Le Mercury N1 £24 ④❷❷
140a Upper St   7354 4088   8–2D
"All the key romantic elements" – "candles, little tables and soft
music" – help make this "cosy" Islington budget veteran very
popular; the bistro fare may be "ordinary", but it comes at "student
prices". / 1 am.

Meson don Felipe SE1 £24 ❸❸❶
53 The Cut   7928 3237   9–4A
"You feel like you're in Spain" at this "jolly" and "buzzing" veteran,
near the Old Vic, which gets "hopelessly overcrowded"; "the world's
longest wine list" (well, almost) accompanies "dependable" tapas.
/ 11 pm; closed Sun; no Amex; no booking after 8 pm.

Meson los Barilles E1 £26 ❸❷④
8a Lamb Street   7375 3136   9–1D
"For a quick City lunch" (or evening bite), this "authentic" Spanish
tapas bar/restaurant near Spitalfields Market "is not the cheapest
place, but good value". / 10.30 pm; closed Sat & Sun D.

Mestizo NW1 £28 ❷❷④
103 Hampstead Rd   7387 4064   8–4C
"Having lived in Mexico, this is finally the real deal!" – all reporters
are impressed by the "legitimacy" of the simple food at this year-
old spot; "pity about the inaccessible location" (near Warren Street
tube), though, and the "lack of ambience". / www.mestizo.com;
11.30 pm; closed Sun L.

sign up for the survey at www.hardens.com

Le Metro
Capital Hotel SW3   £32   ❸❸❷
28 Basil St   7591 1213   5–1D
*"Just round the corner from Harrods", this "pleasant" basement
bar/bistro is well worth knowing about for its "short" but "good-
value" menu and its "choice of wines by the glass". / 9 pm; closed
Sun D; need 5+ to book.*

Metro SW4   £38   ❹❹❷
9a Clapham Common S'side   7627 0632   10–2D
*A younger-scene Clapham bar/restaurant, which serves
"good cocktails" and (somewhat unreliable) "glorified bar food";
the dining tent is "great in summer". / www.metromotel.co.uk; midnight,
Fri & Sat 2 am; closed weekday L; no Amex.*

Metrogusto N1   £44   ❹❶❷
13 Theberton St   7226 9400   8–3D
*Host Ambro presides "with tact and zeal" over this "lively" Islington
favourite; the "fabulous" all-Italian wine list, however, is a more
certain bet than the "interesting" but "irritatingly variable" cooking.
/ 10.30 pm; Mon-Thu D only; booking: max 8, Sat & Sun.*

Mews of Mayfair W1 NEW   £52   ❺❹❹
10-11 Lancashire Ct, New Bond St   7518 9388   3–2B
*Expensively but insipidly decorated, this new restaurant, in a
courtyard just off Bond Street, is presumably meant to be a haven
for ladies-who-lunch; on our early-days visit, however, the food was
poor, the service slow and the bill high. / Rated on Editors' visit;
www.mewsofmayfair.com; 11 pm, Sun 8.30 pm; booking: max 8.*

Meza W1   £35   ❹❹❺
100 Wardour St   7314 4002   3–2D
*Conran's very large Soho tapas bar continues to inspire trivial
feedback; one thing's clear, though: "if you're looking for
a gastronomic experience, this isn't it". / www.conran.com/eat; 1.30 am;
closed Sun L.*

Mezzanine
Royal National Theatre SE1   £40   ❺❹❹
South Bank   7452 3600   2–3D
*The RNT's in-house dining room "survives on its location", to the
extent that some reporters consider it "a disgrace".
/ www.nationaltheatre.org.uk; 11 pm; D only, except Sat open L & D,
closed Sun.*

Michael Moore W1   £45   ❸❸❹
19 Blandford St   7224 1898   2–1A
*"Serious and inventive cooking" wins many fans for Mr M's
"quirky", "cheerful" and "unpretentious" Marylebone dining room
(not least as an informal business destination); results, however,
can be "inconsistent". / www.michaelmoorerestaurant.com; 10.30 pm;
closed Sat L & Sun.*

Mika W11 NEW   £31   ❸❹❸
78 Tavistock Rd   7243 8518   6–1B
*This "haphazard" but "charming" new Notting Hill sushi bar
is hailed as a great little "pit stop" that's "not too expensive
or pretentious". / www.mikalondon.com; 10.30 pm; closed Sun D.*

Mildred's W1 £28 ❷❸❷
45 Lexington St 7494 1634 3–2D
"The perfect place for dating a hippy, especially one who works in meejah" – this "buzzy" Soho stalwart offers "saintly but scrummy" veggie fare (including a "great non-meat burger"). / www.mildreds.co.uk; 11 pm; closed Sun; only Maestro; no booking.

Mimmo d'Ischia SW1 £53 ④❸④
61 Elizabeth St 7730 5406 2–4A
This "old '60s-style trattoria", in Belgravia, can still be "lots of fun, especially when the great man himself is around"; "the only complaint is that's it's too expensive". / www.mimmodischia.co.uk; 11.30 pm; closed Sun.

Mini Mundus SW17 £35 ❸❶❷
218 Trinity Rd 8767 5810 10–2C
A year-old Gallic family-run outfit, in "Nappy Valley"; all reports centre on its "good food, and excellent value for money". / 10.30 pm; closed Mon L.

Mint Leaf SW1 £48 ❷❸❷
Suffolk Pl, Haymarket 7930 9020 2–2C
"The Indian Hakkasan!" – though less famous than its Chinese look-alike, this similarly "sexy" and "night-clubby" basement is a "sophisticated" West End destination, with "superb" and "different" contemporary cuisine. / www.mintleafrestaurant.com; 11 pm; closed Sat L & Sun.

Mirabelle W1 £70 ④❸❸
56 Curzon St 7499 4636 3–4B
"A fading classic"; MPW's Mayfair dowager may still boast an "enormous and exotic" wine list, but its "glamorous" Art Deco-style décor "could use updating", and the cuisine has become plain "lazy". / www.whitestarline.org.uk; 10.30 pm; set weekday L £38 (FP).

Miraggio SW6 £30 ❸④④
510 Fulham Rd 7384 9774 5–4A
This "nice little family-style Italian", near Parson's Green, has already doubled in size ('due to public demand') in its first year of operation, thanks to food that's "traditional and well-done". / www.miraggio.co.uk; 11 pm.

Mirch Masala £20 ❶❸⑤
1416 London Rd, SW16 8679 1828 10–2C
213 Upper Tooting Rd, SW17 8672 7500 10–2D
171-173 The Broadway, UB1 8867 9222 1–3A
111 Commercial Rd, E1 7377 0155 9–2D **NEW**
"They look like greasy spoons", but these "unbeatable" Pakistani canteens – the survey's highest-rated subcontinentals – offer "a complexity of flavours which would grace any Michelin-starred restaurant", and at "ridiculously cheap" prices too. / midnight.

Misato W1 £23 ❷④⑤
11 Wardour St 7734 0808 4–3A
"An authentic Japanese restaurant, run by Japanese people for Japanese people", and located – obviously – in Chinatown; thanks to the "amazing" prices, there's "always a queue". / 11.30 pm; no credit cards.

Missouri Grill EC3 £41 ❸❸④
76 Aldgate High St 7481 4010 9–2D
Fans insist it does "great US food" (including "the best Maryland
crab cakes in town"), but this bravely-sited yearling, opposite
Aldgate tube, seems mainly to have found a rôle as a canteen for
local "suits". / www.missourigrill.com; 11 pm; closed Sat & Sun.

Mitsukoshi SW1 £53 ❷❷⑤
Dorland Hs, 14-20 Lower Regent St 7930 0317 3–3D
It looks "very tired", but this sterile basement (beneath a
department store) remains "a favourite sushi restaurant" for some
reporters, thanks to its "very authentic" cooking and its
"courteous" service. / www.mitsukoshi-restaurant.co.uk; 10 pm.

Miyabi
Great Eastern Hotel EC2 £38
Liverpool St 7618 7100 9–2D
This "surprisingly small" City Japanese changed hands as our
survey for the year was drawing to a close, hence we've left it un-
rated. / www.great-eastern-hotel.co.uk; 10.30 pm; closed Sat L & Sun;
booking: max 6.

Miyama W1 £60 ❷❷⑤
38 Clarges St 7499 2443 3–4B
"Classic Japanese dishes are very well prepared and well served" at
this "excellent" Mayfair fixture (where the lunchtime set deals offer
"outstanding value"); "basic '80s décor" and a "dearth of non-
Japanese diners" all add to its feeling of authenticity. / 10.30 pm;
closed Sat L & Sun L.

Mju
Millennium Knightsbridge SW1 £60 ❸❸⑤
16-17 Sloane St 7201 6330 5–1D
Fans say you can enjoy "15 fine courses, each of individual
brilliance" at this Knightsbridge fusion-restaurant; it's a shame,
then, that a hidden-away location, high prices and "airport lounge"
décor discourage anything resembling a 'following'.
/ www.mju-restaurant.co.uk; 10.30 pm; closed Sun.

Mocotó SW1 [NEW]
145 Knightsbridge 7225 2300 5–1D
On the potentially striking Knightsbridge site that was Isola (RIP) –
this ambitious new Brazilian is set to open as this guide goes to
press; given the recent surge of interest in Latin American cuisine, it
has the chance to be an emblematic newcomer.

Mohsen W14 £25 ❷❷④
152 Warwick Rd 7602 9888 7–1D
The exterior is "unpromising" and the location "grim", but Mrs
Mohsen's "reliable" café (opposite Olympia's Homebase) is a "real
gem", offering "excellent" Persian food at "very reasonable" prices;
BYO too. / midnight; no credit cards.

Momo W1 £50 ④④❷
25 Heddon St 7434 4040 3–2C
An "unmissable" atmosphere still makes Mourad Mazouz's large
party-Moroccan, off Regent Street, a "favourite" for some
reporters; with its "uninspired" food and sometimes "appalling"
service, though, it strikes others as ever more "disappointing".
/ www.momoresto.com; 11 pm; closed Sun L.

Mon Plaisir WC2 £45 ❸❸❷
19-21 Monmouth St   7836 7243   4–2B
For "a slice of Paris in Covent Garden", this "charming", rambling bistro veteran of 50 years' standing is still an "old favourite" for many reporters; more and more, though, "it has its bad days, when the food is a little drab and the staff are surly".
/ www.monplaisir.co.uk; 11.15 pm; closed Sat L & Sun; set weekday L £27 (FP).

Mona Lisa SW10 £23 ❸❷④
417 King's Rd   7376 5447   5–3B
"Working men and Chelsea types mingle for fry-ups" at this "highly-recommended" greasy spoon; by night, it serves "simple, Italian home cooking" at "incredible" prices. / 11 pm; closed Sun D; no Amex.

Monmouth Coffee Company £10 ❶❷❷
27 Monmouth St, WC2   7379 3516   4–2B
2 Park St, SE1   7645 3585   9–4C
A micro-chain serving "the best coffee in London, possibly the world"; "at Borough Market, they do great breakfasts too".
/ www.monmouthcoffee.co.uk; L & afternoon tea only; closed Sun; no Amex; no booking.

Montpeliano SW7 £56 ⑤⑤④
13 Montpelier St   7589 0032   5–1C
This '70s Knightsbridge trattoria has always had a mixed press from reporters – this year, however, saw an upsurge in complaints that it's "snooty", "overpriced" and "disappointing". / midnight; set weekday L £33 (FP).

Monty's W5 £27 ❸❸④
1 The Mall   8567 8122   1–2A
"There are five Monty's curry houses in the area, but this is the best" – this heart-of-Ealing stalwart is a local favourite thanks to grub that's "standard but tasty and reliable".
/ www.montystandoori.co.uk; midnight; set weekday L £16 (FP).

Monza SW3 £42 ❷❸④
6 Yeomans Row   7591 0210   5–2C
"Good, well-priced food" is not that easy to find in Knightsbridge, so this "poorly-located" trattoria – which is, in fact, all of five minutes' walk from Harrods – is well worth seeking out.
/ www.monza.org.uk; 11 pm; closed Mon L; set weekday L £25 (FP).

Mooli SW4 NEW £40 ④❸④
36a Old Town   7627 1166   10–2D
A new Clapham Italian that's had a fair amount of press attention; on our early-days visit, it seemed too expensive to be a handy local, and not good enough to be anything better. / Rated on Editors' visit; 11 pm.

Morel SW4 £42 ❸❸⑤
14 Clapham Park Rd   7627 2468   10–2D
The ambitious cuisine can be "superb" at this Clapham yearling; it suffers from "bleak" décor, however, and can seem "overpriced" (especially when the prix-fixe menu is not available).
/ www.morelrestaurant.co.uk; 10 pm; D only, ex Sun open L & D; no Amex.

The Morgan Arms E3 £40 ❷❸❸
43 Morgan St 8980 6389 1–2D
"A star in the East" – thanks to its *"always interesting and
changing menu"*, this Bow gastro-boozer *"never disappoints"*.
/ www.geronimo-inns.co.uk; 10 pm; closed Sun D; no Amex; booking: max 10.

Morgan M N7 £48 ❶❷④
489 Liverpool Rd 7609 3560 8–2D
*Especially for the "reasonable prices", the quality of Morgan
Meunier's "extraordinary" Gallic cuisine – amongst the best
in London – is "simply amazing"; to sample it, though, you have
to brave a rather "cold" setting in a "plain" former pub in "edgy"
north-Islington.* / www.morganm.com; 10 pm; closed Mon, Tue L,
Sat L & Sun D; no Amex; booking: max 6.

MORO EC1 £40 ❶❷❷
34-36 Exmouth Mkt 7833 8336 9–1A
*"Sensational" Spanish/North African cooking – "always with
an interesting twist" – has won fame for Samantha and Samuel
Clark's "sophisticated" Clerkenwell ten-year-old; by night,
its "energetic" but "laid-back" setting is notoriously "noisy".*
/ www.moro.co.uk; 10.30 pm; closed Sun; booking essential.

Moroccan Tagine W10 £19 ❸❸❸
95 Golborne Rd 8968 8055 6–1A
*For a "cheap and cheerful" meal in Portobello, this "well-priced"
Moroccan café offers an atmospheric pit stop.* / 11 pm; no Amex.

Mosaica
The Chocolate Factory N22 £37 ❷④❸
Unit C005, Clarendon Rd 8889 2400 1–1C
"Worth a visit, but you'll need a map" – this Wood Green factory-
conversion is praised for its *"lovely"* food and its *"spectacular"*
evening atmosphere; the cooking is *"not always consistent"*, though,
and service can be *"haphazard"*. / www.mosaicarestaurant.co.uk;
9.30 pm; closed Mon, Sat L & Sun D.

Mosaico W1 £50 ❸❸④
13 Albemarle St 7409 1011 3–3C
*With its "well-spaced" tables and "reliable" cooking, this "serious"
Italian basement is "hard to beat in Mayfair for business";
it "just about justifies its high prices".* / www.mosaico-restaurant.co.uk;
11 pm; closed Sat L & Sun; set weekday L £32 (FP).

Moshi Moshi £25 ❸❸❸
Waitrose, Canada Pl, E14 7512 9201 11–1C
Unit 24, Liverpool St Station, EC2 7247 3227 9–2D
*With its "solid", "no-nonsense" dishes, London's original Kaiten-
Zushi (conveyor-sushi) chain "beats the living daylights" out of some
of its newer competitors; Liverpool Street is particularly popular.*
/ www.moshimoshi.co.uk; E14 8 pm, Sun 5 pm; Liverpool St 10 pm; Broadgate
4 pm; EC2 closed Sat & Sun; no Amex; E14 & Broadgate no booking.

Motcombs SW1 £48 ④④❸
26 Motcomb St 7235 6382 5–1D
*A long-established Belgravia wine bar-cum-restaurant has a certain
"relaxed", if rather "louche", charm; the food is "acceptable,
but not much more".* / www.motcombs.co.uk; 11 pm; closed Sun D.

Moti Mahal WC2 £43 ❸②④
45 Gt Queen St 7240 9329 4–2D
Despite its "high-quality" cuisine, this rather "traditional" and
"expensive" Indian yearling in Covent Garden has yet to make
much of a splash, and atmosphere can be elusive. / midnight;
closed Sun.

Mr Chow SW1 £63 ④④④
151 Knightsbridge 7589 7347 5–1D
This "old-fashioned" Knightsbridge oriental was originally aimed
at an international crowd, and was quite a famous '70s scene;
it's totally eclipsed nowadays by its NYC offshoots, and attracts little
feedback – presumably because the "OK" food is so "vastly
overpriced". / www.mrchow.com; midnight.

Mr Jerk £18 ❸④④
189 Wardour St, W1 7287 2878 3–1D
19 Westbourne Grove, W2 7221 4678 6–1C
"You can eat well for well under £10" at these "crowded", "no-
frills" Caribbean joints, in Soho and Bayswater – despite the odd
"bland" dish, the scoff is mostly "homely and comforting",
and comes in "generous" portions. / www.mrjerk.co.uk; 11 pm,
Sun 8 pm.

Mr Kong WC2 £26 ❷❸⑤
21 Lisle St 7437 7341 4–3A
"If the staff detect a real interest in the further reaches of the
menu", you'll be very well looked after at this "way above-average"
Chinatown veteran; "avoid downstairs", though (and also the "whip-
through gale" from the front door). / 3 am.

Mr Wing SW5 £42 ❷❷❶
242-244 Old Brompton Rd 7370 4450 5–2A
After two decades in business, this "civilised" Earl's Court Chinese
is still a "fantastic place", with jazz nightly and a "cool basement,
enhanced by tropical fish tanks"; it's "a bit pricey", but few
reporters seem to care. / www.mrwing.com; midnight.

Nahm
Halkin Hotel SW1 £70 ④④⑤
5 Halkin St 7333 1234 2–3A
"Flavours explode in your mouth", say fans of David Thompson's
cuisine at this celebrated Thai restaurant in Belgravia; even they
admit it's a "cold" room, though, and, for its many detractors,
it's just a "poor-value" destination all-round. / www.nahm.como.bz;
10.30 pm; closed Sat L & Sun L.

Naked Turtle SW14 £42 ❸④④
505 Upper Richmond Rd 8878 1995 10–2A
This "buzzy" Sheen wine bar – known for its "singing waitresses" –
has dropped off the map of late; perhaps a recent refurb' will
restore its former notoriety. / 11 pm; D only, ex Sun open L & D; no Amex;
set always available £26 (FP).

Nam Long SW5 £35 ⑤④④
159 Old Brompton Rd 7373 1926 5–2B
"Good for late drinks or people-watching"; this long-standing South
Kensington Vietnamese hang-out serves "average food at high
prices", but serves "top cocktails" and is popular amongst people
"who like to be noticed". / 11.30 pm; D only, closed Sun; no trainers.

sign up for the survey at www.hardens.com

Namo E9 £28 ❷❸④
178 Victoria Park Rd 8533 0639 1–2D
"Excellent Vietnamese food at great prices" wins rave reviews from locals for this "tightly-packed" café near Victoria Park; service, though, can vary. / 11 pm; closed Mon, Tue L & Wed L; set weekday L £18 (FP).

Nancy Lam's Enak Enak SW11 £39 ❸❸❸
56 Lavender Hill 7924 3148 10–1C
"A warm welcome by Nancy and her family" helps win praise for this TV-chef's Battersea dining room, which – say fans – offers "different", "home-cooked" Asian fare; since a refurb a couple of years ago, though, its detractors feel that "prices have rocketed and portions seem to have halved". / www.nancylam.com; 10.30 pm; D only, closed Mon & Sun.

Nando's £21 ④④④
Branches throughout London
"Cheap, cheerful, and the place to go if you like chicken" – this Portuguese-style grill chain makes an "efficient" (and "healthy-ish") stand-by, especially for those with kids in tow. / www.nandos.co.uk; 11.30 pm; no Amex; no booking.

Nanglo SW12 £23 ❷④④
88 Balham High Rd 8673 4160 10–2C
"Some unusual Nepalese dishes" help this Balham subcontinental stand out; service is notably "friendly and generous" too. / 11.30 pm; D only.

Napulé SW6 £35 ❷④❸
585 Fulham Rd 7381 1122 5–4A
"It looks unassuming from the outside", but this lively Italian near Fulham Broadway, "run by Neapolitans", boasts "a delicious antipasti counter" and "excellent, authentic pizza". / 11 pm; closed weekday L; no Amex.

Nathalie SW3 £46 ❷④④
3 Milner St 7581 2848 5–2D
With its "charming" service and "enticing" menu, this "low-profile" Gallic restaurant is "trying hard" in the battle against its hidden-away location (which is, in fact, only a short walk from Brompton Cross). / www.nathalie-restaurant.co.uk; 10.30 pm; closed Mon & Sun.

The National Dining Rooms
National Gallery WC2 NEW £48 ❸④❸
Sainsbury Wing, Trafalgar Sq 7747 2525 2–2C
The NG's relaunched dining room (now run by Oliver Peyton) has had "an OK start" (and is certainly "a great improvement on its predecessor, Crivelli's Garden", RIP); the patriotic British menu is "not cheap" but most reporters consider it "fair value". / www.thenationaldiningrooms.co.uk; Wed 9 pm; closed Mon D, Tue D, Thu D, Fri D, Sat D & Sun D; no Amex.

Nautilus NW6 £25 ❶❶❸
27-29 Fortune Green Rd 7435 2532 1–1B
"Superb fish 'n' chips, in portions to feed the five thousand!" maintains the appeal of this veteran kosher chippie in West Hampstead; service is "lovely", and the setting – "complete with plastic flowers" – is "a total time warp". / 10 pm; closed Sun L; no Amex.

Navarro's W1 £26 ②③②
67 Charlotte St   7637 7713   2–1C
"Beautiful tiled décor" sets the scene at this "authentic" Fitzrovia
tapas bar; thanks to its "fantastic" and "tasty" cooking, it's "always
very busy" (and the noise can be "unbearable"). / www.navarros.co.uk;
10 pm; closed Sat L & Sun.

Neal Street WC2 £58 ⑤⑤⑤
26 Neal St   7836 8368   4–2C
"Ordinary, over-rated and overpriced" – Antonio Carluccio's "tired"
Neal Street flagship Italian seems to trade ever more shamelessly
on the TV-celebrity of its mushroom-mad proprietor.
/ www.carluccios.com; 10.30 pm; closed Sun.

New Culture Revolution £20 ④④⑤
75 Southampton Row, WC1   7436 9708   2–1D
305 King's Rd, SW3   7352 9281   5–3C
157-159 Notting Hill Gate, W11   7313 9688   6–2B
42 Duncan St, N1   7833 9083   8–3D
43 Parkway, NW1   7267 2700   8–3B
This "no-frills" but "good-value" oriental chain serves "dependable
noodles and simple Chinese dishes"; as a "quick, tasty, cheap"
stand-by, it's popular with almost all who comment on it. / 11 pm;
need 4+ to book.

New Mayflower W1 £27 ②③④
68-70 Shaftesbury Ave   7734 9207   4–3A
"Some of the best Cantonese cooking" in the West End is served
at this "lively" fixture on the fringe of Chinatown (though it helps
"if you know your way round the menu"); it's one of the best late-
night eating options in town. / 4 am; D only; no Amex.

New Tayyabs E1 £19 ❶④❸
83 Fieldgate St   7247 9543   9–2D
This "crazily busy" Whitechapel Pakistani is "the real thing",
serving "outstanding" kebabs, lamb chops and curries
at "amazing" prices – "expansion hasn't shortened the queue,
but at least you wait in more style"; BYO. / www.tayyabs.co.uk;
11.30 pm.

New World W1 £28 ❸❸❸
1 Gerrard Pl   7734 0396   4–3A
A "massive" Chinatown institution, known for "entertaining" trolley
service of "the ultimate dim sum" – it otherwise attracts relatively
little commentary. / 11.45 pm; no booking, Sun L.

Newton's SW4 £34 ❸②❸
33 Abbeville Rd   8673 0977   10–2D
A "casual" Clapham stand-by that's a "regular favourite" for local
reporters. / www.newtonsrestaurants.co.uk; 11.30 pm; set dinner £20 (FP).

Nicole's W1 £54 ④❸④
158 New Bond St   7499 8408   3–3C
"A great retreat from Bond Street madness" – despite cooking
that's no more than "reliable", this fashion store basement
"stalwart" makes "a good lunch destination". / 6 pm; L & afternoon
tea only, closed Sun.

sign up for the survey at www.hardens.com

Nikita's SW10 £40 ⑤②❶
65 Ifield Rd 7352 6326 5–3A
"The food is stuck in the '80s" at this dated Russian cellar on the fringe of Chelsea, and the prices can seem "a rip-off" too; who cares, though, if you drink enough of their vodka, or enjoy the "romantic" possibilities afforded by its clandestine booths? / www.nikitasrestaurant.com; 11.30 pm; D only, closed Sun; no Amex.

Niksons SW11 £39
172-174 Northcote Rd 7228 2285 10–2C
Though "a bit more sophisticated than its local rivals", the lofty rear dining room of this "pub-like" Battersea bar seems ever more incidental, and its food is "hit-or-miss". / www.niksons.co.uk; 10 pm; closed Mon L.

No 77 Wine Bar NW6 £30 ❸②
77 Mill Ln 7435 7787 1–1B
Under the same ownership for over two decades, this "lively" and "friendly" wine bar is an ever-handy West Hampstead stand-by. / 11.30 pm; no Amex.

NOBU
METROPOLITAN HOTEL W1 £88 ②
Old Park Ln 7447 4747 3–4A
Mayfair's legendary fusion "classic" still "wows the palate" with its "thrilling" Japanese/Latin American fare (not least "wonderful" sushi); prices, though, are "a laugh", service "should be better", and the setting "needs refreshing". / www.noburestaurants.com; 10.15 pm; booking: max 12; set weekday L £60 (FP).

Nobu Berkeley W1 £88 ❸ ❸
15-16 Berkeley St 7290 9222 3–3C
Mayfair's year-old "walk-in Nobu" – no booking, you wait for your table in the "frenzied" bar – is "younger" and more "chaotic" than the original; "in comparison", the Japanese fusion fare here is "uninspiring", but prices are equally "astronomical". / www.noburestaurants.com; 2 am; D only, closed Sun.

La Noisette SW1 NEW £75 ❸❸❸
164 Sloane St 7750 5000 5–1D
Gordon Ramsay rejigged this Knightsbridge dining room in mid-2006, installing ex-Greenhouse chef Bjorn van der Horst; our early-days visit found it very like its predecessors on the site (Monte's, RIP and Pengelley's, RIP) – a smart but bland operation that's hard to criticise but difficult to love. / Rated on Editors' visit; www.gordonramsay.com; 11.30 pm; closed Sat L & Sun.

Noodle Noodle £22 ❸ ⑤
18 Buckingham Palace Rd, SW1 7931 9911 2–4B
Vauxhall Bridge Rd, SW1 7828 8565 2–4B
"When you're in a hurry... when you're hungry" (and near Victoria), these "simple" pit stops offer cheap sustenance fast. / www.noodle-noodle.co.uk; 10.45 pm; Buckingham Palace Rd closed Sun.

Noor Jahan £33 ❷❷❸
2a Bina Gdns, SW5 7373 6522 5–2B
26 Sussex Pl, W2 7402 2332 6–1D
"Brilliant" curries win widespread satisfaction with this veteran Earl's Court subcontinental – like its recent Bayswater offshoot, it's "always reliable". / 11.30 pm.

North Sea Fish WC1 £28 ❷④④
7-8 Leigh St   7387 5892   8–4C
"It's certainly not a glamour-destination", but this "old-fashioned", "no-frills" Bloomsbury chippie is still "one of the best". / 10.30 pm; closed Sun.

The Northgate N1 £33 ❸❷❸
113 Southgate Rd   7359 7392   1–1C
"Unfancy, but well-executed" dishes (from a "limited menu") make this De Beauvoir gastropub a popular destination; of late, though, its performance has seemed more "hit-and-miss". / 11 pm; closed weekday L; no Amex.

Nosh TW1 £34 ④④❸
139 St Margarets Rd   8891 4188   1–4A
This "simple" St Margaret's spot is "not bad for a little local", and of some note for its "relaxing" atmosphere; it's difficult, though, to avoid the conclusion that "you could do better elsewhere". / 10.30 pm; closed Sun.

Noto £30 ❸❷⑤
2-3 Bassishaw Highwalk, EC2   7256 9433   9–2B
26 King William St, EC4   7929 7879   9–3C **NEW**
"The number of oriental expats speaks volumes" about the authentic (if "unglamorous") style of these "Japanese diners"; notwithstanding the odd "uninspiring" dish, it offers "a good alternative to the usual City fare". / www.noto.co.uk; 9.30pm; closed Sat & Sun; no Amex.

Notting Grill W11 £53 ❸④❸
123a Clarendon Rd   7229 1500   6–2A
Fans of AWT's "convivial" pub-conversion, in a Holland Park backwater, hail it as "a meat-lovers' paradise", with "fabulous steak" and "excellent burgers"; service can be "forgetful", though, and doubters say the place "should do better". / www.awtonline.co.uk; 10.30 pm; closed Mon L.

Notting Hill Brasserie W11 £50 ❶❶❷
92 Kensington Park Rd   7229 4481   6–2B
The "secret" about this "tucked-away" Notting Hill "treasure" now seems to be well and truly out; Mark Jankel's "incredibly accomplished" cooking just gets better, service is "smooth and unobtrusive" and the ambience – pepped up by "gentle live jazz" – is "fabulous" too. / 11 pm; closed Sun D; set weekday L £33 (FP).

Noura £46 ④❸④
122 Jermyn St, SW1   7839 2020   3–3D
16 Hobart Pl, SW1   7235 9444   2–4B
2 William St, SW1   7235 5900   5–1D
16 Curzon St, W1   7495 1050   3–4B
"It's sad to see the decline at this once-fabulous Lebanese"; when it had just one London outlet (in Belgravia), this Paris-based chain was of some note – since the push for West End domination, however, it has risked becoming "very ordinary". / www.noura.co.uk; 12.30 am, William St midnight.

sign up for the survey at www.hardens.com

Nozomi SW3 £62 ⑤④④
15 Beauchamp Pl 7838 1500 5–1C
*This self-promotingly "glamorous" and "trendy" Japanese yearling
in Knightsbridge has induced amazingly little feedback – most of
it to the effect that it's a "huge disappointment", with "outrageous"
prices for food that's "average at best". / 11.30 pm; closed Sun.*

Numero Uno SW11 £34 ❸②②
139 Northcote Rd 7978 5837 10–2C
*A "local favourite" Italian consistently praised by Battersea
reporters for its "decent" cooking, its "friendly" service and its
"great" atmosphere; it's "always full". / 11.30 pm; no Amex.*

Nuovi Sapori SW6 £38 ❷❶④
295 New King's Rd 7736 3363 10–1B
*"Good and well-priced" Italian cooking – twinned with "superb"
service – is helping win quite a following for this "friendly" Fulham
yearling. / 11 pm; closed Sun.*

Nuvo EC4 £9 ❷❷④
68 Cannon St 0800 328 6886 9–3C
*"A City lunchtime revolution"; this year-old take-away is roundly
praised for its "fantastic soup, salad, sandwiches and, in particular,
smoothies". / www.eatnuvo.com; L only, closed Sat & Sun; no Amex.*

Nyonya W11 £25 ❸❸④
2a Kensington Park Rd 7243 1800 6–2B
*Fans extol the "wonderful" and "authentic" Peranakan cuisine
at this "communal but stylish" canteen, near Notting Hill Gate;
its critics just find it "unremarkable", though. / www.nyonya.co.uk;
10.30 pm.*

O'Conor Don W1 £34 ④❸❷
88 Marylebone Ln 7935 9311 3–1A
*OK, but could do better – a fair summary on this cosy Marylebone
pub, which serves hearty Irish fodder. / www.oconordon.com; 10 pm;
closed Sat & Sun.*

O'Zon TW1 £22 ❸❶❸
33-35 London Rd 8891 3611 1–4A
*"An excellent-value, eat-as-much-as-you-like" oriental in downtown
Twickenham; it offers a "good diversity" of Thai, Chinese and
Malaysian dishes, served by "very friendly staff who don't pressure
you". / www.ozon.co.uk; 11 pm.*

The Oak W2
137 Westbourne Park Rd 7221 3355 6–1B
*This vibrant converted boozer in Notting Hill – known for its
fantastic pizza – had a major fire in early-2006; it's still closed
as this guide goes to press, but apparently they plan to re-open
some time soon. / 10 pm; Mon-Thu closed L; no booking.*

Odette's NW1
130 Regent's Park Rd 7586 5486 8–3B
*This gorgeous mirrored romantic favourite – long a fixture
of Primrose Hill – changed hands again this year (and is now
owned by rock promoter Vince Power); the premises are 'dark'
as we go to press – a relaunch is apparently planned for late-2006.*

Odin's W1 £45 ❸⓿⓿

27 Devonshire St 7935 7296 2–1A

For those of an "old-school" bent, this "discreet", "courteous" and "relaxing" Marylebone restaurant – decorated with the art collection of the late Peter Langan – remains "hard to beat"; to younger bloods, though, it can just seem "unimaginative". / www.langansrestaurants.co.uk; 11 pm; closed Sat & Sun; booking: max 10.

Old Parr's Head W14 £19 ❸❷④

120 Blythe Rd 7371 4561 7–1C

"It's so cheap, you don't have to think twice" at this "great" Olympia Thai-in-a-pub; (it's "especially good in summer when you can sit outside"). / www.theoldparrshead.com; 10.45 pm; no Amex.

Old Vic Brasserie SE1 NEW

Mercury Hs, Waterloo Rd awaiting tel 9–4A

The Cheyne Walk Brasserie has made its name by selling elegant 'comfort' food at prices which are high even by Chelsea standards – it will be interesting to see how the same team adapts the formula for this new autumn-2006 opening, in gritty Waterloo.

Ye Olde Cheshire Cheese EC4 £34 ⑤④⓿

145 Fleet St 7353 6170 9–2A

"One of the few pubs in London that justifies the Ye Olde in its name!" – this City-fringe tavern is "a must for visitors"; with its "vacant" service and "very poor" food, however, "it really seems to have gone down in recent times". / www.yeoldecheshirecheese.com; 9.30 pm; closed Sun D; no booking, Sat & Sun.

Oliveto SW1 £43 ❷❸⑤

49 Elizabeth St 7730 0074 2–4A

As close as Belgravia gets to a "neighbourhood restaurant", this "cramped" and "noisy" pizzeria has a very strong local following for its "simple but very tasty" fare; it's best to book. / 11 pm; booking: max 7 at D.

Olivo SW1 £44 ❷❷④

21 Eccleston St 7730 2505 2–4B

This "very good local Sardinian bistro", in Belgravia, may be rather "cramped", but its "genuine" dishes, "interesting" wines and "friendly" service make it enduringly popular locally; look out for a new offshoot in Lower Belgrave Street at the end of 2006. / 11 pm; closed Sat L & Sun L.

Olley's SE24 £31 ❷❷❸

67-69 Norwood Rd 8671 8259 10–2D

"The best fish 'n' chips for miles" is served at this "fantastic" location, in a converted railway arch overlooking Brockwell Park. / www.olleys.info; 10.30 pm; closed Mon L.

1 Blossom Street E1 £46 ④❸❸

1 Blossom St 7247 6530 9–1D

"A stone's throw from the City", this "well-spaced" Italian makes a good business venue, with its "solid" cooking and an "extensive, top-grade" wine list; the basement setting "can seem a bit gloomy" but there's also "a wonderful garden". / www.1blossomstreet.com; 9 pm; closed Sat & Sun.

sign up for the survey at www.hardens.com

1 Lombard Street EC3 £75 ④④④
1 Lombard St 7929 6611 9–3C
*"An ideal location by Bank" have long helped make this
"cavernous" former banking hall a "perfect pinstripe destination";
its cuisine, however, "doesn't inspire like once it did".*
/ www.1lombardstreet.com; 9.45 pm; closed Sat & Sun; no trainers; booking
essential.

One-O-One
Sheraton Park Tower SW1 £73 ❶③⑤
101 Knightsbridge 7290 7101 5–1D
*Pascal Proyart's fish and seafood cooking is "beyond superlative",
and compensates for the "'80s airport lounge" décor of this
"strange" Knightsbridge dining room, where the staff dress
"like refugees from Star Trek".* / 10.15 pm.

OQO Bar N1 £35 ④❸❷
4-6 Islington Grn 7704 2332 8–3D
*For "cool-quotient", this "very minimalistic" Islington yearling –
with its "fantastic" cocktails and "beautiful" bar – rates highly;
the funky oriental fare is increasingly "mediocre", however.*
/ www.oqobar.co.uk; midnight.

Orange Tree N20 £37 ❸④❷
7 Totteridge Ln 8343 7031 1–1B
*"An excellent pub-refurbishment in leafy Totteridge" ("though it's
not much like a pub anymore") – this "slick" new sibling
to Hampstead's Freemason's Arms has gone down a storm locally,
even if results can be a tad "haphazard".*
/ www.theorangetreetotteridge.co.uk; 9.30 pm.

L'Oranger SW1 £77 ❸❸❸
5 St James's St 7839 3774 3–4D
*As a "discreet, efficient venue at which to impress", this St James's
fixture has much going for it – not least "excellent, classical French"
cuisine, "attentive" service and an "elegant" traditional setting;
needless to say, it "doesn't come cheap".* / 11 pm; closed Sat L & Sun;
booking: max 8; set weekday L £48 (FP).

The Oratory SW3 £31 ④④❷
232 Brompton Rd 7584 3493 5–2C
*"Top wines at astonishingly low prices" ensure John Brinkley's
"cosy bistro", near the V&A, is usually "packed"; the food, though,
is "nothing too fancy".* / www.brinkleys.com; 11 pm.

Oriel SW1 £34 ⑤④❷
50-51 Sloane Sq 7730 2804 5–2D
*This brasserie at the centre of the Sloane world is most notable for
its positively "voyeuristic" people-watching potential (especially
al fresco); it's "always fun" for coffee, lunch or brunch, but the food
is at "tourist trap" level.* / www.tragusholdings.com; 10.45 pm; no booking.

Oriental City Food Court NW9 £22 ❷④⑤
399 Edgware Rd 8200 1188 1–1A
*"You can't get bored" on a visit to the overwhelming food court
of this oriental north London shopping mall, where "a fantastic
range of cuisines – from Vietnamese to Thai, Japanese
to Indonesian" – is served "hawker-style at cheap prices".* / 9 pm;
L & early evening only; no Amex.

Origin
The Hospital WC2 NEW £50 ❷❷❸
24 Endell St 7170 9200 4–2C
This new incarnation of Covent Garden's Thyme (RIP) has
succeeded – where its predecessor failed – in showcasing Adam
Byatt's "stimulating" and "original" cuisine (with most dishes
available as starters or mains); it can be "pretty empty" though –
"pity it's so hidden from the street". / www.origin-restaurant.com;
10.30 pm; closed Sat L & Sun.

Original Tajines W1 £30 ❸❸❸
7a Dorset St 7935 1545 2–1A
"Off the beaten track in Marylebone", this neighbourhood café –
with its "interesting" food, "sweet" service and "cosy" setting –
offers a "slightly different" experience. / www.originaltagines.com;
midnight; closed Sat L & Sun; no Amex.

Orrery W1 £68 ❸❷❸
55 Marylebone High St 7616 8000 2–1A
Thanks to its "fabulous", "modern classical French cuisine",
"excellent" wine and "lovely" setting (overlooking a churchyard),
this "formal" Fitzrovian is, for some reporters, "the only good
Conran"; even here, though, prices can seem "difficult to justify".
/ www.orrery.co.uk; 10.45 pm; booking: max 12; set weekday L £38 (FP).

Orso WC2 £43 ④❸④
27 Wellington St 7240 5269 4–3D
"Often overlooked" nowadays, this Italian cellar near Covent
Garden is "a favourite of many years' standing" for many reporters,
who see it as an "always-reliable" venue with "tasty" food and
"efficient" staff; as ever, though, sceptics just find it "adequate but
uninspiring". / midnight; set weekday L £26 (FP).

Oscar
Charlotte Street Hotel W1 £58 ⑤⑤④
15 Charlotte St 7907 4705 2–1C
This attractive muralled dining room (part of a boutique hotel)
looks a "great location", and – for breakfast – it is one too; at other
times, though, "it's incomprehensible why you would choose this
place over its many better Fitzrovia rivals".
/ www.charlottestreethotel.com; 11 pm; closed Sun L.

Oslo Court NW8 £48 ❷❶❸
Charlbert St, off Prince Albert Rd 7722 8795 8–3A
"It's the antithesis of stylish", but everyone – "youngsters as much
as the blue-rinse regulars" – loves this "inimitable" and
"reassuring" time warp, in a Regent's Park mansion block; "nothing
is too much trouble" for staff who deliver a menu that's "a roll-call
of favourites from the '70s and '80s". / 11 pm; closed Sun.

Osteria Antica Bologna SW11 £38 ④④④
23 Northcote Rd 7978 4771 10–2C
This "dated" and "cramped" Battersea Italian has long had
a name for its "authentic" approach; it's still "an old favourite" for
some reporters, but others find it "disappointing". / www.osteria.co.uk;
11 pm.

Osteria Basilico W11 £40 ❷❸❶
29 Kensington Park Rd   7727 9957   6–1A
"Quintessential Notting Hill" – this "festive" Italian favourite
is "always packed and noisy", thanks to its "reliably great" food
(including "super pizzas"); service, though, can be "brusque".
/ www.osteriabasilico.co.uk; 11.30 pm; no booking, Sat L.

Osteria dell'Arancio SW10 £47 ❸❷❷
383 King's Rd   7349 8111   5–3B
An Italian reporter notes he "feels at home" at this atmospheric
revamp of "a former World's End pub", thanks in large part to the
"knowledgable and helpful" service; ditching the set-menu format
has boosted appreciation for its cooking (which is matched with
a "very thoughtful" wine selection). / www.osteriadellarancio.com; 11 pm.

Ottolenghi £36 ❶❸❸
63 Ledbury Rd, W11   7727 1121   6–1B
1 Holland St, W8   7937 0003   5–1A NEW
287 Upper St, N1   7288 1454   8–2D
"Out-of-this-world" salads and "exquisite" cakes are highlights
of the cuisine at these "outstanding" and "genuinely different" deli-
diners – they're "outrageously expensive, but somehow always
worth it". / www.ottolenghi.co.uk; 11 pm, Sun 7 pm; W11 closed Sun;
no Amex; W11 no booking, N1 booking for D only.

(BRASSERIE)
OXO TOWER SE1 £47 ⑤⑤❸
Barge House St   7803 3888   9–3A
If you must check out "the best view in London", the adjacent
brasserie at least charges lower prices than the restaurant –
they are still "exorbitant". / 11 pm; booking: max 8.

(RESTAURANT)
OXO TOWER SE1 £66 ⑤⑤❸
Barge House St   7803 3888   9–3A
"Stunning" views too often "seem the only good thing" about the
8th-floor restaurant of this South Bank landmark – with its "over-
inflated" prices for "barely average" food, and its "appalling"
service, it yet again tops nominations as London's most
disappointing and most overpriced restaurant.
/ www.harveynichols.com; 11 pm; booking: max 14; set weekday L £45 (FP).

Ozer W1 £29 ④❸❸
4-5 Langham Pl   7323 0505   3–1C
"Having moderated its initial high aims", this upmarket relation
of the Sofra Turkish chain makes a handy destination, just north
of Oxford Circus; for a "cheap and cheerful" stand-by, it's quite
"comfortable" too. / www.sofra.co.uk; midnight.

Pacific Bar and Grill W6 NEW £35 ④④❷
320 Goldhawk Rd   8741 1994   7–1B
A very stylishly revamped branch of Café Med, near Stamford
Brook tube, with a "great atmosphere (for families especially)";
fans say its American fare is "reliable", but critics find it downright
inept.

Pacific Oriental EC2 £48 ④④④
1 Bishopsgate 7621 9988 9–2C
*This large pan-Asian joint doesn't attract much interest from
reporters nowadays – "what was once an innovative and welcoming
restaurant has slowly transformed into a noisy after-work City
haunt". / www.orientalrestaurantgroup.co.uk; 9 pm; closed Sat & Sun.*

Page in Pimlico SW1 £29 ❸❷❸
11 Warwick Way 7834 3313 2–4B
*"A little Thai oasis" in a pub – eat in the bar, or "for a quiet meal"
head for the upstairs dining room. / www.frontpagepubs.com; 10 pm.*

Il Pagliaccio SW6 £31 ④❷⓿
182-184 Wandsworth Bridge Rd 7371 5253 10–1B
*The "mad and chaotic" staff are "a blast with kids" (of all ages)
at this "fun and breezy local Italian" in deepest Fulham;
the cooking, however, is "unremarkable". / www.paggs.co.uk; midnight;
no Amex.*

Le Pain Quotidien W1 £22 ❷❸⓿
72 Marylebone High St 7486 6154 2–1A
*"Gosh it's good", say fans of this "relaxing" Belgian bakery import
in Marylebone, where you can eat-in at a large communal table;
"wonderful breads", "amazing chocolate spreads" and "delicious"
coffee (in bowls) are highlights in a wide line up of "yummy"
options; a new South Bank branch is coming soon. / L & afternoon
tea only.*

The Painted Heron £42 ⓿⓿❸
112 Cheyne Walk, SW10 7351 5232 5–3B
205-209 Kennington Ln, SE11 7793 8313 1–3C
*"Still semi-undiscovered", this unlikely Chelsea-and-Kennington duo
deliver "exactly what you want from a posh Indian" – "decent"
décor, "deeply flavoured" dishes and "fabulous" service.
/ www.thepaintedheron.com; SE11 10.30 pm, SW10 11 pm; SW10 closed
Sat L & Sun.*

Le Palais du Jardin WC2 £46 ④④❸
136 Long Acre 7379 5353 4–3C
*Some reporters still see this "glamorous" Covent Garden brasserie
– known for its "impressive seafood platters" – as a "buzzing and
ever-reliable" central stand-by; service has long been "haphazard",
however, and standards generally seem ever more "tired".
/ www.lpdj.co.uk; midnight.*

The Palmerston SE22 £36 ❷❸④
91 Lordship Ln 8693 1629 1–4D
*The food is "a significant notch above pub grub" at this "excellent"
year-old gastropub in East Dulwich – it "has raised the bar
in SE22". / www.thepalmerston.co.uk; 11 pm; closed Sun D; no Amex;
set weekday L £24 (FP).*

Pampa £40 ❸④❸
4 Northcote Rd, SW11 7924 1167 10–2C
60 Battersea Rise, SW11 7924 4774 10–2C
*These "noisy" and "basic" Battersea Argentineans win unanimous
praise for their "consistently great and tasty steaks" – for critics,
though, these are "the only saving grace". / 11 pm; D only; Northcote
Road closed Sun.*

Pan-Asian Canteen
Paxton's Head SW1   £31   ❷❸❸
153 Knightsbridge   7581 6256   5–1D
Oddly sited on the first floor of a palatial pub – this communal-table dining room serves "fresh and tasty oriental treats" that are "very cheap" by Knightsbridge standards. / 10 pm; no Amex.

Papageno WC2   £36   ④④❷
29-31 Wellington St   7836 4444   4–3D
"Kitsch", "gaudy" and "fun", this slightly more handily-sited Covent Garden offshoot of Sarastro offers a less extreme experience than the original (but much of the same "theatrical" charm); its "basic" cuisine is sometimes "better than expected" too.
/ www.papagenorestaurant.com; midnight.

Papillon SW3 NEW   £52   ❸❸❷
96 Draycott Ave   7225 2555   5–2C
Soren Jessen's "fun" Belle Epoque-inspired newcomer has quickly become a natural home for the beautiful people of Brompton Cross; its "classic" haute-brasserie fare is sound enough, but the "very extensive" wine list is perhaps a more notable attraction.
/ www.papillonchelsea.co.uk; midnight; set weekday L £31 (FP).

Pappa Ciccia   £26   ❷0❷
105-107 Munster Rd, SW6   7384 1884   10–1B
41 Fulham High St, SW6   7736 0900   10–1B
90 Lower Richmond Rd, SW15   8789 9040   10–1A
"Excellent" pizzas and "outstanding value" feature in almost all feedback on this "friendly" and "genuinely Italian-feeling" west London mini-chain; at SW6 branches you can BYO (Fulham High Street, wine only). / www.pappaciccia.com; 11 pm.

Pappagallo W1   £47   ❸❷④
54-55 Curzon St   7629 2742   3–4B
"Good food at a reasonable price, for the area" makes this Mayfair Italian a trusty "stand-by" for some reporters; it doesn't seem to be gathering much of a following, though, and the atmosphere can be flat. / midnight; closed Sat L & Sun L.

Paradise by Way
of Kensal Green W10   £34   ❸❷❷
19 Kilburn Ln   8969 0098   1–2B
An "amazing, eclectic, laid-back ambience" has long made this "different" gastropub pioneer "a joy" for its trendy 'outer-Notting Hill' crowd; its "competent" cooking has pepped up a bit in recent times. / 10.30 pm; no Amex.

Paradiso Olivelli   £28   ④④④
3 Gt Titchfield St, W1   7436 0111   3–1C
9 St Christopher's Pl, W1   7486 3196   3–1A
35 Store St, WC1   7255 2554   2–1C
31 Catherine St, WC2   7836 3609   4–2D
61 The Cut, SE1   7261 1221   9–4A
"For a fast and efficient bite", some reporters tip this "handy" chain; arguably, though, it's "adequate in all areas, but not much more". / www.ristoranteparadiso.co.uk; midnight; WC1 Sun.

Al Parco N6 £23 ❷❸④
2 Highgate West Hill 8340 5900 8–1B
*"A little bit of Italy in Parliament Hill"; locals insist that,
for "fantastic thin-crust pizzas", it just can't be beat – "sit inside
by the oven or outside on the pavement". / 10.30 pm; no Amex.*

**Parmigiano the
Italian Kitchen W14** NEW £34 ❸❸❸
238 Blythe Rd 7603 1122 7–1C
*A "friendly" new Italian local, north of Brook Green; its "interesting"
menu delivers the odd "surprisingly clumsy" dish, but the pizza
is reliable, and "cheap" prices (not least a "good-value early bird"
offer) help disarm criticism. / www.snowsonthegreen.co.uk; 11 pm,
Sun 10 pm; closed weekday L; no Amex.*

The Parsee N19 £33 ❸❸⑤
34 Highgate Hill 7272 9091 8–1C
*"Interesting and distinctive" Indian cooking has always been the
compensation for the "sterile" ambience at Cyrus Todiwala's
Highgate five-year-old; of late, however, standard have "fallen".
/ www.theparsee.com; 10.45 pm; D only, closed Sun.*

Pasha SW7 £44
1 Gloucester Rd 7589 7969 5–1B
*This exotic, ultra-"romantic" Moroccan hideaway in South
Kensington was relaunched under new ownership shortly before this
guide went to press; early newspaper reports suggest that the food
and service continue to play second fiddle to the ambience.
/ www.pasha-restaurant.co.uk; midnight; closed Sun L; booking: max 10
at weekends; set weekday L £16 (FP).*

Pasha N1 £35 ④❸④
301 Upper St 7226 1454 8–3D
*This large and "friendly" Turkish fixture, in Islington, offers "reliable
food at a reasonable cost"; "the meze makes a good-value meal
in itself". / 11.30 pm.*

Passione W1 £56 ❸❸④
10 Charlotte St 7636 2833 2–1C
*Gennaro Contaldo's "stylish, hearty and rustic" cooking has made
quite a name for his "intimate" ("cramped") Fitzrovia venture;
it attracts ever more criticism, though, especially for prices which
many reporters find "excessive". / www.passione.co.uk; 10.15 pm; closed
Sat L & Sun.*

Pasta Brown £33 ④④⑤
31-32 Bedford St, WC2 7836 7486 4–3C
35-36 Bow St, WC2 7379 5775 4–2D
*These West End "pit stops" look extremely touristy, but such
feedback as they inspire praises their "decent" pasta and
"good value". / www.pastabrown.com; 11 pm, Sun 6.30 pm; closed Sun D;
no Mastercard.*

Patara £45 ❶❷❸
15 Greek St, W1 7437 1071 4–2A
3-7 Maddox St, W1 7499 6008 3–2C
181 Fulham Rd, SW3 7351 5692 5–2C
9 Beauchamp Pl, SW3 7581 8820 5–1C
*"Gorgeous" cooking – which "takes you right back to Thailand" –
and "polite" staff hit all the right notes at this "simple" and
"calming" small chain; its Soho branch in particular is hailed as a
"rare pearl" in the West End. / 10.30 pm; set weekday L £27 (FP).*

Paternoster Chop House EC4 £50 ⑤④⑤
Warwick Ct, Paternoster Sq 7029 9400 9–2B
"Why are so many Conran places rubbish?"; this "completely soulless" City grill – with its "ho-hum cooking" and its "noisy" ambience – is just a waste of a "great location".
/ www.conran.com/eat; 10.30 pm; closed Sat & Sun D.

Patio W12 £25 ④❷❸
5 Goldhawk Rd 8743 5194 7–1C
"You can't go wrong, except around the waist", say fans of this "homely" Shepherd's Bush "one-off", whose "bustling owner ensures you have a good time", and where the "unbeatable set menu delivers huge portions of Polish staples" at "low" prices; critics, though, find the food plain "dull". / 11.30 pm; closed Sat L.

Pâtisserie Valerie £26 ❸④❷
17 Motcomb St, SW1 7245 6161 5–1D
Hans Cr, SW1 7590 0905 5–1D
105 Marylebone High St, W1 7935 6240 2–1A
162 Piccadilly, W1 7491 1717 3–3C
44 Old Compton St, W1 7437 3466 4–2A
215 Brompton Rd, SW3 7823 9971 5–1C
Duke of York Sq, SW3 7730 7094 5–2D
27 Kensington Church St, W8 7937 9574 5–1A
37 Brushfield St, E1 7247 4906 9–2D
For an "excellent croissant", "scrummy pâtisserie" or "reliable snack", this "Continental"-style veteran chain remains a favourite; the Soho original, Marylebone (originally Maison Sagne) and Knightsbridge branches are the best-known.
/ www.patisserie-valerie.co.uk; 7 pm, Old Compton St & Brushfield St 8 pm, Hans Cr 11.30 pm; no booking.

Patterson's W1 £60 ❷❸④
4 Mill St 7499 1308 3–2C
Raymond & Tom Patterson's "ambitious" and highly popular Mayfair three-year-old is central London's most prominent family-run venture; satisfaction somewhat declined this year, though, particularly as regards its rather "soulless" setting.
/ www.pattersonsrestaurant.com; 11 pm; closed Sat L & Sun.

Paul £28 ❷④④
115 Marylebone High St, W1 7224 5615 2–1A
29-30 Bedford St, WC2 7836 3304 4–3C
73 Gloucester Rd, SW7 7373 1232 5–2B NEW
43 Hampstead High St, NW3 7794 8657 8–1A NEW
147 Fleet St, EC4 7353 5874 9–2A NEW
"Mmmmmm!"; with their "marvellous" pâtisserie, "wonderful" bread and "mouth-watering" sandwiches (not to mention the "awesome hot chocolate"), this fast-expanding café/bakery chain is one of the more welcome French invasions; "shame about the classically Gallic service", though. / 7.30 pm-8.30 pm; no Amex; no booking.

Pearl
Marriot Hotel WC1 £65 ❸❸❸
252 High Holborn 7829 7000 2–1D
Standards at this "grand" and "cavernous" Holborn dining room can "vary from occasion to occasion"; hit lucky, though, and Jan Tanaka's cuisine is "perfectly executed and beautifully presented".
/ www.pearl-restaurant.com; 10 pm; closed Sat L & Sun.

The Peasant EC1 £40 ④④④

240 St John St 7336 7726 8–3D

For fans, this Clerkenwell fixture remains "an excellent gastropub" (in both the "noisier" bar, and the more "formal" upstairs); its ratings are undercut, though, by reports of "over-ambitious" food or of service that's "a let-down". / www.thepeasant.co.uk; 11 pm.

Pellicano SW3 £44 ❸❷❸

19-21 Elystan St 7589 3718 5–2C

"Consistent" cooking and "always-welcoming" service makes this "quiet Italian haven", near Chelsea Green, a "good local stand-by". / 11 pm.

E Pellicci E2 £14 ❸❸❶

332 Bethnal Green Rd 7739 4873 1–2D

In the East End, this "perfect" Art Deco "greasy spoon" – run by the Pellicci family since the '50s – not only offers "a fabulous trip back in time", but is also a "bustling" setting for "an especially brilliant English breakfast". / L only, closed Sun; no credit cards.

The Penthouse WC2 £52 ⑤⑤❸

1 Leicester Sq 7734 0900 4–4A

Fans say "views rival the Oxo Tower's" at this top-floor West End dining room, above a large nightclub; it attracts negligible feedback, though – the variable cuisine is "just too expensive for what it is". / www.thepenthouseclub.co.uk; 11 pm; D only, closed Mon & Sun.

The People's Palace
Royal Festival Hall SE1

South Bank Centre 7928 9999 2–3D

This impressive dining chamber overlooking the Thames was closed as this guide went to press; it is scheduled to re-open in 2007 on completion of the refurbishment of the Royal Festival Hall. / www.peoplespalace.co.uk; 10.45 pm.

The Pepper Tree SW4 £20 ❷❸❸

19 Clapham Common S'side 7622 1758 10–2D

For over a decade now, this "busy little Thai", near Clapham South tube, has delivered "super-quick", "fresh" and "cheap" nosh in a "buzzy" refectory setting. / www.thepeppertree.co.uk; 11 pm; no Amex; no booking at D.

Perc%nto EC4 £47 ⑤⑤⑤

26 Ludgate Hill 7778 0010 9–2B

A seriously complacent City basement Italian, serving "bland and uninspiring food" in a "bland and uninspiring setting"; service is sometimes "totally absent" too. / www.etruscarestaurants.com; 10 pm.

Père Michel W2 £39 ❸❸④

11 Bathurst St 7723 5431 6–2D

A time-warped Gallic outfit, hailed by its small fan club as Bayswater's "best-kept secret"; fish is the highlight. / 11 pm; closed Sat L & Sun.

Perla £30 ④④❸

11 Charlotte St, W1 7436 1744 2–1C
28 Maiden Ln, WC2 7240 7400 4–4D
803 Fulham Rd, SW6 7471 4895 10–1B

These "loud" and "basic" Mexican cantinas aren't about to win any culinary awards; they're "fun", though, with a "short but reliable" menu and "good cocktails" and tequilas. / 10 pm-11 pm; WC2 Sun D only.

sign up for the survey at www.hardens.com

Pescador Too NW3 £34 ❸❷❸
108 Heath St 7443 9500 8–1A
*Some find it "great", others only "average", but there's little doubt
that this "pleasant" Portuguese fish restaurant is one of the
brighter stars in the Hampstead constellation. / 11 pm; closed
weekday L; set Sun L £19 (FP).*

Petersham Nurseries TW10 £54 ❸❹❷
Off Petersham Rd 8605 3627 1–4A
*A trip to this posh Petersham garden centre café – where "top-
notch" food, is served in a "lovely" old glasshouse – offers
"a unique experience" and makes "a great day out" ("book far,
far ahead for a Sunday"); the downside? – it's "so overpriced".
/ www.petershamnurseries.com; Wed-Sun L only, closed Mon & Tue; no Amex;
booking essential.*

Le Petit Auberge N1 £28 ❹❸❸
283 Upper St 7359 1046 8–2D
*This "hectic" and "unpretentious" bistro near Islington's Almeida
Theatre is an "old favourite" for locals, offering "modest" cooking
in a setting some find "romantic". / 11 pm; set weekday L £17 (FP).*

Le Petit Train NW1 🆕 £40 ❸❸❸
40 Chalcot Rd 7483 0077 8–3B
*Fans say this Gallic newcomer, on a difficult Primrose Hill site,
is "small but perfectly formed"; the brasserie-style set menus
certainly offer top value, but our early-days visit left us unsure that
the premium for à la carte would be justified. / Rated on Editors' visit;
10 pm; closed Sun; set always available £24 (FP).*

**PÉTRUS
THE BERKELEY SW1** £84 ❶❶❷
Wilton Pl 7235 1200 5–1D
*Marcus Wareing's "consummately skillful" cuisine just gets better
and better, and, if he goes on improving at this rate, this "soothing"
Belgravia dining room will soon be London's No.
1; the "intimidatingly large" wine list ("with some good mid-priced
options") is also of note, as is the "exemplary" service.
/ www.marcuswareing.com; 10.45 pm; closed Sat L & Sun; no jeans or trainers;
booking: max 10; set weekday L £50 (FP).*

Pham Sushie EC1 £22 ❶❷❸
155 Whitecross St 7251 6336 9–1B
*"Some of the best sushi in London" makes it well worth seeking out
this "top-value", "unassuming" and "friendly" café, near the
Barbican. / 10 pm; closed Sat L & Sun.*

Philpotts Mezzaluna NW2 £43 ❸❸❹
424 Finchley Rd 7794 0455 1–1B
*With its "robust" Italian food and its "interesting" wine, David
Philpott's Childs Hill stalwart is generally hailed by reporters as an
"oasis in a gastronomic desert". / www.philpotts-mezzaluna.com; 11 pm;
closed Mon & Sat L; no Amex.*

Pho EC1 🆕 £22 ❸❷❹
86 St John St 7253 7624 9–1A
*"Steaming bowls of pho" (Vietnamese broth and noodles,
pronounced as in the French 'feu') are "served quickly and with
a smile" at this "cheap" and "crowded" Clerkenwell café.
/ www.phocafe.co.uk; 10 pm; closed Sat & Sun.*

for updates visit www.hardens.com

The Phoenix SW3   £35   ④④❸
23 Smith St   7730 9182   5–2D
"A good gastropub that consistently delivers" – a comment typical of the upbeat but unexceptional feedback on this "relaxed" hangout, just off the King's Road. / www.geronimo-inns.co.uk; 9.45 pm; no Amex.

Phoenix Bar & Grill SW15   £39   ❷❷❷
162-164 Lower Richmond Rd   8780 3131   10–1A
Cooking that is "higher quality than in the past" has helped boost ratings at this "light", "airy" and "welcoming" Putney ten-year-old; go for a table under the outside canopy in summer. / www.sonnys.co.uk; 11 pm.

Phoenix Palace NW1   £30   ❷❸❸
3-5 Glentworth St   7486 3515   2–1A
"Fantastic dim sum" (and other "largely authentic" Cantonese fare) makes this "top-notch" oriental near Baker Street tube a "very popular" choice; "it's always full of Chinese folk". / 11.15 pm.

Picasso's SW3   £32   ⑤④❸
127 King's Rd   7352 4921   5–3C
This "quirky" Italian joint – a real remnant of '60s Chelsea – serves strong coffee and basic but "tasty" snacks. / 11.15 pm.

Pick More Daisies N8   £29   ❸❷❸
12 Crouch End Hill   8340 2288   8–1C
A "groovy" ("California-style") Crouch End yearling, rapidly establishing itself as a neighbourhood favourite for "yummy" burgers, "tasty" salads and the like. / www.pickmoredaisies.com; 10 pm; no Amex.

PIED À TERRE W1   £81   ❷❷❷
34 Charlotte St   7636 1178   2–1C
"It's back – hallelujah!", say fans of David Moore's Fitzrovia townhouse-restaurant, which has arisen "phoenix-like" after a major fire; it's much more "sleek" nowadays, and Shane Osborne's "impressive" cuisine "remains on top form". / www.pied-a-terre.co.uk; 11 pm; closed Sat L & Sun; booking: max 6; set weekday L £48 (FP).

The Pig's Ear SW3   £37   ❸❸❷
35 Old Church St   7352 2908   5–3C
Charmingly located in a Chelsea side street, this "cosy" and "intimate" boozer – done out in Art Nouveau style – is almost unanimously hailed as a "good all-rounder", whether you eat in the bar or upstairs in the dining room. / www.thepigsear.co.uk; 10.30 pm.

Pigalle Club W1 NEW   £48   ④❸❷
215-217 Piccadilly   7734 8142   3–3D
A "great addition to the London scene" – this "beautiful" new Mayfair supper club makes a "fab night out" destination; "go for the experience", though, "rather than the food". / www.thepigalleclub.com; 11.30 pm; D only, closed Sun.

The Pilot W4   £29   ❸❷❷
56 Wellesley Rd   8994 0828   7–2A
"They've got the local gastropub thing just right", say fans of this "buzzing" place, south of Gunnersbury Tube (which "stepped up its game" this year). / 10 pm.

ping pong £27 ❸❸❷
10 Paddington St, W1 7009 9600 2–1A NEW
45 Gt Marlborough St, W1 7851 6969 3–2C
74-76 Westbourne Grove, W2 7313 9832 6–1B NEW
"A cheap and cheerful Yauatcha" – this "gimmicky but fun" dim sum chain has been an instant hit with its "great style and concept"; "intriguing" Jasmine tea and "delicious" cocktails, however, outshine food that – "for the prices" – is only "good enough". / midnight, Sun 10.30 pm.

La Piragua N1 £24 ❷❹❷
176 Upper St 7354 2843 8–2D
"Plate-sized Argentinean steaks at bargain prices" help make this "lively" Islington cantina an ever-"reliable" destination for fun on a budget. / midnight; closed Mon & Sun; no Amex.

El Pirata W1 £32 ❹❸❷
5-6 Down St 7491 3810 3–4B
"'Cheap and cheerful' doesn't usually happen in Mayfair", so it's all the more worth remembering this "chaotic" but "fun" tapas bar, near Shepherd Market. / www.elpirata.co.uk; 11.30 pm; closed Sat L & Sun; set weekday L £14 (FP).

Pissarro's W4 £38 ❸❷❶
Corney Reach Way 8994 3111 10–1A
"A great riverside location" ("on a sleepy stretch of the towpath") guarantees a following for this "informal" bar/restaurant, near Chiswick House; its food is not at all bad, and service is "lovely". / www.pissarro.co.uk; 10.30 pm.

Pizza Metro SW11 £32 ❷❷❷
64 Battersea Rise 7228 3812 10–2C
"Superb pizza by the metre" and "service like you were in Naples" make this "family-friendly" Battersea Italian "a great choice for groups and celebrations"; that's perhaps another way of saying that it can be a bit of a "zoo". / 11 pm; closed Mon, Tue-Fri D only, Sat & Sun open L & D; no Amex.

Pizza on the Park SW1 £35 ❹❹❸
11 Knightsbridge 7235 5273 5–1D
"The mix of good pizza and great music is unbeatable", say fans of the basement jazz venue (entrance charge £20) of this grand PizzaExpress, near Hyde Park Corner; the airy, if dated ground-floor restaurant also makes a "cheery" stand-by. / www.pizzaonthepark.co.uk; 11 pm.

Ciro's Pizza Pomodoro £32 ❹❹❷
51 Beauchamp Pl, SW3 7589 1278 5–1C
7-8 Bishopsgate Churchyard, EC2 7920 9207 9–2D
Regular live music and "cheap" pizza help attract a "boisterous crowd" to these "fun" Italians (particularly the Knightsbridge basement original); they are "good for groups, and as a late eat". / SW3 1 am, EC2 midnight; SW3 D only, EC2 closed Sun.

PizzaExpress £25 ④❸❸

Branches throughout London

It's "a trusted old friend" for its army of fans, but even some supporters concede that the food at this ex-benchmark pizzeria chain is "hardly thrilling" nowadays; it retains two key strengths – "agreeable" branches and "pleasant" staff who "cope well with kids". / www.pizzaexpress.co.uk; 11.30 pm-midnight; most City branches closed all or part of weekend; no booking at most branches.

Pizzeria Castello SE16 £27 ❷❷❸

192-196 Jamaica Rd 7064 4631 11–2A

This Bermondsey pizzeria is run by one of the founders of the celebrated Elephant & Castle institution of the same name; fans say that its pizzas are "the best in town" – even "as good as the original was in its heyday"! / 11 pm; closed Mon, Sat L & Sun.

Pizzeria Castello SE1 £27 ④④④

20 Walworth Rd 7703 2556 1–3C

Feedback on this veteran Elephant & Castle pizzeria is becoming thinner and more mixed – fans still insist it's "consistently great", but, for doubters, it's just "very old-school" ("in a bad way"). / 11 pm; closed Sat L & Sun.

Pizzeria Oregano N1 £29 ❷❷❸

19 St Albans Pl 7288 1123 8–3D

"Packed with Italians, and terrific value" – this "café-like" joint, just off Islington's Upper Street, boasts "tasty" pizzas and "larger-than-life" service. / 10.45 pm; closed Mon, Tue-Fri D only, Sat & Sun open L & D; no Amex.

PJ's SW3 £47 ⑤⑤❸

52 Fulham Rd 7581 0025 5–2C

A "Euro-beautiful" following helps make this South Kensington bar/brasserie an invariably "fun" and "lively" scene (that's especially "great for brunch"); the food and service, though, "have really gone downhill" in recent years. / 11.45 pm.

The Place Below EC2 £18 ❸④❸

St Mary-le-Bow, Cheapside 7329 0789 9–2C

"Still among the best places for a quick City lunch" – this "reliable" self-service cafeteria offers "wholesome" veggie fare in the "atmospheric" crypt of an impressive church; BYO. / www.theplacebelow.co.uk; L only, closed Sat & Sun; no Amex; need 15+ to book.

Planet Hollywood W1 £44 ⑤④⑤

13 Coventry St 7287 1000 4–4A

This movie-themed West End landmark is looking as long in the tooth as its celeb' backers (Stallone, Willis and Schwarzenegger) – it can be "unbelievably bad". / www.planethollywoodlondon.com; 1 am.

Plateau E14 £65 ④④❸

Canada Pl 7715 7100 11–1C

"Futuristic" views create an impressive backdrop at Conran's "bright and airy" fourth-floor vantage point (the only pukka business-lunch venue in the very heart of Canary Wharf); "the food doesn't ascend Olympian heights" though, and "isn't worth the premium". / www.conran.com/eat; 10 pm; closed Sat L & Sun D; set dinner £33 (FP).

Poissonnerie de l'Avenue SW3 £56 ❷❷❸
82 Sloane Ave 7589 2457 5–2C
"A good experience, if a little upmarket and expensive"; this "staid" and somewhat "cramped" South Kensington fish veteran has maintained "excellent quality over the years", which is heartily appreciated by its "ageing crowd". / www.poissonneriedelavenue.co.uk; 11.30 pm; closed Sun.

(Ognisko Polskie)
The Polish Club SW7 £36 ❹❷❷
55 Prince's Gate, Exhibition Rd 7589 4635 5–1C
"Courteous" service and gracefully faded décor "take you back to another age", at this South Kensington émigrés club; its Polish fodder is "unsubtle" but not expensive, and even those who find it "awful" can find a visit worthwhile – "for the experience". / www.ognisko.com; 11 pm; set always available £21 (FP).

Pomegranates SW1 £50 ❹❸❷
94 Grosvenor Rd 7828 6560 2–4C
Patrick Gwynn-Jones makes a "wonderful host" at this "appealingly retro" Pimlico-basement '70s survivor; it's "still going strong", and the "eclectic" food is "sometimes unpredictable, but always interesting". / www.pomegranates-restaurant.co.uk; 11.15 pm; closed Sat L & Sun.

Le Pont de la Tour SE1 £63 ❹❹❸
36d Shad Thames 7403 8403 9–4D
With its "tired" food and "condescending" service, it's impossible to avoid the conclusion that this grand Conran riversider is "going downhill" – it may have "unbeatable views" of Tower Bridge, but the bill can still leave you feeling "slightly ill"! / www.conran.com/eat; 11 pm; closed Sat L.

Le Pont de la Tour Bar & Grill SE1 £49 ❹❹❸
36d Shad Thames 7403 8403 9–4D
"Quality continues to decline" at the Pont's brasserie offshoot; this was once a useful destination, but nowadays you can only be sure of getting "great value" – or anything close to it – by seeking out its "pre-theatre" menus and the like. / www.conran.com/eat; 11 pm; no booking; set always available £27 (FP).

Popeseye £38 ❷❸④
108 Blythe Rd, W14 7610 4578 7–1C
277 Upper Richmond Rd, SW15 8788 7733 10–2A
"Steak, steak and steak" (plus a "properly aged and affordable" wine list) is the "simple" but "perfect" formula of this Olympia and Putney bistro duo; conditions are basic, but "the candlelit setting leads to a feeling of relaxed intimacy". / 10.30 pm; D only, closed Sun; no credit cards.

La Porchetta Pizzeria £23 ❸❸❸
33 Boswell St, WC1 7242 2434 2–1D
141-142 Upper St, N1 7288 2488 8–2D
147 Stroud Green Rd, N4 7281 2892 8–1D
74-77 Chalk Farm Rd, NW1 7267 6822 8–2B
84-86 Rosebery Ave, EC1 7837 6060 9–1A
"Go hungry", if you visit one of these "always full and lively" north London Italians, where "madcap staff" deliver "brilliant-value" dishes (in particular thin-crust pizzas "the size of wagon wheels"); "Finsbury Park is original and best", and the queue there "can be annoying". / 10.30-midnight; WC1 closed Sat L & Sun, N1 Mon-Thu closed L, N4 closed weekday L; no Amex; need 5+ to book.

Portal EC1 £52 ❸❸❸
88 St John St 7253 6950 9–1B
"Delicious" Portuguese-influenced cuisine, "excellent" wine, "delightful" design and "accommodating" service could make this "impressive" Clerkenwell yearling a "potential rival for Moro"…; but first, it needs to sort out too many instances of "amateurish" food and service. / www.portalrestaurant.com; 10.15 pm; closed Sat L & Sun.

La Porte des Indes W1 £51 ❸❸❷
32 Bryanston St 7224 0055 2–2A
"A setting that's hard to beat in central London" – "a cavernous labyrinth", complete with waterfall – makes a visit to this Marble Arch Indian a "captivating" experience; the "French-influenced" food is "delicious", but "very, very pricey" (and quite "unspicy"). / www.pilondon.net; 11.30 pm; closed Sat L; set weekday L £30 (FP).

Porters English Restaurant WC2 £31 ⑤④⑤
17 Henrietta St 7836 6466 4–3D
This "touristy" Covent Garden fixture (known for its pies) is too often "slapdash"; with its native theming, it can seem "a disgrace to English catering". / www.porters.uk.com; 11.30 pm; no Amex.

Il Portico W8 £42 ❸❶❸
277 Kensington High St 7602 6262 7–1D
"You are treated as a valued and welcome guest", say fans of this "rustic" family-run trattoria of long standing, by Odeon Kensington, which serves "good" Italian fare of the old school. / 11.15 pm; closed Sun, & Bank Holidays.

The Portrait
National Portrait Gallery WC2 £45 ④⑤❷
St Martin's Pl 7312 2490 4–4B
"Beautiful views of Trafalgar Square and Big Ben" help make this "stylish" top-floor restaurant quite an "impressive location"; its management can sometimes seem "desperately incompetent", though, and the food is often "bland". / www.searcys.co.uk; Thu-Fri 8.30 pm; Sat-Wed closed D; set pre theatre £22 (FP).

Potemkin EC1 £36 ❸❸④
144 Clerkenwell Rd 7278 6661 9–1A
A "great range of vodkas" and "good" (if "heavy") Russian food wins praise for this simply-decorated Clerkenwell bar and baasement restaurant; it's potentially "a fantastic place for romance", but "boisterous parties can make it unbearable". / www.potemkin.co.uk; 10.30 pm; closed Sat L & Sun.

LA POULE AU POT SW1 £44 ❸❷❶
231 Ebury St 7730 7763 5–2D
"To sweep someone off their feet, there's no destination better"
than one of the "hidden corners" of this "dark" Pimlico stalwart –
yet again the survey's top romantic choice – where "rustic" Gallic
food is served "with a shrug"; "you could be a million miles from
London". / 11 pm; set weekday L £30 (FP).

Prego TW9 £36 ❸④④
106 Kew Rd 8948 8508 1–4A
By Richmond standards, this Italian fixture of 20 years' standing
is worth knowing about ("especially for its pizzas and puddings");
"it's very buzzy at the weekends, but otherwise can be quiet".
/ www.pregorestaurant.co.uk; 11 pm; closed Mon L.

Pret A Manger £9 ❸❷④
Branches throughout London
"First-rate" sandwiches, "terrific soups" and "surprisingly good"
coffee have made London's premier take-away chain so popular it's
almost a "cliché"; "how do the staff remain so cheerful, polite and
attentive?" / www.pret.com; 4 pm-6 pm, Trafalgar Sq 8 pm, St. Martin's
Ln 9 pm; closed Sun (except some West End branches), City branches closed
Sat & Sun; no credit cards; no booking.

The Prince Bonaparte W2 £26 ❷❸❷
80 Chepstow Rd 7313 9491 6–1B
"Innovative and good-quality grub" is part of the all-round appeal
of this straightforward – but "really buzzy" – Bayswater gastropub.
/ www.mbplc.com; 10 pm; no booking.

The Princess EC2 £37 ❷❷❸
76 Paul St 7729 9270 9–1C
"At the top of a spiral staircase", this "tasteful" year-old dining
room over a "stripped-down" Shoreditch bar (a sibling
to Farringdon's Easton) wins all-round praise for its "creative"
cooking, "great" wines and "genial" service. / 10.30 pm; closed
Sat L & Sun.

Princess Garden W1 £55 ❷❷④
8 North Audley St 7493 3223 3–2A
"Unusually attentive" service contributes to the "upmarket"
impression given by this "spacious" Chinese fixture in Mayfair;
its cooking is "very proficient but somewhat expensive".
/ www.princessgardenofmayfair.com; 11.30 pm.

Priory House W14 £28 ❸❸❷
58 Milson Rd 7371 3999 7–1C
"Tucked-away in the backstreets near Olympia", this "quiet" and
stylish bar/restaurant serves "delicious tapas, as well as good
cocktails". / www.priorybars.com; 10 pm; no Amex.

Prism EC3 £62 ④④④
147 Leadenhall St 7256 3888 9–2D
With the "surfeit of local expense-accounts", it's no great surprise
that this "impressive" City banking hall is "overpriced"; this doesn't
excuse the sometimes "appalling" service, though, nor the fact that
the ambience sometimes seems "terrible". / www.harveynichols.com;
10 pm; closed Sat & Sun.

for updates visit www.hardens.com

FSA

The Providores W1 £61 ❸❸❸
109 Marylebone High St 7935 6175 2–1A
"In contrast to the heaving bar below", this "serene" but tightly-packed dining room attracts limited (and less consistent) commentary; fans, though, say its "amazing" cuisine – matched by "interesting" NZ wines – is "reassuringly different". / www.providores.co.uk; 10.30 pm; booking: max 12.

(Tapa Room)
The Providores W1 £35 ❷❸❷
109 Marylebone High St 7935 6175 2–1A
"A marvellous Kiwi twist on great British ingredients" ensures this "cosy" Marylebone café/bar is "always crowded" – particularly at brunch, but also at other times for "delicious" and "substantial" tapas; the "wine list really stands out" too. / www.theprovidores.co.uk; 10.30 pm.

The Pumphouse N8 £37 ❸❷❶
1 New River Ave 8340 0400 1–1C
This "brilliantly converted old pumphouse", in Hornsey, is an "interesting" place with a "very spacious" interior, "easy parking" and a huge bar; at peak times it can seem "boisterous", but its Italian-ish food (including pizza) is "pretty good, considering". / 9.45 pm; closed Mon L.

Putney Station SW15 £29 ❹❸❸
94-98 Upper Richmond Rd 8780 0242 10–2B
This "friendly, quick and easy" wine bar yearling has quickly earned popularity with Putney reporters; as ever with John Brinkley's establishments, it's the "very cheap and extensive" wine list that's the biggest draw. / www.brinkleys.com; 11 pm.

Quadrato
Four Seasons Hotel E14 £64 ❸❸❹
Westferry Circus 7510 1857 11–1B
For a "very good business lunch" (or "excellent brunch"), this smart Canary Wharf dining room – with its dependable Italian cooking – has its fans; it's pricey, though, and the atmosphere can sometimes be rather "dead". / www.fourseasons.com; 10.30 pm.

Quaglino's SW1 £51 ⑤⑤⑤
16 Bury St 7930 6767 3–3D
Conran's "warehouse-like" St James's brasserie is dismissed by many reporters for offering a "bland, boring and cold" experience – "how they keep going is a mystery". / www.conran.com/eat; midnight, Fri & Sat 1 am; set weekday L £31 (FP).

The Quality Chop House EC1 £38 ❸❸❸
94 Farringdon Rd 7837 5093 9–1A
The antique benches are infamously "hard on your bum", at this "quirky", "step-back-in-time" Clerkenwell location – a lovingly restored 'Working Class Caterer'; it makes a "reliable" option for "straightforward" brasserie dishes. / 11 pm; closed Sat L.

Queen's Head W6 £24 ❹❸❷
13 Brook Grn 7603 3174 7–1C
The "gorgeous garden" is the star attraction of this rambling Brook Green tavern; it's still "a real pub", and offers "a wide choice" of "traditional pub fayre". / 10 pm; no booking.

sign up for the survey at www.hardens.com 157

Queen's Head & Artichoke NW1 £36 ❸❸❷
30-32 Albany St 7916 6206 8–4B
"There's a busy bar downstairs, and an elegant, calm upstairs dining room" at this *"relaxing"* pub, near Regent's Park, where the Mediterranean tapas are *"pretty good"*. / www.theartichoke.net; 10.15 pm.

Quilon SW1 £47 ❷❷④
41 Buckingham Gate 7821 1899 2–4B
"Beautiful" south Indian cuisine is let down by the *"sterile"* (if smart) décor of this *"accommodating"* subcontinental, near Victoria; the lunchtime set menu, in particular, is *"cracking value"*. / www.thequilonrestaurant.com; 11 pm; closed Sat L & Sun.

Quirinale SW1 £49 ❶❷❸
North Ct, 1 Gt Peter St 7222 7080 2–4C
"Why doesn't it get more coverage?"; Stefano Favio *"cooks with passion"* at this *"low-profile"* Westminster basement, and service is *"superbly attentive"* too, so perhaps the *"cool"* setting – *"more suitable for a power lunch than a romantic tryst"* – is to blame? / 10.30 pm; closed Sat L & Sun.

Quo Vadis W1 £47 ④④④
26-29 Dean St 7437 9585 4–2A
"For a business lunch", MPW's large Soho veteran still has its fans; it's difficult, though, to avoid the feeling that the pilot has gone AWOL – the room can feel *"dead"*, and the Italianate food is sometimes *"diabolical"*. / www.whitestarline.org.uk; 11 pm; closed Sat L & Sun; set pre theatre £31 (FP).

Racine SW3 £48 ❷❶❷
239 Brompton Rd 7584 4477 5–2C
This *"absolutely fabulous"* and *"truly Parisian"* brasserie in Knightsbridge owes its impressive popularity both to Henry Harris's *"honest cooking done spectacularly well"*, and to service that's *"charming"* and *"supremely professional"*. / 10.30 pm; set always available £32 (FP).

Ragam W1 £30 ❶❶⑤
57 Cleveland St 7636 9098 2–1B
It may be *"basic-looking"*, but this *"tiny"* fixture, near the Telecom Tower, continues to delight reporters with its *"brilliant"* vegetarian South Indian cuisine, served by *"lovely people"*; (licensed or you can BYO). / www.mcdosa.com; 11 pm.

Rainforest Café W1 £34 ⑤⑤④
20 Shaftesbury Ave 7434 3111 3–3D
"Kids love" this *"eco-aware"* theme-restaurant, which comes complete with *"robotic gorillas"* and *"a thunderstorm every 20 minutes"*; the food, however, is *"very bad"*. / www.therainforestcafe.co.uk; 10 pm, Thu-Sat 7.30 pm.

Rajasthan £28 ❷❷❸
49 Monument St, EC3 7626 1920 9–3C
8 India St, EC3 7488 9777 9–2D **NEW**
They may charge *"City prices"*, but these *"good City Indians"* are very popular with those labouring in the Square Mile. / 11 pm; closed Sat & Sun.

Randa W8 £36 ❸❸④
23 Kensington Church St   7937 5363   5–1A
An open grill delivers "fresh" and "well-priced" Lebanese food
at the Maroush group's new Kensington pub-conversion;
the "professional" style of the operation, however, can seem
"sterile". / www.maroush.com; midnight.

Randall & Aubin £39 ❷❸❶
16 Brewer St, W1   7287 4447   3–2D
329-331 Fulham Rd, SW10   7823 3515   5–3B
"Great people-watching" in the heart of Soho makes the "funky"
and "hectic" seafood bar original (with its nicely tiled interior) the
more interesting branch of this micro-chain; the Chelsea spin off
is an "enjoyable" brasserie, but more run-of-the-mill.
/ www.randallandaubin.co.uk; 11 pm; W1 no booking.

Rani N3 £24 ❸❷④
7 Long Ln   8349 4386   1–1B
An "authentic Gujarati", "off the beaten track" in North Finchley;
the buffet is especially recommendable – it's "an interesting
education as well as being good value". / www.raniuk.com; 10 pm;
D only, ex Sun open L & D; no Amex.

Ranoush £31 ❷④④
22 Brompton Rd, SW1   7235 6999   5–1D
338 Kings Rd, SW3   7352 0044   5–3C
43 Edgware Rd, W2   7723 5929   6–1D
86 Kensington High St, W8   7938 2234   5–1A
"The best shwarmas in town" ("kebabs as they should be") and
"great juices" are amongst the "vibrant" and "cheap" dishes
on offer at this "efficient" Lebanese chain; it also offers "awesome
late night people-watching". / www.maroush.com; 1 am-3 am; no credit
cards.

Ransome's Dock SW11 £47 ❸❸❸
35 Parkgate Rd   7223 1611   5–4C
Martin Lam's "extensive and frequently-updated wine list" makes
this "cheerful" Battersea fixture a wine buff's "dream"; the food
is "nothing ground-breaking", but "very dependable".
/ www.ransomesdock.co.uk; 11 pm; closed Sun D.

Raoul's Café £35 ④⑤④
105-107 Talbot Rd, W11   7229 2400   6–1B **NEW**
13 Clifton Rd, W9   7289 7313   8–4A
"The best eggs in London" top the bill at Maida Vale's "bustling"
café linchpin, where locals brave "queues" and "abominable"
service for the "great brunch"; the "casual" new Notting Hill sibling
(on the site of Coins, RIP) is strong on eye-candy, less impressive
elsewhere. / 10 pm.

Rapscallion SW4 £37 ❸④④
75 Venn St   7787 6555   10–2D
"Lots of fresh brunch ideas" are a highlight at this "tiny" and
"cramped" bar/restaurant in Clapham; its other fare is also "nicely
judged", though, and it does "excellent cocktails".
/ www.rapscalliononline.com; 11 pm; booking: max 6.

sign up for the survey at www.hardens.com

Rasa N16 £20 ❶❷❷

55 Stoke Newington Church St   7249 0344   1–1C
"It's worth trekking across town in the rain" to visit this small but
"special" and "very friendly" Stoke Newington Keralan (which is the
original of the group); the "delicious" veggie dishes have "beautiful
flavours", "thrilling textures and colours" and are so so "cheap".
/ www.rasarestaurants.com; 10.30 pm; closed weekday L.

Rasa £35 ❶❷❸

5 Charlotte St, W1   7637 0222   2–1C
6 Dering St, W1   7629 1346   3–2B
Holiday Inn Hotel, 1 Kings Cross, WC1   7833 9787   8–3D
56 Stoke Newington Church St, N16   7249 1340   1–1C
The spin-offs from the Stoke Newington original (see also) deliver
"all the flair of the Zaikas of the world, but at a fraction of the
price" – Dering Street and N16 (Travancore) serve meat, while the
Charlotte Street branch (Samudra) offers "stunning fish curries".
/ www.rasarestaurants.com; 10.45 pm; N16 Mon-Fri closed L, W1 closed
Sun L, N16 D only Mon-Sat.

RASOI VINEET BHATIA SW3 £70 ❶❷❸

10 Lincoln St   7225 1881   5–2D
Vineet Bhatia's "mind-blowing" cuisine – "a phenomenal orgy
of flavours" – puts his "haute Indian" Chelsea townhouse firmly
in London's premier gastronomic league; the setting, however,
though "delightful" to some reporters, is "dreary" to others.
/ www.vineetbhatia.com; 11 pm; closed Sat L & Sun; set weekday L £43 (FP).

Ratchada SE3 £23 ❷❷④

129 Lee Rd   8318 0092   1–4D
This "friendly" and "unfussy" Blackheath Thai has a good name
locally for its "fresh" flavours; its menu includes all the "staples",
but also "more exotic options from the grill". / www.ratchada.co.uk;
11 pm; closed Sun; no Amex.

The Real Greek N1 £38 ❸④❷

15 Hoxton Market   7739 8212   9–1D
This is the venture which "revolutionised our notions of Greek
cooking", and – after a really indifferent patch – this "casual"
(going-on "sloppy") Hoxton spot is again winning praise for some
"eye-opening" dishes; "it's miles better than the souvlaki bar chain".
/ www.therealgreek.com; 10.30 pm; closed Sun; no Amex.

The Real Greek Souvlaki & Bar £25 ⑤⑤④

56 Paddington St, W1   7486 0466   2–1A **NEW**
60/62 Long Acre, WC2   7240 2292   4–2D **NEW**
1-2 Riverside Hs, Southwark Br Rd, SE1   7620 0162   9–3B
31-33 Putney High St, SW15   8788 3270   10–2B **NEW**
140-142 St John St, EC1   7253 7234   9–1A
"The Fake Greek, more like" – "the roll-out of the chain" has
"diluted the concept and quality" of these once-excellent souvlaki
bars, which are now "as real as McDonalds". / www.therealgreek.co.uk;
11 pm; EC1 closed Sun; no Amex.

Rebato's SW8 £30 ❸❶❶

169 South Lambeth Rd   7735 6388   10–1D
"A real little bit of Spain in Stockwell" – this "wonderful old-school"
tapas bar gets "packed" to a "frenzy" at the weekends;
the "throwback" restaurant at the rear is less interesting.
/ www.rebatos.com; 10.45 pm; closed Sat L & Sun.

Red Fort W1 £48 ❷❷❸
77 Dean St 7437 2525 4–2A
"Excellent" Indian cuisine – if "at a price" – is the mainstay of this "consistent" Soho stalwart (which took on a "cool" but "reserved" new look a few years ago); beware mineral water though – it "costs more than at some top hotels!" / www.redfort.co.uk; 11.15 pm; closed Sat L & Sun L.

The Red Pepper W9 £33 ❷④④
8 Formosa St 7266 2708 8–4A
Pizzas "that make you feel like you're in Italy" are a highlight at this "very cramped" and "very busy" Maida Vale linchpin. / 11 pm; closed weekday L; no Amex.

Redmond's SW14 £46 ❸❸④
170 Upper Richmond Rd West 8878 1922 10–2A
Redmond and Pippa Hayward's "very good local restaurant", in East Sheen, has a dedicated fan club who praise its "creative" food and "friendly" service; a few former supporters, though, noted "disappointments" of late – "perhaps the strain of opening their bistro over the river?" / www.redmonds.org.uk; 10 pm; D only, ex Sun L only; no Amex; set pre theatre £29 (FP).

Refettorio
The Crowne Plaza Hotel EC4 £52 ❸❸④
19 New Bridge St 7438 8052 9–3A
The décor is "austere", but this "pricey" dining room by Blackfriars Bridge is often hailed as "ideal for business", thanks not least to its "very good" (if "variable") Tuscan fare – "wonderful cold meats and cheeses" are a highlight. / 10.30 pm; closed Sat L & Sun; booking: max 8.

Refuel
Soho Hotel W1 £50 ④④❷
4 Richmond Mews 7559 3007 3–2D
"You feel like an extra on a film set" at this "cool" boutique hotel, which is "bang in the middle of Soho, although you'd never know it" – given its very central location, it attracts very little commentary, but it has its fans for its bar, for business, or for brunch. / 11 pm; closed Sat L.

Le Relais de Venise L'Entrecôte W1 £33 ④④❸
120 Marylebone Ln 7486 0878 2–1A
"Not a patch on the European branches"; though fans do applaud a "simple and enjoyable", "no-choice" formula – "they only serve steak-frites" – at this Marylebone steakhouse, too many reporters have encountered "oily" or "tasteless" food (or thought the trademark secret sauce "vile"). / www.relaisdevenise.com; 10.45 pm; no Amex.

Le Rendezvous du Café EC1 £37 ❷❷❸
22 Charterhouse Sq 7336 8836 9–1B
"The perfect local bistro"; it's "chaotic", but – if you're looking for a "steak/frites-and-bottle-of-Burgundy" kind of place – this "friendly" Clerkenwell joint is hard to beat. / 10 pm; closed Sat L & Sun; no Amex.

Reubens W1 £43 ④④④
79 Baker St 7486 0035 2–1A
Fans applaud the "excellent choice of dishes" (including "legendary salt beef sandwiches") at this kosher Marylebone deli (and basement restaurant); its décor is a bit "weird and '80s", though, and not everyone is impressed. / www.reubensrestaurant.com; 10 pm; closed Fri D & Sat.

Rhodes 24 EC2 £62 ❸❷❷
25 Old Broad St 7877 7703 9–2C
"Views guaranteed to impress any potential client" help make this 24th-floor dining room "a great business lunch venue in the heart of the City"; "Gary's trademark Mod-Brit" cooking can be "fantastic" too (if sometimes, unsurprisingly, "too expensive"). / www.rhodes24.co.uk; 9 pm; closed Sat & Sun; booking essential.

Rhodes W1
Cumberland Hotel W1 £47 ④④⑤
Gt Cumberland Pl 7479 3838 2–2A
Gary R is now a repeat-offender when it comes to putting his name to disappointing spin-offs – many reporters "expected much more" of this new venture near Marble Arch, which has turned out to be a "hangar"-like space, with "poorly-trained" staff and "very average" food. / 10 pm.

Rib Room & Oyster Bar
Jumeirah Carlton Tower Hotel SW1 £77 ④④⑤
2 Cadogan Pl 7858 7053 5–1D
For "the best Sunday lunch in London with all the trimmings", some reporters tip this traditional Knightsbridge dining room (where roast beef is an all-week speciality); it's "very expensive", though, and the ambience can seem very stilted. / www.jumeirah.com; 10.30 pm.

RIBA Café
Royal Ass'n of Brit' Architects W1 £34 ④❸❶
66 Portland Pl 7631 0467 2–1B
The "glorious" '30s setting – "like a set from Metropolis" – is the star attraction at this institutional café (which also has a "great outside terrace" for the summer); it's a handy destination for "breakfast, brunch, lunch, or afternoon tea". / www.riba-venues.com; L & afternoon tea only; L only, closed Sun.

Riccardo's SW3 £37 ❸❸❸
126 Fulham Rd 7370 6656 5–3B
This "bustling" Chelsea "neighbourhood" Italian offers "simple" dishes in tapas-style portions, and "surprisingly good value for the location". / www.riccardos.it; 11.30 pm.

Richoux £33 ⑤⑤④
172 Piccadilly, W1 7493 2204 3–3C
41a South Audley St, W1 7629 5228 3–3A
86 Brompton Rd, SW3 7584 8300 5–1C
3 Circus Rd, NW8 7483 4001 8–3A
They're "a great place for tea", but these tourist-friendly 'period' café/diners are otherwise slated by most reporters for their "careless" cuisine and high prices. / 10.30 pm, SW3 7.30 pm, W1 Sat 11 pm; W1 no booking Sat & Sun.

Rick's Café SW17   £32   ❷❷❷
122 Mitcham Rd   8767 5219   10–2C
*"Very good food at extremely reasonable prices" makes this
"Tooting's best restaurant" – "assuming you don't want a curry",
of course. / 11 pm; no Amex.*

El Rincón Latino SW4   £28   ❸❶❶
148 Clapham Manor St   7622 0599   10–2D
*"After spending three years in Madrid, this is the closest place
to Spain I've found" – this "brilliant" bar in the backstreets
of Clapham boasts "authentic" cuisine and staff "as friendly as any
in town"; not all regulars, though, are happy about its recent
expansion. / 11.30 pm; closed Mon, Tue-Fri D only, Sat & Sun open L & D.*

The Ritz W1   £93   ❹❸❶
150 Piccadilly   7493 8181   3–4C
*Fans (often of mature years) continue to insist that standards
at this "unique" Louis XVI dining room are "getting better and
better"; overall, however, the volume of complaints – of "dull"
cuisine, "shoddy" service and "ruinous" prices – is as deafening
as ever. / 10.30 pm; jacket & tie required; set weekday L £60 (FP).*

Riva SW13   £47   ❸❸❹
169 Church Rd   8748 0434   10–1A
*In some circles, Andreas Riva's "gloomy" Barnes Venetian is still
hailed as "the best Italian restaurant in London"; non-regulars can
feel "like gate-crashers", however, and even some former fans find
the food "lacklustre" nowadays. / 11.30 pm, Sun 9.30 pm; closed Sat L.*

The River Café W6   £62   ❷❸❸
Thames Wharf, Rainville Rd   7386 4200   7–2C
*"So famous it's practically a cliché", this Thames-side Italian
canteen, in an obscure bit of Hammersmith, continues to serve
up "simple food with great ingredients made divine"; even many
fans, though, are gobsmacked by the "stratospheric" prices.
/ www.rivercafe.co.uk; 9 pm; closed Sun D.*

Riviera
Gabriels Wharf SE1   £37   ❹❹❸
56 Upper Ground   7401 7314   9–3A
*"Stunning views over the Thames" are the prime attraction at this
South Bank spot, which is also of note as "an excellent pre-
National Theatre venue". / 11.30 pm.*

The Rivington Grill EC2   £45   ❷❸❸
28-30 Rivington St   7729 7053   9–1C
*"Simple" English fare is "cooked to perfection" at this "light",
"relaxed" and admirably straightforward Shoreditch corner
brasserie. / www.rivingtongrill.co.uk; 11 pm.*

The Rivington Grill SE10 NEW   £44   ❹❹❺
178 Greenwich High Rd   8293 9270   1–3D
*"The worst thing to have happened to Greenwich in 400 years" –
an over-reaction, perhaps, but one typifying the sense of anticlimax
in reports on this new Caprice-group brasserie, which reporters find
"Spartan" and "distinctly average". / www.rivingtongrill.co.uk; 11 pm;
set weekday L £28 (FP).*

sign up for the survey at www.hardens.com

Roast
The Floral Hall SE1 £46 ④④❸
Stoney St 7940 1300 9–4C
"A fantastic space, ruined by a terrible restaurant" – a harsh but pretty fair verdict on Iqbal Wahhab's much-hyped yearling; it may boast a *"spectacular"* setting, above Borough Market, but its traditional British cooking is too often *"sloppy"*, and service is sometimes *"hopeless"*. / www.roast-restaurant.com; 10.30 pm; closed Sun D.

Rocco EC1 NEW £45 ❸②④
6 Little Britain 7796 3362 9–2B
Early reporters are unanimous that this new Italian, near St Paul's, is *"an undiscovered gem"*, offering an *"interesting"* and *"well-cooked"* menu at *"good-value"* prices; personally, we liked the relaxing setting rather more than the food, but survey sentiment is precisely the opposite! / 10.30 pm; closed Sat L & Sun.

The Rocket W3 £35 ❸④❷
11-13 Churchfield Rd 8993 6123 1–2A
"Acton's only gastropub" is a worthy representative of the breed, with an *"inventive"* menu, *"chilled"* staff, and an attractive rear dining room. / www.therocketw3.co.uk; 10.15 pm; closed Mon L.

Rocket £32 ❸❸❷
4-6 Lancashire Ct, W1 7629 2889 3–2B
Putney Wharf, Brewhouse St, SW15 8789 7875 10–2B
A duo of high-quality, *"fun"* and *"lively"* pizzerias, both of which are equally useful in their different ways – Mayfair is a *"perfect, easy and affordable fallback"* (in a part of town without many such places), while Putney benefits from *"wonderful views over the Thames"*. / www.rocketrestaurants.co.uk; 10.45 pm; W1 closed Sun.

Rodizio Rico £33 ④④④
111 Westbourne Grove, W2 7792 4035 6–1B
77-78 Upper St, N1 7354 1076 8–3D
"For meat and lots of it", these all-you-can-eat Brazilian grills can make a *"fun"* choice; service can be *"slow"* however, and the overall experience sometimes seems lacking in soul. / www.rodizio.co.uk; W2 11.30 pm, N1 midnight; closed weekday L.

Roka W1 £47 ❶❸❸
37 Charlotte St 7580 6464 2–1C
"On a par with big sister, Zuma"; the modern Japanese cuisine – including dishes from a *'robata'* grill – is *"out of this world"*, say fans of this *"big"*, *"bright"* and *"bustling"* Fitzrovia venue, whose ground-floor dining room has *"huge picture windows onto the street"*; downstairs, there's a *"very cool"* bar. / www.rokarestaurant.com; 11.30 pm; closed Sun L; booking: max 8; set weekday L £32 (FP).

Ronnie Scott's W1 NEW £45
47 Frith St 7439 0747 4–2A
The food at the 'old' Ronnie Scott's – London's most famous jazz club – was famous for all the wrong reasons; as this guide goes to press, however, its Soho premises were emerging from a major refit, and boasting a much more ambitious dining operation. / www.ronniescotts.co.uk; 1am; closed Sun.

Rosemary Lane E1 £41 ❶❸④
61 Royal Mint St 7481 2602 11–1A
You'd never guess from the "dingy", east-of-the-City location of this
"chilly-looking" pub that it's a true "temple of gastronomy",
but Christina Anghelescu's cooking really is "marvellous and
creative", and "great value for money" too.
/ www.rosemarylane.btinternet.co.uk; 10 pm; closed Sat L & Sun.

Rosmarino NW8 £44 ⑤④④
1 Blenheim Terrace 7328 5014 8–3A
Since the ownership changed two years ago, ratings for this once-
"useful" St John's Wood spot have nose-dived – some reporters still
hail it as "an above average Italian", but too many say it's "a mere
shadow of its former self". / 10.30 pm; closed Mon in winter.

Rossopomodoro SW10 NEW £27 ❸④❸
214 Fulham Rd 7352 7677 5–3B
Near the Chelsea and Westminster Hospital, this new outpost
of an Italian pizza chain has quickly become a hot Eurotrash
rendezvous; the food was pretty good on our early-days visit,
but you did have to wait for it. / Rated on Editors' visit;
www.rossopomodoro.it; midnight.

Rôtisserie Jules £27 ❸④⑤
6-8 Bute St, SW7 7584 0600 5–2B
133 Notting Hill Gate, W11 7221 3331 6–2B
Who cares that its branches are "super-boring"? – you get
"good French chicken at amazingly low prices" at this "basic"
chain; service, though, can be "painfully slow". / 11 pm.

Roundhouse Café NW1 NEW £31
Chalk Farm Rd 0870 389 9920 8–2B
Relaunched shortly before this guide went to press, this famous
Chalk Farm cultural centre now has a large brasserie attached;
unfortunately we did not have the opportunity to visit, but early
newspaper reports are encouraging. / www.roundhouse.org.uk; 10 pm;
closed Mon & Sun D; no Amex.

ROUSSILLON SW1 £68 ❶❶❷
16 St Barnabas St 7730 5550 5–2D
"Deserving of wider recognition" (and slowly winning it), this "rather
isolated" Pimlico backstreet "masterpiece" combines "spectacular"
cuisine, "very interesting" wines (especially from SW France) and
"superb" service – and all at "reasonable" prices.
/ www.roussillon.co.uk; 10.30 pm; closed Mon L, Sat L & Sun; booking: max 11.

Rowley's SW1 £50 ⑤④④
113 Jermyn St 7930 2707 3–3D
With its "very disappointing and expensive" steaks and grills,
this tiled St James's veteran just strikes some reporters as "really
awful" nowadays; its short-lived Mayfair spin-off is no more.
/ www.rowleys.co.uk; 11.30 pm.

Royal Academy W1 £33 ④⑤❸
Burlington Hs, Piccadilly 7300 5608 3–3C
"Stupendous" surroundings help make this "noisy and crowded"
café "a nice and unthreatening West End rendezvous";
"good salads", however, are the high-point of the "very average"
food, and service can be "poor" to the point of being "hilarious".
/ www.royalacademy.org.uk; Fri 8.15 pm; L only, except Fri & Sat open L & D;
no booking at L.

Royal China Club W1 NEW £60 ❷❷④
40-42 Baker St 7486 3898 2–1A
*"The new 'fine dining' version of Royal China" is "more courteous"
than its stablemates, and has an "upscale" setting adorned with
"tanks of giant crabs and lobsters"; prices are "high-end", but the
"experimental" cooking (including "refined dim sum") can
be "exquisite". / 11 pm; set weekday L £26 (FP).*

Royal China £38 ❷❸④
24-26 Baker St, W1 7487 4688 2–1A
13 Queensway, W2 7221 2535 6–2C
68 Queen's Grove, NW8 7586 4280 8–3A
30 Westferry Circus, E14 7719 0888 11–1B
*"Go early and queue" – "it's worth it", for the "superbly crafted"
lunchtime dim sum (often tipped as London's best) at this
benchmark Chinese group; and as to the "Saturday Night Fever
décor"? – well, "you get used to it". / 10.45 pm, Fri & Sat 11.15 pm;
E14 no bookings Sat & Sun L.*

Royal China SW15 £34 ❷❸❸
3 Chelverton Rd 8788 0907 10–2B
*It shares the same "dodgy smoke-and-mirrors décor", but this
Putney Chinese has only tenuous links to the Royal China chain –
its "excellent dim sum" and "top" cooking generally are, however,
of a similar standard. / 10.30 pm; only Amex.*

Royal Court Bar
Royal Court Theatre SW1 £28 ⑤④❸
Sloane Sq 7565 5061 5–2D
*"What a waste of what's potentially an excellent pre/post-theatre
venue"; this "bunker" under Sloane Square is "surprisingly
attractive", but the "canteen food" is "poor" – "you'll want a drink
to help you forget it". / www.royalcourttheatre.com; 8 pm; closed Sun;
no Amex.*

The Royal Exchange Grand Café
The Royal Exchange EC3 £44 ⑤④❷
Cornhill 7618 2480 9–2C
*It certainly has a "unique location" (the internal courtyard of a City
landmark), but this Conran-run seafood bar gets a big thumbs-
down from reporters for its "outrageously pricey but average"
dishes. / www.conran.com/eat; 11 pm; closed Sat & Sun; no booking.*

Royal Oak E2 NEW £33 ❸❸❷
73 Columbia Rd 7729 2220 1–2D
*"Reliably interesting" scoff makes this "lovely" shabby-chic boozer,
overlooking Columbia Road flower market, very popular (and it's
insanely busy on market days); the "mixed" ("local/gay/straight")
crowd only "adds to the ambience". / www.royaloaklondon.com; 10 pm;
closed weekday L.*

RSJ SE1 £39 ❸❷⑤
33 Coin St 7928 4554 9–4A
*Considering its "bleak" setting, and "competent but unsparkling"
Gallic "country cooking", it's remarkable that this South Bank
fixture has been quite a 'name' for a quarter of a century – it must
be thanks to: 1) being "a reliable pre-RNT stand-by", and 2) its
"wonderfully rich list" of Loire wines. / www.rsj.uk.com; 11 pm; closed
Sat L & Sun.*

Ruby Lounge & Sequoia Bar W11 £36 ④④❶
6-8 All Saints Rd   7243 6363   6–1B
"For a relaxed Sunday afternoon with friends" – or *"as one of the
few lively, late-night joints in W11"* – this chilled bar/restaurant has
its fans; food and service are erratic, though – from *"surprisingly
excellent"* to *"distinctly average"*. / www.ruby.uk.com; 12.30 am, Fri & Sat
2 am; closed weekday L.

Rudland & Stubbs EC1 £44 ❸❸④
35-37 Greenhill Rents, Cowcross St   7253 0148   9–1A
New owners re-launched this long-established Clerkenwell fish
parlour in the spring of 2006; on our early-days visit, the menu was
more adventurous than before, and quality was generally good –
the atmosphere, however, is still rather sterile. / Rated on Editors' visit;
www.rudlandstubbs.co.uk; 10.45 pm; closed Sat & Sun; booking: max 10.

La Rueda £30 ④⑤❸
102 Wigmore St, W1   7486 1718   3–1A
642 King's Rd, SW6   7384 2684   5–4A
66-68 Clapham High St, SW4   7627 2173   10–2D
These *"boisterous"* and *"crowded"* tapas bars have inspired some
uncharacteristically *"disappointing"* reports of late; management
changes may have been to blame – with those behind them,
the coming year will hopefully see a return to form. / 11.30 pm, Sat &
Sun midnight; SW6 1 am.

Rules WC2 £55 ❸❸❶
35 Maiden Ln   7836 5314   4–3D
"Great, in spite of its popularity with tourists"; London's oldest
restaurant (1798), in Covent Garden, continues to delight most
of the people most of the time with its *"plush"* and *"clubby"*
Victorian charm and its *"consistently good traditional English
cooking"* (especially game). / www.rules.co.uk; midnight.

Running Horse W1 £28 ❸❸❸
50 Davies St   7493 1275   3–2A
With its *"great little location, just off Oxford Street"*, this Mayfair
gastropub makes a very handy stand-by – it's surprising it's not
better known. / 9 pm; closed Fri D, Sat D & Sun; need 8+ to book.

S & M Café £22 ❸❷❸
268 Portobello Rd, W10   8968 8898   6–1A
4-6 Essex Rd, N1   7359 5361   8–3D
48 Brushfield St, E1   7247 2252   9–1D
These *"fun"*, if *"gimmicky"*, English *"greasy spoons"* offer a fail-safe
formula of *"fabulous sausages"* (with *"a choice of mash and
gravies"*) in pleasantly *"retro"* surroundings. / www.sandmcafe.co.uk;
10.30 pm-11.30 pm; no Amex; W10 no booking Fri-Sun; N1 & E1 no booking
at L.

Sabai Sabai W6 £24 ❸❸⑤
270-272 King St   8748 7363   7–2B
Arguably *"it's one of London's less-attractive dining rooms"*, but this
friendly Thai eatery in Hammersmith is *"always reliable"* for
a *"cheap and cheerful"* bite. / 11.15 pm; closed Sat L & Sun L.

Sabor N1 £32 ❸❷❷
108 Essex Rd   7226 5551   8–3D
"Far from your usual nachos and a chimichanga" – this *"funky"*
and *"eager-to-please"* Latin joint, in Islington, offers *"varied"* and
"interesting" South American *"staples"* at *"good-value"* prices.
/ www.sabor.co.uk; 10.45 pm; closed Mon; no Amex.

Sabras NW10 £23 ❶④⑤
263 High Rd 8459 0340 1–1A
"Outstanding" vegetarian cooking has made this "front room-like" Willesden Gujarati/south Indian a destination of note for over three decades. / www.sabras.com; 10 pm; D only, closed Mon; no Amex.

Le Sacré-Coeur N1 £28 ❸❷❷
18 Theberton St 7354 2618 8–3D
Just off Islington's Upper Street, this "attractive" Gallic bistro offers "good" food, and general "value-for-money". / 11 pm; set weekday L £16 (FP).

Sagar £25 ❶❶④
157 King St, W6 8741 8563 7–2C
27 York St, TW1 8744 3868 1–4A NEW
It looks decidedly "ordinary", but this Hammersmith shop-conversion is one of the best south Indians in town, serving "dangerously tasty" veggie dishes at "embarrassingly cheap" prices, and service is "excellent" and "friendly" too; it now has a Twickenham offshoot. / 11 pm.

Saigon Saigon W6 £27 ❷❸④
313-317 King St 8748 6887 7–2B
"Excellent-value" and "authentic" Vietnamese cooking keeps this large Hammersmith fixture "deservedly busy", despite a no-frills interior that some find "sterile". / 11 pm; closed Mon.

ST JOHN EC1 £44 ❶❷❷
26 St John St 7251 0848 9–1B
An air of true "conviction" inspires continuing adulation for Fergus Henderson's "stark white" ex-smokehouse in Smithfield; his "robust" British menu of offal and other "arcane" ingredients – squirrel anyone? – is certainly an "eye-opener". / www.stjohnrestaurant.com; 11 pm; closed Sat L & Sun.

St John Bread & Wine E1 £41 ❷❷❸
94-96 Commercial St 7247 8724 9–1D
St John's Spitalfields spin-off offers "simple" but "outstanding" British dishes (often of the "ox arse and pig snoot" variety); you need to "like a certain informality" to get the best from the "canteen-like" setting. / www.stjohnbreadandwine.com; 10.30 pm; closed Sun D.

St Johns N19 £33 ❸❷❶
91 Junction Rd 7272 1587 8–1C
For its vast north London fan club, this "oasis" in Archway – with its "friendly" staff, "fabulous, high-ceilinged" rear dining room and "interesting" menu – "ticks all the boxes" to be a great gastropub; this year's culinary standards, though, have been somewhat "inconsistent". / 11 pm, Sun 9.30 pm; Mon-Thu D only, Fri-Sun open L & D; booking: max 12.

Le Saint Julien EC1 £40 ④❸④
62-63 Long Ln 7796 4550 9–1B
Fans praise this year-old Gallic brasserie by Smithfield Market as an "authentic" place with "good-value" cooking; critics, though, say "it looks the part, but tastes like a Paris tourist trap". / 10 pm; closed Sat & Sun.

St Moritz W1 £40 ②③②
161 Wardour St 7734 3324 3–1D
"If your date likes fondues", this "cosy", "make-believe ski chalet"
in the heart of Soho is the place for you; the Swiss food
is surprisingly accomplished, and the Alpine wines can be "really
good" too. / www.stmoritz-restaurant.co.uk; 11.30 pm; closed Sat L & Sun.

Saki Bar & Food Emporium EC1 NEW £38 ②④④
4 West Smithfield 7489 7033 9–1A
"Extremely slow" (or "chaotic") early-days service has proved
a turn-off for reporters at this new Japanese restaurant in a
Clerkenwell basement; fans insist, however, that its "surprisingly
good" food makes it "worth a visit". / www.saki-food.com; 10.30 pm;
closed Sat & Sun; no Amex.

Sakonis HA0 £18 ②④⑤
129 Ealing Rd 8903 9601 1–1A
Fans say this no-frills Wembley cafeteria is "THE place for proper
Gujarati cooking" ("just like mum makes"); everyone "seems to dive
into the cheap buffet", but the prepared food is arguably a better
bet. / 9.30 pm; no Amex.

Sakura W1 £25 ②⑤③
9 Hanover St 7629 2961 3–2C
"You may have a crowded wait for a table" and "service can be a
nightmare", but this "no-frills" Japanese, off Hanover Square,
attracts "a reassuring number of oriental customers", thanks to the
quality of its "authentic" and "cheap" grub. / 10 pm; set weekday L
£15 (FP).

Sale e Pepe SW1 £45 ③②②
9-15 Pavilion Rd 7235 0098 5–1D
There's "always a good night out" to be had at this "very busy and
noisy" veteran Knightsbridge trattoria; "it hasn't changed over the
years" – "amusing" waiters deliver food that's "ever-reliable" in a
"squashed" and "buzzing" setting. / www.saleepepe.co.uk; 11.30 pm;
closed Sun.

The Salisbury Tavern SW6 £38 ③③③
21 Sherbrooke Rd 7381 4005 10–1B
A "stylish" and "friendly" boozer in deepest Fulham, whose large
dining annexe "feels more like a restaurant" (and boasts
a retractable glass roof); practically all reporters hail its "consistent"
standards and "wholesome" cuisine. / www.thesalisbury.com; 11 pm.

Salloos SW1 £43 ①①④
62-64 Kinnerton St 7235 4444 5–1D
"Pedants know it's Pakistani", yet many fans of this "basic" veteran
subcontinental (hidden-away near Knightsbridge) just think of it
as "the best-value, quality Indian food in London"; service is "with a
smile". / 11.15 pm; closed Sun.

Salt House NW8 £36 ③③②
63 Abbey Rd 7328 6626 8–3A
A "lovely" St John's Wood gastropub which has had its "ups and
downs" (and a number of owners) in recent years; reports are still
somewhat varied, but currently put the food at "decent" or better.
/ 11 pm; no Amex.

sign up for the survey at www.hardens.com 169

Salt Yard W1 £35 **❶❷❸**
54 Goodge St 7637 0657 2–1B
"Magnificent" tapas ("an enticing mix of Italian and Spanish flavours"), an "exciting selection of wines" and "accommodating" staff – not to mention "very sensible prices" – win rave reviews for this "cramped" and "loud" Fitzrovia yearling. / www.saltyard.co.uk; 11 pm; closed Sat L & Sun.

The Salusbury NW6 £35 **❸❸❸**
50-52 Salusbury Rd 7328 3286 1–2B
Even if it's "not as good as it was", this "pleasant" Queen's Park fixture is still "one of the best gastropubs" in the outer NWs. / 10.15 pm; closed Mon L; no Amex.

Sam's Brasserie W4 £39 **❹❸❸**
11 Barley Mow Pas 8987 0555 7–2A
Sam Harrison's large new brasserie is potentially "a top-notch addition to Chiswick" – an "interesting", "industrial-style" space suited to "weekend brunch" and "casual" dining generally; service can be "confused", however, and the "enjoyable" cooking not infrequently "falls short". / www.samsbrasserie.co.uk; 10.30 pm; booking: max 12; set weekday L £26 (FP).

San Carlo N6 £43 **❹❷❸**
2 Highgate High St 8340 5823 8–1B
This upscale, "traditional" trattoria in Highgate seems to be perking up under its new chef – it drew fewer brickbats for "tired" cooking this year, and more bouquets for "five star" results. / 11 pm; closed Mon.

San Daniele del Friuli N5 £29 **❸❶❷**
72 Highbury Park 7226 1609 8–1D
With its "laid-back" atmosphere, "warm" service and "authentic" cooking (with game a speciality), this Highbury Italian is a "classic" local. / 10.30 pm; closed Mon L, Tue L, Sat L & Sun; no Amex.

San Lorenzo SW3 £55 **❹❹❹**
22 Beauchamp Pl 7584 1074 5–1C
This "totally overrated" Knightsbridge trattoria, established in 1963, has certainly had a good innings – it serves "average to-below average" food at prices which often seem a "joke". / 11.30 pm; closed Sun; no credit cards.

San Lorenzo Fuoriporta SW19 £45 **❹❹❹**
38 Worple Road Mews 8946 8463 10–2B
San Lorenzo's down-to-earth 'country cousin' (in Wimbledon Town) pleases most reporters with its "pretty good" food, "pleasant" service and "happy" (if slightly dated) ambience; it is, however, rather "overpriced". / www.sanlorenzo.com; 10.45 pm; set weekday L £25 (FP).

Santa Lucia SW10 £34 **❸❸❷**
2 Hollywood Rd 7352 8484 5–3B
"A real Italian atmosphere" buoys up this Chelsea-fringe joint – a hit locally thanks to its "delicious" and "authentic" pizza. / 11.30 pm; closed weekday L; no Amex.

Santa Maria de Buen Ayre E8 £29 ❷❶❷
50 Broadway Mkt 7275 9900 1–2D
"A meat-eaters' paradise" that's "spectacular in its simplicity" –
this Hackney BBQ has "fantastic Argentinean staff" and a "funky"
vibe, and serves "the best steaks this side of Buenos Aires"; grilled
on the parilla, they come with "amazing zingy sauces".
/ www.buenayre.co.uk; 10.30 pm; closed weekday L.

Santini SW1 £60 ❹❸❸
29 Ebury St 7730 4094 2–4B
A glamorous reputation precedes this Belgravia Italian, whose
"spacious yet cosy" style is – say fans – particularly "good for
business"; it's panned by its critics, though, who say it's a "clinical"
joint charging "laughable" prices for "bog-standard" cooking.
/ 11.30 pm; closed Sat L & Sun L; set weekday L £36 (FP).

Santore EC1 NEW £35 ❸❸❹
59-61 Exmouth Mkt 7812 1488 9–1A
At its best on a sunny day (when the front opens onto the street),
this unpretentious Clerkenwell newcomer offers satisfying Italian
dishes at prices that won't break the bank. / Rated on Editors' visit;
11 pm; closed Sun.

Sapori WC2 £30 ❹❸❸
43 Drury Ln 7836 8296 4–2D
A "simple" Italian whose "friendly" and "efficient" staff help make
it "a good Covent Garden stand-by". / 11.30 pm.

Saran Rom SW6 NEW £40 ❸❸❷
Imperial Wharf 7751 3111 5–4B
A "beautiful" interior and "high-quality" cuisine have made this
"wallet-heavy" Thai newcomer – in an "off-the-beaten-track"
riverside development in Fulham – popular with most early-days
reporters. / www.saranrom.com; midnight.

Sarastro WC2 £37 ❺❺❸
126 Drury Ln 7836 0101 2–2D
A "totally OTT", opera-themed Theatreland "kitsch"-fest that can
be really "good for a laugh" (especially in a group);
"uncomfortable" seating, "non-existent" service and "slapdash"
food, though, make some reporters feel the joke's on them.
/ www.sarastro-restaurant.com; midnight.

Sardo W1 £43 ❷❷❸
45 Grafton Way 7387 2521 2–1B
"Lovely" Sardinian cooking – with a good range of "fascinating"
wines to match – has made quite a name for this "dependable"
north-Fitzrovian. / www.sardo-restaurant.com; 11 pm; closed Sat L & Sun.

Sardo Canale NW1 £44 ❷❷❷
42 Gloucester Ave 7722 2800 8–3B
"A great neighbourhood all-rounder" – this "intimate" Primrose Hill
yearling has earned quite a name with its "original and punchy"
Sardinian food and "impassioned, if occasionally wayward" service;
there's a "heavenly" terrace. / www.sardocanale.com; 10 pm; closed
Mon L; set weekday L £31 (FP).

Sargasso Sea N21 £48 ❷❷❷
10 Station Rd 8360 0990 1–1C
Though "not overly cheap", this "wonderful gem" in the wilds of Winchmore Hill delivers a "superb eating experience" – it combines "excellent" fish with "great" service and a "relaxed" setting. / www.sargassosea.co.uk; 10.30 pm; closed Mon, Tue L, Wed L, Sat L & Sun D; set Sun L £30 (FP).

Sarkhel's £28 ❷❷❸
199 Upper Richmond Road West, SW14 8876 6220 10–2B
199 Replingham Rd, SW18 8870 1483 10–2B
"Unbelievably tasty" Indian dishes from a "stunningly diverse" menu have won a huge following for Udit Sarkhel's ordinary-looking Southfields curry house; the East Sheen spin-off wins more mixed praise, but is usually hailed as "a successful extension of his empire". / www.sarkhels.com; 10.30 pm; closed Mon; no Amex.

Sarracino NW6 £35 ❸❷❸
186 Broadhurst Gdns 7372 5889 1–1B
"Just what you want around the corner" – a "friendly local Italian" in West Hampstead, where "excellent" pizza by the metre is the star attraction. / 11 pm; closed weekday L.

Sartoria W1 £55 ❹❸❹
20 Savile Row 7534 7000 3–2C
"Plenty of space between tables" and an "extensive" wine list are among the features which make this tailoring-themed Mayfair Italian "an adaptable venue for business"; many reporters still consider it a typical Conran operation – "mediocre" and "full of itself" – but its ratings materially improved this year. / www.conran.com/eat; 11 pm; closed Sun.

Satsuma W1 £27 ❸❸❹
56 Wardour St 7437 8338 3–2D
"Great for a quick, cheap bite", this heart-of-Soho canteen – likened by some to "a nicer but pricier Wagamama" – offers a "wide" selection of "tasty" Japanese dishes. / www.osatsuma.com; 11 pm; no booking.

Satu Bar & Kitchen EC2 £29 ❸❹❷
10 Cutlers Gardens Arc, Devonshire Sq 7283 7888 9–2D
A large and "stylish" City basement that's "tucked-away, but worth knowing about"; it serves very "passable" oriental food at "reasonable" prices. / www.satu-bar-kitchen.co.uk; 10.30 pm; closed Sat & Sun.

Sauterelle
Royal Exchange EC3 NEW £49 ❹❹❸
Bank 7618 2483 9–2C
Conran's "pleasant" City newcomer, has a "fantastic" location, looking down on the internal courtyard of the Royal Exchange; it inspired few and mixed early reports (including recommendations, of course, as "an excellent place for business"). / www.conran.com/eat; 10 pm; closed Sat & Sun.

Savarona EC2 £31 ❸❹❹
66 Gt Eastern St 7739 2500 9–1D
This Turkish yearling – in a large and quite comfy basement on the fringe of Hoxton – hasn't set the world on fire, but wins praise for its "great meze and mixed grills". / www.savarona.co.uk; 11 pm; closed Sat L & Sun.

(Banquette)
Savoy Hotel WC2   £49   ④❷❸
Strand 7420 2392 4–3D
This Ramsay group 'diner' – serving a "simple and classy grill menu" – was better rated this year, in particular for "fine-dining pre- or post-theatre" and its "great-value Sunday champagne jazz brunch"; not all reporters are impressed, though, and the ambience can still seem "cold". / www.marcuswareing.com; 11 pm; booking: max 8.

(Savoy Grill)
Savoy Hotel WC2   £78   ❸❸❸
Strand 7592 1600 4–3D
Under Marcus Wareing's three-year-old régime, this "so very British" bastion has largely maintained its reputation as a "power venue" par excellence; it can seem "overpriced", though, and doubters find the cuisine "uninspired". / www.marcuswareing.com; 11 pm; jacket required; set weekday L £50 (FP).

Scalini SW3   £58   ❸❸❸
1-3 Walton St 7225 2301 5–2C
"A lively international crowd" drives the "vibrant" ("indescribably noisy") atmosphere at this "trendy" Knightsbridge Italian; fans still say it's "wonderful", but there was growing dissent this year, in particular about "extortionate" prices. / midnight.

Scarlet Dot E1 NEW   £39   ④④⑤
4 Crispin Sq 7375 0880 9–1D
Our early-days visit to this trendy Indian newcomer, by Spitalfields, left us mightily unimpressed; one early reporter, however, insists that it's a good place with an "original" menu (but we've rated it on our editors' assessment). / Rated on Editors' visit; www.scarletdot.co.uk; 11.30 pm.

Scarpetta TW11   £30   ❸❷❷
78 High St 8977 8177 1–4A
Teddington reporters are delighted with this Italian yearling; with its "great pizza" (and other fare), its "excellent" service and its "fabulous" interior, they say it's "a dream local". / 11 pm; no shorts.

The Scarsdale W8   £32   ④❸❶
23a Edwardes Sq 7937 1811 7–1D
A "fantastic" terrace overlooking a "graceful" square – plus the ambience of a "country pub" – ensures that this Kensington hostelry is "always crowded", even if the food is no more than "adequate". / 10 pm.

Scoffers SW11   £31   ④❷❷
6 Battersea Rise 7978 5542 10–2C
The "wonderful tree in the middle" creates a fantastic ambience at this "fun" and "reasonably-priced" Battersea stand-by, which is most popular as a breakfast/brunch destination. / 11 pm.

Scott's W1 NEW
20 Mount St 7629 5248 3–3A
Traditionally one of London's grandest fish and seafood restaurants, this Mayfair landmark is to be the subject of a major relaunch by the people behind J Sheekey (and also The Ivy, Le Caprice and so on) in late-2006.

sign up for the survey at www.hardens.com

The Sea Cow £30 ❷❸④

676 Fulham Rd, SW6   7610 8020   10–1B **NEW**
37 Lordship Ln, SE22   8693 3111   1–4D
57 Clapham High St, SW4   7622 1537   10–2D
*"How could fish 'n' chips be done better?" – this growing chain
of "updated", "refectory-style" chippies (which feature "a wonderful
selection of seafood") goes down a storm with reporters.*
/ www.theseacow.co.uk; 10.30 pm, Sun 8.30 pm; SW4 closed Mon.

Seafresh SW1 £28 ❸④④

80-81 Wilton Rd   7828 0747   2–4B
*"Better than ever since the refurbishment", this veteran Pimlico
chippie offers "fresh" fish in "enormous" portions.* / 10.30 pm;
closed Sun.

Searcy's Brasserie EC2 £51 ④④④

Level 2, Barbican Centre   7588 3008   9–1B
*For business or before a concert, this "consistent", "quiet" and
"restrained" City venue has its advocates; it feels "quite clinical",
though, and critics say that the location – which has a decent view
– "deserves better".* / www.barbican.org.uk; 10.30 pm; closed Sat L & Sun.

Seashell NW1 £32 ❷④⑤

49 Lisson Grove   7224 9000   8–4A
*It's an ambience-free zone, but – for "really fresh fish and generous
chips" – this legendary (and touristy) Marylebone chippie is still
tipped as "the best" by many reporters.* / www.seashellrestaurant.co.uk;
10.30 pm; closed Sun.

The Sequel SW4 £39 ❸❶❸

75 Venn St   7622 4222   10–2D
*"For an endless Sunday lunch" or mellow evening occasion,
this Clapham fixture provides "a good place for lingering",
with dependable grub and "the best cocktails".* / 11 pm; closed Mon,
Tue-Fri D only, Sat & Sun open L & D.

Serafino W1 £48 ④❸④

8 Mount St   7629 0544   3–3B
*Ignore the "overpriced" ground floor of this "traditional" Italian
near the Connaught – it's the "cheap and cheerful" basement
that's really worth seeking out.* / 10.45 pm; closed Sat L & Sun.

Settle Inn SW11 £28 ❸❷❷

186 Battersea Bridge Rd   7228 0395   10–1C
*"Great roasts" are the menu highlight at this "fun" and "laid-back"
boozer, a short stroll from Battersea Park.* / www.frontpagepubs.com;
10 pm.

Seven Stars WC2 £32 ❸❸❷

53 Carey St   7242 8521   2–2D
*"Barking" service – presided over by Full-On Food presenter,
Roxy Beaujolais – adds life to this 400-year-old inn behind the Royal
Courts of Justice, which serves a good selection of "fresh, seasonal
dishes".*

Shakespeare's Globe SE1 £38 ④❷❷

New Globe Walk   7928 9444   9–3B
*The food is still only "average", but this first-floor dining room –
with its "attentive" service, its "lovely riverside location" and its view
of St Paul's – generated much better reports this year.* / 9.30 pm;
closed Mon D & Sun D.

Shampers W1 £34 ❸❷❷
4 Kingly St 7437 1692 3–2D
It may "reek of the '70s", but this "unreconstructed" Soho wine bar, with its "charming" owner, is just so "relaxed and friendly"; critics say the "comfort food" is a "throwback", but fans say it's "well-priced", and complements the "excellent" wines. / 11 pm; closed Sun (& Sat in Aug).

Shanghai E8 £28 ❷❷❸
41 Kingsland High St 7254 2878 1–1C
"A unique conversion of a former pie and eel shop" provides the setting for this Chinese restaurant in Dalston; it's "vastly improved in recent times", and – for dim sum in particular – "worth a long detour". / www.wengwahgroup.com; 11 pm.

Shanghai Blues WC1 £46 ❷❸❷
193-197 High Holborn 7404 1668 4–1D
In its second year, "Holborn's answer to Hakkasan" has come into its own; the food – especially the "gorgeous" dim sum – is often "very good", and a tastefully-converted civic building provides the "classy" setting in which to enjoy it. / www.shanghaiblues.co.uk; 11.30 pm.

J SHEEKEY WC2 £56 ❶❷❷
28-32 St Martin's Ct 7240 2565 4–3B
It's not just "London's best fish and seafood" which has made this "classy" and "utterly reliable" Theatreland "Golden Oldie" the survey's most talked-about destination; it's now so totally eclipsed its stablemate, the Ivy, that it even attracts "a better class of celebrity"! / www.j-sheekey.co.uk; midnight; set dinner £38 (FP).

Shepherd's SW1 £44 ④❷❸
Marsham Ct, Marsham St 7834 9552 2–4C
"For the suits of Westminster", Richard Shepherd's "discreet" and "clubby" veteran of the "old school" makes an "ideal lunch venue"; if you like "stodgy" and "unimaginative", the "old-fashioned British cooking" is "fine". / www.langansrestaurants.co.uk; 11 pm; closed Sat & Sun.

Shikara SW3 £27 ❸❸❸
87 Sloane Ave 7581 6555 5–2C
For a new place just a few yards from Brompton Cross, this year-old Indian has created remarkably little interest; nonetheless, it's voted a "value-for-money" spot in this chichi bit of town. / 11.30 pm.

The Ship SW18 £30
41 Jews Row 8870 9667 10–2B
This riverside pub by Wandsworth Bridge is known for its "excellent outdoor BBQ" and its "great vibe on sunny days"; as the Gotto family prepared to give it back to Young's brewery, however, standards have been "going down, down, down" – maybe, with the handover completed, they can be revived? / www.theship.co.uk; 10.30 pm; no booking, Sun L.

Shish £23 ❸❸❷
75 Bishops Bridge Rd, W2 7229 7300 6–1C
2-6 Station Pde, NW2 8208 9290 1–1A
313 Old St, EC1 7749 0990 9–1D
*"Taking the humble kebab to new heights" – this funky trio
"use quality ingredients" and serve them "in a clean and modern
setting"; though it's in distant Willesden Green, the "relaxed"
original attracts most reviews. / www.shish.com; 11.30 pm; need 8+
to book.*

Shogun W1 £53 ❶❶④
Adam's Row 7493 1255 3–3A
*"Quite simply, the best sushi/sashimi in London" – a not
unreasonable claim for this "un-trendy but great" Japanese
basement, "tucked-away" in Mayfair. / 11 pm; D only, closed Mon.*

Siam Central W1 NEW £22 ④❷❸
14 Charlotte St 7436 7460 2–1C
*A handy Fitzrovia corner newcomer; on an early-days visit, its Thai
fare didn't strike us as anything special, but the prices are
reasonable, the service welcoming and the setting chic. / Rated
on Editors' visit; 11 pm.*

Signor Sassi SW1 £50 ④❷④
14 Knightsbridge Grn 7584 2277 5–1D
*There's "always a buzz" at this "traditional" Knightsbridge Italian,
which – with its "crazy" waiters – is cherished as a "fun"
destination by many reporters; critics, though, just find it "loud,
chaotic and average". / 11.30 pm; closed Sun.*

Signor Zilli W1 £45 ❸❷❸
41 Dean St 7734 3924 4–2A
*"Very friendly" staff add to the attractions of Aldo Zilli's "cramped"
original venture in Soho, where the Italian fare can sometimes
be "very good". / 11.30 pm; closed Sat L & Sun.*

Silka SE1 £28 ❸❷④
6-8 Southwark St 7378 6161 9–4C
*This Indian basement in Borough Market has yet to hit the big
time, but satisfies all who report on it; it serves "well-spiced" and
"good-value" dishes, based on Ayurvedic principles. / www.silka.co.uk;
11.30 pm; closed Sun.*

Silks & Spice £27 ❸❷❸
95 Chiswick High Rd, W4 8995 7991 7–2B
28 Chalk Farm Rd, NW1 7482 2228 8–2B
Temple Ct, 11 Queen Victoria St, EC4 7248 7878 9–2C
*This "unpretentious" chain attracts consistent praise for its decent
Thai/Malaysian food and its "cheerful" style. / www.silksandspice.net;
11 pm, EC4 Thu & Fri 2 am; EC4 closed Sat & Sun, W4 L only Mon-Fri;
no Amex.*

Simpson's Tavern EC3 £26 ④❸❶
38 1/2 Ball Ct, Cornhill 7626 9985 9–2C
*"For a boozy City lunch with friends", this "bawdy" Dickensian
chop-house – offering "filling", "school dinners" fare at "sensible
prices" – is, on most accounts, simply "great".
/ www.simpsonsofmayfair.com; L only, closed Sat & Sun.*

Simpsons-in-the-Strand WC2 £57 ④❸④
100 Strand 7836 9112 4–3D
Nowadays, most feedback on this famous Victorian temple to the Roast Beef of Olde England concentrates on the fact that, to start the day, it offers "the best posh fry-up in the world"; otherwise, it is often dismissed as a "tourist time warp", trading "on past glories". / www.fairmont.com/simpsons; 10.45 pm, Sun 9 pm; no jeans or trainers.

Singapore Garden NW6 £35 ❷❷❸
83a Fairfax Rd 7624 8233 8–2A
"Vastly improved" after a recent refurbishment, this Swiss Cottage "old-timer" now has "very swish" premises, which provide a much more elegant showcase for its "interesting" and "well presented" array of Singaporean/Malay dishes. / www.singaporegarden.co.uk; 11 pm.

Singapura £34 ❸❸❸
31 Broadgate Circle, EC2 7256 5045 9–2D
78-79 Leadenhall St, EC3 7929 0089 9–2D
1-2 Limeburner Ln, EC4 7329 1133 9–2A
"Delicious" food and "friendly" service makes these City orientals "reliable" destinations for most reporters – "for both business and pleasure". / www.singapuras.co.uk; 10.30 pm; closed Sat & Sun, EC2 & EC3 L only.

606 Club SW10 £35 ⑤④❶
90 Lots Rd 7352 5953 5–4B
"Great" jazz is the draw to this celebrated hole-in-the-wall – a hard-to-find cellar, near Chelsea Harbour; its "sloppy" cuisine is at best incidental. / www.606club.co.uk; midnight; D only.

06 St Chad's Place WC1 £31 ❷④❷
6 St Chad's Pl 7278 3355 8–3D
"A lovely space" – a converted shed by a railway line – whose "good" light menu makes it all the more welcome near King's Cross; service can be "poor", though. / www.6saintchadsplace.com; 9.30 pm; closed Sat & Sun; no Amex.

Six-13 W1 £49 ❷❸④
19 Wigmore St 7629 6133 3–1B
"Kosher food that gentiles will also enjoy" helps make this smartish venture, just north of Oxford Street, a useful option for business. / www.six13.com; 10.30 pm; closed Fri D, Sat & Sun.

(Gallery)
Sketch W1 £50 ⑤⑤④
9 Conduit St 0870 777 4488 3–2C
"Unless you're a huge fan of strange loos", this kooky Barbarella-style Mayfair venue is best left to people who have "more money than sense", or who "want to be seen, not to eat". / www.sketch.uk.com; 11 pm, Thu-Sat 2 am; D only, closed Sun; booking: max 12.

(Glade)
Sketch W1 £37 ⑤⑤⑤
9 Conduit St 0870 777 4488 3–2C
Hipsters insist that the lunch-only section of Momo's Mayfair palazzo is "very funky", but more of the (few) reports say it's just a "dowdy" place – "like a disused Parisian apartment" – serving "really disappointing" dishes. / www.sketch.uk.com; L only, closed Sun.

(Lecture Room)
Sketch W1 £115 ⑤④④

9 Conduit St   0870 777 4488   3–2C

It's "a sublime eating experience" to its fans, but the vast majority of reporters are scathing about Mourad Mazouz's & Pierre Gagnaire's ultra-luxurious Mayfair dining room – they find the overall style "up itself", the "overly-rich" cuisine to be "trying too hard", and the prices "criminal". / www.sketch.uk.com; 10.30 pm; closed Mon, Sat L & Sun; booking: max 8; set weekday L £52 (FP).

(Parlour)
Sketch W1 £34 ④④④

9 Conduit St   0870 777 4488   3–2C

Supporters laud the "creative and beautiful" pastries and "great" atmosphere of this "lovely" café and lunch spot, off the main foyer of Momo's Mayfair palace; sceptics, though, can see only an "expensive and pompous" place, offering "tiny portions of over-fussy food". / www.sketch.uk.com; 10 pm; closed Sun; no booking.

(Dining Room)
Smiths of Smithfield EC1 £35 ❸❸❸

67-77 Charterhouse St   7251 7997   9–1A

The "metropolitan buzz" makes conversation "a challenge" in the brasserie on the second floor of this Clerkenwell warehouse-complex; its "simple" and "reliable" food is "just the ticket for an informal business lunch". / www.smithsofsmithfield.co.uk; 10.45 pm; closed Sat L & Sun.

(Ground Floor)
Smiths of Smithfield EC1 £23 ④④❷

67-77 Charterhouse St   7251 7997   9–1A

Lazy Sunday brunches (ideally with a hangover) are "an institution" at this "cavernous" bar overlooking Smithfield Market – "arrive early to avoid a long wait for a table"; "you go more for the atmosphere than the cooking", though, and service is "not a strong point". / www.smithsofsmithfield.co.uk; L only.

(Top Floor)
Smiths of Smithfield EC1 £58 ❷❸❷

67-77 Charterhouse St   7251 7950   9–1A

"A great view, especially at night" – ideally from the terrace – is one of the features which helps make this "smart" top-floor steakhouse a "very reliable" destination; its "fine" steaks are "superb" too, but they do taste best "on expenses".
/ www.smithsofsmithfield.co.uk; 10.45 pm; closed Sat L; booking: max 10.

Smollensky's £41 ⑤④④

105 Strand, WC2   7497 2101   4–3D
Bradmore Hs, Ham'smith B'way, W6   8741 8124   7–2C
22-24 York St, TW1   8891 5200   1–4A
Unit 1 Reuters Plaza, Canary Wharf, E14   7719 0101   11–1C
22 Wapping High St, E1   7680 1818   11–1A

"Everything is average" at this long-established, "middle-of-the-road" and vaguely American-theme chain; its Strand HQ has recently been given a contemporary new look. / www.smollenskys.co.uk; 10.30 pm, W6 Fri & Sat 2 am; W6 & E14 closed Sun.

Snows on the Green W6 £40 ❷❷❸
166 Shepherd's Bush Rd 7603 2142 7–1C
"A safe bet every-time" – Brook Green's "favourite local" offers
"really reliable" Mediterranean cuisine at "reasonable" prices;
service is "attentive" too. / 10.45 pm; closed Sat L & Sun.

Sofra £30 ④④④
1 St Christopher's Pl, W1 7224 4080 3–1A
18 Shepherd St, W1 7493 3320 3–4B
36 Tavistock St, WC2 7240 3773 4–3D
11 Circus Rd, NW8 7586 9889 8–3A
21 Exmouth Mkt, EC1 7833 1111 9–1A
"Tasty" Turkish food makes this "cheap" chain a popular stand-by
for its many fans; for doubters, though, it's just "bland" and
"unexciting". / www.sofra.co.uk; midnight.

Soho Japan W1 £31 ❷❸④
52 Wells St 7323 4661 2–1B
An excellent no-frills north-Soho spot, offering "extremely well-
priced" Japanese food of "high quality" to a "substantially expat
clientèle"; (licensed or you can BYO). / www.sohojapan.co.uk; 10.30 pm;
closed Sat L & Sun.

Soho Spice W1 £32 ④④❸
124-126 Wardour St 7434 0808 3–1D
A "buzzing" ambience, and "late opening" are plus points of this
"relatively cheap" modern Indian in Soho; some still see it as
a "good stand-by" – others just find the food too "blah" these days.
/ www.sohospice.co.uk; midnight, Sun 10.30 pm; set weekday L £20 (FP).

Solly's Exclusive NW11 £31 ④④④
148 Golders Green Rd 8455 0004 1–1B
"You feel like you're in the Middle East" at this "interesting" Golders
Green Israeli (which has a restaurant upstairs, and a café/take-
away below); regulars insist it's "always fun", but the uninitiated can
simply find it "disappointing". / 11 pm, Sat 1 am; closed Fri D & Sat L;
no Amex.

Somerstown Coffee House NW1 NEW £34 ④④④
60 Chalton St 7691 9136 8–3C
This new French-owned pub is reasonably "good value", but is
of most interest as a tolerable rendezvous in the very thin area
to the west of King's Cross station. / 11 pm; closed Sun D.

Sông Quê E2 £25 ❶④④
134 Kingsland Rd 7613 3222 1–2D
"Saigon meets Shoreditch" at this "no-frills" café – the best-known
of the many Vietnamese places in the area; "the best beef pho"
is the highlight of its "amazing-value" menu. / 11 pm.

Sonny's SW13 £42 ④❸❸
94 Church Rd 8748 0393 10–1A
Some Barnes locals still tout this textbook 'modern brasserie'
as "the finest local restaurant you could wish for"; it's looking ever
more "tired" nowadays, though, and the food has "fluctuated" this
year – let's hope the new chef can steady the ship!
/ www.sonnys.co.uk; 11.45 pm; closed Sun D; set dinner £22 (FP).

Sophie's Steakhouse SW10 £34 ❸❸❶
311-313 Fulham Rd 7352 0088 5–3B
"There's always a wait for tables" – during which you can hang out in the bar – at this "packed and lively" Chelsea linchpin, which offers "great" burgers but "variable" steaks.
/ www.sophiessteakhouse.com; 11.45 pm; no booking; set weekday L £24 (FP).

Sotheby's Café W1 £39 ❷❶❷
34 New Bond St 7293 5077 3–2C
"Charming for a light lunch" – the "quirky" café off the foyer of the Mayfair auction house provides a "quality" menu (of "limited" length), "very friendly" service and "major people-watching opportunities". / www.sothebys.com; L only, closed Sat & Sun.

Souk WC2 £25 ❺❺❷
27 Litchfield St 7240 1796 4–3B
With its "plentiful nooks and crannies" and cheapish north African fodder, this "bazaar"-style dive near The Ivy makes "a popular central destination for big groups"; the cooking can be "poor", though, and service "too slow". / www.soukrestaurant.co.uk; midnight.

Souk Medina WC2 NEW £30 ❸❸❷
1A Short Gdns 7240 1796 4–2B
With its "fabulous pseudo-Moroccan atmosphere", this "pumping" new Covent Garden-fringe spot makes an ideal party destination; let's hope standards hold up a bit better than at its Litchfield Street sibling. / www.soukrestaurant.co.uk; 11.30 pm.

Spacca Napoli W1 £26 ❷❶❸
101 Dean St 7437 9440 3–1D
"It's only a few yards from Oxford Street, so people assume it's no good", but in fact this is a "really nice" and "good-value" Soho Italian, with "authentic Neapolitan pizza". / www.spaccanapoli.co.uk; 11 pm.

Spago SW7 £27 ❷❷❸
6 Glendower Pl 7225 2407 5–2B
"South Kensington's best cheap and cheerful Italian" offers "authentic and really tasty" pizza (and other fare) in a "good buzzy atmosphere". / 11.30 pm.

The Spencer Arms SW15 NEW £37 ❸❸❷
237 Lower Richmond Rd 8788 0640 10–1B
Fans are happy to overlook "occasional lapses" at this "lovely" (and "very family-friendly") Shaker-style pub-conversion by Putney Heath, which offers an "imaginative" twist on "British pub grub". / 10 pm; no Amex.

La Spiga W1 £40 ❸④④
84-86 Wardour St 7734 3444 3–2D
"It seems to have lost most of its ambience", but this "very noisy" Soho Italian is still the "ultimate stand-by" for many reporters, thanks to its "heavenly" pizza. / 11 pm; closed Sun L.

La Spighetta W1 £40 ❸❸⑤
43 Blandford St 7486 7340 2–1A
New owners seem to be reviving this Marylebone Sardinian (which has quite a name for its pizza); the "noisy" basement setting, though, still strikes some reporters as "horrid". / www.spighetta.co.uk; 10.30 pm.

Spoon at Sanderson
Sanderson W1 £77 ⑤⑤⑤
50 Berners St 7300 1444 3–1D
"Completely over-rated and poncy" – this Fitzrovia design-hotel
dining room offers *"shockingly poor"* cooking at *"ridiculous"* prices.
/ www.morganshotelgroup.com; 11 pm.

The Spread Eagle SE10 £44 ❸❷❷
1-2 Stockwell St 8853 2333 1–3D
If you want *"cute and cosy"*, look no further than this Greenwich
coaching inn, which is full of *"intimate snugs"*; its *"friendly"* French
staff deliver *"classic"* (if *"rather rich"*) Gallic dishes. / 10 pm;
no Amex.

THE SQUARE W1 £88 ❷❷④
6-10 Bruton St 7495 7100 3–2C
Philip Howard's *"memorable"* cooking and an *"awesome"* wine list
make this *"formal"* Mayfair dining room the *"perfect place
to impress on business"*; presumably to please the Michelin men,
the décor has recently been *"polished up"*, but (or should that read
'therefore'?) the ambience remains *"a bit boring"*.
/ www.squarerestaurant.com; 10.45 pm; closed Sat L & Sun L.

Square Pie Company £9 ❷❸④
Selfridges Food Hall, W1 7318 2460 3–1A
1 Canada Sq, Jubilee Line Mall, E14 7519 6071 11–1C
16 Horner Sq, Old Spitalfields Mkt, E1 7377 1114 9–1D
The name does not lie – it is the *"superb variety"* of *"hot"*,
"honest" and *"tasty"* pies that make this small eat-in/take-away
chain universally popular with reporters. / www.squarepie.com;
E14 5 pm; W1 8 pm; E1 3pm, Sun 6 pm; E1 closed Sat, E14 closed Sun.

Sree Krishna SW17 £19 ❶❷❸
192-194 Tooting High St 8672 4250 10–2C
"London's longest-established south Indian restaurant" –
this Tooting *"golden oldie"* still retains many fans for its *"amazing-
value"* fare (not all of which is meat-free). / www.sreekrishna.co.uk;
10.45 pm, Fri & Sat midnight; set weekday L £12 (FP).

Sri Nam E14 £31 ❸④④
10 Cabot Sq 7715 9515 11–1C
The Canary Wharf outpost of the Sri Thai chain; though not
as highly-rated as its siblings, it wins consistent praise for its *"tasty"*
grub. / www.orientalrestaurantgroup.co.uk; 10 pm; closed Sat & Sun; booking
essential.

Sri Siam City EC2 £37 ❸❸④
85 London Wall 7628 5772 9–2C
It is *"a bit dull"*, but this well-established Thai basement maintains
quite a strong City following, thanks to cooking that's *"solid"*
(if *"pricey"*). / www.orientalrestaurantgroup.co.uk; 10.30 pm; closed
Sat & Sun.

Sri Thai City EC4 £35 ❸❷❸
3 Queen Victoria St 7827 0202 9–3C
A *"cavernous"* Thai restaurant, hailed by most reporters as *"a great
cheap City option"*. / www.orientalrestaurantclub.co.uk; 10.30 pm; closed
Sat & Sun.

Sri Thai Soho W1   £37   ❸❸④
16 Old Compton St   7434 3544   4–2A
*"A cut above most other Thai restaurants" – in Soho, anyway –
this ever-handy destination is particularly good "for a quick meal".
/ www.orientalrestaurantgroup.co.uk; 11 pm; closed Sun L.*

Standard Tandoori W2   £22   ❷④⑤
21-23 Westbourne Grove   7229 0600   6–1C
*Founded in 1968, this aptly-named Bayswater institution is –
"warts 'n' all" – "still one of London's best-value Indians".
/ 11.45 pm.*

Star Café W1   £24   ❸❷❸
22 Gt Chapel St   7437 8778   3–1D
*"It should have a blue plaque", say regulars at this old-style Soho
Italian café, which is a haunt of "many well-known media folk";
"the most amazing full English" is a top attraction.
/ www.thestarcafesoho.co.uk; L only, closed Sat & Sun.*

Star of India SW5   £38   ❷❸④
154 Old Brompton Rd   7373 2901   5–2B
*As an "Indian with a difference", this family-run South Kensington
curry-house has a fine tradition of "delicate" and "interesting"
cooking; the "flamboyant" muralled décor, however, has now
"gone past shabby-chic and needs work". / 11.45 pm.*

Starbucks   £11   ④❸④
Branches throughout London
*"I know I am supposed to hate it, but I genuinely like their coffee!"
– reporters are shamefaced in their addiction to this "functional"
US import; the "in-store goodies", though, are "grossly overpriced".
/ www.starbucks.com; 6.30 pm-11 pm; most City branches closed all or part
of weekend; no booking.*

The Sterling EC3   £34   ❸❷❸
30 St Mary Axe   7929 3641   9–2D
*We left unimpressed by its thoroughly anonymous style, but early-
days reporters seem to like this new bar, at the foot of the
'Gherkin', which is praised for its "busy but efficient" feel and its
"honest" food. / www.lewisandclarke.com; 11 pm; closed Sat & Sun.*

Stick & Bowl W8   £16   ❸❸⑤
31 Kensington High St   7937 2778   5–1A
*With its "hilariously uncomfortable shared tables and stools",
plus "delicious" and "cheap" Chinese scoff, this long-established
Kensington canteen is "a great-value no-frills solution in a part
of town that's difficult on a budget". / 11 pm; no credit cards; no booking.*

Sticky Fingers W8   £35   ⑤⑤④
1a Phillimore Gdns   7938 5338   5–1A
*This former-favourite Kensington burger joint has "gone seriously
downhill" – service can be "completely disorganised" these days,
and they "must do better" on the food. / www.stickyfingers.co.uk;
midnight.*

Stock Pot £15 ④④④
40 Panton St, SW1 7839 5142 4–4A
18 Old Compton St, W1 7287 1066 4–2A
273 King's Rd, SW3 7823 3175 5–3C
The food's "akin to school dinners 25 years ago", but who cares? –
at the "unbelievably cheap" prices, "you just can't go wrong"
at these "hearty, fill-you-up bistros". / 11 pm-midnight; W1 no credit
cards, SW3 no Amex; some booking restrictions apply.

Stone Mason's Arms W6 £29 ④④❸
54 Cambridge Grove 8748 1397 7–2C
This "welcoming" gastropub used to be notable for transcending its
trafficky Hammersmith location; "standards have dropped", though
– it's "nothing special as a gastro-venue" nowadays. / 11 pm.

Story Deli
The Old Truman Brewery E1 £20 ❶④❷
3 Dray Walk 7247 3137 1–2D
"A real buzz" distinguishes this young East End fashionistas'
favourite, which offers "the best pizza north of Naples";
much service is refectory-style. / 10 pm during summer (D only during
summer); L only.

Strada £31 ④❸❸
15-16 New Burlington St, W1 7287 5967 3–2C
31 Marylebone High St, W1 7935 1004 2–1A
9-10 Market Pl, W1 7580 4644 3–1C
6 Gt Queen St, WC2 7405 6295 4–1D
237 Earl's Court Rd, SW5 7835 1180 5–2A
175 New King's Rd, SW6 7731 6404 10–1B
105-106 Upper St, N1 7226 9742 8–3D
4 South Grove, N6 8347 8686 8–1B
40-42 Parkway, NW1 7428 9653 8–3B
11-13 Battersea Rise, SW11 7801 0794 10–2C
375 Lonsdale Rd, SW13 8392 9216 10–1A
102-104 Clapham High St, SW4 7627 4847 10–2D
8-10 Exmouth Mkt, EC1 7278 0800 9–1A
"With its modern contemporary feel" – and a menu of "simple",
"solid" Italian fare, including "thin and crispy" pizza – this fast-
growing chain is emerging as "a better alternative to the Asks and
PizzaExpresses of the world". / www.strada.co.uk; 11 pm; some booking
restrictions apply.

Stratford's W8 £41 ❷❷❸
7 Stratford Rd 7937 6388 5–2A
In a Kensington backwater, this "welcoming" and "old-fashioned"
restaurant serves "simply-prepared" but "reliable" fish dishes; it's a
particular "favourite" of those who like their ambience "quiet".
/ 11 pm; closed Sun; set dinner £25 (FP).

Sugar Hut SW6 £43 ④④❶
374 North End Rd 7386 8950 5–3A
A "chilled" and "divinely romantic" Fulham Thai, where "the food
is forgettable, but the bill is not"; "the best bit is the bar with the
bed-seats". / www.sugarhutgroup.com; 1 am; D only; booking essential.

sign up for the survey at www.hardens.com

Sugar Reef W1 £38 ⑤⑤⑤
42-44 Gt Windmill St   7851 0800   3–2D
*Reporters don't waste many words on this vast Soho nite-club;
for those counting the pennies, though, its 'offer' meals – "a bizarre
concept that's a total bargain at the start of the week" – are worth
knowing about.* / www.sugarreef.net; 1 am; closed Mon L, Tue L,
Wed L & Sun; set weekday L £24 (FP).

Sukho Thai Cuisine SW6 £37 ❶❷❸
855 Fulham Rd   7371 7600   10–1B
*It's "unpretentious" in style, but this "cheery little Thai place" has
developed a strong Fulham following, thanks to its "delightful" staff,
its "fabulous" food and its "affordable" prices.* / 11 pm.

Sumosan W1 £75 ❸④④
26b Albemarle St   7495 5999   3–3C
*This minimalist Mayfair Japanese still has many fans for whom it's
"just as good as Nobu or Zuma"; it's been "slipping" recently
though – service can be "clueless", and the food seems ever-more
"achingly expensive".* / www.sumosan.com; 11.30 pm; closed
Sat L & Sun L.

The Sun & Doves SE5 £26 ❸④❷
61 Coldharbour Ln   7733 1525   1–4C
*A "great" garden ("complete with totem pole and fairy lights") adds
interest to this "friendly" converted boozer – still the best of the
amazingly few decent spots in Camberwell; "the cooking is not
always top-notch, but the overall experience is very good".*
/ www.sunanddoves.co.uk; 10.30 pm; no Amex; need 10+ to book.

Le Suquet SW3 £51 ❷④❸
104 Draycott Ave   7581 1785   5–2C
*"It's like walking straight into Cannes' old town" when you visit this
"classy" and "unchanging" Brompton Cross veteran, where
"comically French" staff serve "beautiful seafood platters" (and fish
dishes).* / 11.30 pm; set weekday L £31 (FP).

Sushi Hiroba WC2 NEW £28 ❶❷❸
50-54 Kingsway   7430 1888   2–2D
*It has a soulless location on the fringe of Covent Garden, but this
atmospheric new London outpost of a Korean-backed conveyor-
sushi chain impressed on our summer-2006 visit – everything
we sampled was beautifully fresh, brilliantly-realised, and came
at very user-friendly prices.* / Rated on Editors' visit.

Sushi-Hiro W5 £37 ❶❷④
1 Station Pde   8896 3175   1–3A
*From the street, it may "resemble a dental practice", but this "tiny"
and "truly authentic" Japanese (near Ealing Common tube) serves
"incredibly fresh" sushi to a "primarily oriental clientèle"; "bring
cash, and book in advance".* / 9 pm; closed Mon; no credit cards.

Sushi-Say NW2 £36 ❷❶④
33b Walm Ln   8459 7512   1–1A
*Aficionados of Japanese cuisine (sushi addicts especially) say
"it's well worth the hike" to sample the "outstanding" and
"authentic" dishes at the Shimizu family's basic Willesden Green
outfit; "I have to eat in Nobu regularly for business – for pleasure,
give me Sushi-Say any time!"* / 10.30 pm; closed Mon.

The Swag & Tails SW7 £40 ❸❷❷
10-11 Fairholt St 7584 6926 5–1C
"An oasis away from the noise and bustle of Knightsbridge" –
this "delightful mews pub with a tiny restaurant" serves a "limited"
menu of "quality gastro-bar food". / www.swagandtails.com; 10 pm;
closed Sat & Sun.

The Swan W4 £33 ❷❸❷
119 Acton Ln 8994 8262 7–1A
A "heaven-sent" garden is not the only attraction at this "first-rate"
local on the Chiswick/Acton borders – the food is "above average",
there's "a great wine list" and the interior retains the "cosy" and
"unpretentious" feel of "a real pub". / 10.30 pm; closed weekday L;
no Amex; no booking.

Sweetings EC4 £43 ❷❷⓿
39 Queen Victoria St 7248 3062 9–3B
This true "old school classic" – a "quaint" Victorian parlour –
is "still the City's best place for seafood", and has a "hustling and
bustling" atmosphere that's "second to none"; no booking,
so "get there early". / L only, closed Sat & Sun; no booking.

Taberna Etrusca EC4 £42 ⑤④④
9 Bow Churchyard 7248 5552 9–2C
Reporters split 50/50 on this long-standing Italian: to fans it's
a "great place" with a "lovely" atmosphere – to doubters just
"an efficient factory for emptying City boys' wallets" ("and, worse,
they seem to enjoy it!"). / www.etruscarestaurants.com; L only, closed
Sat & Sun.

The Table SE1 NEW £20 ❷❸④
83 Southwark St 7401 2760 9–4B
Surely the leading firm of architects of whose offices this new café
forms part could have done a better job on its "cramped" design? –
"for a tasty and freshly prepared lunch", however, the place makes
a handy South Bank destination. / Rated on Editors' visit; Mon-Thu 6 pm,
Fri 11 pm; closed Sat & Sun; no Amex.

Taiwan Village SW6 £25 ❷⓿❸
85 Lillie Rd 7381 2900 5–3A
"A smorgasbord of tastes" – "and that's just from the set menu!" –
rewards visitors to this relatively unknown Fulham two-year-old,
which specialises in the cuisines of Taiwan, Hunan and Sichuan;
"the food, the value and the welcome are all amazing".
/ www.taiwanvillage.com; 11.30 pm, Sun 10.30 pm; closed Mon L.

Talad Thai SW15 £24 ⓿❷④
320 Upper Richmond Rd 8789 8084 10–2A
"Fresh-tasting" Thai dishes come "fast" and "cheap" at this
brilliantly-rated canteen, adjoining an oriental supermarket
in Putney. / www.taladthai.co.uk; 10.30 pm; no Amex.

Taman gang W1 £75 ④④⓿
141 Park Ln 7518 3160 2–2A
This "stunning" basement bar/restaurant, near Marble Arch, is –
say fans – a "cool" place for "beautiful people" to eat
"imaginative" Asian-fusion fare; critics just find it "pretentious",
and "far too expensive". / www.tamangang.com; 11.30 pm; D only, ex Sun
open L & D; booking: max 6.

Tamarai WC2 NEW
167 Drury Ln   awaiting tel   4–1C
*Under the same ownership as Chor Bizarre, this ambitious new
pan-Asian is scheduled to open around the publication date of this
guide; Covent Garden is not a natural location for a restaurant
as trendy as this place aims to be, so it will be interesting to see
how it fares.*

Tamarind W1   £58   ❷❷❸
20 Queen St   7629 3561   3–3B
*Alfred Pasad's "sophisticated" and "delicate" cuisine continues
to win wide acclaim for this grand Mayfair nouvelle Indian;
some reporters, however, are "not overly keen" on its basement
setting. / www.tamarindrestaurant.com; 11.15 pm; closed Sat L;
set weekday L £36 (FP).*

tamesa@oxo
Oxo Tower SE1 NEW   £35   ④④❸
2nd Fl, Oxo Tower Wharf, Barge House St   7633 0088   9–3A
*Can Dominic Ford (who used to run 'Oxo Tower', six floors up)
make a go of this bright newcomer – equally blessed with "fantastic
views" – on the 'graveyard' second floor?; like its fans, we found
"fresh" brasserie fare and an "enjoyable" all-round experience –
but others have encountered "mediocre" food and "amateurish"
service. / 11.30 pm.*

Tampopo SW10   £27   ❸④④
140 Fulham Rd   7370 5355   5–3B
*"Like Wagamama but classier", this Chelsea canteen – the London
outpost of a national chain – is unanimously acclaimed by reporters
for its "very fresh and light" Asian fare. / www.tampopo.co.uk; 11 pm.*

Tandoori Lane SW6   £26   ❸❷❸
131a Munster Rd   7371 0440   10–1B
*This Indian veteran in deepest Fulham won extremely consistent
praise this year for its "reliable" curries. / 11.30 pm; no Amex.*

Tandoori Nights SE22   £27   ❶❶❸
73 Lordship Ln   8299 4077   1–4D
*South East London fans say this East Dulwich curry-house
is "the best-ever Indian", thanks to its "fresh and delicious" cooking
and its "very attentive" service; its "cramped" and "slightly boring"
interior is "always packed". / 11.30 pm; closed weekday L & Sat L.*

Tangawizi TW1   £34   ❷❷❷
406 Richmond Rd   8891 3737   1–4A
*"Well-spiced food, with rich, multi-various flavours" make this
"stylish" Indian a big hit down Twickenham way; (Tangawizi,
of course, is Swahili for ginger tea). / www.tangawizi.co.uk; 11 pm;
D only, closed Sun.*

Tapas Brindisa SE1   £39   ❷❸❸
18-20 Southwark St   7357 8880   9–4C
*It's "cramped and chaotic" (and "a shame you can't book"),
but this "brilliant" Borough Market café (allied to the famous
Iberian food importers) serves "amazing" tapas that are "pricey
but worth it". / www.brindisa.com; 11 pm; closed Sun L; no Amex.*

Taqueria W11 £28 ❸❸④
139-143 Westbourne Grove 7229 4734 6–1B
A "fun" café in Notting Hill – a "trustafarian" hang-out of the
moment – which "does some justice" to Mexico's cuisine; "delicious
tacos and margaritas are highlights of a "refreshingly different"
selection that "sometimes borders on excellence".
/ www.comcoolchilli.co.uk; 11 pm; no Amex; no booking.

Taro £21 ❸❸④
10 Old Compton St, W1 7439 2275 4–2B
61 Brewer St, W1 7734 5826 3–2D
"Very cheap, very cheerful, very quick" – Mr Taro's Soho canteens
are praised by all reporters for their "good fresh sushi" and their
"huge bowls of tasty ramen". / 10.30 pm, Sun 9.30 pm; no Amex;
no booking.

Tartine SW3 £36 ④❸❸
114 Draycott Ave 7589 4981 5–2C
"For a light lunch or brunch" near Brompton Cross, some reporters
tip this "stylish" pit stop, which serves "glorified toasties on Poilâne
bread"; "the people-watching is the main reason to go".
/ www.tartine.co.uk; 11 pm; need 6+ to book at D.

Tas £31 ❸❷❸
22 Bloomsbury St, WC1 7637 4555 2–1C NEW
33 The Cut, SE1 7928 2111 9–4A
72 Borough High St, SE1 7403 7200 9–4C
97-99 Isabella St, SE1 7620 6191 9–4A
37 Farringdon Rd, EC1 7430 9721 9–1A NEW
"Tasty Turkish food at very reasonable prices" – served in "handily-
located", and "always-buzzy" branches – have made a huge
success of this "authentic"-feeling chain. / www.tasrestaurant.com;
11.30 pm.

Tas Ev SE1 £26 ❸❷❷
97-99 Isabella St 7620 6191 9–4A
"The odd rumbling train adds to the ambience" of "the best Tas
group outlet yet" – a "spacious" and "buzzy" bar/deli/restaurant
in railway arches near Southwark tube, offering "cheap" and
"tasty" Turkish fare. / www.tasrestaurant.com; 11.30 pm.

Tas Pide SE1 £29 ④❸❷
20-22 New Globe Walk 7928 3300 9–3B
Pide (Turkish-style pizza) forms a large part of the "simple" menu
of this "decently-priced" South Bank Anatolian; dishes can be a
trifle "bland" – an accusation that could certainly not be levelled
at the "memorable" interior. / www.tasrestaurant.com; 11.30 pm;
set always available £29 (FP).

La Tasca £27 ⑤⑤④
23-24 Maiden Ln, WC2 7240 9062 4–4C
404-406 Chiswick High Rd, W4 8994 4545 7–2A
18-19 The Mall, W5 8840 2041 1–2A
21 Essex Rd, N1 7226 3272 –
West India Quay, E14 7531 9990 11–1C
15-17 Eldon St, EC2 7256 2381 9–2C
Even fans concede it's "formulaic", but for most reporters this
"buzzing" tapas chain offers an "enjoyable" experience; ratings are
undercut, though, by those critics who think its food "an insult
to Spanish cuisine". / www.latasca.co.uk; 11 pm, E14 10.45 pm; need 8+
to book.

Tate Britain SW1 £42 ④❸❷
Millbank 7887 8825 2–4C
Whistler's famous murals, together with an "amazing" wine list
(which has some "terrific bargains") are the reasons to visit this
"civilised" museum dining room; the "acceptable" food is very much
in a supporting role. / www.tate.org.uk; L & afternoon tea only.

(Café (Level 2))
Tate Modern SE1 £32 ④④❸
Bankside 7401 5014 9–3B
"It's pricey for what it is", but the "stylish" café at the foot of Tate
Modern is a "pleasant surprise" for many reporters,
with "surprisingly tasty" food. / www.tate.org.uk; Fri 9.30 pm; L & tea only,
except Fri & Sat open L&D.

(Restaurant (Level 7))
Tate Modern SE1 £37 ④④❷
Bankside 7401 5020 9–3B
The view from this "airy and spacious" museum café is "as good
as at Oxo Tower" – perhaps even better; sadly, the usual rooms-
with-a-view rules apply: service tends to be "unenthusiastic" and
the food is "pricey for what it is". / www.tate.org.uk; 5.30 pm, Fri & Sat
9.30 pm; Sat-Thu closed D.

Tatsuso EC2 £80 ❷❸④
32 Broadgate Circle 7638 5863 9–2D
"You could be in Tokyo", at this "very serious" City "veteran", which
has quite a name as "THE client lunch place" (no doubt explaining
why it's "exceptionally expensive"); upstairs "they cook in front
of you" at the teppan-yaki – in the sombre cellar, it's sushi and
so on. / 9.30 pm; closed Sat & Sun.

Tawana W2 £32 ❷❷④
3 Westbourne Grove 7229 3785 6–1C
A Bayswater Thai, handily located a few yards from Queensway –
the setting's "dull", but the food's "authentic". / www.tawana.co.uk;
11 pm; no Amex.

The Tea Palace W11 £38 ④❸④
175 Westbourne Grove 7727 2600 6–1B
"The best range of teas in London" makes this "expensive" year-old
Notting Hill salon-de-thé a "great place for a girly tea party"
(or "a super spot to take mum"); the food "could be more
imaginative", though, and the ambience is a tad "sterile".
/ www.teapalace.co.uk; 6.30 pm; L & afternoon tea only.

Teca W1 £48 ❷❷④
54 Brooks Mews 7495 4774 3–2B
This "chic", if "stark", Italian "jewel", off Bond Street, enjoys
a limited profile, but can make a great find, especially for business;
its modern cooking is created with "flair", and well-matched by the
"brilliant" wines and "very efficient" service. / 10.30 pm; closed
Sat L & Sun.

Ten Ten Tei W1 £33 ❷❸⑤
56 Brewer St 7287 1738 3–2D
An "authentic" but "dingy" Soho Japanese, where you get "terrific
sushi for the price"; "the cooked dishes rate a mention" too.
/ 10 pm; closed Sun; no Amex.

Tendido Cero SW5 £35 ❷❸❷
174 Old Brompton Rd   7370 3685   5–2B
"Frantic but fun" staff serve up "excellent" tapas in "generous portions" – and "at extremely reasonable prices" – at this "authentic" South Kensington bar; sadly, though, "you can no longer BYO". / www.cambiodetercio.co.uk; 11 pm.

Tentazioni SE1 £50 ❶❷❸
2 Mill St   7394 5248   11–2A
"Many well-heeled Italians at dinner" speak for the quality of the "excellent, authentic regional Italian cooking" at this "hidden gem", in a backstreet near Tower Bridge; service is "helpful and knowledgeable" too. / www.tentazioni.co.uk; 10.45 pm; closed Sat L & Sun.

The Tenth
Royal Garden Hotel W8 £69 ❸❷❶
Kensington High St   7361 1910   5–1A
You get "wonderful views" over Kensington Gardens from this top-floor hotel dining room; even more amazingly, "the food matches up" and service is "sooooo good". / www.royalgardenhotel.co.uk; 10.30 pm; closed Sat L & Sun; set weekday L £45 (FP).

Terminus
Great Eastern Hotel EC2 £40
40 Liverpool St   7618 7400   9–2D
This handy – but, under Conran's management, dismal – Liverpool Street brasserie changed hands as this year's survey was drawing to a close (so we've left it un-rated); it will be interesting to see if the new régime can do better. / www.terminus-restaurant.co.uk; 11 pm.

The Terrace WC2 NEW £39 ④④⑤
Lincoln's Inn Fields   7430 1234   2–2D
"It was a cute idea, putting a hut in the middle of Lincoln's Inn Fields" (and with "lovely views of the greenery and tennis courts" too); the food is "pretty ordinary", though ("save for a few Caribbean dishes"), and "expensive" too – "given the room's distinct lack of frills". / www.theterrace.info; 9 pm; closed Sun; set weekday L £22 (FP).

Texas Embassy Cantina SW1 £36 ⑤④④
1 Cockspur St   7925 0077   2–2C
A "very central" location helps win some support for this large operation, near Trafalgar Square; it's a pretty "tacky" destination, though, and the "quasi-Tex/Mex" food is too often "bland and tasteless". / www.texasembassy.com; 11 pm.

TGI Friday's £35 ⑤⑤⑤
25-29 Coventry St, W1   7839 6262   4–4A
6 Bedford St, WC2   7379 0585   4–4C
Fulham Broadway, SW6   7385 1660   5–4A
96-98 Bishops Bridge Rd, W2   7229 8600   6–1C
"Thank God we had a 50%-off voucher, otherwise it wouldn't have been worth it"; this All-American chain – with its "irritatingly jolly" staff – serves "average US slop, but not at US prices..." / www.tgifridays.co.uk; 11.30 pm.

Thai Bistro W4 £25 ❷❸④
99 Chiswick High Rd   8995 5774   7–2B
This "consistently great", "canteen-style" Chiswick Thai wins praise for its "fresh" and "inexpensive" fare; "ambience is not high on the agenda". / 11 pm; closed Tue L & Thu L; no Amex.

sign up for the survey at www.hardens.com

Thai Café SW1   £25   ③④⑤
22 Charlwood St   7592 9584   2–4C
"Friendly" prices justify the "unflagging popularity" of this "cheap and cheerful" Pimlico Thai. / 10.30 pm; closed Sat L & Sun L.

Thai Corner Café SE22   £22   ③②④
44 North Cross Rd   8299 4041   1–4D
The option to BYO adds to the "cheap and cheerful" appeal of this "noisy" East Dulwich oriental favourite. / 10.30 pm; no credit cards.

Thai Elephant TW10   £34   ③②③
1 Wakefield Rd   8940 5114   1–4A
This rather old-fashioned Richmond Thai can be "very enjoyable" and its lunch deals in particular are "well-priced". / www.thaielephantrichmond.co.uk; 11 pm; set weekday L £20 (FP).

Thai Garden SW11   £25   ③②③
58 Battersea Rise   7738 0380   10–2C
"Polite and smiling staff" add to the charm of this "reassuring" Battersea veteran, whose food is hailed as "excellent if un-innovative". / 11 pm; D only.

Thai on the River SW11   £39   ③③②
2 Lombard Rd   7924 6090   5–4B
A "wonderful setting, especially in summer" is the headline feature of this Thai restaurant, by the Thames in Battersea, but the food is also consistently well-rated. / www.thaiontheriver.com; 11 pm.

Thai Pot WC2   £32   ④③④
1 Bedfordbury   7379 4580   4–4C
It has "an awkward layout" and its fare is "standard", but this "reliable" and quite "cheap" Thai fixture, behind the Coliseum, makes a good place for a "quick pre- or post-theatre supper". / www.thaipot.co.uk; 11.15 pm; closed Sun.

Thai Square   £29   ④④③
21-24 Cockspur St, SW1   7839 4000   2–3C
5 Princes St, W1   7499 3333   3–1C
148 Strand, WC2   7497 0904   2–2D
19 Exhibition Rd, SW7   7584 8359   5–2C
347-349 Upper St, N1   7704 2000   8–3D
2-4 Lower Richmond Rd, SW15   8780 1811   10–1A
136-138 Minories, EC3   7680 1111   9–3D
1-7 Gt Thomas Apostle, EC4   7329 0001   9–3B
"Solid" (but "dumbed-down") food, "average" service and "great interior design" – that's the formula which has won success for this oriental chain; the "lovely" Putney Bridge branch (originally the restaurant of that name, RIP) enjoys "fantastic views". / www.thaisq.co.uk; between 10 and 11.30 pm, SW1 open til 1am Fri & Sat; EC3 & EC4 closed Sat & Sun, W1 & WC2 closed Sun.

Thailand SE14   £26   ①②③
15 Lewisham Way   8691 4040   1–3D
"Recently expanded, but still quite small" – this "charming" and "unbelievable-value" New Cross fixture maintains its "local gem" status, thanks to its "consistently lovely" Thai/Laotian fare. / 11.30 pm; set always available £15 (FP).

The Thatched House W6 £31 ❸❹❷
115 Dalling Rd 8748 6174 7–1B
"You could take anyone" ("from your mates to your maiden aunt") to this "friendly" revamped pub, which – "unlike some of the Hammersmith Porsche-pullers" – still feels like a local; its "solid" grub is "just a tad different", and "the beer's good" too. / www.thatchedhouse.com; 10 pm; no Amex.

Theo Randall
InterContinental Hotel W1 NEW
1 Hamilton Pl 7409 3131 3–4A
This grand but formerly very '70s hotel at Hyde Park Corner is set to emerge from a major refurbishment in the autumn of 2006; Theo Randall has been head chef of the fabled River Café for many years, so this really should be one to watch. / www.london.interconti.com.

Thomas Cubitt SW1 NEW £44 ❸❷❷
44 Elizabeth St 7730 6060 2–4A
"A superb addition to Belgravia", this "beautiful", understated boozer has quickly established itself as the social centre the area formerly lacked; the food – whether on the "casual" ground floor, or in the smarter dining room above – is "pretty good" too. / www.thethomascubitt.co.uk; 10 pm.

3 Monkeys SE24 £30 ❸❸❹
136-140 Herne Hill 7738 5500 1–4C
"Tasty and delicate" cuisine has helped make quite a name for this "cavernous" contemporary Indian, in Herne Hill; it's not currently up to its best past standards, but some locals feel the cooking is "improving". / www.3monkeysrestaurant.com; 11 pm; D only.

Tiger Tiger SW1 £37 ⑤⑤❹
29 Haymarket 7930 1885 4–4A
Some reporters "have nothing good to say" about this large, raucous West End pick-up joint, which incorporates multiple bars and a restaurant; off-peak, though, "inexpensive deals" can make it "handy for a quick bite". / www.tigertiger-london.co.uk; 11 pm.

Timo W8 £50 ❸❷❹
343 Kensington High St 7603 3888 7–1D
Thanks to its "honest" and "accomplished" Italian cuisine, reporters seem prepared to overlook the "clinical" and "stilted" ambience of this neighbourhood spot, on the Kensington/Olympia borders. / www.timorestaurant.net; 11 pm; closed Sat L; booking: max 8.

Tobia NW3 £27 ❷❷⑤
1st Floor, 2a Lithos Rd 7431 4213 1–1B
This "great" family-run Ethiopian restaurant may be situated above a community hall ("and looks it"), but all reporters agree that a meal here is "an amazing experience". / www.tobiarestaurant.co.uk; midnight.

Toff's N10 £26 ❷❷❹
38 Muswell Hill Broadway 8883 8656 1–1B
"Good traditional fish 'n' chips" – in "huge" portions – has won a widespread north London fan club for this Muswell Hill institution; there's "always a queue". / www.toffsfishandchips.co.uk; 10 pm; closed Sun; no booking, Sat.

Toku
Japan Centre W1 £23 ❸④④
212 Piccadilly 7255 8255 3–3D
"The hustle and bustle makes you feel like you're in Tokyo",
when you visit this handy "pit stop" by Piccadilly Circus; "you may
have to wait", but – "for a quick bite" of "authentic", "no-frills"
Japanese food at "sensible" prices – it's hard to beat.
/ www.japancentre.com; 10 pm, Sun 8 pm; no Amex.

Tokyo City EC2 £36 ❷④④
46 Gresham St 7726 0308 9–2B
"Stick to the Japanese offering" ("the Thai menu isn't as good"),
and "you won't go wrong" at this unpretentious spot, near the Bank
of England. / www.tokyocity.co.uk; 10 pm; closed Sat & Sun.

Tokyo Diner WC2 £17 ❸❸④
2 Newport Pl 7287 8777 4–3B
This "quick" and "easy" Chinatown veteran offers "filling and
basic" Japanese scoff; "no fuss, free tea, low prices, no tips and
365-day opening" are all part of the formula. / www.tokyodiner.com;
midnight; no Amex; no booking, Fri & Sat.

TOM AIKENS SW3 £82 ❸❷❸
43 Elystan St 7584 2003 5–2C
Tom Aikens's fans say that the "mind-blowing" cuisine at his
"brightly-lit" Chelsea "Foodie Paradise" is "the best in town";
his approach can often seem "too clever by half", though, with a
lot of his creations striking reporters as "over-elaborate".
/ www.tomaikens.co.uk; 11 pm; closed Sat & Sun; jacket and/or tie; booking:
max 8; set weekday L £42 (FP).

Tom's W11 £26 ④④❷
226 Westbourne Grove 7221 8818 6–1B
"Relaxed weekend breakfasts and brunches" are the forte of Tom
Conran's cramped deli in the heart of Notting Hill; otherwise it can
seem "slightly overpriced". / L only; no Amex; no booking.

Tom's Kitchen SW3 NEW
27 Cale St 7823 3652 5–2C
Tom Aikens (see entry) has teemed up with chef Ollie Couillard –
who was brilliant at La Trompette, less so at the Dorchester Grill –
to create this new informal eatery, near Chelsea Green; it should
be one of the openings of late-2006.

Tootsies £30 ④④④
35 James St, W1 7486 1611 3–1A
177 New King's Rd, SW6 7736 4023 10–1B
107 Old Brompton Rd, SW7 7581 8942 5–2B
120 Holland Park Ave, W11 7229 8567 6–2A
148 Chiswick High Rd, W4 8747 1869 7–2A
196-198 Haverstock Hill, NW3 7431 3812 8–2A
1 Battersea Rise, SW11 7924 4935 10–2C
Putney Wharf, 30 Brewhouse St, SW15 8788 8488 10–2B
48 High St, SW19 8946 4135 10–2B
36-38 Abbeville Rd, SW4 8772 6646 10–2D
"A great family destination" – this "unassuming" chain remains
known for its "decent" burgers and "hearty" brunches; since mid-
2006, it has been part of the same stable as Gourmet Burger
Kitchen. / www.tootsiesrestaurants.co.uk; 11 pm; some booking restrictions
apply.

Tosa W6 NEW   £25   ❷❷❸
332 King St   8748 0002   7–2B
This "authentic" Japanese newcomer (on the "awkward" site that
was once Nanking, RIP) is a useful addition to Hammersmith's
main drag; "sweet" staff serve "well-executed" and "flavoursome"
dishes at "very reasonable" prices. / www.eatattosatosa.net; 11 pm;
closed Mon; no Amex.

Toto's SW1   £65   ❷❷❷
Lennox Gardens Mews   7589 0075   5–2C
"Flattering" staff and a "spacious" setting help create a "delightful"
atmosphere at this "discreet" Knightsbridge Italian, which feels
"very sophisticated in a rather old-fashioned way"; it's unsurprisingly
"pricey", but the cooking is "top-notch". / 11 pm; set weekday L
£46 (FP).

Trader Vics
Hilton Hotel W1   £64   ⑤④❸
22 Park Ln   7208 4113   3–4A
This basement tiki kitsch-fest may have "been around for donkeys
years" but it can still be "fun for themed drinks" – "the kitchen's
theory seems to be that after a couple of Singapore Slings it'll all
taste the same anyway". / www.tradervics.com; 12.30 am; closed
Sat L & Sun L.

The Trading House EC1 NEW   £38   ❸❷④
12-13 Grenville St   7831 0697   9–1A
We enjoyed our early-days visit to this small and "friendly"
newcomer, near Holborn, which is perhaps best suited to informal
business dining. / www.thetradinghouse.net; 10 pm; closed Sat & Sun.

The Trafalgar Tavern SE10   £36   ④④❷
Park Row   8858 2909   1–3D
"There's nothing better than a drink on the riverside terrace" of this
huge and "historic" pub, by the Thames at Greenwich; the food
is "fine, if nothing more" and perhaps "a tad pricey" for what it is.
/ 10 pm; closed Sun D; no Amex; no booking, Sun L.

Tree House SW13   £37   ④❸❸
73 White Hart Ln   8392 1617   10–1A
This "attractive" converted boozer, on the fringe of Barnes,
generally offers OK food in a "friendly" environment.
/ www.treehousepeople.com; L only; no Amex.

Trinity SW4 NEW
4 The Polygon   7622 1199   10–2D
On the rather hidden-away Clapham site formerly occupied
by Polygon (RIP), a late-2006 newcomer with the involvement
of Adam (Origin) Byatt; no further details were available as this
guide went to press.

Trinity Stores SW12 NEW   £12   ❷❷❸
5-6 Balham Station Rd   8673 3773   10–2C
A new Balham deli – early reports, though few, are a hymn
of praise to its "great coffee and cakes" and "home-made" lunches
and dinners, all served at a communal table. / www.trinitystores.co.uk;
L only.

sign up for the survey at www.hardens.com

Troika NW1 £26 ④④❸
101 Regent's Park Rd 7483 3765 8–2B
This "bustling" Russian café remains something of a Primrose Hill landmark; the food isn't art, but it is inexpensive and usually "tasty". / www.troika.co.uk; 10.30 pm.

Les Trois Garçons E1 £64 ④❸❶
1 Club Row 7613 1924 1–2D
This "kitsch-classic" East End pub-conversion – "I wanted to take home the stuffed bulldog in a tiara" – has an "irresistible craziness" which makes it "perfect for a date"; the "rich" Gallic fare is secondary, though, and comes at "heavy" prices. / www.lestroisgarcons.com; 10.30 pm; D only, closed Sun.

LA TROMPETTE W4 £52 ❶❶❷
5-7 Devonshire Rd 8747 1836 7–2A
This "flawless and unfaltering" Turnham Green "masterwork" (sibling to Wandsworth's legendary Chez Bruce) wins almost universal praise for its "excellent" Gallic cooking, "lovely" setting, "very friendly" service and "outstanding" wine list. / www.latrompette.co.uk; 10.30 pm; booking: max 6.

Troubadour SW5 £30 ④④❶
265 Old Brompton Rd 7370 1434 5–3A
Especially for breakfast, Earl's Court's "quirky" and "Bohemian" café/pub/coffee shop truly is an institution – even a reporter who says the comfort cooking is "terrible" and the service "worse" admits: "I keep going back". / www.troubadour.co.uk; 11 pm; no Amex.

La Trouvaille W1 £47 ④❸❸
12a Newburgh St 7287 8488 3–2C
Many reporters still vaunt this Soho five-year-old as "a little French gem that's perfect for seduction"; even some fans, though, find it "not as good as in previous years", with "less imaginative food", and with "the atmosphere damaged by the addition of a cellar bar". / www.latrouvaille.co.uk; 11 pm; closed Sat L & Sun; set weekday L £30 (FP).

Truc Vert W1 £44 ❸❸❸
42 North Audley St 7491 9988 3–2A
With its "adventurous" Gallic bites, its "terrific" brunches and its "smashing" coffee, this "charming, country-chic" deli/bistro makes "a wonderful refuge from Oxford Street". / www.trucvert.co.uk; 9.30 pm; closed Sun D.

Tsunami SW4 £35 ❶❸❸
5-7 Voltaire Rd 7978 1610 10–1D
"I still can't believe that this is in Clapham!"; this "terrific local Japanese" – run by an "ex-Nobu chef" – offers "inspirational" dishes at "excellent prices". / 11 pm, Sun 9 pm; closed weekday L.

Tugga SW3 £47 ⑤⑤④
312-314 King's Rd 7351 0101 5–3C
This "fun and psychedelic" Chelsea Portuguese tapas bar/restaurant (opened in mid-2005) has failed to live up to its initial promise – service can be "less than attentive", and the food is often "poor". / www.tugga.com; 1 am; closed Mon, Tue-Fri D only, Sat & Sun open L & D; set weekday L £24 (FP).

Tuttons WC2 £39 ⑤④④
11-12 Russell St 7836 4141 4–3D
Thanks to its "terrifically central location" and its "great views of Covent Garden's piazza", this attractive brasserie is "naturally overpriced"; as you'd expect, the cooking is "unmemorable" too. / 11.30 pm; set pre theatre £25 (FP).

Two Brothers N3 £29 ❷❷④
297-303 Regent's Park Rd 8346 0469 1–1B
"The Manzi brothers have created an institution", and there's "usually a queue" at this north London stalwart, which serves "top quality fish 'n' chips in generous portions". / www.twobrothers.co.uk; 10.15 pm; closed Mon & Sun; no booking at D.

202
Nicole Farhi W11 £39 ❸❸❶
202 Westbourne Grove 7727 2722 6–1B
"A lovely place for weekend brunch"; this "half-café/half-clothes shop" has "just the right bobo (bourgeois/Bohemian) Notting Hill atmosphere", and the food is surprisingly good too – "expect to queue". / L & afternoon tea only; no booking.

Ubon E14 £90 ❷④④
34 Westferry Circus 7719 7800 11–1B
"It may not be Park Lane, but at least you can get a table without weeks of waiting" – Nobu's lower-key Canary Wharf sibling offers almost the same standards as in Mayfair, plus "amazing views". / www.noburestaurants.com; 10.15 pm; closed Sat L & Sun.

Uli W11 £29 ❷❶❷
16 All Saints Rd 7727 7511 6–1B
"A winner every time"; the "fabulous host" (Michael) gives "the friendliest service you could ever hope for" at this "homely" Notting Hill outfit, which serves "very good-value and tasty Chinese/fusion food"; the garden is "an extra plus". / www.uli-oriental.co.uk; 11 pm; D only; no Amex.

Ultimate Burger £22 ④④⑤
98 Tottenham Court Rd, W1 7436 5355 2–1B NEW
334 New Oxford St, WC1 7436 6641 4–1C NEW
82 Fortis Green Rd, N10 8883 6198 8–1C NEW
"Ultimate may be an overstatement" – this "simple" chain serves "tasty" enough burgers, but they are "no match for GBK". / www.ultimateburger.co.uk; 10.30 pm.

Umu W1 £100 ❸❸④
14-16 Bruton Pl 7499 8881 3–2C
Marlon Abela's "outrageously expensive" Kyoto-style Mayfair yearling polarises reporters; critics deride it as a "pretentious" place – "are we supposed to pray over its miniscule offerings?" – whereas fans vaunt its "exquisite" dishes, and say it's "the best Japanese in London". / www.umurestaurant.com; 11 pm; closed Sat L & Sun; booking: max 14; set weekday L £43 (FP).

The Union Café W1 £39 ❸❸❸
96 Marylebone Ln 7486 4860 3–1A
The "plain and airy" Marylebone outpost of the John Brinkley group is "always busy" – the "best-value wines around" are the special draw, but the "reliable" cooking plays an honourable supporting rôle. / www.brinkleys.com; 11 pm; closed Sun D.

Uno SW1 £37 ❸④④
1 Denbigh St 7834 1001 2–4B
"A bright restaurant, serving good-quality Italian food", in the heart
of Pimlico; *"the acoustics are poor"*, though, and *"everyone shouts"*.
/ www.uno1.co.uk; 11 pm; set always available £25 (FP).

Upper Glas N1 NEW
359 Upper St 7359 1932 8–3D
A late-2006 newcomer, taking over the former site of Lola's
(RIP) above Islington's Antiques Market; the aim is a Swedish
'fine dining' counterpart to the original Glas, by Borough Market.

Upstairs Bar SW2 NEW £35 ❷❶❷
89b Acre Ln (door on Branksome Rd) 7733 8855 10–2D
"A revelation for Brixton!" – this *"tucked-away-upstairs"* newcomer
makes a *"fantastic find"*, thanks to its *"simple"* but *"excellent"*
French cuisine, its *"very personal"* service and its *"intimate"* and
"stylish" setting; surprisingly *"great"* views too. / 10.30 pm; closed Mon,
Tue–Sat D only, closed Sun D; no Amex.

Le Vacherin W4 £38 ❷❷❸
76-77 South Pde 8742 2121 7–1A
Malcolm John's *"perfect evocation of a provincial Gallic restaurant"*
– complete with proper *"ultra-staid"* décor – makes
an *"astonishing"* find in deepest Chiswick; the bourgeois dishes are
suitably *"fabulous"* and *"hearty"*, and service is *"attentive"*.
/ www.levacherin.co.uk; 10.30 pm; closed Mon L; no Amex.

Vama SW10 £43 ❶❷❸
438 King's Rd 7351 4118 5–3B
Inspirations *"conventional and modern"* – in *"just the right mix"* –
lead to the creation of some *"exquisite"* and *"refined"* dishes at this
"upmarket" (but *"slightly overcrowded"*) World's End
subcontinental. / www.vama.co.uk; 11 pm.

Vasco & Piero's Pavilion W1 £44 ❷❶❷
15 Poland St 7437 8774 3–1D
It's been in business for 35 years, but this *"fabulous old-school
Italian"* can still be *"a real find"* on the fringe of Soho; seating
is *"tight"*, but the cooking is *"first-rate"*, and *"the staff are keen
to send you home smiling"*. / www.vascosfood.com; 10.30 pm; closed
Sat L & Sun.

Veeraswamy W1 £46 ❷❷❷
Victory Hs, 99-101 Regent St 7734 1401 3–3D
With its *"fantastic"* and *"colourful"* new look (which is in fact
"more classical in style" than the '90s-minimalism it replaced),
London's oldest Indian has boldly *"moved into the 21st century"*;
all aspects of the operation – not least the *"truly delicious"* food
and *"friendly"* service – are *"much improved"*. / www.veeraswamy.com;
10.30 pm; booking: max 12; set pre theatre £29 (FP).

El Vergel SE1 £17 ❶❷❷
8 Lant St 7357 0057 9–4B
"Delicious" and *"stupidly cheap"* Latin American fare helps make
this *"very friendly"* Borough *"hidden gem"* a *"great place for
a quick lunch"* – *"shame it's not open in the evenings!"*
/ www.elvergel.co.uk; breakfast & L only, closed Sat & Sun; no credit cards.

Vertigo
Tower 42 EC2 £40 ④④❶
20-25 Old Broad St 7877 7842 9–2C
"Dreadfully overpriced food" and "very '80s décor" aside,
this "unique" 42nd-floor City vantage point offers "phenomenal"
views and is an "ideal place to impress your other half" (or a
client); you must book ahead to gain entry. / www.vertigo42.co.uk;
11 pm; closed Sat & Sun; booking essential.

Vesbar W12 £25 ④❸❸
15-19 Goldhawk Rd 8762 0215 7–1C
This welcoming bar in a grotty bit of Shepherd's Bush makes
a relaxing place to "hang out", or enjoy a "hungover Sunday
brunch"; "the food is decent burger/salad stuff". / 11 pm.

Via Condotti W1 NEW £65 ④❷④
23 Conduit St 7493 7050 3–2C
The latest addition to Claudio Pulze's Italian stable, this summer-
2006 newcomer occupies the site of the short-lived Mayfair branch
of Rowley's (RIP); there wasn't much actively wrong with the place
on our early-days visit, but the whole experience was pretty bland.
/ *Rated on Editors' visit.*

Vic Naylors EC1 £40 ④④❸
38 & 42 St John St 7608 2181 9–1B
It's no foodie hotspot, but for a "casual" evening (especially after
work), this bar/restaurant near Smithfield Market offers OK food
and a "lively" atmosphere. / www.vicnaylor.com; 12.30 am; closed
Sat L & Sun.

Il Vicolo SW1 £40 ❷❸④
3-4 Crown Passage 7839 3960 3–4D
It suffers from "very busy, compact and noisy" quarters, but –
with its "good" service and "distinctive" Sardinian dishes –
this "little Italian tucked-away in the heart of St James's" feels very
"authentic". / 10 pm; closed Sat & Sun.

The Victoria SW14 £41 ❸④❸
10 West Temple 8876 4238 10–2A
"A good gastropub... at restaurant prices"; this attractive Sheen
venture, "tucked-away" near Richmond Park, incorporates a "huge,
light conservatory" (that can seem "a bit stark at night"); "avoid
at weekends if you don't like children". / www.thevictoria.net; 10 pm.

Viet Garden N1 £23 ❷❷④
207 Liverpool Rd 7700 6040 8–2D
With its "fresh and fragrant" food, "great-value" prices and
"very friendly family service", this "unpretentious" Islington local is,
for its fans, "the best Vietnamese this side of Hoxton". / 11 pm;
no Amex.

Viet Hoa E2 £22 ❸❸④
70-72 Kingsland Rd 7729 8293 1–2D
"Very tasty" Vietnamese food at "very affordable" prices wins
consistent praise for this grungy Shoreditch canteen; it still draws
a few "Hoxton trendies", but doesn't seem to be the vogue
destination it once was. / 11.30 pm.

Viet-Anh NW1 £17 ❸❶④
41 Parkway 7284 4082 8–3B
A "welcoming" but basic Camden Town café, where "freshly
cooked" Vietnamese fare is served in "large quantities". / 11 pm;
no Amex.

Vijay NW6 £26 ❷❷❸
49 Willesden Ln 7328 1087 1–1B
A Kilburn veteran that's "almost always crowded", thanks to its
"great" south Indian food and its "exceptionally friendly" service.
/ 10.45 pm.

Villa Bianca NW3 £46 ④❸❷
1 Perrins Ct 7435 3131 8–2A
This long-established Hampstead Italian is "always busy", thanks
not least to its "romantic" setting in an ultra-cute lane; reporters
differ on whether it's "consistently good" or "consistently average".
/ www.villabiancanw3.com; 11.30 pm; set weekday L £30 (FP).

Village East SE1 NEW £44 ❸④❷
171-173 Bermondsey St 7357 6082 9–4D
"Very NYC" in style, this interestingly-configured and (rather self-
consciously) "trendy" bar/restaurant is hailed by most reporters
as a "great addition" to Bermondsey; prices, though, give nothing
away. / www.villageeast.co.uk; 10.30 pm.

Villandry W1 £46
170 Gt Portland St 7631 3131 2–1B
Now under the same management as Hush, this once-celebrated
Marylebone deli is to emerge from a major refurbishment – as a
brasserie – around the publication date of this guide; it's difficult
to see how the newcomer can't be an improvement on what went
before. / www.villandry.com; 10.30 pm; closed Sun D; booking: max 12.

The Vine NW5 £31 ④⑤④
86 Highgate Rd 7209 0038 8–1B
Kentish Town's first gastropub is "resting on its laurels nowadays",
and continues to attract mixed reviews; it does have its good days,
though, and there's "a nice courtyard at the back".
/ www.thevinelondon.co.uk; 11 pm.

Vingt-Quatre SW10 £33 ④④❸
325 Fulham Rd 7376 7224 5–3B
"Just right for a casual meal at an odd hour" – this "trendy" 24/7
feature of the Chelsea 'Beach' is "good for breakfast at any time
of day". / www.vingtquatre.co.uk; no booking.

Vinoteca EC1 NEW £31 ❸❶❶
7 St John St 7253 8786 9–1B
"A great concept"; this "pioneering" new Clerkenwell "gem" offers
"the best-value wine list around", plus "gutsy" bistro cooking, in a
"cosy" and "buzzy" setting; "the only problem is that it's getting far
too popular". / www.vinoteca.co.uk; 10 pm; closed Sun; no Amex.

Vivat Bacchus EC4 £43 ❸❶❸
47 Farringdon St 7353 2648 9–2A
The "walk-in wine cellar" (showcasing "fabulous South African
wines") and "captivating" cheese room are highlights at this City-
fringe basement restaurant, whose "good balance between
formality and informality" suits it well for business; a ground-floor
wine bar is a recent addition. / www.vivatbacchus.co.uk; 9.30 pm; closed
Sat & Sun.

Volt SW1 £55 ❸❸❷
17 Hobart Pl 7235 9696 2–4B
"Nightclub-style décor" sets the scene at this Belgravia newcomer, which offers a clubby night out for thirtysomethings (and beyond); the cooking is of the "good but pricey" variety. / www.voltlounge.com; midnight; closed Sat L & Sun.

Vrisaki N22 £29 ❸④④
73 Myddleton Rd 8889 8760 1–1C
This meze-tastic Bounds Green taverna is notorious for its "enormous" portions; the food is not art, but it comes at "good prices". / midnight; closed Sun.

W'sens SW1 £55 ❸❸❷
12 Waterloo Pl 7484 1355 2–3C
"Superb" cuisine from new chef Clement Bonano is helping disarm early gripes about the "pretentious" style and "bills that spiral" at the Pourcel brothers' St James's yearling – the "potential is there for it to be a funky and extremely stylish dining experience". / www.wsens.co.uk; 11 pm; closed Sat L & Sun.

Wagamama £23 ④❸④
8 Norris St, SW1 7321 2755 4–4A
Harvey Nichols, Knightsbridge, SW1 7201 8000 5–1D
101a Wigmore St, W1 7409 0111 3–1A
10a Lexington St, W1 7292 0990 3–2D
4a Streatham St, WC1 7323 9223 2–1C
1 Tavistock St, WC2 7836 3330 4–3D
14a Irving St, WC2 7839 2323 4–4B
26a Kensington High St, W8 7376 1717 5–1A
The N1 Centre, Parkfield St, N1 7226 2664 8–3D
11 Jamestown Rd, NW1 7428 0800 8–3B
Royal Festival Hall, SE1 7021 0877 2–3D
50-54 Putney High St, SW15 8785 3636 10–2B
46-48 Wimbledon Hill Rd, SW19 8879 7280 10–2B **NEW**
Jubilee Place, 45 Bank St, E14 7516 9009 11–1C
1a Ropemaker St, EC2 7588 2688 9–1C
22 Old Broad St, EC2 7256 9992 9–2C
Tower Pl, EC3 7283 5897 9–3D
109 Fleet St, EC4 7583 7889 9–2A
30 Queen St, EC4 7248 5766 9–3B
For "a quick bowl" of "clean"-tasting noodles, these "fast and efficient" refectories – known for their "peak time queues" – remain a benchmark; most reporters feel they've "maintained standards over the years", but the ratings give some support to those who say they're in "gentle decline". / www.wagamama.com; 10 pm-11 pm; EC4 & EC2 closed Sat & Sun; no booking.

Wakaba NW3 £45 ❷④⑤
122a Finchley Rd 7586 7960 8–2A
"Unwelcoming", "tired" and "sparse" décor and an "uninviting exterior" have long been defining features of this Japanese veteran opposite Finchley Road tube; most reporters, though, still "love the food". / 11 pm; closed Sun.

The Walmer Castle W11 £30 ❸④❷
58 Ledbury Rd 7229 4620 6–1B
"Above a hectic Notting Hill boozer", this "spacious and attractive" dining room serves "reliable" and "reasonably-priced" Thai scoff. / 10.30 pm; closed weekday L.

sign up for the survey at www.hardens.com

Walnut NW6 £33 ❷❷❸
280 West End Ln 7794 7772 1–1B
This five-year-old "neighbourhood" spot in West Hampstead is hailed by locals as "a real gem", thanks to its "friendly" staff and its "interesting modern European-ish food". / www.walnutwalnut.com; 11 pm; closed Mon, Tue-Sun D only; no Amex.

Wapping Food E1 £46 ❸❸❶
Wapping Power Station, Wapping Wall 7680 2080 11–1A
With its "beautiful" and "dramatic" setting, this "funky" and "laid-back" former pumping station makes a "super-cool" destination (especially for brunch); the food is "good" too, but eclipsed by the "stonking" Aussie wine selection. / www.thewappingproject.com; 10.30 pm; closed Sun D.

The Waterloo Fire Station SE1 £36 ④⑤④
150 Waterloo Rd 7620 2226 9–4A
This "busy and bustling" bar/restaurant, by Waterloo, is an "interesting" site with lots of potential, but "bad" service and so-so, "pub-type" food make it no more than a stand-by nowadays. / 10.45 pm.

The Waterway W9 £37 ❸⑤❸
54 Formosa St 7266 3557 8–4A
A "chilled" and "contemporary" pub-conversion, which boasts an "excellent" terrace by Regent's Canal; the food – the summer BBQ in particular – is "great"… "when it finally emerges". / www.thewaterway.co.uk; 10.30 pm; booking: max 12.

The Well EC1 £38 ❸❸❸
180 St John St 7251 9363 9–1A
"Chilled" and "very reliable" – this Clerkenwell hang-out is "always packed" and "buzzy", thanks to the "real gastropub food" offered by its "regularly-changing menu". / www.downthewell.com; 10.30 pm.

The Wells NW3 £44 ❸❸❷
30 Well Walk 7794 3785 8–1A
"A very pretty spot by the Heath" sets the scene at this "friendly" Hampstead gastropub; a new chef arrived in spring 2006 – early reports suggest he is set to take the "satisfying" food up a notch. / www.thewellshampstead.co.uk; 10 pm; no Amex; booking: max 8.

Weng Wah House NW3 £32 ④④❸
240 Haverstock Hill 7794 5123 8–2A
"Better than average", or "westernised" and "nothing special"? – opinions divide on this long-established Belsize Park Chinese, which put in a more mixed performance this year. / www.wengwahgroup.com; 11.30 pm.

The Westbourne W2 £33 ❸④❶
101 Westbourne Park Villas 7221 1332 6–1B
"Hang with the chic crowd" at this "heaving" trustafarian hang-out, on the Bayswater/Notting Hill border; "if you can get a table" – especially on the "unmissable" summer terrace – the food "always hits the spot". / www.thewestbourne.com; 10 pm; closed Mon L; no Amex; need 4+ to book.

The Wharf TW11 £41 ⑤④❷
22 Manor Rd 8977 6333 1–4A

This "riverside" bar/restaurant boasts a "special location" – with a huge terrace – near Teddington Lock; even fans agree it's "pricey", though, and critics complain of "poor" food and "inexperienced" service. / www.walk-on-water.co.uk; 10 pm.

White Cross TW9 £23 ④④❷
Water Ln 8940 6844 1–4A

It's the "nice setting" – downstream of Richmond Bridge – which makes this large Young's pub (and beer garden) worth remembering; the food has no great aspirations, but dishes are "freshly prepared". / www.youngs.co.uk; 9.30 pm; closed Sat D & Sun D; no Amex; no booking.

White Horse SW6 £34 ❸❸❷
1-3 Parsons Grn 7736 2115 10–1B

The "Sloaney Pony" has a "great location" on Parson's Green (complete with terrace), an "extensive" range of ales and "very good wine"; foodwise, it's best-known for its "fantastic" summer BBQ, but the upstairs dining room has seemed "much improved" of late. / www.whitehorsesw6.com; 10.30 pm.

The White Swan EC4 £44 ❷❸④
108 Fetter Ln 7242 9696 9–2A

"Great food in a convivial, no-nonsense setting" isn't that easy to find on the fringes of the City, helping explain the high popularity of this "smart" second-floor dining room, above a Holborn pub; you can grab a bite in the bar too. / www.thewhiteswanlondon.com; 10 pm; closed Mon D, Sat & Sun.

Whits W8 £44 ❸❶❸
21 Abingdon Rd 7938 1122 5–1A

"Decent" food at "reasonable" prices is winning a wider following for this "improving" Kensington local, which is particularly distinguished by its "charming" and "personal" service. / www.whits.co.uk; 10.30 pm; closed Mon, Sat L & Sun.

William IV N1 NEW £32 ❸❸❸
7 Shepherdess Walk 3119 3012 8–3D

This all-white gastropub is a brave new venture, in an 'emerging' part of Hoxton; the food is not ambitious, but most reports confirm our early-days impression that it's pretty competent. / 10 pm; no Amex.

William IV NW10 £32 ④❸❷
786 Harrow Rd 8969 5944 1–2B

It has an "unlikely setting" – in distant Kensal Green – but this large boozer remains a popular destination (especially in summer, for the "lovely" garden); the new tapas format "pleasantly surprises" most reporters, but can also seem a bit "hit-and-miss". / www.williamivlondon.com; 10.30 pm.

Willie Gunn SW18 £36 ④④❸
422 Garratt Ln 8946 7773 10–2B

This "attractive" neighbourhood hang-out has long been a feature of Earlsfield life (especially for a "relaxing brunch"); some local reporters, though, now find it "disappointing" and "lazy". / 11 pm.

sign up for the survey at www.hardens.com

Wiltons SW1 £81 ❸❷❷
55 Jermyn St   7629 9955   3–3C
"Q. Why does this dinosaur survive? A. Because it's very good";
this "formal" clubland institution uses only "the finest produce"
(including "the best seafood in town"), cooked "without
complication" by the last of the 'old-time' Connaught chefs (Jerome
Ponchelle), and sold at prices verging on "ludicrous".
/ www.wiltons.co.uk; 10.30 pm; closed Sat & Sun; jacket required.

The Windmill W1 £33 ❸❸❸
6-8 Mill St   7491 8050   3–2C
"Award-winning pies" are the highlight of the "real British pub
grub" served at this admirably "old-fashioned" Mayfair hostelry;
it has "good beer too". / www.windmillmayfair.co.uk; 9.30 pm; closed
Sat D & Sun.

The Windsor Castle W8 £26 ❹❹❶
114 Campden Hill Rd   7243 9551   6–2B
With its marvellous "traditional" interior and "pleasant" walled
garden, this ancient "diamond" of a coaching inn, off Notting Hill
Gate, makes an enjoyable year-round choice; its pub fare
is somewhere between "good" and "average".
/ www.windsor-castle-pub.co.uk; 11 pm; no booking.

Wine Factory W11 £31 ❹❷❸
294 Westbourne Grove   7229 1877   6–1B
As with all John Brinkley's establishments, it is the "extremely good-
value wine list" which is the star at this "relaxed" Notting Hill pizza
parlour. / www.brinkleys.com; 11 pm.

Wine Gallery SW10 £31 ❺❸❷
49 Hollywood Rd   7352 7572   5–3B
John Brinkley's stalwart Chelsea hang-out is "always a winner" for
those who value its "bargain" wine, "fun" atmosphere and
"cute garden" – the food, though, is "distinctly average".
/ www.brinkleys.com; 11 pm; booking: max 12.

The Wine Library EC3 £24 ❺❷❶
43 Trinity Sq   7481 0415   9–3D
The "incredible wine list" (at "retail prices" and served
by "knowledgeable" but "unpatronising" staff) fuels a "great
atmosphere" in these interesting City vaults; the "basic" buffet
accompaniment (cheese, paté, etc) is incidental.
/ www.winelibrary.co.uk; 8 pm, Mon 6 pm; L & early evening only, closed
Sat & Sun.

Winkles E2 £38 ❷❷❺
238 Roman Rd   8880 7450   1–2D
"An excellent find in Bethnal Green" – a bare modern café where
"chatty" staff take "evident pleasure" in providing "simple" and
"beautifully fresh" fish and seafood; however, "it's not a place
to linger". / www.winkles.co.uk; 10.30 pm; closed Mon L.

Wizzy SW6 £34 ❷❺❺
616 Fulham Rd   7736 9171   10–1B
The "intriguing" Korean cooking at Wizzy Chung's brave Fulham
yearling is prepared "with obvious thought and care"; the ambience
"could use attention", though, and the "friendly" service can end
up "totally overwhelmed". / www.wizzyrestaurant.co.uk; 11.30 pm;
no Maestro.

Wódka W8　　　　　　　　　　　£42　❸❷❷
12 St Alban's Grove　7937 6513　5–1B
"Amazing" vodkas fuel the "fun" and "lively" atmosphere of this
"tucked-away" Kensington fixture, but the Polish cuisine – served
"with a flourish" – is "good and wholesome" too. / www.wodka.co.uk;
11.15 pm; closed Sat L & Sun L; set always available £26 (FP).

Wolfe's WC2　　　　　　　　　　£35　❸❸④
30 Gt Queen St　7831 4442　4–1D
"Delicious Kobe burgers" are the headline feature of the
"extensive" menu of this venerable, American-style Covent Garden
'family-restaurant'; "pity the atmosphere's so boring".
/ www.wolfes-grill.net; 11.45 pm, Sun 8.45 pm.

THE WOLSELEY W1　　　　　　£50　❸❷❷
160 Piccadilly　7499 6996　3–3C
"A smattering of celebs" add to the "vibrancy" of Messrs Corbin
and King's "magnificent" 'grand café', near the Ritz; for the
ultimate breakfast, afternoon tea or brunch it's "unbeatable" –
otherwise, the cooking is sometimes good, sometimes "shaky".
/ www.thewolseley.com; midnight.

Wong Kei W1　　　　　　　　　£20　❸⑤④
41-43 Wardour St　7437 8408　4–3A
It's worth running the gauntlet of the "manic" staff, the "shared
tables" and "hectic" ambience of this legendary Chinatown "dive" –
it offers "ample", "tasty" and "piping hot" scoff at "brilliant" prices.
/ 11 pm; no credit cards; no booking.

Woodlands　　　　　　　　　　£29　❶❷④
37 Panton St, SW1　7839 7258　4–4A
77 Marylebone Ln, W1　7486 3862　2–1A
12-14 Chiswick High Rd, W4　8994 9333　7–2B
102 Heath St, NW3　7794 3080　8–1A NEW
"Outstanding" Indian veggie fare – "from mild to spicy, from light
to filling" – is winning an ever more enthusiastic following for this
long-established but rather "soulless", chain.
/ www.woodlandsrestaurant.co.uk; 10.45 pm.

Wright Brothers
Oyster & Porter House SE1 NEW　£34　❶❷❶
11 Stoney St　7403 9554　9–4C
"A great new addition to Borough Market" – this "bustling" oyster
bar offers a "simple" but "perfect" formula of "immaculately fresh"
seafood, "good" wines and a "special selection" of ales, all served
by "keen" and "knowledgeable" staff. / 11pm, Sun 5pm.

Xich-lô EC1 NEW　　　　　　　£37　④❷④
103 St John St　7253 0323　9–1A
A large three-level Vietnamese newcomer in Clerkenwell (backed,
bizarrely, by a restaurateur from Oslo); service on our early visit
was charming, but we couldn't see anything in the formula that
would begin to attract enough customers. / Rated on Editors' visit;
11 pm; closed Sat L & Sun; no Amex.

XO NW3 NEW
29 Belsize Ln　Awaiting tel　8–2A
Will Ricker – he of E&O and Eight Over Eight – has yet to put
a foot wrong, so his first north London opening (on the site of the
former Belsize Tavern, RIP) should be one of the openings of late-
2006.

sign up for the survey at www.hardens.com

Yakitoria W2 NEW £46 ②③②
25 Sheldon Sq   3214 3000   6–1C
"They've really gone to town" on the sleek, "Bond-esque" décor of this "very out-of-the-way" new Japanese, by the canal in the new Paddington Basin development; the food (sushi, yakitori and more) is "delicious" and the cocktails "amazing", but the big question is: "will the Nobu and Zuma crowd make the trek?"
/ www.yakitoria.co.uk; 11 pm; closed Sat D & Sun.

Yas W14 £29 ④④⑤
7 Hammersmith Rd   7603 9148   7–1D
This small café, opposite Olympia, is best-known for being "alive" into the wee hours; its "traditional Persian food", though, can seem "too plain to be interesting". / 5 am.

YAUATCHA W1 £50 ①③②
Broadwick Hs, 15-17 Broadwick St   7494 8888   3–2D
"You only get 90 minutes, but the most delicious 90 minutes ever", say fans of the "heavenly morsels" on offer at Alan Yau's Soho dim sum phenomenon; opinions divide on whether to opt for the "groovy" cellar or the "airy" ground floor tea room (with its "amazing jewel-like cakes"); watch out for "pushy" service.
/ 11.45 pm.

Yelo £24 ③②③
136a Lancaster Rd, W11   7243 2220   6–1A
8-9 Hoxton Sq, N1   7729 4626   9–1D
This "cheap", "cheerful" and "friendly" Thai duo are praised by most, if not quite all, reporters for their "scrumptious" fare; (the Hoxton Square branch has some particularly nice alfresco tables). / www.yelothai.com; N1 11 pm, W1 10.30 pm; no booking.

Yi-Ban £29 ②③②
Imperial Wharf, Imperial Rd, SW6   7731 6606   5–4B
Regatta Centre, Dockside Rd, E16   7473 6699   11–1D
It's the East End branch of this oriental mini-chain – with its "superb dim sum at lunch time, and fantastic view of London City Airport across the docks" – which is most worth seeking out; its pricier year-old spin-off in Fulham (in a "sterile new development") seems "over-priced". / www.yi-ban.co.uk; 11 pm; SW6 closed Sun.

Yming W1 £33 ②①③
35-36 Greek St   7734 2721   4–2A
"All the more pleasant for being just outside the mad scrum of Chinatown" – Christine Yau's "refined" Soho Chinese not only provides "wonderfully considerate and charming" service but also many "unusual" and "memorable" dishes. / www.yminglondon.com; 11.45 pm; closed Sun; set pre theatre £17 (FP).

Yo! Sushi £28 ⑤④④
St Albans House, 57 Haymarket, SW1   7930 7557   4–4A
Harvey Nichols, Knightsbridge, SW1   7201 8641   5–1D
15 Woodstock St, W1   7629 0051   3–1B
Trocadero, 17 Rupert St, W1   7434 2724   3–3D
Selfridges, 400 Oxford St, W1   7318 3944   3–1A
52 Poland St, W1   7287 0443   3–1D
myhotel, 11-13 Bayley St, WC1   7636 0076   2–1C
Fulham Broadway Centre, SW6   7385 6077   5–4A
Unit 7 Paddington Station, W2   7706 9550   6–1C
Whiteley's, 151 Queensway, W2   7727 9392   6–1C
N1 Centre, 37 Parkfield St, N1   7359 3502   8–3D
02 Centre, 255 Finchley Rd, NW3   7431 4499   8–2A
Unit 3b Belvedere Rd, SE1   7928 8871   2–3D
95 Farringdon Rd, EC1   7841 0785   9–1A
"Novelty factor" makes them "a winner with the kids", but these
"pricey" conveyor-sushi joints are a pretty "poor excuse for
Japanese food". / www.yosushi.co.uk; 10 pm-11 pm; no booking.

Yoshino W1 £38 ❶❷④
3 Piccadilly Pl   7287 6622   3–3D
"In a gloomy alley", near Piccadilly Circus, this small outfit attracts
a clientèle largely composed of "Japanese nationals" with its
"wonderful sushi" and its "reliably excellent" other fare. / 10 pm;
closed Sun.

Yum Yum N16 £24 ❷❷❷
183-187 Stoke Newington High St   7254 6751   1–1D
"A great big welcome back!" to this "reincarnated" Stoke
Newington Thai (which has now – finally! – decamped to new
premises just around the corner); it can sometimes seem "too vast
and cold", but most reporters say this is a "stunning" destination,
with "fantastic" food. / www.yumyum.co.uk; 11 pm; no Amex.

Yuzu NW6 £34 ❷④④
102 Fortune Green Rd   7431 6602   1–1B
You don't pick this West Hampstead Japanese for its "cramped"
conditions or its variable service; its "fresh-tasting" noodles and
"great sushi", however, come at "cheap" prices.
/ www.yuzu-restaurants.com; 10.30 pm; D only, closed Mon.

ZAFFERANO SW1 £56 ❷❷❸
15 Lowndes St   7235 5800   5–1D
Recent expansion – "there's a new glitzy bit, as well as the old,
bricky part" – has made the setting of this famous Belgravian
"less cramped" than it used to be; it's long been hailed as "the best
Italian in London", but some reporters feel it's "slipped a notch"
in the upheaval. / www.zafferanorestaurant.com; 11 pm.

Zaika W8 £50 ❷❸❸
1 Kensington High St   7795 6533   5–1A
Sanjay Dwivedi's "incredibly creative" cooking wins rave reviews for
this converted banking hall, opposite Kensington Gardens – one of
London's top "nouvelle Indians"; the "spacious" setting
is somewhere between "stylish" and "soulless".
/ www.zaika-restaurant.co.uk; 10.45 pm; closed Sat L; set weekday L £30 (FP).

sign up for the survey at www.hardens.com

Zakudia SE1 £27 ❸❷❸
2a Southwark Bridge Rd   7021 0085   9–3B
It's no culinary hotspot, but this year-old bar – with its wonderful Thames views, good cocktail menu and generously priced selection of filling bar snacks – is a worthwhile budget option, near Shakespeare's Globe. / Rated on Editors' visit; www.zakudia.com; 11.30 pm; booking essential.

Zamzama NW1 £25 ❸④❸
161-163 Drummond St   7387 6699   8–4C
For its fans this high-tech curry house is "the best in Little India"; service "can be perfunctory" but the cuisine is "cheap", "varied" and "unusual". / www.zamzama.co.uk; 11.15 pm; closed Sat L & Sun.

Zen Central W1 £43 ❷❷❸
20-22 Queen St   7629 8089   3–3B
Opinions differ as to whether the stark, period-piece '80s décor of this grand Mayfair spot needs a make-over; in all other respects, however – including the quality of the "authentic" Chinese cuisine – commentary, though sparse, is invariably upbeat. / www.zencentralrestaurant.com; 11.30 pm.

ZeNW3 NW3 £37 ❸④④
83 Hampstead High St   7794 7863   8–2A
This striking '80s Chinese veteran, in the heart of Hampstead, has had its ups and downs over the years; it can still, on occasion, deliver "interesting", if "expensive", food, but feedback remains pretty mixed. / www.zenw3.com; 10.45 pm; no Amex.

Zero Degrees SE3 £27 ❸❸❸
29-31 Montpelier Vale   8852 5619   1–4D
"It's always difficult to choose between the bucket-sized moules-frites and the huge wood-fired pizzas" at this "chilled" but "buzzing" Blackheath microbrewery; "great home brews" too. / www.zerodegrees.co.uk; midnight.

Zero Quattro SW19 NEW £40 ❸❸④
28 Ridgway   8946 4840   10–2B
In Wimbledon – "an area incredibly lacking in 'proper' restaurants" – this "bright" and "cheerful" new Italian has made quite a splash; even fans, though, can find food standards a touch "variable". / www.zeroquattro.co.uk; midnight.

The Zetter EC1 £40 ④④❸
St John's Sq, 86-88 Clerkenwell Rd   7324 4455   9–1A
Leaving aside the "very decent brunch", the Italian food at this "chilled" Clerkenwell boutique hotel is "no better than OK" (and can be plain "bad") – how distant all that launch hype now seems! / www.thezetter.com; 11 pm.

Ziani SW3 £41 ❸❷❷
45-47 Radnor Walk   7352 2698   5–3C
"Mad chaos and joie de vivre" characterise the "great", "buzzy" atmosphere of this small Chelsea Italian "classic", where "owner Roberto is legendarily accommodating and kind". / www.zianiuk.com; 10.30 pm.

Zilli Fish W1 £52 ❸❸④
36-40 Brewer St 7734 8649 3–2D
"Great simple fish dishes" win quite a following for Aldo Zilli's *"lively"* Soho corner spot – *"a restaurant full of big flavours and fun"*; a much-needed refurb was completed as the survey was drawing to a close. / www.zillialdo.com; 11.30 pm; closed Sun.

Zimzun SW6 £30 ❸④❸
Fulham Broadway Centre 7385 4555 5–4A
For a quick bite near Fulham Broadway, you could do worse than this surprisingly OK oriental, in the shopping mall over the tube. / www.zimzun.co.uk; 10.30 pm.

Zinc £41 ④④④
21 Heddon St, W1 7255 8899 3–2C
11 Jerdan Pl, SW6 7386 2250 5–4A
Despite their handy locations (including just off Regent Street) and "pleasant" outside tables, these "straightforward" modern brasseries attract hardly any reporter feedback; such as there is proclaims them very "average". / www.conran.com; 11 pm, W1 Thu-Sat midnight, SW6 Fri & Sat 1 am; W1 closed Sun.

Zizzi £29 ④④❸
110-116 Wigmore St, W1 7935 2336 3–1A
33-41 Charlotte St, W1 7436 9440 2–1C
35-38 Paddington St, W1 7224 1450 3–1A
20 Bow St, WC2 7836 6101 4–2D
73-75 Strand, WC2 7240 1717 4–4D
194-196 Earl's Court Rd, SW5 7373 0126 5–2A
231 Chiswick High Rd, W4 8747 9400 7–2A
202-208 Regent's Park Rd, N3 8371 6777 1–1B
1-3 Hampstead Ln, N6 8374 0090 8–1B
87 Allitsen Rd, NW8 7722 7296 8–3A
35-37 Battersea Rise, SW11 7924 7311 10–2C
4-5 King St, TW9 8332 2809 1–4A
33 Westferry Circus, E14 7512 9257 11–1B
With its "lively" and "pleasant" branches and "very child-friendly attitude", this pizza-and-pasta group is a "favourite chain" for many reporters (rating similarly overall to stablemates PizzaExpress and Ask!). / www.askcentral.co.uk; 11 pm; some booking restrictions apply.

Zuccato £30 ④❸④
02 Centre, 255 Finchley Rd, NW3 7431 1799 8–2A
41 Bow Ln, EC4 7329 6364 9–2C
Arguably they are "soulless", but this funny Italian duo (in the City and a Finchley shopping mall) rarely inspire harsh criticisms, and make an "efficient" choice for an "informal" bite; pizza is the best bet. / NW3 11.30 pm, EC4 10.30 pm; EC4 closed Sat & Sun.

ZUMA SW7 £60 ❶❸❶
5 Raphael St 7584 1010 5–1C
"On a par with Nobu, and the whole experience is probably better"; this Knightsbridge hotspot continues to deliver *"amazing fusion food"* to a *"Eurotrashy"* clientèle, who are *"all tall, thin and beautiful"* – the bar in particular is *"jumping"*. / www.zumarestaurant.com; 11 pm; booking: max 8.

INDEXES

BREAKFAST
(with opening times)

Central
Amato *(8)*
Apostrophe: *Barrett St W1, Tottenham Ct Rd W1, WC2 (7)*
Asia de Cuba *(7)*
Atrium *(8)*
Baker & Spice: *all branches (7)*
Balans: *all branches (8)*
Bank Aldwych *(Mon-Fri 7, Sat & Sun 11.30)*
Bar Italia *(7)*
Benugo: *all central branches (7.30)*
Bistro 1: *Beak St W1 (Sun 11)*
Brasserie Roux *(6.30, Sat & Sun 7)*
The Brown's, Grill *(7)*
Café Bohème *(8)*
Café in the Crypt *(Mon-Sat 8)*
Caramel *(8)*
Carluccio's Caffè: *all central branches (8)*
Cecconi's *(7)*
Chez Gérard: *Chancery Ln WC2 (8)*
Christopher's *(Sat & Sun 11.30)*
The Cinnamon Club *(Mon-Fri 7.30)*
City Café *(6.30, Sat & Sun 7)*
The Club Bar & Dining *(10.30 am)*
Connaught (Angela Hartnett) *(7)*
Cork & Bottle *(11)*
Eagle Bar Diner *(Sat 10, Sun 11)*
Eat & Two Veg *(8, Sun 10)*
Exotika *(7.30)*
The Fifth Floor Café *(Mon-Sat 8)*
5 Cavendish Square *(8)*
Flat White *(8, Sun 10)*
Fortnum's, The Fountain *(8.30)*
Franco's *(Mon-Fri 7, Sat 7.30)*
La Fromagerie Café *(Mon 10.30, Tue-Fri 8, Sat 9, Sun 10)*
Fuzzy's Grub: *SW1 (7)*
Galvin at Windows *(7)*
Giraffe: *all branches (7.45, Sat & Sun 9)*
The Goring Hotel *(7)*
Homage *(Mon-Sat 9)*
Hush *(Mon-Fri 7.30)*
Indigo *(6.30)*
Inn the Park *(8)*
Jaan *(6.30)*
Konditor & Cook: *WC1 (9.30)*
Ladurée *(8)*
The Lanesborough *(7)*
Leon: *W1 (8)*
Loch Fyne: *all branches (9)*
Maison Bertaux *(8.30)*
Maison Blanc Vite: *W1 (8)*
Maroush: *V) 3-4 Vere St W1 (8)*
Mash *(8, Sat 11.30)*
Maxwell's: *WC2 (Sat & Sun 9.30)*
Mediterranean Kitchen: *WC2 (10)*
Mju *(7)*
Monmouth Coffee Company: *WC2 (8)*
Nicole's *(10)*
One-O-One *(7)*
Oriel *(8.30)*
Oscar *(7, Sat & Sun 8)*

Le Pain Quotidien *(7, Sun 9)*
Pasta Brown: *Bedford St WC2 (Mon-Sat 8)*
Pâtisserie Valerie: *all branches (7.30)*
Paul: *all central branches (7.30)*
Pearl *(6.30)*
The Portrait *(10)*
The Providores *(9, Sat & Sun 10)*
Providores (Tapa Room) *(9, Sat & Sun 10)*
Ranoush: *all branches (9)*
Refuel *(7, Sun 8)*
Rhodes W1 *(6.30, Sat & Sun 7)*
Rib Room *(7, Sun 8)*
RIBA Café *(8)*
Richoux: *all branches (8)*
The Ritz *(7, Sun 8)*
Royal Academy *(10)*
Serafino *(7)*
Simpsons-in-the-Strand *(Mon-Fri 7.30)*
06 St Chad's Place *(8)*
Sketch (Parlour) *(Mon-Fri 8, Sat 10)*
Sotheby's Café *(9.30)*
Spoon at Sanderson *(7)*
Square Pie Company: *W1 (10)*
Star Café *(7)*
Stock Pot: *SW1 (7); W1 (8)*
Tate Britain *(10)*
The Terrace *(8)*
Tootsies: *W1 (Sat & Sun 11)*
Truc Vert *(7.30, Sun 9.30)*
Tuttons *(9.30)*
The Union Café *(Sun 11)*
Villandry *(8.30)*
The Wolseley *(7, Sat & Sun 9)*
Yauatcha *(10)*

West
Abbaye: *SW7 (9)*
Adams Café *(7.30, Sat 8.30)*
Annie's: *all branches (Tue-Sun 10)*
Aquasia *(7)*
Aubaine *(8, Sun 9)*
Aziz *(8.30, Sun 9)*
Babes 'n' Burgers *(11)*
Baker & Spice: *all branches (7)*
Balans West: *all branches (8)*
Beach Blanket Babylon *(Sat & Sun 9.30)*
Beaufort House *(9.30)*
Bedlington Café *(8)*
Beirut Express *(7)*
Bistrot 190 *(Mon-Fri 7)*
Blakes *(7.30)*
Blue Kangaroo *(9.30)*
Bluebird Café *(8, Sun 10)*
La Brasserie *(8, Sat & Sun 9)*
Britannia *(10.30)*
Brunello *(7)*
Bush Garden Café *(8, Sat 9)*
Café Crêperie de Hampstead: *SW7 (10)*
Café Laville *(10)*
Carluccio's Caffè: *all west branches (8)*
Chelsea Bun Diner *(7, Sun 9)*
Chelsea Kitchen *(7.30)*
Chez Kristof (Deli) *(8)*

Cowshed *(Sat 9, Sun 10)*
Duke on the Green *(10)*
Ed's Easy Diner: *SW3 (Sat & Sun 9)*
Electric Brasserie *(8)*
11 Abingdon Road *(8)*
Fresco *(8)*
Ghillies: *all branches (10)*
Giraffe: *all branches (7.45, Sat & Sun 9)*
Gravy *(Sat & Sun 10)*
The Grove *(10)*
Hammersmith Café *(9)*
Harlem: *W2 (10.30)*
Hugo's: *all branches (9.30)*
I Thai *(7)*
Joe's Brasserie *(Sat & Sun 11)*
Joe's Café *(9.30)*
Julie's *(9)*
Julie's Wine Bar *(9)*
Langan's Coq d'Or Bar &
   Grill *(Sat & Sun 10.30)*
Leon: *SW3 (Mon-Fri 8, Sat 9, Sun 10)*
Lisboa Pâtisserie *(7.30)*
Loco Locale: *SW6 (Sat & Sun 11)*
Lucky Seven *(10)*
Lundum's *(9)*
Maroush: *I) 21 Edgware Rd W2 (10)*
Mediterranean Kitchen: *SW7, both
   W8 (10)*
Le Metro *(7.30)*
Mona Lisa *(6.30)*
Ottolenghi: *W11 (8, Sun 9)*
Pâtisserie Valerie: *all branches (7.30)*
Picasso's *(7)*
Ranoush: *all branches (9)*
Raoul's Café: *W9 (8.30); W11 (8.30,
   Sun 9)*
Richoux: *all branches (8)*
The Rocket *(Sat & Sun 10)*
Ruby Lounge & Sequoia Bar *(Sat
   & Sun 11)*
S & M Café: *all branches (7.30)*
Sam's Brasserie *(Sat & Sun 9)*
Shish: *all branches (Sat & Sun 10)*
Sophie's Steakhouse *(Sat & Sun 11)*
Stock Pot: *SW3 (8)*
Tartine *(11)*
The Tea Palace *(10)*
Tom's *(8, Sun 9)*
Tootsies: *SW7, W4 (Sat & Sun 10);
   SW6 (Sat & Sun 10.30); W11 (Sat & Sun
   9)*
Troubadour *(9)*
202 *(Sun 8.30)*
Vesbar *(Sat & Sun 9)*
Vingt-Quatre *(open 24 hours)*
White Horse *(Sat & Sun 11)*
Zinc: *SW6 (Sat & Sun 10)*

North

The Almeida *(9, summer only)*
The Arches *(11.30)*
Baker & Spice: *all branches (7)*
Banners *(9, Sat & Sun 10)*
Base: *NW3 (8)*
Café Mozart *(9)*
Carluccio's Caffè: *all north
   branches (8)*
Chamomile *(7)*
The Elk in the Woods *(10)*
Fifteen Trattoria *(7.30; Sun 9)*

Fig *(Sat & Sun 10)*
Florians *(Sat & Sun 11)*
Gail's Bread *(7, Sat & Sun 8)*
Gallipoli: *Upper St N1, Upper St
   N1 (10.30)*
Giraffe: *all branches (7.45, Sat & Sun 9)*
The Green *(Sat & Sun 11.30)*
Harry Morgan's *(11.30)*
Hugo's: *all branches (9.30)*
Kenwood (Brew House) *(9)*
Landmark (Winter Garden) *(7)*
Little Earth Café *(10)*
Mediterranean Kitchen: *N1 (10)*
Oriental City *(10)*
Ottolenghi: *N1 (8, Sun 9)*
Al Parco *(8)*
Pick More Daisies *(10)*
Richoux: *all branches (8)*
S & M Café: *all branches (7.30)*
Shish: *all branches (Sat & Sun 10)*
Strada: *N6 (9)*
Tootsies: *NW3 (Sat & Sun 10)*
Troika *(8.30)*
Zuccato: *NW3 (10.30)*

South

Amano Café *(7, Sat & Sun 9)*
Amici *(Sat & Sun 11)*
Annie's: *all branches (Tue-Sun 10)*
Balham Kitchen & Bar *(8)*
Bar du Musée *(Sat & Sun 11)*
Bar Estrela *(9)*
Bermondsey Kitchen *(Sat & Sun
   9.30)*
The Blue Pumpkin *(11.30)*
Boiled Egg *(9)*
Le Bouchon Bordelais *(10)*
Café Portugal *(6.30)*
Canyon *(Sat & Sun 11)*
Carluccio's Caffè: *SW15 (8)*
Le Chardon *(Sat & Sun 9.30)*
Delfina Studio Café *(8)*
Eco Brixton: *SW9 (8.30)*
Ferrari's *(10)*
Garrison *(Mon-Fri 7.45, Sat & Sun 8.45)*
Gastro *(8)*
Ghillies: *all branches (10)*
Giraffe: *all branches (7.45, Sat & Sun 9)*
Greenwich Park *(11)*
Hudson's *(10)*
The Inn at Kew Gardens *(7)*
Inside *(Sat 11)*
Joanna's *(10)*
Loch Fyne: *all branches (9)*
Monmouth Coffee
   Company: *SE1 (7.30)*
Mooli *(Sat & Sun 11)*
Putney Station *(Sat & Sun noon)*
Rapscallion *(10.30)*
El Rincón Latino *(Sat & Sun 11)*
Roast *(7)*
Scoffers *(10.30)*
The Table *(8 am)*
Tapas Brindisa *(Fri & Sat 9)*
Tate Restaurant *(10)*
Tate Café *(10)*
Tootsies: *SW19 (9); SW15, SW4 (Sat &
   Sun 10); SW11 (Sat & Sun 9.30)*
Tree House *(10)*

Trinity Stores (8, Sat 9, Sun 10)
El Vergel (8.30)
The Victoria (7)

East
Addendum (Brasserie 7)
Ambassador (8.30 am)
Apostrophe: all east branches (7)
Bar Capitale: all branches (6)
Benugo: all east branches (7.30)
Bleeding Heart (7 pm)
Bonds (7)
Brick Lane Beigel Bake (24 hrs)
Canteen (Sat & Sun 9)
Carluccio's Caffè: EC1 (10); E14 (8)
Chez Gérard: EC2, EC4 (8)
Club Mangia (7)
Comptoir Gascon (8)
Coq d'Argent (Mon-Fri 7.30)
Curve (Mon 6.30)
The Diner (8)
Epicurean Pizza Lounge (11)
Flâneur (8.30, Sat & Sun 10)
Fox & Anchor (7)
The Gun (Sat & Sun 10.30)
Hadley House (10)
Hilliard (8.30)
Hope & Sir Loin (7)
Leon: EC4 (7); E1 (8, Sun 10)
Lilly's (Sat & Sun 11)
Maison Blanc Vite: EC3 (7)
Malmaison Brasserie (7, Sat & Sun 8)
Nuvo (6.30)
Paternoster Chop House (Mon-Fri 10.30)
Pâtisserie Valerie: all branches (7.30)
E Pellicci (6.15)
Perc%nto (6.45)
The Place Below (7.30)
Prism (Mon-Fri 8)
Quadrato (6.30, Sat & Sun 8)
The Quality Chop House (Mon-Fri 7.30)
The Royal Exchange (8)
S & M Café: all branches (7.30)
St John Bread & Wine (9, Sat & Sun 10)
Scarlet Dot (Sun 10)
Shish: all branches (Sat & Sun 10)
Smiths (Ground Floor) (7)
Square Pie Company: E14 (7)
The Sterling (8)
Story Deli (9)
Terminus (7, Sat & Sun 7.30)
Wapping Food (Sat & Sun 10)
The Well (10.30)
The Zetter (7, Sat & Sun 11)
Zuccato: EC4 (8)

BRUNCH MENUS

Central
Amato
Aurora
The Avenue
Balans: all branches
Bank Aldwych
Boisdale
Boxwood Café

Brasserie Roux
Le Caprice
Caramel
Christopher's
Circus
City Café
The Fifth Floor Café
La Fromagerie Café
Fuzzy's Grub: SW1
Galvin at Windows
Giraffe: all branches
Hush
Indigo
Inn the Park
The Ivy
Joe Allen
Ladurée
The Lanesborough
Mash
The National Dining Rooms
Nicole's
Oriel
Pâtisserie Valerie: Marylebone High St W1, Old Compton St W1
La Perla: WC2
The Portrait
The Providores
Providores (Tapa Room)
Rainforest Café
RIBA Café
Serafino
Tootsies: W1
Villandry
The Wolseley

West
The Abingdon
Admiral Codrington
Aquasia
Aubaine
Balans West: all branches
Beach Blanket Babylon
Beaufort House
Bistrot 190
Blue Elephant
Bluebird
Bluebird Café
Bodean's: SW6
La Brasserie
Bush Bar & Grill
Cactus Blue
Café Laville
Chelsea Bun Diner
Cheyne Walk Bras'
Chez Kristof (Deli)
Chutney Mary
Cross Keys
The Crown & Sceptre
Duke on the Green
Electric Brasserie
The Enterprise
L'Etranger
First Floor
Giraffe: all branches
Gravy
Henry J Beans
Joe's Brasserie
Joe's Café

sign up for the survey at www.hardens.com

Le Gavroche
Gordon Ramsay at Claridge's
The Goring Hotel
Green's
The Greenhouse
The Guinea Grill
Hakkasan
Homage
Hush
Incognico
Indigo
The Ivy
Jaan
Just St James
Ken Lo's Memories
The Lanesborough
Langan's Brasserie
Lindsay House
Locanda Locatelli
Luciano
Mango Tree
Matsuri: *all branches*
Mirabelle
Miyama
Mon Plaisir
Mosaico
Neal Street
Nicole's
Nobu
Odin's
One-O-One
L'Oranger
Origin
Orrery
Le Palais du Jardin
Patterson's
Pearl
Pétrus
Pied à Terre
Quilon
Quirinale
Quo Vadis
Refuel
Rhodes W1
Rib Room
RIBA Café
Roka
Roussillon
Rules
Santini
Sartoria
Savoy Grill
Scott's
J Sheekey
Shepherd's
Simpsons-in-the-Strand
Six-13
The Square
Tamarind
Teca
Theo Randall
Veeraswamy
Il Vicolo
Wiltons
The Wolseley
Zafferano
Zen Central

West
Aubergine
Bibendum
Bluebird Club & Dining Rooms
The Capital Restaurant
Clarke's
1880
Gordon Ramsay
Launceston Place
The Ledbury
Poissonnerie de l'Av.
Racine
The Tenth
Tom Aikens
La Trompette
Zuma
North
Frederick's
Landmark (Winter Garden)
South
Blueprint Café
Butlers W'f Chop-house
Chez Gérard: *SE1*
Delfina Studio Café
Oxo Tower (Brass')
Oxo Tower (Rest')
Le Pont de la Tour
Roast
East
Addendum
Amerigo Vespucci
Aurora
Bar Bourse
Bevis Marks
Bleeding Heart
Boisdale of Bishopsgate
Bonds
Café du Marché
Caravaggio
Chamberlain's
The Chancery
Chez Gérard: *EC2, EC3*
City Miyama
The Clerkenwell Dining Room
Club Gascon
Coq d'Argent
Curve
Dine
The Don
Eyre Brothers
Gow's
Imperial City
Just Gladwins
Lanes
Malmaison Brasserie
Moro
1 Blossom Street
1 Lombard Street
Pacific Oriental
Paternoster Chop House
Plateau
Portal
Prism
Quadrato
Refettorio
Rhodes 24
St John

ENTERTAINMENT
(Check times before you go)

sign up for the survey at www.hardens.com

Jaan
(live music, Wed & Thu)
Joe Allen
(pianist, Mon-Sat; jazz, Sun)
Kai Mayfair
(harpist, Sat)
Kettners
(pianist, nightly; live music, Thu-Sat)
The Lanesborough
(dinner dance, Fri & Sat; jazz, Sun brunch)
Langan's Brasserie
(jazz, nightly)
Levant
(belly dancer, nightly)
Little Italy
(DJ, Fri & Sat)
Mamounia
(belly dancer, nightly)
Maroush: V) 3-4 Vere St W1
(music & dancing, nightly)
Mash
(DJ, Thu-Sat)
Mint Leaf
(DJ/jazz, Fri D)
Mirabelle
(pianist, Tue-Sat & Sun L)
Momo
(live world music, Tue & Wed)
Noura: Jermyn St SW1
(DJ, Thu-Sat)
Oscar
(film club, Sun)
Pigalle Club
(live music, nightly)
Pizza on the Park
(jazz, nightly)
Planet Hollywood
(DJ, nightly)
La Porte des Indes
(jazz, Sun brunch)
Quaglino's
(jazz, nightly; pianist, Sat & Sun brunch)
Rainforest Café
(nightclub, Thu-Sat)
Red Fort
(DJ, Thu-Sat)
Rhodes W1
(DJ, Thu-Sat)
Rib Room
(pianist, Mon-Sat)
The Ritz
(string quartet, Mon-Thu; live music, Fri & Sat)
Roka
(DJ, Thu-Sat)
Ronnie Scott's
(jazz, nightly)
Royal Academy
(jazz, Fri)
Sarastro
(opera, Sun & Mon D)
Sartoria
(pianist, Fri & Sat)
Savoy Grill
(pianist, nightly)
Simpsons-in-the-Strand
(pianist, nightly)
Sketch (Gallery)
(DJ, Fri & Sat)
Smollensky's: WC2
(pianist, Mon-Sat; jazz, Sun)
Soho Spice
(DJ, Fri & Sat)
Souk
(belly dancer, live music & DJ, Thu-Sat)
Taman gang
(DJ, Wed-Sat)

Thai Square: SW1
(DJ, Fri & Sat)
Trader Vics
(guitarist, nightly)
Volt
(DJ)

West
Aquasia
(singer & pianist, Mon-Sat; jazz, Sun)
Aziz
(belly dancer, Thu-Sat)
Azou
(belly dancer, Fri; live music, Sun)
Belvedere
(pianist, nightly)
Benugo: SW7
(jazz, Wed)
Big Easy
(live music, nightly)
Bombay Brasserie
(pianist & singer, nightly)
Cactus Blue
(DJ, Thu-Sat)
Café Lazeez: SW7
(classical music or jazz, Fri & Sat)
Chutney Mary
(jazz, nightly)
(Ciro's) Pizza Pomodoro: SW3
(live music, nightly)
The Collection
(DJ, nightly)
Cristini:
(jazz, Wed)
Da Mario
(disco, Wed-Sat; magician, Wed)
Deep
(DJ, Fri D)
1880
(pianist, nightly)
Frankie's: W4
*(magician, Thu-Sat); SW3
(magician, Wed, Fri & Sat)*
Harwood Arms
(quiz night, Tue)
Levantine
(belly dancer, nightly)
Lowiczanka
(live music, Fri & Sat)
Maroush: I) 21 Edgware Rd W2
(music & dancing, nightly)
Mr Wing
(jazz, Fri & Sat)
Nikita's
(Russian music, Fri & Sat)
Notting Hill Brasserie
(jazz, nightly)
Nozomi
(DJ, Tue-Sat)
Pacific Bar and Grill
(jazz, Sun)
The Prince Bonaparte
(DJ, Fri-Sun)
The Rocket
(DJ, Sun)
Ruby Lounge & Sequoia Bar
(DJ, Thu-Sun)
La Rueda: SW6
(live music, Tue)
606 Club
(live music, nightly)
Smollensky's: W6
(jazz, Sun)
Sticky Fingers
(magician & face painter, Sat & Sun)
Sugar Hut
(DJ, Fri & Sat)

Tugga
(DJ, nightly)
William IV
(DJ, Fri & Sat)
Zinc: *SW6*
(DJ, Fri & Sat; jazz, Sun L)

North
Cottons: *NW1*
(live music, Sun; DJ, Fri & Sat)
Don Pepe
(singer & organist, Fri & Sat)
Florians
(jazz, Sun D)
Fratelli la Bufala
(live classical singing, Thu-Sat)
Gilgamesh
(DJ, nightly)
Globe Restaurant
(drag cabaret, Thu)
The Haven
(jazz, Mon-Wed)
Hoxton Square Bar & Kitchen
(music, nightly)
Hugo's: *NW6*
(piano, Thu & Fri; jazz, Sun)
The Island
(DJ, Sun D)
Landmark (Winter Garden)
(pianist & musicians, daily)
The Living Room: *N1*
(live music, Thu-Sat, Sun L)
Mestizo
(DJ, Tue, Thu, Sat & Sun)
Shish: *NW2*
(DJ, Fri)
Silks & Spice: *NW1*
(live music, Sun & Thu)
Thai Square: *N1*
(DJ, Thu-Sat)
Troika
(Russian music, Fri & Sat)
Villa Bianca
(guitarist, twice weekly; pianist, Sat & Sun)
Weng Wah House
(karaoke, nightly)

South
Archduke Wine Bar
(jazz, Tue-Sat)
Balham Kitchen & Bar
(DJ, Fri & Sat)
Baltic
(jazz, Sun D)
Bengal Clipper
(pianist, nightly)
Cantina del Ponte
(live music, Thu)
Canyon
(jazz, Wed)
Ghillies: *SW18*
(jazz, Sun L)
The Gowlett
(DJ, Sun)
Grafton House
(DJ, Fri & Sat; jazz, Sun)
Greenwich Park
(jazz, Fri)
Harlem: *SW9*
(DJ, Mon-Sat)
The Hartley
(live music, Tue)
INC Bar & Restaurant
(DJ, Fri & Sat; bongo player, Fri & Sat)
La Lanterna
(live music, Fri)
Meson don Felipe
(guitarist, nightly)

Naked Turtle
(live jazz, Tue-Sat D)
Le Pont de la Tour
Bar & Grill
(pianist, nightly)
Rocket Riverside: *SW15*
(live music, Sun, Sept-June only)
La Rueda: *SW4*
(Spanish music & dancing, Fri & Sat)
The Spencer Arms
(live music every other Friday)
The Sun & Doves
(live music, Sun)
Tas: *The Cut SE1, Borough High St SE1*
(guitarist, nightly); Isabella St SE1
(live music, Mon-Sat)
Tas Pide
(guitarist, Mon-Sat)
Thai Square: *SW15*
(DJ, Fri & Sat)
Thailand
(karaoke, Mon, Thu-Sat)
Tree House
(live music, Tue)
The Waterloo Fire Station
(jazz, Fri)
Zakudia
(DJ, Thu-Sat; jazz, Tue)

East
Anakana
(DJ)
Aurora
(pianist, nightly)
The Bar & Grill
(live music, Thu; DJ, Fri)
Barcelona Tapas: *EC4*
(disco, Thu & Fri)
Bavarian Beerhouse
(accordian, Thu)
Bistrothèque
(transvestite show, Wed; cabaret, Wed-Sat)
Café du Marché
(pianist & bass, nightly)
Cat & Mutton
(DJ, Sun)
(Ciro's) Pizza Pomodoro: *EC2*
(live music, Mon-Fri; DJ, Sat)
Coq d'Argent
(pianist, Sat; jazz, Fri & Sun L)
Les Coulisses
(DJ, Thu-Fri)
$
(DJ, Fri & Sat)
The Drunken Monkey
(DJ, Wed-Sun)
Elephant Royale
(live music, Thu-Sat)
Epicurean Pizza Lounge
(DJ, Fri & Sat)
Green & Red Bar & Cantina
(DJ, Fri & Sat)
The Gunmakers
(quiz night, Sun)
Home
(DJ, Thu-Sat)
Lightship
(jazz, Mon & Wed)
LMNT
(opera, Sun)
Medcalf
(DJ, Fri)
1 Lombard Street
(jazz, Fri D)
Pacific Oriental
(disco, Thu & Fri)

Shish: *EC1*
(DJ, Thu & Fri)
Silks & Spice: *EC4*
(DJ, Thu & Fri)
Smiths (Ground Floor)
(DJ, Wed-Sat)
Smollensky's: *E1*
(DJ, Fri & Sat)
Sri Nam
(disco, Fri)
Thai Square City: *EC3*
(DJ, Fri)
Tokyo City
(karaoke, Thu & Fri)
The Trading House
(jazz, Fri)
The Well
(DJ, Fri)
Yi-Ban: *E16*
(live music, Fri & Sat)

LATE

(open till midnight or later as shown; may be earlier Sunday)

Central

Al Sultan
Asia de Cuba
Automat *(1 am)*
The Avenue *(midnight, Fri & Sat 12.30 am)*
Balans: *Old Compton St W1 (24 hours); Old Compton St W1 (5 am, Sun 1 am)*
Bar Italia *(open 24 hours, Sun 3 am)*
Beiteddine
Bohème Kitchen
Boulevard
Browns: *WC2*
Café Bohème *(2.45 am)*
Café du Jardin
Café Lazeez: *W1 (Fri & Sat 1.30 am)*
Café Pacifico
Le Caprice
Cecconi's
China Tang
Circus
The Club Bar & Dining
Cyprus Mangal
Le Deuxième
Dover Street *(2 am)*
Eagle Bar Diner *(Thu-Sat 1 am)*
Ed's Easy Diner: *both W1 (midnight, Fri & Sat 1 am)*
Fakhreldine
Floridita *(2 am)*
Gaby's
Garlic & Shots *(Thu-Sat 12.15 am)*
Gaucho Grill: *W1*
Golden Dragon
Greig's
Hakkasan *(midnight, ex Mon & Sun)*
Harbour City *(12.30 am)*
Hard Rock Café *(1 am)*
Ishtar
Itsu: *all central branches (Fri & Sat midnight)*
The Ivy
Joe Allen *(12.45 am)*
Just Oriental
Kazan
Kettners

Langan's Brasserie
Little Italy *(4 am)*
Maroush: *V) 3-4 Vere St W1 (12.30 am)*
Maxwell's: *all branches*
Melati, Gt Windmill St *(Fri & Sat midnight)*
Moti Mahal
Mr Chow
Mr Kong *(3 am)*
New Mayflower *(4 am)*
Nobu Berkeley *(2 am)*
Noura: *Jermyn St SW1, William St SW1 ; W1 (12.30 am); Hobart Pl SW1 (12.30am, Thu-Sat 1am)*
Original Tajines
Orso
Ozer
Le Palais du Jardin
Papageno
Pappagallo
Paradiso Olivelli: *all branches*
The Penthouse *(1 am)*
ping pong: *all branches*
Pizza on the Park
Planet Hollywood *(1 am)*
Quaglino's *(midnight, Fri & Sat 1 am)*
Ranoush: *SW1*
Ronnie Scott's *(1 am)*
La Rueda: *all branches (Sat & Sun midnight)*
Rules
Sarastro
Satsuma *(Fri & Sat midnight)*
Savoy Hotel (Banquette)
J Sheekey
Sketch (Gallery) *(Thu-Sat 2 am)*
Smollensky's: *WC2 (Thu-Sat midnight 12.15 am)*
Sofra: *all branches*
Soho Spice
Souk
La Spiga *(Wed-Sat midnight)*
Stock Pot: *W1*
Sugar Reef *(1 am)*
TGI Friday's: *all branches (Fri & Sat midnight)*
Tokyo Diner
Trader Vics *(12.30 am)*
Volt
The Wolseley
Yo! Sushi: *Poland St W1*

West

Alounak: *W14*
Balans: *W4, W8 ; SW5 (2 am)*
Beach Blanket Babylon
Beirut Express *(1 am)*
Best Mangal
Big Easy *(Fri & Sat 12.20 am)*
Bistrot 190
Blue Elephant
Buona Sera: *all branches*
The Cabin
Cactus Blue
Café Lazeez: *SW7 (12.30 am)*
Cheyne Walk Bras'
(Ciro's) Pizza Pomodoro: *SW3 (1 am)*
Ed's Easy Diner: *SW3 (Fri & Sat 1 am)*
Fairuz: *W2*

The Grove
Halepi
Harlem: *all branches (2 am)*
Henry J Beans
The Ifield
Kandoo
Khan's of Kensington *(Fri & Sat midnight)*
Khyber Pass
Lou Pescadou
Lowiczanka *(Sat 1 am)*
Maroush: *I) 21 Edgware Rd W2 (1.45 am); IV) 68 Edgware Rd W2 (12.30 am); SW3 (3.30 am)*
Meza *(1.30 am)*
Mohsen
Montpeliano
Monty's
Mr Wing
Il Pagliaccio
Papillon
Pasha
ping pong: *all branches*
Randa
Ranoush: *SW3 ; W8 (1.30 am); W2 (2.30 am)*
Rossopomodoro
Ruby Lounge & Sequoia Bar *(12.30 am, Fri & Sat 2 am)*
La Rueda: *all branches (Sat & Sun midnight)*
Saran Rom
Scalini
606 Club
Sticky Fingers
Sugar Hut *(1 am)*
TGI Friday's: *all branches (Fri & Sat midnight)*
Tugga *(1 am)*
Vingt-Quatre *(24 hours)*
Yas *(5 am)*

North
Ali Baba
Cuba Libre *(Fri & Sat midnight)*
The Fox Reformed *(Sat & Sun midnight)*
Gallipoli: *all branches (Fri & Sat midnight)*
Gaucho Grill: *NW3*
Istanbul Iskembecisi *(5 am)*
Izgara
Kovalam *(Fri & Sat midnight)*
Landmark (Winter Garden) *(1 am)*
Maxwell's: *all branches*
Le Mercury *(1 am)*
Mestizo
OQO Bar
Pasha *(Fri & Sat midnight)*
La Piragua
La Porchetta Pizzeria: *all north branches*
Rodizio Rico: *N1*
Sofra: *all branches*
Solly's Exclusive *(Sat 1 am)*
Tobia
Vrisaki

South
Balham Kitchen & Bar
Buona Sera: *all branches*

Firezza: *SW11*
Fujiyama
Gastro
The Gowlett
Hara The Circle Bar
Harlem: *all branches (2 am)*
Matilda's
Metro *(midnight, Fri & Sat 2 am)*
Mirch Masala: *all south branches*
Paradiso Olivelli: *all branches*
La Rueda: *all branches (Sat & Sun midnight)*
Sree Krishna *(Fri & Sat midnight)*
Zero Degrees
Zero Quattro

East
Barcelona Tapas: *EC4 (2.30 am)*
Brick Lane Beigel Bake *(24 hours)*
Cellar Gascon
(Ciro's) Pizza Pomodoro: *EC2 (midnight)*
$
Itsu: *Level 2, Cabot Place East E14 (Fri & Sat midnight)*
Lahore Kebab House
Mangal Ocakbasi
La Porchetta Pizzeria: *EC1*
Sofra: *all branches*
Vic Naylors *(12.30 am)*

OUTSIDE TABLES
(* particularly recommended)

Central
About Thyme
Al Hamra
Al Sultan
Albannach
Andrew Edmunds
Apostrophe: *Barrett St W1, WC2*
Archipelago
L'Artiste Musclé
Atrium
Auberge: *W1*
Aurora
Back to Basics
Baker & Spice: *SW1*
Balans: *Old Compton St W1*
Bam-Bou
Bank Westminster
Bar Italia
Benugo: *all branches*
Berkeley Square
Bertorelli's: *both W1*
Bistro 1: *Beak St W1, WC2*
Black & Blue: *W1*
Blandford Street
Bohème Kitchen
Boisdale
Boudin Blanc
Boulevard
Boulevard Bar & Dining Room
Brian Turner
Busaba Eathai: *WC1*
Café Bohème
Café des Amis du Vin
Café du Jardin
Café Emm

Base: *all branches*
Beach Blanket Babylon
Beaufort House
Bedlington Café
Belvedere
Benugo: *all branches*
Bibendum Oyster Bar
Big Easy
Black & Blue: *all west branches*
Bluebird Café
The Bollo House
Bombay Brasserie
La Bouchée
The Brackenbury
La Brasserie
Brinkley's
Brunello
The Builder's Arms
Bush Bar & Grill
Bush Garden Café
Cactus Blue
Café Crêperie de
 Hampstead: *SW7*
Café Laville
Café Lazeez: *SW7*
Cambio de Tercio
Chelsea Bun Diner
Chelsea Kitchen
Chez Kristof
Chez Kristof (Deli)
Cibo
Le Colombier
Coopers Arms
Costa's Grill
Crazy Homies
Cristini: *all branches*
The Crown & Sceptre*
Crussh: *W12*
Daphne's
De Cecco*
Deep
Devonshire House
The Dove
Duke on the Green*
E&O
Ealing Park Tavern
Edera
Electric Brasserie
Elistano
Esenza
Il Falconiere
La Famiglia
The Farm
Fat Boy's: *W5*
First Floor
Fishworks: *W4*
Frankie's: *W4*
Friends
The Gate
El Gaucho: *SW3*
Geale's
Giraffe: *all branches*
Glaisters
Gourmet Burger Kitchen: *W4*
Gravy
The Grove
Haandi

The Havelock Tavern
Henry J Beans
Hole in the Wall
Hosteria Del Pesce
Hugo's: *all branches*
I Thai
Indian Zing
Jim Thompson's: *SW6**
Joe's Brasserie
Joe's Café
Julie's
Julie's Wine Bar
kare kare
Karma
Ken Lo's Memories
Kensington Arms
Khan's of Kensington
The Ladbroke Arms
Latymers
The Ledbury
Lillo e Franco
Lisboa Pâtisserie
Locanda Ottoemezzo
Loco Locale: *SW6*
Lowiczanka
Luna Rossa
Lundum's
Ma Goa: *SW6*
Made in Italy
The Mall Tavern
Manicomio
Matriciano
Mediterranean Kitchen: *SW7, both
 W8*
Mediterraneo
Mika
Miraggio
Mohsen
Mona Lisa
Monza
Moroccan Tagine
Noor Jahan: *W2*
Notting Grill
The Oak
Old Parr's Head
The Oratory
Osteria Basilico
Osteria dell'Arancio
Pacific Bar and Grill
Il Pagliaccio
The Painted Heron: *all branches*
Papillon
Pappa Ciccia: *all branches*
Paradise by Way of Kensal
 Green
Parmigiano
Pâtisserie Valerie: *all west branches*
Pellicano
Père Michel
The Phoenix
Picasso's
The Pilot
Poissonnerie de l'Av.
Ognisko Polskie
Il Portico
Priory House
Queen's Head
Randall & Aubin: *SW10*

Solly's Exclusive
Somerstown Coffee House
Strada: *N1*
Tootsies: *NW3*
Troika
Viet-Anh
Villa Bianca
The Vine
Walnut
The Wells
Yelo: *N1*
Yum Yum
Yuzu
Zuccato: *NW3*

South
The Abbeville
Al Forno: *SW19*
Amano Café
Amici
The Anchor & Hope
Annie's: *all branches*
Antipasto & Pasta
Antipasto e Pasta
Arancia
Auberge: *all south branches*
The Aviary
Balham Kitchen & Bar
Baltic
Bar du Musée
Bar Estrela
Barcelona Tapas: *SE22*
Beauberry House
The Blue Pumpkin
Bodean's: *SW4*
Boiled Egg
Le Bouchon Bordelais
Bread & Roses
Brew Wharf*
The Bridge
Browns: *all south branches*
Brula
Buchan's
Buona Sera: *SW11*
Butcher & Grill*
Butlers W'f Chop-house
La Buvette
Café Portugal
Cantina del Ponte
Il Cantuccio di Pulcinella
Canyon
The Castle
Le Chardon
Chez Gérard: *SE1*
Chutney
Cinnamon Cay
The Dartmouth Arms
The Depot*
Dexter's Grill
Dish Dash
don Fernando's
Duke of Cambridge
Earl Spencer
Eco: *all branches*
Everest Inn
Fat Boy's: *W4*; *TW1*
Feng Sushi: *SE1*
The Fentiman Arms

Ferrari's
Fine Burger Company: *SW12*
Firezza: *SW11*
Fish Club
fish!
Four Regions
The Fox & Hounds
Franklins
The Freemasons
Fuego Pizzeria
Ganapati
Gastro
Ghillies: *SW18*
Giraffe: *all branches*
Gourmet Burger Kitchen: *SW11*
Gourmet Pizza Co.: *SE1*
The Gowlett
Greenwich Park
The Greyhound at Battersea
Hara The Circle Bar
Hot Stuff
Hudson's
The Inn at Kew Gardens
Joanna's
Kwan Thai
La Lanterna
The Lavender: *all branches*
The Light House
The Little Bay: *SW11*
Loch Fyne: *TW2*
Loco Mensa: *SE1*
Louvaine
Ma Cuisine: *all branches*
The Mason's Arms
Matilda's
Metro*
Mini Mundus
Mooli
Naked Turtle
Nancy Lam's Enak Enak
Newton's
Niksons
Nosh
Numero Uno
Ost. Antica Bologna
Oxo Tower (Brass')
Oxo Tower (Rest')
The Painted Heron: *all branches*
The Palmerston
Pappa Ciccia: *all branches*
Paradiso Olivelli: *SE1*
The Pepper Tree
Petersham Nurseries*
Phoenix
Pizza Metro
Pizzeria Castello
Le Pont de la Tour*
Le Pont de la Tour
    Bar & Grill
Popeseye: *SW15*
Prego
Putney Station
Ransome's Dock
Rapscallion
Ratchada
Real Greek Souvlaki & Bar: *SE1*
Riva

Riviera
The Rivington Grill
Rocket Riverside: *SW15**
RSJ
La Rueda: *all branches*
San Lorenzo Fuoriporta
Scoffers
The Sequel
Settle Inn
The Ship
The Spencer Arms
The Spread Eagle
Strada: *SW11*
The Sun & Doves
The Table
Tas: *The Cut SE1, Isabella St SE1*
Thai on the River
Thai Square: *SW15*
Thailand
Tootsies: *all south branches*
The Trafalgar Tavern
Tree House
Tsunami
El Vergel
The Victoria
The Waterloo Fire Station
The Wharf*
White Cross
Willie Gunn
Zero Degrees
Zizzi: *SW11*

East
Ambassador
Amerigo Vespucci*
Apostrophe: *EC2*
Arkansas Café
Armadillo
Bar Capitale: *all branches*
Benugo: *all branches*
Bevis Marks
Bleeding Heart
Browns: *E14*
Carluccio's Caffè: *all east branches*
Carnevale
Cat & Mutton
Chamberlain's
Cicada
(Ciro's) Pizza Pomodoro: *EC2*
Coach & Horses
Comptoir Gascon
Coq d'Argent
Curve*
$
The Eagle
Elephant Royale*
Epicurean Pizza Lounge
The Evangelist
El Faro*
La Figa
First Edition
Fish Shop
The Fox
Frocks
Gourmet Pizza Co.: *E14*
The Gun
The Gunmakers
Hadley House

Hawksmoor
Just The Bridge
Kolossi Grill
Leon: *EC4*
Lightship
Lilly's
The Little Bay: *EC1*
LMNT
Medcalf
Memsaheb on Thames
Meson los Barilles
The Morgan Arms
Moro
Namo
New Tayyabs
1 Blossom Street
Paternoster Chop House
Pâtisserie Valerie: *E1*
The Peasant
The Place Below
Plateau
La Porchetta Pizzeria: *EC1*
Quadrato
The Real Greek Souvlaki: *EC1*
Royal China: *E14*
The Royal Exchange
Royal Oak
Rudland & Stubbs
S & M Café: *E1*
Santa Maria de Buen Ayre
Santore
Scarlet Dot
Shish: *all branches*
Singapura: *EC2*
Smiths (Top Floor)
Smiths (Ground Floor)
Sofra: *EC1*
The Sterling*
Story Deli
Taberna Etrusca
La Tasca: *E14**
Vinoteca
Wapping Food
The Well
Winkles
Yi-Ban: *all branches*
The Zetter

PRIVATE ROOMS
**(for the most comprehensive
listing of venues for functions –
from palaces to pubs – visit
www.hardens.com/party, or buy
Harden's London Party, Event &
Conference Guide, available in all
good bookshops)**
* particularly recommended

Central
About Thyme *(45)*
Adam Street *(60,40,15)*
The Admiralty *(30, 60)*
Alastair Little *(25)*
Albannach *(20)*
Alloro *(16)*
Amaya *(14)*
Aperitivo *(35)*

Taberna Etrusca *(40)*
Tatsuso *(8)*
Les Trois Garçons *(10)*
Vinoteca *(30)*
Vivat Bacchus *(45)*
The Well *(70)*
Xich-lô *(40)*
Yi-Ban: *E16 (30)*
The Zetter *(10,50)*

ROMANTIC

Central
Andrew Edmunds
Archipelago
Asia de Cuba
Aurora
Bam-Bou
Bohème Kitchen
Boisdale
Boudin Blanc
Café Bohème
Le Caprice
Cecconi's
Le Cercle
Chor Bizarre
Clos Maggiore
Il Convivio
Crazy Bear
CVO Firevault
Diverso
Elena's L'Etoile
L'Escargot
L'Escargot (Picasso Room)
French House
Galvin at Windows
Le Gavroche
Gay Hussar
Gordon Ramsay at Claridge's
Gordon's Wine Bar
The Greenhouse
Hakkasan
Hush
The Ivy
Kettners
The Lanesborough
Langan's Bistro
Langan's Brasserie
Levant
Lindsay House
The Little Square
Locanda Locatelli
Mimmo d'Ischia
Mirabelle
Momo
Mon Plaisir
Nobu
Odin's
L'Oranger
Orrery
Pétrus
Pied à Terre
Pigalle Club
Pomegranates
La Porte des Indes
La Poule au Pot
The Ritz
Roussillon

Rules
St Moritz
Sarastro
J Sheekey
Souk
Souk Medina
Taman gang
Toto's
La Trouvaille
Vasco & Piero's Pavilion
Volt
The Wolseley
Zafferano

West
The Ark
Assaggi
Babylon
Beach Blanket Babylon
Belvedere
Bibendum
Blakes
Blue Elephant
La Bouchée
The Brackenbury
Brinkley's
Café Laville
Chez Kristof
Clarke's
Le Colombier
Daphne's
E&O
Eight Over Eight
La Famiglia
Ffiona's
Gordon Ramsay
I Thai
Julie's
Julie's Wine Bar
Launceston Place
The Ledbury
Lundum's
Maggie Jones's
Mediterraneo
Mr Wing
Nam Long
Nikita's
Notting Hill Brasserie
Osteria Basilico
Papillon
Paradise by Way of Kensal Green
Pasha
Patio
Pissarro's
Ognisko Polskie
Racine
The River Café
Star of India
Sugar Hut
Le Suquet
La Trompette
Tugga
Le Vacherin
Wódka
Zuma

North
Anglo Asian Tandoori

L'Aventure
La Cage Imaginaire
The Engineer
Fig
Frederick's
Gilgamesh
Mango Room
Le Mercury
Odette's
OQO Bar
Oslo Court
San Carlo
Sardo Canale
Villa Bianca

South
A Cena
Arancia
Bar du Musée
Beauberry House
Brula
Champor-Champor
Le Chardon
Chez Bruce
The Depot
Ditto
Enoteca Turi
The Glasshouse
Joanna's
Lobster Pot
Louvaine
Metro
Oxo Tower (Brass')
Oxo Tower (Rest')
Petersham Nurseries
Le Pont de la Tour
Ransome's Dock
Scoffers
The Spread Eagle
Tree House
Upstairs Bar

East
Bleeding Heart
Café du Marché
Club Gascon
Elephant Royale
Frocks
The Han of Nazz
Lightship
LMNT
Moro
Potemkin
Les Trois Garçons
Vertigo

ROOMS WITH A VIEW

Central
Fakhreldine
Foliage
Galvin at Windows
Inn the Park
The National Dining Rooms
Orrery
The Penthouse
The Portrait
The Terrace

West
Aquasia
Babylon
Belvedere
Café Laville
Pissarro's
The Tenth

South
Blueprint Café
Butlers W'f Chop-house
Cantina del Ponte
Carluccio's Caffè: SW15
The Depot
Ghillies: SW18
Gourmet Pizza Co.: SE1
Kwan Thai
Oxo Tower (Brass')
Oxo Tower (Rest')
The People's Palace
Le Pont de la Tour
Le Pont de la Tour
  Bar & Grill
Riviera
Rocket Riverside: SW15
Shakespeare's Globe
tamesa@oxo
Tate Restaurant
Thai on the River
Thai Square: SW15
The Trafalgar Tavern
Upstairs Bar
Zakudia

East
Coq d'Argent
Curve
Elephant Royale
The Grapes
Just The Bridge
Plateau
Rhodes 24
Searcy's Brasserie
Smiths (Top Floor)
Ubon
Vertigo
Yi-Ban: E16

NOTABLE WINE LISTS

Central
Adam Street
Andrew Edmunds
Arbutus
Bedford & Strand
Boisdale
Café des Amis du Vin
Camerino
Le Cercle
Cigala
Clos Maggiore
Connaught (Angela Hartnett)
The Contented Vine
Cork & Bottle
The Ebury
L'Escargot
The Fifth Floor Restaurant
Fino
Foliage

Fortnum's, The Fountain
La Fromagerie Café
Le Gavroche
Gordon Ramsay at Claridge's
Gordon's Wine Bar
The Greenhouse
Hardy's
The Ivy
Kai Mayfair
Locanda Locatelli
Mirabelle
Olivo
Orrery
Pétrus
Pied à Terre
The Providores
Quo Vadis
Roussillon
St Moritz
Savoy Grill
Shampers
Sotheby's Café
The Square
Tate Britain
Teca
The Union Café
Zafferano

West
Bibendum
Brinkley's
Brunello
Clarke's
Le Colombier
L'Etranger
Gordon Ramsay
Le Metro
The Oratory
Osteria dell'Arancio
Papillon
Racine
The River Café
Tom Aikens
La Trompette
White Horse
Wine Factory
Wine Gallery

North
Cru
Metrogusto
The Real Greek

South
Cantina Vinopolis
Chez Bruce
Enoteca Turi
The Glasshouse
The Greyhound at Battersea
Le Pont de la Tour
Putney Station
Ransome's Dock
Redmond's
Riva
RSJ
Tentazioni

East
Alba
Ambassador

Bleeding Heart
Cellar Gascon
Club Gascon
Coq d'Argent
The Don
Moro
Vinoteca
Vivat Bacchus
Wapping Food
The Wine Library

CUISINE INDEXES

An asterisk (*) after an
entry indicates exceptional
or very good cooking

AMERICAN

Central
All Star Lanes (WC1)
Automat (W1)
Bodean's (W1)
Christopher's (WC2)
Hard Rock Café (W1)
Joe Allen (WC2)
Maxwell's (WC2)
Planet Hollywood (W1)
Rainforest Café (W1)
Smollensky's (WC2)
TGI Friday's (W1, WC2)

West
Babes 'n' Burgers (W11)
Big Easy (SW3)
Bodean's (SW6)
Harlem (W2)
Lucky Seven (W2)*
PJ's (SW3)
Smollensky's (W6)
Sticky Fingers (W8)
TGI Friday's (SW6, W2)

North
Maxwell's (NW3)
Pick More Daisies (N8)

South
Bodean's (SW4)
Harlem (SW9)
Smollensky's (TW1)

East
Arkansas Café (E1)*
Christopher's In The City (EC3)
The Diner (EC2)
Missouri Grill (EC3)
Smollensky's (E1, E14)

AUSTRALIAN

Central
The Easton (WC1)*

South
Cinnamon Cay (SW11)*
Naked Turtle (SW14)

East
The Princess (EC2)*

BELGIAN

Central
Belgo Centraal (WC2)

West
Abbaye (SW7)

North
Belgo Noord (NW1)

East
Abbaye (EC1)

BRITISH, MODERN

Central
About Thyme (SW1)
Adam Street (WC2)
Alastair Little (W1)*
Andrew Edmunds (W1)
Atrium (SW1)
Aurora (W1)
The Avenue (SW1)
Axis (WC2)
Bank Aldwych (WC2)
Bank Westminster (SW1)
Bellamy's (W1)
Berkeley Square (W1)
Blandford Street (W1)
Brian Turner (W1)
British Museum (WC1)
The Brown's, Grill (W1)
Café du Jardin (WC2)
Le Caprice (SW1)*
The Club Bar & Dining (W1)
The Contented Vine (SW1)
The Cuckoo Club (W1)
CVO Firevault (W1)
Le Deuxième (WC2)
Ebury Wine Bar (SW1)
Embassy (W1)
The Fifth Floor Restaurant (SW1)
Footstool (SW1)
French House (W1)
Homage (WC2)
Hush (W1)
Indigo (WC2)
Inn the Park (SW1)
The Ivy (WC2)
Just St James (SW1)
Konstam at the Prince
   Albert (WC1)
The Lanesborough (SW1)
Langan's Brasserie (W1)
Lindsay House (W1)
The Little Square (W1)
Living Room W1 (W1)
Mash (W1)
Nicole's (W1)
Origin (WC2)*
Oscar (W1)
Patterson's (W1)*
Pigalle Club (W1)
The Portrait (WC2)
Quaglino's (SW1)
Refuel (W1)
Rhodes W1 (W1)
RIBA Café (W1)
Ronnie Scott's (W1)
Royal Court Bar (SW1)
Six-13 (W1)*
Sotheby's Café (W1)*
Tate Britain (SW1)
The Terrace (WC2)

Thomas Cubitt (SW1)
Tuttons (WC2)
The Union Café (W1)
Villandry (W1)
The Wolseley (W1)
Zinc (W1)

West
The Abingdon (W8)
Admiral Codrington (SW3)
The Anglesea Arms (W6)*
The Anglesea Arms (SW7)
Babylon (W8)
Beach Blanket Babylon (W11)
Belvedere (W8)
Bibendum Oyster Bar (SW3)
Bistrot 190 (SW7)
Bluebird (SW3)
The Bollo House (W4)
The Brackenbury (W6)*
Brinkley's (SW10)
Britannia (W8)
The Builder's Arms (SW3)
Bush Bar & Grill (W12)
Clarke's (W8)*
The Collection (SW3)
Coopers Arms (SW3)
The Crown & Sceptre (W12)
Devonshire House (W4)
The Dove (W6)
Duke on the Green (SW6)
Ealing Park Tavern (W5)
1880 (SW7)
11 Abingdon Road (W8)
The Farm (SW6)
First Floor (W11)
Formosa Dining Room (W9)
The Frontline Club (W2)
Gravy (W4)
Harwood Arms (SW6)
The Havelock Tavern (W14)*
High Road Brasserie (W4)
Hole in the Wall (W4)
The Ifield (SW10)
Island (W2)
Joe's Brasserie (SW6)
Joe's Café (SW3)
Julie's (W11)
Julie's Wine Bar (W11)
Kensington Place (W8)
The Ladbroke Arms (W11)*
Launceston Place (W8)
Lots Road (SW10)
The Mall Tavern (W8)
Le Metro (SW3)
Notting Hill Brasserie (W11)*
The Oratory (SW3)
Pacific Bar and Grill (W6)
Paradise by Way of Kensal
   Green (W10)
The Phoenix (SW3)
The Pig's Ear (SW3)
The Pilot (W4)
Pissarro's (W4)
PJ's (SW3)

The Prince Bonaparte (W2)*
Raoul's Café (W9)
The Rocket (W3)
Ruby Lounge & Sequoia
   Bar (W11)
The Salisbury Tavern (SW6)
Sam's Brasserie (W4)
Snows on the Green (W6)*
Sophie's Steakhouse (SW10)
Stone Mason's Arms (W6)
The Tea Palace (W11)
The Tenth (W8)
The Thatched House (W6)
Tom's Kitchen (SW3)
Vingt-Quatre (SW10)
The Waterway (W9)
The Westbourne (W2)
White Horse (SW6)
Whits (W8)

North
The Barnsbury (N1)*
Bastille (N1)
Bradley's (NW3)
The Bull (N6)
Café Med (NW8)
The Chapel (NW1)
Crown & Goose (NW1)
The Drapers Arms (N1)
The Duke of Cambridge (N1)
The Elk in the Woods (N1)
The Engineer (NW1)*
Fig (N1)
Frederick's (N1)
Freemasons Arms (NW3)
The Garden Café (NW1)
Globe Restaurant (NW3)
The Green (NW2)
The Greyhound (NW10)
The Haven (N20)
The Hill (NW3)
Holly Bush (NW3)
The House (N1)
The Island (NW10)*
The Junction Tavern (NW5)
The Lansdowne (NW1)
The Lock Dining Bar (N17)*
The Lord Palmerston (NW5)*
Mango Room (NW1)*
Mosaica (N22)*
No 77 Wine Bar (NW6)
The Northgate (N1)
Odette's (NW1)
The Pumphouse (N8)
Roundhouse Café (NW1)
The Vine (NW5)
Walnut (NW6)*
The Wells (NW3)
William IV (N1)
Landmark (Winter
   Garden) (NW1)

South
The Abbeville (SW4)
Alma (SW18)

Archduke Wine Bar (SE1)
The Aviary (SW20)
Balham Kitchen & Bar (SW12)
Bankside (SE1)
The Blue Pumpkin (SW17)
Blueprint Café (SE1)
Bread & Roses (SW4)
The Bridge (SW13)
Buchan's (SW11)
Cantina Vinopolis (SE1)
Canyon (TW10)
The Castle (SW11)
Chapter Two (SE3)*
Chez Bruce (SW17)*
The Dartmouth Arms (SE23)
The Depot (SW14)
Ditto (SW18)*
Earl Spencer (SW18)*
The Fentiman Arms (SW8)
The Fire Stables (SW19)
Franklins (SE22)*
The Freemasons (SW18)
Garrison (SE1)
The Glasshouse (TW9)*
Grafton House (SW4)
Greenwich Park (SE10)
The Greyhound at
   Battersea (SW11)
The Hartley (SE1)
INC Bar & Restaurant (SE10)
The Inn at Kew Gardens (TW9)
Inside (SE10)*
Kew Grill (TW9)*
Lamberts (SW12)*
The Lavender (SE11, SW11, SW9)
The Mason's Arms (SW8)
Menier Chocolate Factory (SE1)
Mezzanine (SE1)
Oxo Tower (Rest') (SE1)
The Palmerston (SE22)*
The People's Palace (SE1)
Petersham Nurseries (TW10)
Phoenix (SW15)*
Le Pont de la Tour (SE1)
Ransome's Dock (SW11)
Redmond's (SW14)
The Rivington Grill (SE10)
RSJ (SE1)
Scoffers (SW11)
The Sea Cow (SE22)*
Shakespeare's Globe (SE1)
Sonny's (SW13)
The Spencer Arms (SW15)
The Sun & Doves (SE5)
The Table (SE1)*
tamesa@oxo (SE1)
The Trafalgar Tavern (SE10)
Tree House (SW13)
Trinity (SW4)
The Victoria (SW14)
The Waterloo Fire Station (SE1)
The Wharf (TW11)
Willie Gunn (SW18)

East
Addendum (EC3)
Ambassador (EC1)
Bankside (EC2)
The Bar & Grill (EC1)
Bar Bourse (EC4)
Bevis Marks (EC3)*
Bistrothèque (E2)
Bleeding Heart (EC1)*
Cat & Mutton (E8)
The Chancery (EC4)*
Club Mangia (EC4)
Coach & Horses (EC1)*
The Don (EC4)*
The Evangelist (EC4)
The Fox (EC2)
Frocks (E9)
Gow's (EC2)
The Gun (E14)
The Gunmakers (EC1)
Hadley House (E11)
Hilliard (EC4)*
Home (EC2)*
Just Gladwins (EC3)
Just The Bridge (EC4)
Lanes (E1)
LMNT (E8)
Medcalf (EC1)*
The Morgan Arms (E3)*
Moro (EC1)*
1 Lombard Street (EC3)
The Peasant (EC1)
Prism (EC3)
The Quality Chop House (EC1)
Rhodes 24 (EC2)
The Rivington Grill (EC2)*
Royal Oak (E2)
Searcy's Brasserie (EC2)
Smiths (Top Floor) (EC1)*
Smiths (Ground Floor) (EC1)
The Sterling (EC3)
Terminus (EC2)
The Trading House (EC1)
Vic Naylors (EC1)
Vinoteca (EC1)
Wapping Food (E1)
The Well (EC1)
The White Swan (EC4)*

BRITISH, TRADITIONAL

Central
Boisdale (SW1)
Boxwood Café (SW1)
Brian Turner (W1)
Chimes (SW1)
Dorchester Grill (W1)
The Endurance (W1)
Fortnum's, The Fountain (W1)
Fuzzy's Grub (SW1)*
Gordon's Wine Bar (WC2)
The Goring Hotel (SW1)
Green's (SW1)
Greig's (W1)

Grenadier *(SW1)*
The Guinea Grill *(W1)**
Mews of Mayfair *(W1)*
The National Dining
   Rooms *(WC2)*
Odin's *(W1)*
Porters English
   Restaurant *(WC2)*
Rib Room *(SW1)*
Rules *(WC2)*
Savoy Grill *(WC2)*
Shepherd's *(SW1)*
Simpsons-in-the-Strand *(WC2)*
Square Pie Company *(W1)**
Wiltons *(SW1)*
The Windmill *(W1)*

West
Bluebird Club & Dining
   Rooms *(SW3)*
Ffiona's *(W8)*
Kensington Arms *(W8)*
Maggie Jones's *(W8)*
Le Metro *(SW3)*
Queen's Head *(W6)*
S & M Café *(W10)*
The Windsor Castle *(W8)*

North
The Marquess Tavern *(N1)*
S & M Café *(N1)*
St Johns *(N19)*
Two Brothers *(N3)**

South
The Anchor & Hope *(SE1)**
Browns *(SE1)*
Butlers W'f Chop-house *(SE1)*
Roast *(SE1)*
Settle Inn *(SW11)*
The Trafalgar Tavern *(SE10)*

East
Boisdale of Bishopsgate *(EC2)*
Canteen *(E1)*
Fox & Anchor *(EC1)*
Fuzzy's Grub *(EC4)**
George & Vulture *(EC3)*
Hope & Sir Loin *(EC1)*
Ye Olde Cheshire Cheese *(EC4)*
Paternoster Chop House *(EC4)*
The Quality Chop House *(EC1)*
S & M Café *(E1)*
St John *(EC1)**
St John Bread & Wine *(E1)**
Simpson's Tavern *(EC3)*
Square Pie Company *(E1, E14)**
Sweetings *(EC4)**
The Wine Library *(EC3)*

DANISH

West
Lundum's *(SW7)**

EAST & CENT. EUROPEAN

Central
Gay Hussar *(W1)*
The Wolseley *(W1)*

North
Café Mozart *(N6)*
Troika *(NW1)*

FISH & SEAFOOD

Central
Back to Basics *(W1)**
Belgo Centraal *(WC2)*
Bentley's *(W1)**
Café Fish *(W1)*
The Ebury *(SW1)*
Fishworks *(W1)**
Fung Shing *(WC2)**
Green's *(SW1)*
Livebait *(WC2)*
Loch Fyne *(WC2)*
Manzi's *(WC2)*
One-O-One *(SW1)**
Le Palais du Jardin *(WC2)*
Quaglino's *(SW1)*
Randall & Aubin *(W1)**
Rib Room *(SW1)*
Scott's *(W1)*
Seafresh *(SW1)*
J Sheekey *(WC2)**
Wiltons *(SW1)*
Zilli Fish *(W1)*

West
Big Easy *(SW3)*
The Cow *(W2)**
Deep *(SW6)*
Fish Hook *(W4)**
Fishworks *(W4)**
Ghillies *(SW6)*
Hosteria Del Pesce *(SW6)*
Lou Pescadou *(SW5)**
Mandarin Kitchen *(W2)**
Poissonnerie de l'Av. *(SW3)**
Stratford's *(W8)**
Le Suquet *(SW3)**

North
Belgo Noord *(NW1)*
Bradley's *(NW3)*
Chez Liline *(N4)**
Fishworks *(N1, NW1)**
Hoxton Square Bar &
   Kitchen *(N1)*
Nautilus *(NW6)**
Pescador Too *(NW3)*
Sargasso Sea *(N21)**

South
Balham Kitchen & Bar *(SW12)*
Fish Club *(SW11)**
fish! *(SE1)*
Fishworks *(TW9)**
Gastro *(SW4)*
Ghillies *(SW18)*

Livebait (SE1)
Lobster Pot (SE11)*
Loch Fyne (TW2)
Matilda's (SW11)
Le Pont de la Tour
   Bar & Grill (SE1)
Tas Ev (SE1)
Wright Brothers (SE1)*

East
Chamberlain's (EC3)
Curve (E14)
The Evangelist (EC4)
Fish Central (EC1)
Fish Shop (EC1)
Fishmarket (EC2)
Gow's (EC2)
The Grapes (E14)*
Rudland & Stubbs (EC1)
Sweetings (EC4)*
Vertigo (EC2)
Winkles (E2)*

FRENCH

Central
The Admiralty (WC2)
Annex 3 (W1)
Arbutus (W1)*
L'Artiste Musclé (W1)
L'Atelier de Robuchon (WC2)
Auberge (W1)
Bellamy's (W1)
Beotys (WC2)
Berkeley Square (W1)
Boudin Blanc (W1)
Brasserie Roux (SW1)
Café Bagatelle (W1)
Café Bohème (W1)
Café des Amis du Vin (WC2)
Le Cercle (SW1)*
Chez Gérard (SW1, W1, WC2)
Circus (W1)
Clos Maggiore (WC2)
Dover Street (W1)
Drones (SW1)
The Ebury (SW1)
Elena's L'Etoile (W1)
L'Entrecôte Café de Paris (W1)
L'Escargot (W1)*
L'Escargot (Picasso Room) (W1)
L'Estaminet (WC2)
Foliage (SW1)*
Gabrielles (W1)
Galvin at Windows (W1)*
Galvin Bistrot de Luxe (W1)*
Le Gavroche (W1)*
Gordon Ramsay at
   Claridge's (W1)
The Greenhouse (W1)
Incognico (WC2)
Ladurée (SW1)
Langan's Bistro (W1)
maze (W1)*
Mirabelle (W1)

Mju (SW1)
Mon Plaisir (WC2)
La Noisette (SW1)
L'Oranger (SW1)
Orrery (W1)
Le Pain Quotidien (W1)*
Le Palais du Jardin (WC2)
Pearl (WC1)
Pétrus (SW1)*
Pied à Terre (W1)*
La Poule au Pot (SW1)
Randall & Aubin (W1)*
Le Relais de Venise (W1)
The Ritz (W1)
Roussillon (SW1)*
Sketch (Lecture Rm) (W1)
Sketch (Gallery) (W1)
Sketch (Glade) (W1)
The Square (W1)*
La Trouvaille (W1)
Villandry (W1)
W'sens (SW1)

West
Aubaine (SW3)
Aubergine (SW10)*
Base (SW3)
Belvedere (W8)
Bibendum (SW3)
La Bouchée (SW7)*
La Brasserie (SW3)
Brasserie St Quentin (SW3)
Café Crêperie de
   Hampstead (SW7)*
The Capital Restaurant (SW3)*
Charlotte's Place (W5)
Cheyne Walk Bras' (SW3)
Chez Kristof (W6)
Le Colombier (SW3)
Ealing Park Tavern (W5)
1880 (SW7)
11 Abingdon Road (W8)
L'Etranger (SW7)*
Fish Hook (W4)*
Gordon Ramsay (SW3)*
Langan's Coq d'Or Bar &
   Grill (SW5)
The Ledbury (W11)*
Lou Pescadou (SW5)*
Nathalie (SW3)*
Notting Hill Brasserie (W11)*
Papillon (SW3)
Père Michel (W2)
Poissonnerie de l'Av. (SW3)*
Racine (SW3)*
Randall & Aubin (SW10)*
Le Suquet (SW3)*
Tartine (SW3)
Tom Aikens (SW3)
La Trompette (W4)*
Le Vacherin (W4)*
Whits (W8)

North
The Almeida (N1)

Les Associés (N8)*
L'Aventure (NW8)*
Base (NW1, NW3)
Bastille (N1)
Bistro Aix (N8)
Bradley's (NW3)
The Bull (N6)
Café Crêperie de
  Hampstead (NW3)*
La Cage Imaginaire (NW3)
Le Mercury (N1)
Morgan M (N7)*
Oslo Court (NW8)*
Le Petit Auberge (N1)
Le Petit Train (NW1)
Le Sacré-Coeur (N1)
Somerstown Coffee
  House (NW1)
The Wells (NW3)

South
Auberge (SE1)
Bar du Musée (SE10)
Le Bouchon Bordelais (SW11)*
La Brasserie Ma Cuisine (TW1)
Brew Wharf (SE1)
Brula (TW1)*
La Buvette (TW9)*
Le Chardon (SE22)*
Chez Gérard (SE1)
Chez Lindsay (TW10)
Emile's (SW15)
The Food Room (SW8)*
Gastro (SW4)
Louvaine (SW11)
Ma Cuisine (TW1, TW9)
Mini Mundus (SW17)
Morel (SW4)
Niksons (SW11)
Old Vic Brasserie (SE1)
Rick's Café (SW17)*
Riviera (SE1)
The Spread Eagle (SE10)

East
Auberge (EC3)
Aurora (EC2)
Bistrothèque (E2)
Bleeding Heart (EC1)*
Café du Marché (EC1)*
Cellar Gascon (EC1)*
Chez Gérard (EC2, EC3, EC4)
Club Gascon (EC1)*
Comptoir Gascon (EC1)*
Coq d'Argent (EC3)
Les Coulisses (EC2)
Dans le Noir (EC1)
Dine (EC4)
First Edition (E14)
The Gun (E14)
Malmaison Brasserie (EC1)
Plateau (E14)
Le Rendezvous du Café (EC1)*
Rosemary Lane (E1)*
The Royal Exchange (EC3)

Le Saint Julien (EC1)
Sauterelle (EC3)
The Trading House (EC1)
Les Trois Garçons (E1)

FUSION

Central
Archipelago (W1)*
Asia de Cuba (WC2)
Bam-Bou (W1)
CVO Firevault (W1)
Eddalino (W1)
Jaan (WC2)*
Mju (SW1)
Nobu (W1)*
Nobu Berkeley (W1)
The Providores (W1)
Providores (Tapa Room) (W1)*
Spoon at Sanderson (W1)

West
Aquasia (SW10)
I Thai (W2)

North
Hoxton Square Bar &
  Kitchen (N1)
Queen's Head &
  Artichoke (NW1)

South
Beauberry House (SE21)
Champor-Champor (SE1)*
Cinnamon Cay (SW11)*
Rapscallion (SW4)
Silka (SE1)
Tsunami (SW4)*
Village East (SE1)

East
First Edition (E14)
Ubon (E14)*

GAME

Central
Boisdale (SW1)
Dorchester Grill (W1)
Rules (WC2)
Wiltons (SW1)

North
San Daniele (N5)

East
Boisdale of Bishopsgate (EC2)
Gow's (EC2)

GERMAN

East
Bavarian Beerhouse (EC1)

GREEK

Central
Beotys (WC2)

Real Greek Souvlaki & Bar (W1, WC2)

West
As Greek As It Gets (SW5)
Costa's Grill (W8)
Halepi (W2)

North
Daphne (NW1)
Lemonia (NW1)
The Real Greek (N1)
Vrisaki (N22)

South
Real Greek Souvlaki & Bar (SW15)
Real Greek Souvlaki & Bar (SE1)

East
Kolossi Grill (EC1)
The Real Greek Souvlaki (EC1)

HUNGARIAN

Central
Gay Hussar (W1)

INTERNATIONAL

Central
Balans (W1)
Bedford & Strand (WC2)
Bohème Kitchen (W1)
Boulevard (WC2)
Boulevard Bar & Dining Room (W1)
Browns (W1, WC2)
Café Emm (W1)
Café in the Crypt (WC2)
City Café (SW1)
Cork & Bottle (WC2)
Eat & Two Veg (W1)
Exotika (WC2)*
Garlic & Shots (W1)
Giraffe (W1)
Gordon's Wine Bar (WC2)
Grumbles (SW1)
Hardy's (W1)
Michael Moore (W1)
Motcombs (SW1)
O'Conor Don (W1)
Oriel (SW1)
Papageno (WC2)
Pomegranates (SW1)
Running Horse (W1)
Sarastro (WC2)
Savoy Hotel (Banquette) (WC2)
Seven Stars (WC2)
Shampers (W1)
Star Café (W1)
Stock Pot (SW1, W1)
Sugar Reef (W1)
Tiger Tiger (SW1)

West
Annie's (W4)
Balans West (SW5, W4, W8)

Beaufort House (SW3)
Blakes (SW7)
Blue Kangaroo (SW6)
The Cabin (SW6)
Café Laville (W2)
Chelsea Bun Diner (SW10)
Chelsea Kitchen (SW3)
Coopers Arms (SW3)
Cowshed (W11)
Electric Brasserie (W11)
The Enterprise (SW3)
Foxtrot Oscar (SW3)
The Gate (W6)*
Giraffe (W4, W8)
Glaisters (SW10)
Mona Lisa (SW10)
The Scarsdale (W8)
606 Club (SW10)
Stock Pot (SW3)
The Swag & Tails (SW7)
202 (W11)
Vesbar (W12)
The Windsor Castle (W8)
Wine Gallery (SW10)
Zinc (SW6)

North
The Arches (NW6)
Banners (N8)
Browns (N1)
The Fox Reformed (N16)
Giraffe (N1, NW3)
The Haven (N20)
Hoxton Apprentice (N1)
Kaz Kreol (NW1)
The Living Room (N1)
Orange Tree (N20)
Two Brothers (N3)*

South
Annie's (SW13)
Bread & Roses (SW4)
Browns (TW9)
Delfina Studio Café (SE1)*
Duke of Cambridge (SW11)
Giraffe (SE1, SW11)
Hudson's (SW15)
Joanna's (SE19)
Laughing Gravy (SE1)
The Light House (SW19)
Metro (SW4)
Morel (SW4)
Naked Turtle (SW14)
Newton's (SW4)
Nosh (TW1)
Putney Station (SW15)
The Sequel (SW4)
The Ship (SW18)
Tate Café (SE1)
Tate Restaurant (SE1)
Upstairs Bar (SW2)*
The Wharf (TW11)
White Cross (TW9)

East
Browns (E14, EC2)

Club Mangia *(EC4)*
$ *(EC1)*
Lilly's *(E1)*
Les Trois Garçons *(E1)*
Vivat Bacchus *(EC4)*

IRISH

Central
O'Conor Don *(W1)*

ITALIAN

Central
Al Duca *(SW1)*
Alloro *(W1)**
Amato *(W1)*
Aperitivo *(W1)*
Bertorelli's *(WC2)*
Bertorelli's *(W1)*
Caffè Caldesi *(W1)*
Caldesi *(W1)*
Camerino *(W1)*
Caraffini *(SW1)**
Carluccio's Caffè *(W1)*
Cecconi's *(W1)*
Ciao Bella *(WC1)*
Cipriani *(W1)*
Como Lario *(SW1)*
Il Convivio *(SW1)**
Cristini *(W2)*
Delfino *(W1)**
Diverso *(W1)*
Eddalino *(W1)*
Fiore *(SW1)*
5 Cavendish Square *(W1)*
Franco's *(SW1)*
Frankie's Italian Bar & Grill *(W1)*
Getti *(SW1, W1)*
Giardinetto *(W1)*
Incognico *(WC2)*
L'Incontro *(SW1)*
Italian Kitchen *(WC1)*
Latium *(W1)**
Little Italy *(W1)*
Locanda Locatelli *(W1)**
Luciano *(SW1)*
Luigi's *(WC2)*
Mimmo d'Ischia *(SW1)*
Mosaico *(W1)*
Neal Street *(WC2)*
Oliveto *(SW1)**
Olivo *(SW1)**
Orso *(WC2)*
Pappagallo *(W1)*
Paradiso Olivelli *(W1, WC2)*
Passione *(W1)*
Pasta Brown *(WC2)*
Pizza on the Park *(SW1)*
La Porchetta Pizzeria *(WC1)*
Quirinale *(SW1)**
Quo Vadis *(W1)*
Sale e Pepe *(SW1)*
Salt Yard *(W1)**

Santini *(SW1)*
Sapori *(WC2)*
Sardo *(W1)**
Sartoria *(W1)*
Serafino *(W1)*
Signor Sassi *(SW1)*
Signor Zilli *(W1)*
Spacca Napoli *(W1)**
La Spiga *(W1)*
La Spighetta *(W1)*
Strada *(W1, WC2)*
Teca *(W1)**
Theo Randall *(W1)*
Toto's *(SW1)**
Uno *(SW1)*
Vasco & Piero's Pavilion *(W1)**
Via Condotti *(W1)*
Il Vicolo *(SW1)**
Volt *(SW1)*
Zafferano *(SW1)**
Zilli Fish *(W1)*
Zizzi *(W1, WC2)*

West
L'Accento Italiano *(W2)*
Aglio e Olio *(SW10)**
The Ark *(W8)*
Arturo *(W2)*
Assaggi *(W2)**
Brunello *(SW7)*
Buona Sera *(SW3)*
Carluccio's Caffè *(SW10, SW7, W5)*
Carpaccio's *(SW3)*
Cibo *(W14)*
Da Mario *(SW7)*
Daphne's *(SW3)*
De Cecco *(SW6)*
La Delizia *(SW3)*
Edera *(W11)*
11 Abingdon Road *(W8)*
Elistano *(SW3)*
Esenza *(W11)*
Est Est Est *(W4)*
Il Falconiere *(SW7)*
La Famiglia *(SW10)*
Frankie's *(SW3, W4)*
Frantoio *(SW10)*
Friends *(SW10)*
The Green Olive *(W9)*
Lillo e Franco *(W8)**
Locanda Ottoemezzo *(W8)*
Loco Locale *(SW6)*
Lucio *(SW3)*
Luna Rossa *(W11)*
Made in Italy *(SW3)**
Manicomio *(SW3)*
Matriciano *(SW6)*
Mediterraneo *(W11)**
Miraggio *(SW6)*
Montpeliano *(SW7)*
Monza *(SW3)**
Napulé *(SW6)**
Nuovi Sapori *(SW6)**
The Oak *(W2)*
Osteria Basilico *(W11)**

Osteria dell'Arancio *(SW10)*
Ottolenghi *(W11, W8)**
Il Pagliaccio *(SW6)*
Pappa Ciccia *(SW6)**
Parmigiano *(W14)*
Pellicano *(SW3)*
Picasso's *(SW3)*
Il Portico *(W8)*
The Red Pepper *(W9)**
Riccardo's *(SW3)*
The River Café *(W6)**
Rossopomodoro *(SW10)*
San Lorenzo *(SW3)*
Santa Lucia *(SW10)*
Scalini *(SW3)*
Spago *(SW7)**
Strada *(SW5, SW6)*
Timo *(W8)*
Wine Factory *(W11)*
Ziani *(SW3)*
Zizzi *(SW5, W4)*

North
Artigiano *(NW3)*
L'Artista *(NW11)*
La Brocca *(NW6)*
Cantina Italia *(N1)**
Carluccio's Caffè *(N1, NW3, NW8)*
Casale Franco *(N1)*
La Collina *(NW1)*
Fifteen Restaurant *(N1)*
Fifteen Trattoria *(N1)*
Florians *(N8)*
Fratelli la Bufala *(NW3)*
Marine Ices *(NW3)*
Metrogusto *(N1)*
Ottolenghi *(N1)**
Al Parco *(N6)**
Philpotts Mezzaluna *(NW2)*
Pizzeria Oregano *(N1)**
La Porchetta Pizzeria *(N1, N4, NW1)*
Rosmarino *(NW8)*
Salt House *(NW8)*
The Salusbury *(NW6)*
San Carlo *(N6)*
San Daniele *(N5)*
Sardo Canale *(NW1)**
Sarracino *(NW6)*
Strada *(N1, N6, NW1)*
Villa Bianca *(NW3)*
Zizzi *(N3, N6, NW8)*
Zuccato *(NW3)*

South
A Cena *(TW1)**
Al Forno *(SW15, SW19)*
Amici *(SW17)*
Antipasto & Pasta *(SW11)*
Antipasto e Pasta *(SW4)*
Arancia *(SE16)**
Buona Sera *(SW11)*
Café Mamma *(TW9)*
Cantina del Ponte *(SE1)*
Il Cantuccio di Pulcinella *(SW11)**
Carluccio's Caffè *(SW15)*

Enoteca Turi *(SW15)**
Est Est Est *(SW17, SW19)*
Ferrari's *(SW17)*
Frankie's Italian Bar & Grill *(SW15)*
La Lanterna *(SE1)*
Loco Locale *(SE3)*
Loco Mensa *(SE1)*
Mooli *(SW4)*
Numero Uno *(SW11)*
Ost. Antica Bologna *(SW11)*
Pappa Ciccia *(SW15)**
Pizza Metro *(SW11)**
Pizzeria Castello *(SE16)**
Pizzeria Castello *(SE1)*
Prego *(TW9)*
Rick's Café *(SW17)**
Riva *(SW13)*
Riviera *(SE1)*
San Lorenzo Fuoriporta *(SW19)*
Scarpetta *(TW11)*
Strada *(SW11, SW13, SW4)*
Tentazioni *(SE1)**
Zero Quattro *(SW19)*
Zizzi *(SW11, TW9)*

East
Alba *(EC1)**
Amerigo Vespucci *(E14)*
Bertorelli's *(EC3, EC4)*
Il Bordello *(E1)**
Caravaggio *(EC3)*
Carluccio's Caffè *(E14, EC1)*
La Figa *(E14)*
Flâneur *(EC1)*
1 Blossom Street *(E1)*
E Pellicci *(E2)*
Perc%nto *(EC4)*
La Porchetta Pizzeria *(EC1)*
Quadrato *(E14)*
Refettorio *(EC4)*
Rocco *(EC1)*
Santore *(EC1)*
Strada *(EC1)*
Taberna Etrusca *(EC4)*
The Zetter *(EC1)*
Zizzi *(E14)*
Zuccato *(EC4)*

MEDITERRANEAN

Central
About Thyme *(SW1)*
Connaught (Angela Hartnett) *(W1)*
Bistro 1 *(W1, WC2)*
Caramel *(SW1)*
The Fifth Floor Café *(SW1)*
Hummus Bros *(W1)*
Ishtar *(W1)*
Leon *(W1)**
Mediterranean Kitchen *(WC2)*
La Noisette *(SW1)*
Rocket *(W1)*
Salt Yard *(W1)**

06 St Chad's Place (WC1)*
Truc Vert (W1)
Tuttons (WC2)
W'sens (SW1)

West
Aquasia (SW10)
The Atlas (SW6)*
Cross Keys (SW3)
The Grove (W6)
Leon (SW3)*
Little Bay (SW6)
Locanda Ottoemezzo (W8)
Made in Italy (SW3)*
Mediterranean Kitchen (SW7, W11, W8)
Mediterraneo (W11)*
Meza (W1)
Priory House (W14)
Raoul's Café (W9)
Raoul's Café & Deli (W11)
Snows on the Green (W6)*
The Swan (W4)*
Tom's (W11)
Troubadour (SW5)
William IV (NW10)

North
Camden Brasserie (NW1)
The Chapel (NW1)
Cru (N1)
The Little Bay (NW6)
Mediterranean Kitchen (N1)
The Pumphouse (N8)
The Vine (NW5)

South
Bar Estrela (SW8)
Bermondsey Kitchen (SE1)
Fish in a Tie (SW11)
The Fox & Hounds (SW11)*
The Little Bay (SW11)
Oxo Tower (Brass') (SE1)
Rocket Riverside (SW15)
The Wharf (TW11)

East
Ambassador (EC1)
Bonds (EC2)
The Clerkenwell Dining Room (EC1)
The Eagle (EC1)
Eyre Brothers (EC2)
Flâneur (EC1)
Leon (E1, EC4)*
The Little Bay (EC1)
The Peasant (EC1)
Portal (EC1)
Le Saint Julien (EC1)
Vinoteca (EC1)

ORGANIC

Central
Leon (W1)*
Le Pain Quotidien (W1)*

West
Babes 'n' Burgers (W11)
Bush Garden Café (W12)
Lillo e Franco (W8)*

North
The Duke of Cambridge (N1)

South
The Hartley (SE1)
Tandoori Nights (SE22)*

East
Smiths (Dining Rm) (EC1)
Story Deli (E1)*

POLISH

West
Daquise (SW7)
Lowiczanka (W6)
Ognisko Polskie (SW7)
Patio (W12)
Wódka (W8)

South
Baltic (SE1)

PORTUGUESE

West
Lisboa Pâtisserie (W10)*
Tugga (SW3)

North
Pescador Too (NW3)

South
Bar Estrela (SW8)
Café Portugal (SW8)*

East
El Faro (E14)
Portal (EC1)

RUSSIAN

West
Nikita's (SW10)

North
Troika (NW1)

South
Zakudia (SE1)

East
Potemkin (EC1)

SCANDINAVIAN

Central
Garbo's (W1)

West
Lundum's (SW7)*

North
Upper Glas (N1)

South
Glas (SE1)*

East
Lightship (E1)

SCOTTISH

Central
Albannach (WC2)
Boisdale (SW1)

South
Buchan's (SW11)

East
Boisdale of Bishopsgate (EC2)

SPANISH

Central
Cigala (WC1)
Fino (W1)*
Goya (SW1)
Navarro's (W1)*
El Pirata (W1)
La Rueda (W1)
Salt Yard (W1)*
La Tasca (WC2)

West
Cambio de Tercio (SW5)*
La Copita (W12)
Galicia (W10)
L-Restaurant & Bar (W8)
Meza (W1)
La Rueda (SW6)
La Tasca (W4, W5)
Tendido Cero (SW5)*

North
Don Pepe (NW8)*
The Islington Tapas Bar (N1)

South
Barcelona Tapas (SE22)
don Fernando's (TW9)
La Mancha (SW15)
Meson don Felipe (SE1)
Rebato's (SW8)
Rick's Café (SW17)*
El Rincón Latino (SW4)
La Rueda (SW4)
Tapas Brindisa (SE1)*

East
Barcelona Tapas (E1, EC3, EC4)
Eyre Brothers (EC2)
Meson los Barilles (E1)
Moro (EC1)*
La Tasca (E14, EC2)

STEAKS & GRILLS

Central
Astor Bar & Grill (W1)
Black & Blue (W1)
Bodean's (W1)
Chez Gérard (SW1, W1, WC2)
Christopher's (WC2)
L'Entrecôte Café de Paris (W1)
Gaucho Grill (W1, WC2)
The Guinea Grill (W1)*
Ishtar (W1)
Kettners (W1)
Quaglino's (SW1)
Rowley's (SW1)
Seafresh (SW1)
Smollensky's (WC2)
Texas Embassy Cantina (SW1)
Wolfe's (WC2)

West
Black & Blue (SW7, W8)
Bodean's (SW6)
El Gaucho (SW3, SW7)*
Gaucho Grill (SW3)
Notting Grill (W11)
Popeseye (W14)*
Rôtisserie Jules (SW7, W11)
Smollensky's (W6)
Sophie's Steakhouse (SW10)
Sticky Fingers (W8)

North
Black & Blue (NW3)
Camden Brasserie (NW1)
Gaucho Grill (NW3)
Haché (NW1)*
Hoxton Square Bar &
   Kitchen (N1)
Pick More Daisies (N8)

South
Barnes Grill (SW13)
Bermondsey Kitchen (SE1)
Black & Blue (SE1)
Bodean's (SW4)
Butcher & Grill (SW11)*
Chez Gérard (SE1)
Kew Grill (TW9)*
Matilda's (SW11)
La Pampa (SW11)
Le Pont de la Tour
   Bar & Grill (SE1)
Popeseye (SW15)*
Smollensky's (TW1)

East
Arkansas Café (E1)*
The Bar & Grill (E1)
Chez Gérard (EC2, EC3, EC4)
Christopher's In The City (EC3)
Epicurean Pizza Lounge (EC1)
Fox & Anchor (EC1)
Gaucho Grill (E14, EC2, EC3)
Hawksmoor (E1)
Hope & Sir Loin (EC1)
Lilly's (E1)
Missouri Grill (EC3)
Santa Maria de Buen Ayre (E8)*
Simpson's Tavern (EC3)
Smiths (Top Floor) (EC1)*
Smiths (Dining Rm) (EC1)
Smiths (Ground Floor) (EC1)
Smollensky's (E1, E14)

SWISS

Central
St Moritz *(W1)**

VEGETARIAN

Central
Al Hamra *(W1)*
Food for Thought *(WC2)**
India Club *(WC2)*
The Lanesborough *(SW1)*
Malabar Junction *(WC1)*
Masala Zone *(W1)*
Mildred's *(W1)**
Rasa Samudra *(W1)**
Woodlands *(SW1, W1)**

West
Blah! Blah! Blah! *(W12)**
Blue Elephant *(SW6)*
The Gate *(W6)**
Masala Zone *(SW5)*
Woodlands *(W4)**

North
Chutneys *(NW1)*
Diwana B-P House *(NW1)*
Geeta *(NW6)**
Jashan *(HA0, N8)**
Little Earth Café *(NW3)**
Manna *(NW3)*
Masala Zone *(N1)*
Rani *(N3)*
Rasa *(N16)**
Sabras *(NW10)**
Sakonis *(HA0)**
Vijay *(NW6)**
Woodlands *(NW3)**

South
Kastoori *(SW17)**
Le Pont de la Tour *(SE1)*
Sree Krishna *(SW17)**

East
Carnevale *(EC1)**
The Place Below *(EC2)*
Sri Siam City *(EC2)*

AFTERNOON TEA

Central
Brasserie Roux *(SW1)*
The Fifth Floor Café *(SW1)*
Fortnum's, The Fountain *(W1)*
Ladurée *(SW1)*
The Lanesborough *(SW1)*
Pâtisserie Valerie *(SW1, W1)*
Richoux *(W1)*
The Ritz *(W1)*
Royal Academy *(W1)*
Sketch (Parlour) *(W1)*
Villandry *(W1)*
The Wolseley *(W1)*
Yauatcha *(W1)**

West
Daquise *(SW7)*
Pâtisserie Valerie *(SW3, W8)*
Richoux *(SW3)*
The Tea Palace *(W11)*

North
Richoux *(NW8)*

BURGERS, ETC

Central
Black & Blue *(W1)*
Eagle Bar Diner *(W1)*
Ed's Easy Diner *(W1, WC2)*
Fine Burger Company *(W1)*
Hamburger Union *(W1, WC2)*
Hard Rock Café *(W1)*
Joe Allen *(WC2)*
Kettners *(W1)*
Maxwell's *(WC2)*
Planet Hollywood *(W1)*
Rainforest Café *(W1)*
Savoy Hotel (Banquette) *(WC2)*
Tootsies *(W1)*
The Ultimate Burger *(W1, WC1)*
Wolfe's *(WC2)*

West
Babes 'n' Burgers *(W11)*
Big Easy *(SW3)*
Black & Blue *(SW7, W8)*
Ed's Easy Diner *(SW3)*
Electric Brasserie *(W11)*
Foxtrot Oscar *(SW3)*
Gourmet Burger Kitchen *(SW6, W2, W4)**
Henry J Beans *(SW3)*
Joe's Café *(SW3)*
Lucky Seven *(W2)**
Notting Grill *(W11)*
PJ's *(SW3)*
Sticky Fingers *(W8)*
Tootsies *(SW6, SW7, W11, W4)*

North
Black & Blue *(NW3)*
Fine Burger Company *(N1, N10, NW3)*
Gourmet Burger Kitchen *(NW3, NW6)**
Haché *(NW1)**
Maxwell's *(NW3)*
No 77 Wine Bar *(NW6)*
Tootsies *(NW3)*
The Ultimate Burger *(N10)*

South
Black & Blue *(SE1)*
Dexter's Grill *(SW17)*
Fine Burger Company *(SW12)*
Gourmet Burger Kitchen *(SW11, SW15)**
Matilda's *(SW11)*
Tootsies *(SW11, SW15, SW19, SW4)*

East
Arkansas Café *(E1)**

The Bar & Grill *(EC1)*
$ *(EC1)*
Smiths (Dining Rm) *(EC1)*

CRÊPES

West
Bluebird Café *(SW3)*
Café Crêperie de
  Hampstead *(SW7)**

North
Café Crêperie de
  Hampstead *(NW3)**

South
Chez Lindsay *(TW10)*

FISH & CHIPS

Central
Fryer's Delight *(WC1)*
Golden Hind *(W1)**
Harry Ramsden's *(W1)*
North Sea Fish *(WC1)**
Seafresh *(SW1)*

West
Bibendum *(SW3)*
Geale's *(W8)*
Sea Cow *(SW6)**

North
Nautilus *(NW6)**
Seashell *(NW1)**
Toff's *(N10)**
Two Brothers *(N3)**

South
Brady's *(SW18)*
Fish Club *(SW11)**
Olley's *(SE24)**
The Sea Cow *(SE22, SW4)**

East
Faulkner's *(E8)**

ICE CREAM

North
Marine Ices *(NW3)*

PIZZA

Central
Delfino *(W1)**
Fire & Stone *(WC2)*
Frankie's Italian Bar & Grill *(W1)*
Gourmet Pizza Co. *(W1)*
Kettners *(W1)*
Mash *(W1)*
Oliveto *(SW1)**
Paradiso Olivelli *(W1, WC1, WC2)*
Pizza on the Park *(SW1)*
La Porchetta Pizzeria *(WC1)*
Rocket *(W1)*
Sapori *(WC2)*
La Spiga *(W1)*

La Spighetta *(W1)*
Strada *(W1, WC2)*
Zizzi *(W1, WC2)*

West
Basilico *(SW6)**
Buona Sera *(SW3)*
Da Mario *(SW7)*
La Delizia *(SW3)*
Firezza *(W11, W4)**
Frankie's *(SW3, W4)*
Friends *(SW10)*
Made in Italy *(SW3)**
Osteria Basilico *(W11)**
Parmigiano *(W14)*
(Ciro's) Pizza Pomodoro *(SW3)*
Spago *(SW7)**
Strada *(SW5, SW6)*
Wine Factory *(W11)*
Zizzi *(SW5, W4)*

North
Basilico *(N1, NW3)**
La Brocca *(NW6)*
Cantina Italia *(N1)**
Firezza *(N1)**
Furnace *(N1)*
Marine Ices *(NW3)*
Al Parco *(N6)**
Pizzeria Oregano *(N1)**
La Porchetta Pizzeria *(N1, N4, NW1)*
Strada *(N1, N6, NW1)*
Zizzi *(N3, N6, NW8)*

South
Al Forno *(SW15, SW19)*
Amano Café *(SE1)*
Basilico *(SW11, SW14)**
Buona Sera *(SW11)*
Eco *(SW4)*
Eco Brixton *(SW9)*
Firezza *(SW11, SW18)**
Frankie's Italian Bar &
  Grill *(SW15)*
Fuego Pizzeria *(SW8)*
Gourmet Pizza Co. *(SE1)*
The Gowlett *(SE15)*
La Lanterna *(SE1)*
Paradiso Olivelli *(SE1)*
Pizza Metro *(SW11)**
Pizzeria Castello *(SE16)**
Pizzeria Castello *(SE1)*
Rocket Riverside *(SW15)*
Strada *(SW11, SW13, SW4)*
Zero Degrees *(SE3)*
Zizzi *(SW11, TW9)*

East
Bar Capitale *(EC2, EC4)*
Il Bordello *(E1)**
Epicurean Pizza Lounge *(EC1)*
Gourmet Pizza Co. *(E14)*
(Ciro's) Pizza Pomodoro *(EC2)*
La Porchetta Pizzeria *(EC1)*
Strada *(EC1)*
Zizzi *(E14)*

SANDWICHES, CAKES, ETC

Central
Amato (W1)
Apostrophe (SW1, W1, WC2)*
Baker & Spice (SW1)*
Bar Italia (W1)
Benugo (W1)*
Crussh (W1)*
Flat White (W1)*
La Fromagerie Café (W1)*
Fuzzy's Grub (SW1)*
Konditor & Cook (W1, WC1)*
Ladurée (SW1)
Maison Bertaux (W1)*
Maison Blanc Vite (W1)
Monmouth Coffee
 Company (WC2)*
Le Pain Quotidien (W1)*
Pâtisserie Valerie (SW1, W1)
Paul (W1, WC2)*
Richoux (W1)
Royal Academy (W1)
Sketch (Parlour) (W1)

West
Aubaine (SW3)
Baker & Spice (SW3)*
Benugo (SW7)*
Bluebird Café (SW3)
Café Crêperie de
 Hampstead (SW7)*
Chez Kristof (Deli) (W6)
Crussh (W12, W8)*
Hugo's (SW7)
Joe's Café (SW3)
Lisboa Pâtisserie (W10)*
Pâtisserie Valerie (SW3, W8)
Paul (SW7)*
Richoux (SW3)
Tom's (W11)
Troubadour (SW5)

North
Baker & Spice (NW6)*
Café Crêperie de
 Hampstead (NW3)*
Chamomile (NW3)
Gail's Bread (NW3)
Hugo's (NW6)
Kenwood (Brew House) (NW3)
Al Parco (N6)*
Paul (NW3)*
Richoux (NW8)

South
Boiled Egg (SW11)
Konditor & Cook (SE1)*
Monmouth Coffee
 Company (SE1)*
Trinity Stores (SW12)*

East
Apostrophe (EC2, EC4)*
Benugo (EC1)*
Brick Lane Beigel Bake (E1)
Crussh (E14, EC3, EC4)*

Fuzzy's Grub (EC4)*
Maison Blanc Vite (EC3)
Nuvo (EC4)*
Pâtisserie Valerie (E1)
Paul (EC4)*

ARGENTINIAN

Central
Gaucho Grill (W1, WC2)

West
El Gaucho (SW3, SW7)*
Gaucho Grill (SW3)

North
Gaucho Grill (NW3)

South
La Pampa (SW11)

East
Gaucho Grill (E14, EC2, EC3)
Santa Maria de Buen Ayre (E8)*

BRAZILIAN

Central
Mocoto (SW1)

West
Rodizio Rico (W2)

North
Rodizio Rico (N1)

CUBAN

Central
Floridita (W1)

North
Cuba Libre (N1)

MEXICAN/TEXMEX

Central
Café Pacifico (WC2)
La Perla (W1, WC2)
Texas Embassy Cantina (SW1)

West
Crazy Homies (W2)
La Perla (SW6)
Taqueria (W11)

North
Mestizo (NW1)*

East
Green & Red Bar &
 Cantina (E1)*

PERUVIAN

South
Fina Estampa (SE1)

SOUTH AMERICAN

West
Cactus Blue (SW3)
1492 (SW6)

North
La Piragua (N1)*
Sabor (N1)

South
El Vergel (SE1)*

East
Armadillo (E8)*

AFRO-CARIBBEAN

Central
Calabash (WC2)
Mr Jerk (W1)
The Terrace (WC2)

West
Mr Jerk (W2)

North
Cottons (NW1)
The Green (NW2)
Mango Room (NW1)*

East
Cottons (EC1)

ETHIOPIAN

North
Tobia (NW3)*

MOROCCAN

Central
Mamounia (W1)
Momo (W1)
Original Tajines (W1)
Souk Medina (WC2)

West
Adams Café (W12)*
Aziz (SW6)
Moroccan Tagine (W10)
Pasha (SW7)

NORTH AFRICAN

Central
Mamounia (W1)
Souk (WC2)

West
Azou (W6)

East
Moro (EC1)*

SOUTH AFRICAN

South
Chakalaka (SW15)
Naked Turtle (SW14)

TUNISIAN

West
Adams Café (W12)*

EGYPTIAN

North
Ali Baba (NW1)

ISRAELI

Central
Gaby's (WC2)

North
Harry Morgan's (NW8)
Solly's Exclusive (NW11)

KOSHER

Central
Reubens (W1)
Six-13 (W1)*

North
Kaifeng (NW4)
Solly's Exclusive (NW11)

East
Bevis Marks (EC3)*

LEBANESE

Central
Al Hamra (W1)
Al Sultan (W1)
Beiteddine (SW1)
Fairuz (W1)*
Fakhreldine (W1)
Ishbilia (SW1)*
Levant (W1)
Mamounia (W1)
Maroush (W1)
Noura (SW1, W1)
Ranoush (SW1)*

West
Al Bustan (SW7)
Al-Waha (W2)
Beirut Express (W2)*
Chez Marcelle (W14)*
Fairuz (W2)*
Fresco (W2)*
Levantine (W2)
Maroush (SW3)
Café Maroush (W2)
Randa (W8)
Ranoush (SW3, W2, W8)*

PERSIAN

West
Alounak (W14, W2)*
Kandoo (W2)
Mohsen (W14)*
Yas (W14)

South
Dish Dash (SW12)

SYRIAN

West
Abu Zaad (W12)*

TURKISH

Central
Cyprus Mangal (SW1)*
Efes Restaurant (W1)
Ishtar (W1)
Kazan (SW1)
Ozer (W1)
Sofra (W1, WC2)
Tas (WC1)

West
Best Mangal (W14)*
Shish (W2)

North
Gallipoli (N1)
Istanbul Iskembecisi (N16)
Izgara (N3)*
Pasha (N1)
Shish (NW2)
Sofra (NW8)

South
Tas Ev (SE1)
Tas Pide (SE1)

East
The Han of Nazz (E2)
Haz (E1)
Mangal Ocakbasi (E8)*
Savarona (EC2)
Shish (EC1)
Sofra (EC1)
Tas (EC1)

AFGHANI

North
Afghan Kitchen (N1)*

BURMESE

West
Mandalay (W2)*

CHINESE

Central
Bar Shu (W1)*
China Tang (W1)
The Chinese Experience (W1)*
Chuen Cheng Ku (W1)
Fung Shing (WC2)*
Golden Dragon (W1)
Hakkasan (W1)
Harbour City (W1)
Hunan (SW1)*
Imperial China (WC2)

Jade Garden (W1)
Jenny Lo's (SW1)*
Joy King Lau (WC2)
Kai Mayfair (W1)*
Ken Lo's Memories (SW1)*
Laureate (W1)
Mekong (SW1)
Mr Chow (SW1)
Mr Kong (WC2)*
New Culture Revolution (WC1)
New Mayflower (W1)*
New World (W1)
Princess Garden (W1)*
Royal China (W1)*
Royal China Club (W1)*
Shanghai Blues (WC1)*
Six-13 (W1)*
Taman gang (W1)
Wong Kei (W1)
Yauatcha (W1)*
Yming (W1)*
Zen Central (W1)*

West
Choys (SW3)
The Four Seasons (W2)*
Good Earth (SW3)*
Ken Lo's Memories (W8)*
Made in China (SW10)*
Mandarin Kitchen (W2)*
Mao Tai (SW6)*
Mr Wing (SW5)*
New Culture Rev'n (SW3, W11)
Royal China (W2)*
Stick & Bowl (W8)
Taiwan Village (SW6)*
Yi-Ban (SW6)*

North
Good Earth (NW7)*
Gung-Ho (NW6)*
Kaifeng (NW4)
New Culture Rev'n (N1, NW1)
OQO Bar (N1)
Phoenix Palace (NW1)*
Royal China (NW8)*
Sakonis (HA0)
Singapore Garden (NW6)*
Weng Wah House (NW3)
ZeNW3 (NW3)

South
Dalchini (SW19)*
Dragon Castle (SE17)*
Four Regions (TW9)
O'Zon (TW1)
Royal China (SW15)*

East
The Drunken Monkey (E1)
Imperial City (EC3)*
The Lotus (E14)
Royal China (E14)*
Shanghai (E8)*
Yi-Ban (E16)*

CHINESE, DIM SUM

Central
The Chinese Experience *(W1)**
Chuen Cheng Ku *(W1)*
dim T *(W1)*
Golden Dragon *(W1)*
Hakkasan *(W1)*
Harbour City *(W1)*
Jade Garden *(W1)*
Joy King Lau *(WC2)*
Laureate *(W1)*
New World *(W1)*
ping pong *(W1)*
Royal China *(W1)**
Royal China Club *(W1)**
Shanghai Blues *(WC1)**
Yauatcha *(W1)**

West
ping pong *(W2)*
Royal China *(W2)**

North
dim T café *(NW3)*
Phoenix Palace *(NW1)**
Royal China *(NW8)**

South
Royal China *(SW15)**

East
The Drunken Monkey *(E1)*
The Lotus *(E14)*
Royal China *(E14)**
Shanghai *(E8)**

INDIAN

Central
Amaya *(SW1)**
Benares *(W1)**
Café Lazeez *(W1)*
Chor Bizarre *(W1)**
Chowki *(W1)*
The Cinnamon Club *(SW1)**
Deya *(W1)**
Gopal's of Soho *(W1)*
Imli *(W1)*
India Club *(WC2)*
Malabar Junction *(WC1)*
Masala Zone *(W1)*
Mela *(WC2)*
Mint Leaf *(SW1)**
Moti Mahal *(WC2)*
La Porte des Indes *(W1)*
Rasa Samudra *(W1)**
Red Fort *(W1)**
Soho Spice *(W1)*
Tamarind *(W1)**
Veeraswamy *(W1)**
Woodlands *(SW1, W1)**

West
Agni *(W6)**
Anarkali *(W6)*
Bombay Bicycle Club *(W11)**
Bombay Brasserie *(SW7)*

Bombay Palace *(W2)**
Brilliant *(UB2)**
Café Lazeez *(SW7)*
Chutney Mary *(SW10)**
Five Hot Chillies *(HA0)**
Ginger *(W2)*
Haandi *(SW7)**
Indian Zing *(W6)**
kare kare *(SW5)**
Karma *(W14)*
Khan's *(W2)**
Khan's of Kensington *(SW7)*
Khyber Pass *(SW7)**
Love India *(SW3)**
Ma Goa *(SW6)**
Madhu's *(UB1)**
Malabar *(W8)**
Masala Zone *(SW5)*
Memories of India *(SW7)*
Monty's *(W5)*
Noor Jahan *(SW5, W2)**
The Painted Heron *(SW10)**
Rasoi Vineet Bhatia *(SW3)**
Shikara *(SW3)*
Standard Tandoori *(W2)**
Star of India *(SW5)**
Tandoori Lane *(SW6)*
Vama *(SW10)**
Woodlands *(W4)**
Zaika *(W8)**

North
Anglo Asian Tandoori *(N16)*
Bombay Bicycle Club *(NW3)**
Chutneys *(NW1)*
Diwana B-P House *(NW1)**
Eriki *(NW3)**
Geeta *(NW6)**
Great Nepalese *(NW1)**
Jashan *(HA0, N8)**
Kovalam *(NW6)**
Masala Zone *(N1)*
The Parsee *(N19)*
Rani *(N3)*
Rasa *(N16)**
Sabras *(NW10)**
Sakonis *(HA0)**
Vijay *(NW6)**
Woodlands *(NW3)**
Zamzama *(NW1)*

South
Babur Brasserie *(SE23)**
Bengal Clipper *(SE1)*
Bombay Bicycle Club *(SW12)**
Chutney *(SW18)**
Dalchini *(SW19)**
Everest Inn *(SE3)**
Ganapati *(SE15)*
Hara The Circle Bar *(SE1)**
Hot Stuff *(SW8)**
Indian Ocean *(SW17)**
Kastoori *(SW17)**
Ma Goa *(SW15)**
Mirch Masala *(SW16, SW17, UB1)**

Nanglo *(SW12)**
The Painted Heron *(SE11)**
Sagar *(TW1)**
Sarkhel's *(SW14, SW18)**
Silka *(SE1)*
Sree Krishna *(SW17)**
Tandoori Nights *(SE22)**
Tangawizi *(TW1)**
3 Monkeys *(SE24)*

East
Anakana *(EC1)*
Bengal Quay *(E14)*
Café Spice Namaste *(E1)**
The Gaylord *(E14)**
Kasturi *(EC3)*
Lahore Kebab House *(E1)**
Lime *(E14)*
Memsaheb on Thames *(E14)**
Mirch Masala *(E1)**
New Tayyabs *(E1)**
Rajasthan II *(EC3)**
Scarlet Dot *(E1)*

INDIAN, SOUTHERN

Central
India Club *(WC2)*
Malabar Junction *(WC1)*
Quilon *(SW1)**
Ragam *(W1)**
Rasa *(W1)**
Rasa Maricham *(WC1)**
Woodlands *(SW1, W1)**

West
Agni *(W6)**
Sagar *(W6)**
Woodlands *(W4)**

North
Chutneys *(NW1)*
Geeta *(NW6)**
Kovalam *(NW6)**
Rani *(N3)*
Rasa *(N16)**
Rasa Travancore *(N16)**
Sabras *(NW10)**
Vijay *(NW6)**
Woodlands *(NW3)**

South
Kastoori *(SW17)**
Sree Krishna *(SW17)**

INDONESIAN

Central
Melati, Peter St *(W1)*
Melati, Gt Windmill St *(W1)*
Trader Vics *(W1)*

West
Mawar *(W2)*

South
Nancy Lam's Enak Enak *(SW11)*

JAPANESE

Central
Abeno *(WC1)*
Abeno Too *(WC2)**
Benihana *(W1)*
Chisou *(W1)**
Defune *(W1)**
Edokko *(WC1)**
Feng Sushi *(SW1)*
Gili Gulu *(WC2)*
Hazuki *(WC2)*
Ikeda *(W1)**
Ikkyu *(W1)*
Itsu *(W1)**
Kulu Kulu *(W1, WC2)**
Matsuri *(SW1, WC1)**
Misato *(W1)**
Mitsukoshi *(SW1)**
Miyama *(W1)**
Mju *(SW1)*
Nobu *(W1)**
Nobu Berkeley *(W1)*
Roka *(W1)**
Sakura *(W1)**
Satsuma *(W1)*
Shogun *(W1)**
Soho Japan *(W1)**
Sumosan *(W1)*
Sushi Hiroba *(WC2)**
Taman gang *(W1)*
Taro *(W1)*
Ten Ten Tei *(W1)**
Toku *(W1)*
Tokyo Diner *(WC2)*
Umu *(W1)*
Wagamama *(SW1, W1, WC1, WC2)*
Yo! Sushi *(SW1, W1, WC1)*
Yoshino *(W1)**

West
Benihana *(SW3)*
L'Etranger *(SW7)**
Feng Sushi *(SW10, W11, W8)*
Inaho *(W2)**
Itsu *(SW3)**
Kisso *(SW5)*
Kulu Kulu *(SW7)**
Mika *(W11)*
Nozomi *(SW3)*
Sushi-Hiro *(W5)**
Tosa *(W6)**
Wagamama *(W8)*
Yakitoria *(W2)**
Yo! Sushi *(SW6, W2)*
Zuma *(SW7)**

North
Benihana *(NW3)*
Café Japan *(NW11)**
Feng Sushi *(NW3)*
Jin Kichi *(NW3)**
Sushi-Say *(NW2)**
Wagamama *(N1, NW1)*
Wakaba *(NW3)**
Yo! Sushi *(N1, NW3)*

Yuzu (NW6)*
ZeNW3 (NW3)

South
Feng Sushi (SE1)
Fujiyama (SW9)*
Inshoku (SE1)
Tsunami (SW4)*
Wagamama (SE1, SW15, SW19)
Yo! Sushi (SE1)

East
City Miyama (EC4)*
 City Noto (EC4)
Itsu (E14)*
K10 (EC2)*
Kurumaya (EC4)*
Miyabi (EC2)
Moshi Moshi (E14, EC2)
Noto (EC2)
Pham Sushie (EC1)*
Saki Bar & Food
  Emporium (EC1)*
Tatsuso (EC2)*
Tokyo City (EC2)*
Ubon (E14)*
Wagamama (E14, EC2, EC3, EC4)
Yo! Sushi (EC1)

KOREAN

Central
Asadal (WC1)
Jindalle (SW1)
Koba (W1)*

West
Wizzy (SW6)*

MALAYSIAN

Central
Melati, Peter St (W1)
Melati, Gt Windmill St (W1)

West
Awana (SW3)
Mawar (W2)
Nyonya (W11)

North
Café de Maya (NW3)
Singapore Garden (NW6)*

South
Champor-Champor (SE1)*

East
Ekachai (EC2)*
Singapura (EC2, EC3, EC4)

PAKISTANI

Central
Salloos (SW1)*

South
Mirch Masala (SW16, SW17, UB1)*

East
Lahore Kebab House (E1)*
Mirch Masala (E1)*
New Tayyabs (E1)*

PAN-ASIAN

Central
Cocoon (W1)
dim T (W1)
Hare & Tortoise (WC1)
Just Oriental (SW1)
Katana (WC2)
Noodle Noodle (SW1)
Pan-Asian Canteen (SW1)*
The Penthouse (WC2)
Tamarai (WC2)

West
E&O (W11)*
Eight Over Eight (SW3)*
Hare & Tortoise (W14, W5)
Jim Thompson's (SW6)
Tampopo (SW10)
Uli (W11)*
Zimzun (SW6)

North
dim T café (NW3)
Gilgamesh (NW1)
Jim Thompson's (N21)
Oriental City (NW9)*
XO (NW3)

South
The Banana Leaf
  Canteen (SW11)*
Hare & Tortoise (SW15)
Nancy Lam's Enak Enak (SW11)

East
Apium (EC1)
Cicada (EC1)*
Gt Eastern Dining Rm (EC2)*
Pacific Oriental (EC2)
Satu Bar & Kitchen (EC2)

THAI

Central
Blue Jade (SW1)
Busaba Eathai (W1, WC1)*
Chiang Mai (W1)*
Crazy Bear (W1)*
Mango Tree (SW1)
Mekong (SW1)
Nahm (SW1)
Page in Pimlico (SW1)
Patara (W1)*
Siam Central (W1)
Sri Thai Soho (W1)
Thai Café (SW1)
Thai Pot (WC2)
Thai Square (SW1, W1, WC2)

West
Bangkok (SW7)*

Bedlington Café (W4)
Ben's Thai (W9)
Blue Elephant (SW6)
Busabong (SW10)
Café 209 (SW6)
Churchill Arms (W8)*
Esarn Kheaw (W12)*
Fat Boy's (W5)
Hammersmith Café (W6)
Latymers (W6)
Old Parr's Head (W14)
Patara (SW3)*
Sabai Sabai (W6)
Saran Rom (SW6)
Silks & Spice (W4)
Sugar Hut (SW6)
Sukho Thai Cuisine (SW6)*
Tawana (W2)*
Thai Bistro (W4)*
Thai Square (SW7)
The Walmer Castle (W11)
Yelo Thai Canteen (W11)
Zimzun (SW6)

North
Café de Maya (NW3)
Isarn (N1)*
Silks & Spice (NW1)
Thai Square (N1)
Yelo (N1)
Yum Yum (N16)*

South
Amaranth (SW18)*
Fat Boy's (TW1, TW8, W4)
Four Regions (TW9)
Kwan Thai (SE1)
The Pepper Tree (SW4)*
Ratchada (SE3)*
Talad Thai (SW15)*
Thai Corner Café (SE22)
Thai Elephant (TW10)
Thai Garden (SW11)
Thai on the River (SW11)
Thai Square (SW15)
Thailand (SE14)*

East
Ekachai (EC2)*
Elephant Royale (E14)
Gt Eastern Dining Rm (EC2)*
Silks & Spice (EC4)
Sri Nam (E14)
Sri Siam City (EC2)
Sri Thai City (EC4)
Thai Square (EC4)
Thai Square City (EC3)

North
Huong-Viet (N1)*
Viet Garden (N1)*
Viet-Anh (NW1)

East
Cây Tre (EC1)*
Namo (E9)*
Pho (EC1)
Sông Quê (E2)*
Viet Hoa (E2)
Xich-lô (EC1)

VIETNAMESE

Central
Bam-Bou (W1)
Mekong (SW1)

West
Nam Long (SW5)
Saigon Saigon (W6)*

AREA OVERVIEWS

CENTRAL

Soho, Covent Garden & Bloomsbury
(Parts of W1, all WC2 and WC1)

£70+	Lindsay House	British, Modern	③③②
	Savoy Grill	British, Traditional	③③③
	Asia de Cuba	Fusion	④④③
£60+	Axis	British, Modern	③③④
	L'Escargot (Picasso Room)	French	③②①
	Pearl	"	③③③
	Astor Bar & Grill	Steaks & grills	⑤④④
	Matsuri	Japanese	②②④
£50+	Christopher's	American	⑤⑤④
	Adam Street	British, Modern	③③②
	Alastair Little	"	②②⑤
	Indigo	"	③②②
	The Ivy	"	③②②
	Origin	"	②②③
	Refuel	"	④④②
	Rules	British, Traditional	③③①
	Simpsons-in-the-Strand	"	④③④
	J Sheekey	Fish & seafood	①②②
	Zilli Fish	"	③③④
	The Admiralty	French	④④③
	Clos Maggiore	"	③②①
	Jaan	Fusion	②②④
	Little Italy	Italian	④④③
	Neal Street	"	⑤⑤⑤
	Albannach	Scottish	④⑤④
	Floridita	Cuban	⑤⑤③
	Yauatcha	Chinese	①③②
	The Penthouse	Pan-Asian	⑤⑤③
£40+	Joe Allen	American	④③①
	Smollensky's	"	⑤④④
	Bank Aldwych	British, Modern	④④④
	Café du Jardin	"	④③④
	Le Deuxième	"	③③④
	French House	"	③③②
	Homage	"	④③②
	The Portrait	"	④⑤②
	Ronnie Scott's	"	– – –
	The National Dining Rooms	British, Traditional	③④③
	Livebait	Fish & seafood	④④⑤
	Manzi's	"	③③③
	Beotys	French	④②③
	Café des Amis du Vin	"	④④④
	Chez Gérard	"	⑤④④
	Circus	"	– – –
	L'Escargot	"	②②②
	L'Estaminet	"	③③③
	Incognico	"	③③③
	Mon Plaisir	"	③③②

	Name	Cuisine			
	Le Palais du Jardin	"	④	④	❸
	La Trouvaille	"	④	❸	❸
	Savoy Hotel (Banquette)	International	④	❷	❸
	Bertorelli's	Italian	⑤	④	④
	Luigi's	"	⑤	④	④
	Orso	"	④	❸	④
	Quo Vadis	"	④	④	④
	Signor Zilli	"	❸	❷	❸
	Vasco & Piero's Pavilion	"	❷	⓿	❷
	Cigala	Spanish	④	❸	④
	Gaucho Grill	Steaks & grills	❸	④	④
	St Moritz	Swiss	❷	❸	❷
	Planet Hollywood	Burgers, etc	⑤	④	⑤
	La Spiga	Pizza	❸	④	④
	Shanghai Blues	Chinese	❷	❸	❷
	Moti Mahal	Indian	❸	❷	④
	Red Fort	"	❷	❷	❸
	Asadal	Korean	❸	④	④
	Patara	Thai	⓿	❷	❸
£35+	TGI Friday's	American	⑤	⑤	⑤
	Aurora	British, Modern	❸	❸	❷
	British Museum	"	–	–	–
	Konstam at the Prince Albert	"	④	❷	❸
	The Terrace	"	④	④	⑤
	Tuttons	"	⑤	④	④
	Loch Fyne	Fish & seafood	❸	④	④
	Arbutus	French	❷	❷	❸
	Café Bohème	"	④	❸	⓿
	Randall & Aubin	"	❷	❸	⓿
	Gay Hussar	Hungarian	④	❸	❷
	Bohème Kitchen	International	❸	④	❸
	Boulevard	"	④	❸	④
	Boulevard Bar & Dining Room	"	❸	④	❸
	Papageno	"	④	④	❷
	Sarastro	"	⑤	⑤	❸
	Sugar Reef	"	⑤	⑤	⑤
	Italian Kitchen	Italian	❸	❷	❸
	Meza	Spanish	④	④	⑤
	Wolfe's	Burgers, etc	❸	❸	④
	Kettners	Pizza	④	④	❷
	Bar Shu	Chinese	❷	④	④
	Imperial China	"	❸	❷	❸
	Malabar Junction	Indian	❸	❸	❷
	Rasa Maricham	Indian, Southern	⓿	❷	❸
	Sri Thai Soho	Thai	❸	❸	④
£30+	All Star Lanes	American	④	④	❷
	Bodean's	"	❸	❸	❸
	Belgo Centraal	Belgian	④	④	❸
	Andrew Edmunds	British, Modern	❸	⓿	⓿
	The Endurance	British, Traditional	④	④	❸
	Porters English Restaurant	"	⑤	④	⑤
	Balans	International	⑤	④	❸
	Bedford & Strand	"	④	❸	④

	Browns	"	⑤⑤④
	Cork & Bottle	"	⑤④❶
	Garlic & Shots	"	④④④
	Seven Stars	"	❸❸❷
	Shampers	"	❸❷❷
	Amato	Italian	❸❷❸
	Aperitivo	"	❸❸❸
	Ciao Bella	"	❸❶❷
	Pasta Brown	"	④④⑤
	Sapori	"	④❸❸
	Strada	"	④❸❸
	Mediterranean Kitchen	Mediterranean	⑤⑤④
	06 St Chad's Place	"	❷④❷
	Rainforest Café	Burgers, etc	⑤⑤④
	Fire & Stone	Pizza	❸❸❷
	Café Pacifico	Mexican/TexMex	④④❷
	La Perla	"	④④❸
	Souk Medina	Moroccan	❸❸❷
	Sofra	Turkish	④④④
	Tas	"	❸❷❸
	The Chinese Experience	Chinese	❷❶❸
	Fung Shing	"	❷❸④
	Yming	"	❷❶❸
	Café Lazeez	Indian	❸❸❸
	Mela	"	❸❸❸
	Soho Spice	"	④④❸
	Abeno	Japanese	❸❷④
	Abeno Too	"	❷❷❷
	Edokko	"	❶❶❸
	Hazuki	"	❸❷④
	Ten Ten Tei	"	❷❸⑤
	Katana	Pan-Asian	④④④
	Chiang Mai	Thai	❷④④
	Thai Pot	"	④❸④
£25+	Maxwell's	American	④④❸
	The Easton	Australian	❷④❷
	Real Greek Souvlaki & Bar	Greek	⑤⑤④
	Spacca Napoli	Italian	❷❶❸
	Zizzi	"	④④❸
	Leon	Mediterranean	❷❸❸
	La Tasca	Spanish	⑤⑤④
	Mildred's	Vegetarian	❷❸❷
	Harry Ramsden's	Fish & chips	④④④
	North Sea Fish	"	❷④④
	Paradiso Olivelli	Pizza	④④④
	Pâtisserie Valerie	Sandwiches, cakes, etc	❸④❷
	Paul	"	❷④④
	Souk	North African	⑤⑤❷
	Gaby's	Israeli	❸❷⑤
	Chuen Cheng Ku	Chinese	❸④④
	Golden Dragon	"	❸④④
	Harbour City	"	❸❸❸
	Jade Garden	"	❸④❸

	Laureate	"	④④④
	Mr Kong	"	❷❸⑤
	New Mayflower	"	❷❸④
	New World	"	❸❸❸
	ping pong	Chinese, Dim sum	❸❸❷
	Chowki	Indian	❸④④
	Gopal's of Soho	"	❸❸④
	Imli	"	❸❷❸
	Itsu	Japanese	❷❸❸
	Satsuma	"	❸④④
	Sushi Hiroba	"	❶❷❸
	Yo! Sushi	"	⑤④④
	Melati, Gt Windmill St	Malaysian	④❸⑤
	Busaba Eathai	Thai	❷❸❷
	Thai Square	"	④④❸
£20+	Café Emm	International	④❸❸
	Café in the Crypt	"	⑤④❸
	Exotika	"	❷❷④
	Gordon's Wine Bar	"	⑤❸❶
	Star Café	"	❸❷❸
	La Porchetta Pizzeria	Italian	❸❸❸
	Ed's Easy Diner	Burgers, etc	④❸❷
	Hamburger Union	"	❸④④
	The Ultimate Burger	"	④④⑤
	Calabash	Afro-Caribbean	❸④⑤
	Joy King Lau	Chinese	❸④④
	New Culture Revolution	"	④④⑤
	Wong Kei	"	❸⑤④
	India Club	Indian	④④④
	Masala Zone	"	❸❸❸
	Melati, Peter St	Indonesian	❸❸⑤
	Gili Gulu	Japanese	④⑤⑤
	Kulu Kulu	"	❷④⑤
	Misato	"	❷④⑤
	Taro	"	❸❸④
	Wagamama	"	④❸④
	Hare & Tortoise	Pan-Asian	❸❸④
£15+	Stock Pot	International	④④④
	Bistro 1	Mediterranean	④❷❸
	Food for Thought	Vegetarian	❷④④
	Bar Italia	Sandwiches, cakes, etc	④❷❶
	Konditor & Cook	"	❶④④
	Mr Jerk	Afro-Caribbean	❸④④
	Tokyo Diner	Japanese	❸❸④
£10+	Hummus Bros	Mediterranean	❸❷④
	Apostrophe	Sandwiches, cakes, etc	❷❸❸
	Monmouth Coffee Company	"	❶❷❷
£5+	Fryer's Delight	Fish & chips	❸❸⑤
	Flat White	Sandwiches, cakes, etc	❷❷❷
	Maison Bertaux	"	❷❷❷

Mayfair & St James's (Parts of W1 and SW1)

£120+	Le Gavroche	French	②⓪②
£110+	Sketch (Lecture Rm)	French	⑤④④
£100+	Umu	Japanese	❸❸④
£90+	The Ritz	French	④❸⓪
£80+	Dorchester Grill	British, Traditional	④④④
	Wiltons	"	❸②②
	G Ramsay at Claridges	French	❸②②
	The Greenhouse	"	❸②④
	The Square	"	②②④
	Nobu	Japanese	②④④
	Nobu Berkeley	"	❸④❸
£70+	The Brown's, Grill	British, Modern	④②④
	Mirabelle	French	④❸❸
	L'Oranger	"	❸❸❸
	Cipriani	Italian	⑤⑤④
	Connaught (Angela Hartnett)	Mediterranean	❸❸❸
	Hakkasan	Chinese	❸④②
	Taman gang	"	④④⓪
	Sumosan	Japanese	❸④④
£60+	Bellamy's	British, Modern	❸②❸
	Berkeley Square	"	– – –
	Brian Turner	"	④④⑤
	The Cuckoo Club	"	⑤④❸
	Patterson's	"	②❸④
	Galvin at Windows	French	②②❸
	Cecconi's	Italian	❸❸②
	Via Condotti	"	④②④
	China Tang	Chinese	④④❸
	Trader Vics	Indonesian	⑤④❸
	Ikeda	Japanese	②❸⑤
	Matsuri	"	②②④
	Miyama	"	②②⑤
	Cocoon	Pan-Asian	❸④②
£50+	Le Caprice	British, Modern	②⓪⓪
	Embassy	"	④④⑤
	Hush	"	④④❸
	Just St James	"	❸④④
	Nicole's	"	④❸④
	Quaglino's	"	⑤⑤⑤
	The Wolseley	"	❸②②
	Green's	British, Traditional	❸②❸
	Mews of Mayfair	"	⑤④④
	Bentley's	Fish & seafood	②②❸
	Dover Street	French	⑤⑤❸
	maze	"	②❸❸
	Sketch (Gallery)	"	⑤⑤④
	W'sens	"	❸❸②
	Giardinetto	Italian	❸②⑤
	Mosaico	"	❸❸④

	Sartoria	"	④❸④
	The Guinea Grill	Steaks & grills	❷❸❷
	Rowley's	"	⑤④④
	Mamounia	Moroccan	④❷❷
	Momo	"	④④❷
	Fakhreldine	Lebanese	❸❸❸
	Kai Mayfair	Chinese	❶❷❸
	Princess Garden	"	❷❷④
	Benares	Indian	❷❷❸
	Tamarind	"	❷❷❸
	Benihana	Japanese	④④④
	Chisou	"	❷❸④
	Mitsukoshi	"	❷❷⑤
	Shogun	"	❶❶④
£40+	Automat	American	④④❸
	The Avenue	British, Modern	④④④
	Inn the Park	"	④⑤❸
	Langan's Brasserie	"	④❸❷
	Pigalle Club	"	④❸❷
	Rhodes W1	"	④④⑤
	Six-13	"	❷❸④
	Zinc	"	④④④
	Greig's	British, Traditional	④④④
	Café Fish	Fish & seafood	❸④⑤
	Boudin Blanc	French	❸❸❷
	Brasserie Roux	"	❸❸❸
	Chez Gérard	"	⑤④④
	Gabrielles	"	④⑤④
	Alloro	Italian	❷❷❷
	Diverso	"	④④⑤
	Fiore	"	❸❷④
	Franco's	"	④④④
	Frankie's Italian Bar & Grill	"	⑤⑤④
	Getti	"	⑤④⑤
	Luciano	"	❸④❸
	Pappagallo	"	❸❷④
	Serafino	"	④❸④
	Teca	"	❷❷④
	Il Vicolo	"	❷❸④
	Truc Vert	Mediterranean	❸❸❸
	Gaucho Grill	Steaks & grills	❸④④
	Al Hamra	Lebanese	④⑤④
	Levant	"	④④❶
	Noura	"	④❸④
	Zen Central	Chinese	❷❷❸
	Chor Bizarre	Indian	❷❸❸
	Mint Leaf	"	❷❸❷
	Veeraswamy	"	❷❷❷
	Quilon	Indian, Southern	❷❷④
	Patara	Thai	❶❷❸
£35+	The Little Square	British, Modern	④❸❷
	Living Room W1	"	④④④
	Sotheby's Café	"	❷❶❷

			Ratings
	Fortnum's, The Fountain	British, Traditional	4 3 3
	Sketch (Glade)	French	5 5 5
	Tiger Tiger	International	5 5 4
	Al Duca	Italian	3 3 4
	Al Sultan	Lebanese	3 2 4
	Rasa	Indian	1 2 3
	Yoshino	Japanese	1 2 4
£30+	The Windmill	British, Traditional	3 3 3
	L'Artiste Musclé	French	4 2 2
	Browns	International	5 5 4
	Strada	Italian	4 3 3
	Rocket	Mediterranean	3 3 2
	El Pirata	Spanish	4 3 2
	Hard Rock Café	Burgers, etc	4 3 2
	Delfino	Pizza	2 2 3
	Richoux	Sandwiches, cakes, etc	5 5 4
	Royal Academy	"	4 5 3
	Sketch (Parlour)	"	4 4 4
	Sofra	Turkish	4 4 4
	Just Oriental	Pan-Asian	3 2 4
£25+	Running Horse	International	3 3 3
	Pâtisserie Valerie	Sandwiches, cakes, etc	3 4 2
	Ishtar	Turkish	4 4 3
	Woodlands	Indian	1 2 4
	Itsu	Japanese	2 3 3
	Sakura	"	2 5 3
	Yo! Sushi	"	5 4 4
	Jindalle	Korean	3 4 4
	Busaba Eathai	Thai	2 3 2
	Thai Square	"	4 4 3
£20+	Gourmet Pizza Co.	Pizza	4 4 4
	Maison Blanc Vite	Sandwiches, cakes, etc	3 4 4
	Toku	Japanese	3 4 4
	Wagamama	"	4 3 4
	Noodle Noodle	Pan-Asian	3 4 5
£15+	Stock Pot	International	4 4 4
£10+	Benugo	Sandwiches, cakes, etc	2 3 4
	Crussh	"	2 2 4
£5+	Fuzzy's Grub	Sandwiches, cakes, etc	1 1 3

Fitzrovia & Marylebone (Part of W1)

			Ratings
£80+	Pied à Terre	French	2 2 2
£70+	Spoon at Sanderson	Fusion	5 5 5
£60+	Orrery	French	3 2 3
	The Providores	Fusion	3 3 3
	5 Cavendish Square	Italian	4 4 3
	Royal China Club	Chinese	2 2 4
	Defune	Japanese	2 4 5
£50+	Oscar	British, Modern	5 5 4

			Ratings
	Caldesi	*Italian*	❸④④
	Eddalino	"	❸❸④
	Locanda Locatelli	"	❷❷❷
	Passione	"	❸❸④
	La Porte des Indes	*Indian*	❸❸❷
£40+	Blandford Street	*British, Modern*	④❸④
	CVO Firevault	"	❸❸⓿
	Mash	"	⑤⑤⑤
	Odin's	*British, Traditional*	❸⓿⓿
	Back to Basics	*Fish & seafood*	⓿❸④
	Fishworks	"	❷④④
	Annex 3	*French*	⑤⑤❷
	Café Bagatelle	"	⑤⑤⓿
	Elena's L'Etoile	"	④❸❷
	Galvin Bistrot de Luxe	"	❷❷❷
	Villandry	"	— — —
	Archipelago	*Fusion*	❷⓿⓿
	Hardy's	*International*	④❷❸
	Michael Moore	"	❸❸④
	Bertorelli's	*Italian*	⑤④④
	Caffè Caldesi	"	④④④
	Camerino	"	❸❷④
	Getti	"	⑤④⑤
	Latium	"	⓿❷❸
	Sardo	"	❷❷❸
	La Spighetta	"	❸❸⑤
	Fino	*Spanish*	❷⓿❷
	Black & Blue	*Steaks & grills*	❸❸④
	Reubens	*Kosher*	④④④
	Fairuz	*Lebanese*	❷❸④
	Maroush	"	❸④⑤
	Deya	*Indian*	❷❷④
	Roka	*Japanese*	⓿❸❸
	Koba	*Korean*	❷⓿❷
	Crazy Bear	*Thai*	❷❷⓿
	Bam-Bou	*Vietnamese*	❸❸⓿
£35+	The Union Café	*British, Modern*	❸❸❸
	Auberge	*French*	⑤④④
	Providores (Tapa Room)	*Fusion*	❷❸❷
	Salt Yard	*Mediterranean*	⓿❷❸
	Garbo's	*Scandinavian*	④❸⑤
	Royal China	*Chinese*	❷❸④
	Rasa Samudra	*Indian*	⓿❷❸
£30+	RIBA Café	*British, Modern*	④❸⓿
	Langan's Bistro	*French*	❸❷❷
	Le Relais de Venise	"	④④❸
	Eat & Two Veg	*International*	⑤⑤④
	Giraffe	"	④❸❸
	O'Conor Don	*Irish*	④❸❷
	Strada	*Italian*	④❸❸
	La Rueda	*Spanish*	④⑤❸
	L'Entrecôte Café de Paris	*Steaks & grills*	④④④
	Tootsies	*Burgers, etc*	④④④

	La Fromagerie Café	*Sandwiches, cakes, etc*	❶②②
	La Perla	*Mexican/TexMex*	④④③
	Original Tajines	*Moroccan*	❸❸❸
	Sofra	*Turkish*	④④④
	Ragam	*Indian, Southern*	❶❶⑤
	Soho Japan	*Japanese*	❷③④
£25+	Real Greek Souvlaki & Bar	*Greek*	⑤⑤④
	Carluccio's Caffè	*Italian*	④④❸
	Zizzi	*"*	④④❸
	Navarro's	*Spanish*	❷❸❷
	Eagle Bar Diner	*Burgers, etc*	❸④❷
	Paradiso Olivelli	*Pizza*	④④④
	Pâtisserie Valerie	*Sandwiches, cakes, etc*	❸④❷
	Paul	*"*	❷④④
	Efes II	*Turkish*	④④❸
	Ozer	*"*	④❸❸
	ping pong	*Chinese, Dim sum*	❸❸❷
	Woodlands	*Indian*	❶❷④
	Ikkyu	*Japanese*	❸④④
	Yo! Sushi	*"*	⑤④④
	dim T	*Pan-Asian*	④④❸
£20+	Fine Burger Company	*Burgers, etc*	❸❸④
	The Ultimate Burger	*"*	④④⑤
	Le Pain Quotidien	*Sandwiches, cakes, etc*	❷❸❶
	Wagamama	*Japanese*	④❸④
	Siam Central	*Thai*	④❷❸
£15+	Golden Hind	*Fish & chips*	❶❷❸
£10+	Apostrophe	*Sandwiches, cakes, etc*	❷❸❸
	Benugo	*"*	❷❸④
£5+	Square Pie Company	*British, Traditional*	❷❸④

Belgravia, Pimlico, Victoria & Westminster (SW1, except St James's)

£80+	Pétrus	*French*	❶❶❷
£70+	The Lanesborough	*British, Modern*	④❷❶
	Rib Room	*British, Traditional*	④④⑤
	One-O-One	*Fish & seafood*	❶❸⑤
	Foliage	*French*	❷❷❸
	La Noisette	*"*	❸❸❸
	Nahm	*Thai*	④④⑤
£60+	The Goring Hotel	*British, Traditional*	❸❶❶
	Mju	*French*	❸❸⑤
	Roussillon	*"*	❶❶❷
	Santini	*Italian*	④❸❸
	Toto's	*"*	❷❷❷
	Mr Chow	*Chinese*	④④④
£50+	The Fifth Floor Restaurant	*British, Modern*	④④⑤
	Boxwood Café	*British, Traditional*	④❸④
	Pomegranates	*International*	④❸❷
	L'Incontro	*Italian*	❸❸❸

for updates visit www.hardens.com

	Mimmo d'Ischia	"	④❷④
	Signor Sassi	"	④❷④
	Volt	"	❸❸❷
	Zafferano	"	❷❷❸
	Boisdale	Scottish	❸❷❶
	Ladurée	Afternoon tea	❸④❸
	Amaya	Indian	❶❸❷
	The Cinnamon Club	"	❷❸❷
£40+	Atrium	British, Modern	⑤⑤④
	Bank Westminster	"	④④❸
	Ebury Wine Bar	"	❸❸❷
	Tate Britain	"	④❸❷
	Thomas Cubitt	"	❸❷❷
	Shepherd's	British, Traditional	④❷❸
	Chez Gérard	French	⑤④④
	Drones	"	④④④
	The Ebury	"	④④❸
	La Poule au Pot	"	❸❷❶
	Motcombs	International	④④❸
	Caraffini	Italian	❷❶❷
	Il Convivio	"	❷❶❸
	Olivo	"	❷❷④
	Quirinale	"	❶❷❸
	Sale e Pepe	"	❸❶❷
	Oliveto	Pizza	❷❸⑤
	Beiteddine	Lebanese	❸❸④
	Noura	"	④❸④
	Hunan	Chinese	❶❶④
	Ken Lo's Memories	"	❷❷❷
	Salloos	Pakistani	❶❶④
	Mango Tree	Thai	❸❸④
£35+	The Contented Vine	British, Modern	④④④
	Footstool	"	⑤⑤④
	Grenadier	British, Traditional	④④❷
	Le Cercle	French	❶❷❷
	City Café	International	④❷❸
	Grumbles	"	❸❷❸
	Como Lario	Italian	④④④
	Pizza on the Park	"	④④❸
	Uno	"	❸④④
	About Thyme	Mediterranean	④④④
	The Fifth Floor Café	"	⑤⑤④
	Baker & Spice	Sandwiches, cakes, etc	❷④④
	Texas Embassy Cantina	Mexican/TexMex	⑤④④
	Ishbilia	Lebanese	❷❷④
£30+	Oriel	International	⑤④❷
	Goya	Spanish	④❷❸
	Ranoush	Lebanese	❷④④
	Kazan	Turkish	❸❷❸
	Pan-Asian Canteen	Pan-Asian	❷❸❸
£25+	Royal Court Bar	British, Modern	⑤④❸
	Chimes	British, Traditional	⑤④④

	Caramel	*Mediterranean*	④❸❷
	Seafresh	*Fish & chips*	❸④④
	Pâtisserie Valerie	*Sandwiches, cakes, etc*	❸④❷
	Feng Sushi	*Japanese*	❸❸❸
	Yo! Sushi	*"*	⑤④④
	Blue Jade	*Thai*	④❷④
	Page in Pimlico	*"*	❸❷❸
	Thai Café	*"*	❸④⑤
£20+	Cyprus Mangal	*Turkish*	❶❸④
	Jenny Lo's	*Chinese*	❶❷❸
	Wagamama	*Japanese*	④❸④
	Mekong	*Vietnamese*	❸❷❸
£10+	Apostrophe	*Sandwiches, cakes, etc*	❷❸❸

WEST

Chelsea, South Kensington, Kensington, Earl's Court & Fulham (SW3, SW5, SW6, SW7, SW10 & W8)

Price	Restaurant	Cuisine	Ratings
£100+	Blakes	International	④❸❶
£90+	Hosteria Del Pesce	Fish & seafood	– – –
	Aubergine	French	❷❷❸
	Gordon Ramsay	"	❶❶❷
£80+	Tom Aikens	French	❸❷❸
£70+	The Capital Restaurant	French	❷❷❸
	1880	"	❸❸❷
	Brunello	Italian	⑤⑤❸
	Rasoi Vineet Bhatia	Indian	❶❷❸
£60+	The Collection	British, Modern	④⑤❸
	The Tenth	"	❸❷❶
	Bibendum	French	❸❷❷
	Nozomi	Japanese	⑤④④
	Zuma	"	❶❸❶
£50+	Babylon	British, Modern	④④❶
	Bluebird	"	⑤⑤⑤
	Clarke's	"	❶❶❸
	Kensington Place	"	❸❸④
	Launceston Place	"	❸❸❷
	Deep	Fish & seafood	– – –
	Poissonnerie de l'Av.	"	❷❷❸
	Le Suquet	"	❷④❸
	Belvedere	French	❸❷❶
	Cheyne Walk Bras'	"	❸❸❶
	L'Etranger	"	❷❷❸
	Papillon	"	❸❸❷
	Aquasia	Fusion	④④④
	Carpaccio's	Italian	⑤⑤❸
	Daphne's	"	❸❸❷
	Montpeliano	"	⑤⑤④
	San Lorenzo	"	④④④
	Scalini	"	❸❸❸
	Timo	"	❸❷④
	Locanda Ottoemezzo	Mediterranean	④④❷
	Bombay Brasserie	Indian	❸❸❸
	Chutney Mary	"	❷❷❷
	Zaika	"	❷❸❸
	Benihana	Japanese	④④④
£40+	Big Easy	American	❸❸❸
	PJ's	"	⑤⑤❸
	The Abingdon	British, Modern	❸❷❷
	Admiral Codrington	"	❸❸❸
	11 Abingdon Road	"	④❸④
	Joe's Café	"	❸④④
	Whits	"	❸❶❸

	Name	Cuisine	Ratings
	Bluebird Club	British, Traditional	④④④
	Maggie Jones's	"	④❸❶
	Lundum's	Danish	❷⓪⓪
	Lou Pescadou	Fish & seafood	❷❷❸
	Stratford's	"	❷❷❸
	La Bouchée	French	❷❸❷
	La Brasserie	"	④④❷
	Brasserie St Quentin	"	❸❷❸
	Le Colombier	"	❸❷❷
	Nathalie	"	❷⓪④
	Racine	"	❷⓪❷
	The Enterprise	International	④❷❷
	The Swag & Tails	"	❸❷❷
	Zinc	"	④④④
	The Ark	Italian	④❸❷
	La Famiglia	"	④④❸
	Frankie's	"	⑤⑤④
	Lucio	"	❸❷❸
	Manicomio	"	❸④❸
	Monza	"	❷❸④
	Osteria dell'Arancio	"	❸❷❷
	Pellicano	"	❸❷❸
	Il Portico	"	❸⓪❸
	Ziani	"	❸❷❷
	Cross Keys	Mediterranean	④④❸
	Wódka	Polish	❸❷❷
	Tugga	Portuguese	⑤⑤④
	Nikita's	Russian	⑤❷⓪
	Cambio de Tercio	Spanish	❷❸❸
	L-Restaurant & Bar	"	❸❷④
	Black & Blue	Steaks & grills	❸❸④
	Gaucho Grill	"	❸④④
	Pasha	Moroccan	– – –
	Maroush	Lebanese	❸④⑤
	Good Earth	Chinese	❷❷❸
	Ken Lo's Memories	"	❷❷❸
	Mao Tai	"	❷❷❸
	Mr Wing	"	❷❷⓪
	The Painted Heron	Indian	⓪⓪❸
	Vama	"	⓪❷❸
	Kisso	Japanese	❸④④
	Awana	Malaysian	❸❸④
	Eight Over Eight	Pan-Asian	⓪❷❷
	Blue Elephant	Thai	❸❷⓪
	Patara	"	⓪❷❸
	Saran Rom	"	❸❸❷
	Sugar Hut	"	④④⓪
£35+	Sticky Fingers	American	⑤⑤④
	TGI Friday's	"	⑤⑤⑤
	Bibendum Oyster Bar	British, Modern	❸❸❸
	Bistrot 190	"	⑤⑤④
	Britannia	"	❸❷❸
	Duke on the Green	"	❸④❸

	The Farm	"	– – –
	The Ifield	"	④❸❸
	Lots Road	"	– – –
	The Mall Tavern	"	❸④❸
	The Phoenix	"	④④❸
	The Pig's Ear	"	❸❸❷
	The Salisbury Tavern	"	❸❸❸
	Ffiona's	British, Traditional	④❶❶
	Ghillies	Fish & seafood	④④❸
	Langan's Coq d'Or	French	❸❷❸
	Randall & Aubin	"	❷❸❶
	Tartine	"	④❸❸
	Beaufort House	International	④❸❷
	The Cabin	"	❸❷❸
	Foxtrot Oscar	"	⑤⑤④
	606 Club	"	⑤④❶
	De Cecco	Italian	❸❷❸
	Elistano	"	④④④
	Il Falconiere	"	④❸④
	Frantoio	"	❸❷❷
	Made in Italy	"	❷⑤④
	Matriciano	"	❸❸❸
	Napulé	"	❷④❸
	Nuovi Sapori	"	❷❶④
	Ottolenghi	"	❶❸❸
	Riccardo's	"	❸❸❸
	Polish Club (Ognisko Polskie)	Polish	④❷❷
	Tendido Cero	Spanish	❷❸❷
	El Gaucho	Steaks & grills	❷④④
	Aubaine	Sandwiches, cakes, etc	⑤⑤❸
	Baker & Spice	"	❷④④
	Cactus Blue	South American	⑤④④
	1492	"	❸④❸
	Aziz	Moroccan	④④❷
	Al Bustan	Lebanese	❸④⑤
	Randa	"	❸❸④
	Made in China	Chinese	❷❷⑤
	Haandi	Indian	❷❸④
	kare kare	"	❷❷④
	Love India	"	❷❷④
	Star of India	"	❷❸④
	Sukho Thai Cuisine	Thai	❶❷❸
	Nam Long	Vietnamese	⑤④④
£30+	Bodean's	American	❸❸❸
	Abbaye	Belgian	④④④
	Brinkley's	British, Modern	④❸❷
	The Builder's Arms	"	❸❸❶
	Harwood Arms	"	❸❷❷
	Joe's Brasserie	"	❸❸❷
	Le Metro	"	❸❸❷
	The Oratory	"	④④❷
	Vingt-Quatre	"	④④❸
	White Horse	"	❸❸❷

	Kensington Arms	British, Traditional	❸❸④
	Base	French	❸④❸
	Balans	International	⑤④❸
	Giraffe	"	④❸❸
	Glaisters	"	④④❷
	The Scarsdale	"	④❸❶
	Wine Gallery	"	⑤❸❷
	Aglio e Olio	Italian	❷❸❸
	Buona Sera	"	❸❷❷
	Da Mario	"	❸❸❸
	Loco Locale	"	④❸❸
	Miraggio	"	❸④④
	Il Pagliaccio	"	④❷❶
	Picasso's	"	⑤④❸
	Santa Lucia	"	❸❸❷
	Strada	"	④❸❸
	The Atlas	Mediterranean	❷❸❷
	Mediterranean Kitchen	"	⑤⑤④
	La Rueda	Spanish	④⑤❸
	Sophie's Steakhouse	Steaks & grills	❸❸❶
	Tootsies	Burgers, etc	④④④
	Sea Cow	Fish & chips	❷❸④
	Basilico	Pizza	❷❸④
	Friends	"	④❷❸
	(Ciro's) Pizza Pomodoro	"	④④❷
	Bluebird Café	Sandwiches, cakes, etc	⑤⑤④
	Hugo's	"	④④❷
	Richoux	"	⑤⑤④
	Troubadour	"	④④❶
	La Perla	Mexican/TexMex	④④❸
	Ranoush	Lebanese	❷④④
	Choys	Chinese	④❸④
	Café Lazeez	Indian	❸❸❸
	Ma Goa	"	❶❶❷
	Malabar	"	❷❷❸
	Noor Jahan	"	❷❷❸
	Wizzy	Korean	❷⑤⑤
	Jim Thompson's	Pan-Asian	⑤⑤❸
	Zimzun	"	❸④❸
	Bangkok	Thai	❷❷④
	Busabong	"	④④④
£25+	The Anglesea Arms	British, Modern	❸❷❷
	Blue Kangaroo	International	④④④
	Coopers Arms	"	④④④
	The Windsor Castle	"	④④❶
	Carluccio's Caffè	Italian	④④❸
	Lillo e Franco	"	❷❷④
	Pappa Ciccia	"	❷❶❷
	Rossopomodoro	"	❸④❸
	Spago	"	❷❷❸
	Zizzi	"	④④❸
	Leon	Mediterranean	❷❸❸
	Daquise	Polish	④④❸

			Rating
	Rôtisserie Jules	Steaks & grills	③④⑤
	Henry J Beans	Burgers, etc	④④❸
	Geale's	Fish & chips	④❸④
	Pâtisserie Valerie	Sandwiches, cakes, etc	❸④❷
	Paul	"	❷④④
	Taiwan Village	Chinese	❷⓿❸
	Yi-Ban	"	❷❸❷
	Khan's of Kensington	Indian	❸❷④
	Khyber Pass	"	❷❷④
	Memories of India	"	❸❷❸
	Shikara	"	❸❸❸
	Tandoori Lane	"	❸❷❸
	Feng Sushi	Japanese	❸❸❸
	Itsu	"	❷❸❸
	Yo! Sushi	"	⑤④④
	Tampopo	Pan-Asian	❸④④
	Thai Square	Thai	④④❸
£20+	As Greek As It Gets	Greek	④④⑤
	Chelsea Bun Diner	International	❸❷❸
	Mona Lisa	"	❸❷④
	Little Bay	Mediterranean	❸❷❷
	Ed's Easy Diner	Burgers, etc	④❸❷
	Gourmet Burger Kitchen	"	❷④④
	Café Crêperie	Crêpes	❷④④
	La Delizia	Pizza	❸④④
	New Culture Rev'n	Chinese	④④⑤
	Masala Zone	Indian	❸❸❸
	Kulu Kulu	Japanese	❷④⑤
	Wagamama	"	④❸④
£15+	Costa's Grill	Greek	④❷❸
	Chelsea Kitchen	International	④❸④
	Stock Pot	"	④④④
	Stick & Bowl	Chinese	❸❸⑤
	Café 209	Thai	❸❸⓿
	Churchill Arms	"	❷④❸
£10+	Benugo	Sandwiches, cakes, etc	❷❸④
	Crussh	"	❷❷④

Notting Hill, Holland Park, Bayswater, North Kensington & Maida Vale (W2, W9, W10, W11)

			Rating
£60+	The Ledbury	French	⓿⓿❷
	I Thai	Fusion	⑤⑤④
£50+	Notting Hill Brasserie	British, Modern	⓿⓿❷
	Assaggi	Italian	⓿⓿❷
	Notting Grill	Steaks & grills	❸④❸
£40+	Beach Blanket Babylon	British, Modern	⑤⑤❷
	The Frontline Club	"	④❷❷
	Island	"	❸⓿❸
	Julie's	"	④④⓿
	Julie's Wine Bar	"	④④❷
	Electric Brasserie	International	④④❷

	Arturo	*Italian*	④④④
	Edera	"	④③④
	Esenza	"	❸②❸
	Mediterraneo	"	②②❸
	Osteria Basilico	"	❷❸❶
	Fairuz	*Lebanese*	❷❸④
	Café Maroush	"	❸④⑤
	Bombay Palace	*Indian*	❶❶❸
	Yakitoria	*Japanese*	❷❸❷
	E&O	*Pan-Asian*	❶②❶
£35+	Harlem	*American*	⑤⑤④
	TGI Friday's	"	⑤⑤⑤
	First Floor	*British, Modern*	④②❶
	Formosa Dining Room	"	❸❸❸
	The Ladbroke Arms	"	❷④❷
	Raoul's Café	"	④⑤④
	Ruby Lounge & Sequoia Bar	"	④④❶
	The Tea Palace	"	④❸④
	The Waterway	"	❸⑤❸
	The Cow	*Fish & seafood*	❷④❷
	Père Michel	*French*	❸❸④
	Halepi	*Greek*	❸④❸
	202	*International*	❸❸❶
	L'Accento Italiano	*Italian*	❸❸❸
	Cristini	"	❸❸④
	The Green Olive	"	❸❸❸
	Luna Rossa	"	④⑤④
	Ottolenghi	"	❶❸❸
	Raoul's Café & Deli	*Mediterranean*	④⑤④
	Crazy Homies	*Mexican/TexMex*	❸⑤❷
	Levantine	*Lebanese*	④④❸
	Royal China	*Chinese*	❷❸④
	Bombay Bicycle Club	*Indian*	❷❸④
£30+	Lucky Seven	*American*	❷❸❷
	Paradise, Kensal Green	*British, Modern*	❸②❷
	The Westbourne	"	❸④❶
	The Red Pepper	*Italian*	❷④④
	Wine Factory	"	④②❸
	Mediterranean Kitchen	*Mediterranean*	⑤⑤④
	Tootsies	*Burgers, etc*	④④④
	Rodizio Rico	*Brazilian*	④④④
	Al-Waha	*Lebanese*	❸❸④
	Ranoush	"	❷④④
	Mandarin Kitchen	*Chinese*	❶④④
	Ginger	*Indian*	❸❸④
	Noor Jahan	"	❷❷❸
	Inaho	*Japanese*	❶⑤⑤
	Mika	"	❸④❸
	Tawana	*Thai*	❷❷④
	The Walmer Castle	"	❸④❷
£25+	The Prince Bonaparte	*British, Modern*	❷❸❷
	Café Laville	*International*	④❸❷
	Cowshed	"	❸❸❸

	Galicia	Spanish	❸❷❷
	Rôtisserie Jules	Steaks & grills	❸④⑤
	Tom's	Sandwiches, cakes, etc	④④❷
	Taqueria	Mexican/TexMex	❸❸④
	The Four Seasons	Chinese	❷⑤⑤
	ping pong	Chinese, Dim sum	❸❸❷
	Feng Sushi	Japanese	❸❸❸
	Yo! Sushi	"	⑤④④
	Nyonya	Malaysian	❸❸④
	Uli	Pan-Asian	❷⓪❷
£20+	Babes 'n' Burgers	American	❸④❸
	S & M Café	British, Traditional	❸❷❸
	Gourmet Burger Kitchen	Burgers, etc	❷④④
	Firezza	Pizza	❷❷❸
	Beirut Express	Lebanese	❷④④
	Alounak	Persian	❷④❸
	Kandoo	"	❸❷❸
	Shish	Turkish	❸❸❷
	New Culture Rev'n	Chinese	④④⑤
	Standard Tandoori	Indian	❷④⑤
	Mawar	Malaysian	❸④⑤
	Ben's Thai	Thai	❸④❸
	Yelo Thai Canteen	"	❸❷❸
£15+	Mr Jerk	Afro-Caribbean	❸④④
	Moroccan Tagine	Moroccan	❸❸❸
	Fresco	Lebanese	❷⓪❸
	Mandalay	Burmese	⓪⓪④
	Khan's	Indian	❷④④
£5+	Lisboa Pâtisserie	Sandwiches, cakes, etc	❷❸❸

Hammersmith, Shepherd's Bush, Olympia, Chiswick & Ealing (W4, W5, W6, W12, W14)

£60+	The River Café	Italian	❷❸❸
£50+	La Trompette	French	⓪⓪❷
£40+	Smollensky's	American	⑤④④
	High Road Brasserie	British, Modern	– – –
	Snows on the Green	"	❷❷❸
	Fish Hook	Fish & seafood	❷❸④
	Fishworks	"	❷④④
	Charlotte's Place	French	❸❸④
	Cibo	Italian	❸❷④
	Frankie's	"	⑤⑤④
£35+	The Brackenbury	British, Modern	❷❷❷
	Bush Bar & Grill	"	– – –
	Devonshire House	"	④❸④
	Ealing Park Tavern	"	❸❷❷
	Gravy	"	④④④
	The Havelock Tavern	"	⓪⑤❸
	Hole in the Wall	"	❸❸❷

	Pacific Bar and Grill	"	④④②
	Pissarro's	"	❸②❶
	The Rocket	"	❸④②
	Sam's Brasserie	"	④❸❸
	Chez Kristof	French	❸❸②
	Le Vacherin	"	❷❷❸
	Annie's	International	④❷❷
	Est Est Est	Italian	– – –
	The Grove	Mediterranean	④④❸
	Popeseye	Steaks & grills	❷❸④
	The Gate	Vegetarian	❷❸④
	Sushi-Hiro	Japanese	❶②④
£30+	The Anglesea Arms	British, Modern	❷④②
	The Bollo House	"	④④❸
	The Thatched House	"	❸④②
	Balans	International	⑤④❸
	Giraffe	"	④❸❸
	Parmigiano	Italian	❸❸❸
	The Swan	Mediterranean	❷❸②
	Tootsies	Burgers, etc	④④④
	Brilliant	Indian	❷❷❷
	Madhu's	"	❶❷❷
£25+	The Crown & Sceptre	British, Modern	❸④❸
	The Dove	"	④④❷
	The Pilot	"	❸❷❷
	Stone Mason's Arms	"	④④❸
	Vesbar	International	④❸❸
	Carluccio's Caffè	Italian	④④❸
	Zizzi	"	④④❸
	Priory House	Mediterranean	❸❸②
	Lowiczanka	Polish	④④⑤
	Patio	"	④❷❸
	La Tasca	Spanish	⑤⑤④
	Blah! Blah! Blah!	Vegetarian	❷❸❸
	Adams Café	Moroccan	❷❶❸
	Azou	North African	❸②❸
	Chez Marcelle	Lebanese	❶④⑤
	Mohsen	Persian	❷❷④
	Yas	"	④④⑤
	Anarkali	Indian	❸❷④
	Indian Zing	"	❷❶❸
	Karma	"	❸❷④
	Monty's	"	❸❸④
	Woodlands	"	❶②④
	Sagar	Indian, Southern	❶❶④
	Tosa	Japanese	❷❷❸
	Esarn Kheaw	Thai	❶②⑤
	Fat Boy's	"	❸❸❸
	Silks & Spice	"	❸②❸
	Thai Bistro	"	❷❸④
	Saigon Saigon	Vietnamese	❷❸④
£20+	Queen's Head	British, Traditional	④❸②
	La Copita	Spanish	❸❸④

	Gourmet Burger Kitchen	*Burgers, etc*	②④④
	Firezza	*Pizza*	②②③
	Chez Kristof (Deli)	*Sandwiches, cakes, etc*	③④③
	Alounak	*Persian*	②④③
	Best Mangal	*Turkish*	②③④
	Agni	*Indian*	①①④
	Mirch Masala	*"*	①③⑤
	Hare & Tortoise	*Pan-Asian*	③③④
	Bedlington Café	*Thai*	③④④
	Latymers	*"*	③④⑤
	Sabai Sabai	*"*	③③⑤
£15+	Abu Zaad	*Syrian*	②③③
	Hammersmith Café	*Thai*	③②④
	Old Parr's Head	*"*	③②④
£10+	Bush Garden Café	*Organic*	③③②
	Crussh	*Sandwiches, cakes, etc*	②②④

NORTH

Hampstead, West Hampstead, St John's Wood, Regent's Park, Kilburn & Camden Town (NW postcodes)

£50+	Landmark (Winter Gdn)	British, Modern	④❸❷
	L'Aventure	French	❷❷❶
	Benihana	Japanese	④④④
£40+	Bradley's	British, Modern	❸❸④
	The Engineer	"	❷④❷
	Globe Restaurant	"	❸❷④
	The Wells	"	❸❸❷
	Fishworks	Fish & seafood	❷④④
	Oslo Court	French	❷❶❸
	Le Petit Train	"	❸❸❸
	Artigiano	Italian	④④④
	Philpotts Mezzaluna	"	❸❸④
	Rosmarino	"	⑤④④
	Sardo Canale	"	❷❷❷
	Villa Bianca	"	④❸❷
	Black & Blue	Steaks & grills	❸❸④
	Gaucho Grill	"	❸④④
	Good Earth	Chinese	❷❷❸
	Kaifeng	"	❸❷④
	Wakaba	Japanese	❷④⑤
	Gilgamesh	Pan-Asian	④❷❶
£35+	Café Med	British, Modern	④④❸
	Freemasons Arms	"	④④❸
	The Hill	"	④④❸
	The Lansdowne	"	❸④❷
	Queen's Head & Artichoke	Fusion	❸❸❷
	La Collina	Italian	❸❸❸
	Salt House	"	❸❸❷
	The Salusbury	"	❸❸❸
	Sarracino	"	❸❷❸
	Camden Brasserie	Mediterranean	④④④
	Baker & Spice	Sandwiches, cakes, etc	❷④④
	Cottons	Afro-Caribbean	④④❷
	Mango Room	"	❷❸❶
	Royal China	Chinese	❷❸④
	ZeNW3	"	❸④④
	Bombay Bicycle Club	Indian	❷❸④
	Sushi-Say	Japanese	❷❶④
	Singapore Garden	Malaysian	❷❷❸
£30+	Belgo Noord	Belgian	④④❸
	The Chapel	British, Modern	④❸❸
	The Green	"	❸❸❸
	The Greyhound	"	④❸❸
	Holly Bush	"	❸❸❷
	The Island	"	❷❸❸
	The Junction Tavern	"	❸❷❷
	The Lord Palmerston	"	❷❸❷

Name	Cuisine	Ratings
No 77 Wine Bar	"	④❸❷
Roundhouse Café	"	– – –
The Vine	"	④⑤④
Walnut	"	❷❷❸
Base	French	❸④❸
La Cage Imaginaire	"	❸❷❷
Somerstown Coffee House	"	④④④
Lemonia	Greek	④❷❶
The Arches	International	④❷❷
Giraffe	"	④❸❸
Fratelli la Bufala	Italian	④❸❸
Strada	"	④❸❸
Zuccato	"	④❸④
William IV	Mediterranean	④❸❷
Pescador Too	Portuguese	❸❷❸
Manna	Vegetarian	❸❷❸
Tootsies	Burgers, etc	④④④
Seashell	Fish & chips	❷④⑤
Basilico	Pizza	❷❸④
Hugo's	Sandwiches, cakes, etc	④④❷
Richoux	"	⑤⑤④
Harry Morgan's	Israeli	❸❸⑤
Solly's Exclusive	"	④④④
Sofra	Turkish	④④④
Gung-Ho	Chinese	❷❷❷
Phoenix Palace	"	❷❸❸
Weng Wah House	"	④④❸
Eriki	Indian	❶❶❷
Jin Kichi	Japanese	❶❷④
Yuzu	"	❷④④
£25+ Maxwell's	American	④④❸
Crown & Goose	British, Modern	❸❸❷
The Garden Café	"	④④❶
Daphne	Greek	❸❷❷
Kaz Kreol	International	– – –
L'Artista	Italian	❸❷❸
La Brocca	"	④❸❷
Carluccio's Caffè	"	④④❸
Marine Ices	"	④❷❷
Zizzi	"	④④❸
Troika	Russian	④④❸
Don Pepe	Spanish	❷❷❸
Nautilus	Fish & chips	❶❶❸
Paul	Sandwiches, cakes, etc	❷④④
Mestizo	Mexican/TexMex	❷❷④
Tobia	Ethiopian	❷❷⑤
Great Nepalese	Indian	❷❷⑤
Vijay	"	❷❷❸
Woodlands	"	❶❷④
Zamzama	"	❸④❸
Café Japan	Japanese	❶❷⑤
Feng Sushi	"	❸❸❸
Yo! Sushi	"	⑤④④

			Ratings
	dim T café	*Pan-Asian*	④④❸
	Café de Maya	*Thai*	④❷④
	Silks & Spice	*"*	❸❷❸
£20+	La Porchetta Pizzeria	*Italian*	❸❸❸
	The Little Bay	*Mediterranean*	❸❷❷
	Haché	*Steaks & grills*	❷❷❷
	Fine Burger Company	*Burgers, etc*	❸❸④
	Gourmet Burger Kitchen	*Burgers, etc*	❷④④
	Café Crêp de Hampst.	*Crêpes*	❷④④
	Kenwood (Brew House)	*Sandwiches, cakes, etc*	④❸❷
	Ali Baba	*Egyptian*	❸❸④
	Shish	*Turkish*	❸❸❷
	New Culture Revolution	*Chinese*	④④⑤
	Chutneys	*Indian*	❸④④
	Diwana B-P House	*"*	❸④⑤
	Five Hot Chillies	*"*	❶❶❸
	Jashan	*"*	❶❶④
	Sabras	*"*	❶④⑤
	Kovalam	*Indian, Southern*	❷❷⑤
	Wagamama	*Japanese*	④❸④
	Oriental City	*Pan-Asian*	❷④⑤
£15+	Little Earth Café	*Vegetarian*	❷❸④
	Chamomile	*Sandwiches, cakes, etc*	❸❷④
	Geeta	*Indian*	❷❷⑤
	Sakonis	*"*	❷④⑤
	Viet-Anh	*Vietnamese*	❸❶④
£10+	Gail's Bread	*Sandwiches, cakes, etc*	❸❷④

Hoxton, Islington, Highgate, Crouch End, Stoke Newington, Finsbury Park, Muswell Hill & Finchley (N postcodes)

£80+	Fifteen Restaurant	*Italian*	⑤④④
£40+	The Bull	*British, Modern*	④④❸
	Frederick's	*"*	❸❸❷
	The House	*"*	❸❸❸
	Fishworks	*Fish & seafood*	❷④④
	Sargasso Sea	*"*	❷❷❷
	The Almeida	*French*	④④④
	Morgan M	*"*	❶❷④
	Fifteen Trattoria	*Italian*	❸❷❷
	Metrogusto	*"*	④❶❷
	San Carlo	*"*	④❷❸
	Cru	*Mediterranean*	④④❷
£35+	The Drapers Arms	*British, Modern*	❸④❸
	The Duke of Cambridge	*"*	❸④❸
	The Elk in the Woods	*"*	❸❸❶
	Fig	*"*	❸❷❸
	The Lock Dining Bar	*"*	❷❷④
	Mosaica	*"*	❷④❸
	The Pumphouse	*"*	❸❷❶
	The Marquess Tavern	*British, Traditional*	❸❸❷

	Chez Liline	Fish & seafood		❶❸⑤
	Bistro Aix	French		❸❸④
	The Real Greek	Greek		❸④❷
	Hoxton Apprentice	International		④④❸
	The Living Room	"		④④④
	Orange Tree	"		❸④❷
	Casale Franco	Italian		④❸❸
	Ottolenghi	"		❶❸❸
	Pasha	Turkish		④❸④
	OQO Bar	Chinese		④❸❷
	Rasa Travancore	Indian, Southern		❶❷❸
£30+	The Barnsbury	British, Modern		❷❷❷
	The Haven	"		❸❷❷
	The Northgate	"		❸❷❸
	William IV	"		❸❸❸
	St Johns	British, Traditional		❸❷❶
	Bastille	French		④④④
	Hoxton Square	Fusion		❸④❸
	Banners	International		❸❶❶
	Browns	"		⑤⑤④
	The Fox Reformed	"		④❸❷
	Giraffe	"		④❸❸
	Cantina Italia	Italian		❷❷❷
	Florians	"		④❷❸
	Strada	"		④❸❸
	Mediterranean Kitchen	Mediterranean		⑤⑤④
	Basilico	Pizza		❷❸④
	Furnace	"		❸④❸
	Rodizio Rico	Brazilian		④④④
	Cuba Libre	Cuban		④④❸
	Sabor	South American		❸❷❷
	The Parsee	Indian		❸❸⑤
	Jim Thompson's	Pan-Asian		⑤⑤❸
	Isarn	Thai		❷❶❷
£25+	Pick More Daisies	American		❸❷❸
	Café Mozart	East & Cent. European		④❸❸
	Le Petit Auberge	French		④❸❸
	Le Sacré-Coeur	"		❸❷❷
	Vrisaki	Greek		❸④④
	Carluccio's Caffè	Italian		④④❸
	Pizzeria Oregano	"		❷❷❸
	San Daniele	"		❸❶❷
	Zizzi	"		④④❸
	The Islington Tapas Bar	Spanish		⑤⑤④
	Toff's	Fish & chips		❷❷④
	Two Brothers	"		❷❷④
	Yo! Sushi	Japanese		⑤④④
	Thai Square	Thai		④④❸
£20+	S & M Café	British, Traditional		❸❷❸
	Les Associés	French		❷❷❷
	Le Mercury	"		④❷❷
	Al Parco	Italian		❷❸④
	La Porchetta Pizzeria	"		❸❸❸

Fine Burger Company	Burgers, etc	❸❸④
The Ultimate Burger	"	④④⑤
Firezza	Pizza	❷❷❸
La Piragua	South American	❷④❷
Gallipoli	Turkish	❸❸❷
Istanbul Iskembecisi	"	❸❸④
Izgara	"	❷❸❸
Afghan Kitchen	Afghani	❷④④
New Culture Rev'n	Chinese	④④⑤
Anglo Asian Tandoori	Indian	❸❷❸
Jashan	"	❶❶④
Masala Zone	"	❸❸❸
Rani	"	❸❷④
Rasa	"	❶❷❷
Wagamama	Japanese	④❸④
Yelo	Thai	❸❷❸
Yum Yum	"	❷❷❷
Huong-Viet	Vietnamese	❷⑤④
Viet Garden	"	❷❷④

SOUTH

South Bank (SE1)

Price	Name	Cuisine	Rating
£60+	Oxo Tower (Rest')	British, Modern	⑤⑤③
	Le Pont de la Tour	"	④④③
£50+	Butlers W'f Chop-house	British, Traditional	④③③
	Tentazioni	Italian	⓪②③
£40+	Blueprint Café	British, Modern	④④③
	Cantina Vinopolis	"	④④④
	Mezzanine	"	⑤④④
	Roast	British, Traditional	④④③
	Livebait	Fish & seafood	④④⑤
	Chez Gérard	French	⑤④④
	Champor-Champor	Fusion	②②⓪
	Village East	"	③④②
	Cantina del Ponte	Italian	⑤⑤⑤
	Oxo Tower (Brass')	Mediterranean	⑤⑤③
	Baltic	Polish	③③②
	Glas	Scandinavian	②②④
	Black & Blue	Steaks & grills	③③④
	Le Pont de la Tour Bar & Grill	"	④④③
	Hara The Circle Bar	Indian	②④④
£35+	Garrison	British, Modern	③③⓪
	RSJ	"	③②⑤
	Shakespeare's Globe	"	④②②
	tamesa@oxo	"	④④③
	The Waterloo Fire Station	"	④⑤④
	fish!	Fish & seafood	③④④
	Auberge	French	⑤④④
	Riviera	"	④④③
	Delfina Studio Café	International	②⓪②
	Laughing Gravy	"	– – –
	Tate Restaurant	"	④④②
	Tapas Brindisa	Spanish	②③③
	Fina Estampa	Peruvian	④③②
	Kwan Thai	Thai	③②④
£30+	Archduke Wine Bar	British, Modern	⑤②③
	The Hartley	"	④④③
	Menier Chocolate Factory	"	④③②
	The Anchor & Hope	British, Traditional	②③②
	Browns	"	⑤⑤④
	Wright Brothers	Fish & seafood	⓪②⓪
	Brew Wharf	French	④⑤④
	Giraffe	International	④③③
	Tate Café	"	④④③
	La Lanterna	Italian	③⓪②
	Loco Mensa	"	④③③
	Bermondsey Kitchen	Mediterranean	④④③
	Tas	Turkish	③②③
	Bengal Clipper	Indian	③③②

£25+	Bankside	British, Modern	④④④
	Real Greek Souvlaki & Bar	Greek	⑤⑤④
	Zakudia	Russian	❸②❸
	Amano Café	Pizza	❸④❷
	Paradiso Olivelli	"	④④④
	Pizzeria Castello	"	④④④
	Tas Pide	Turkish	④❸❷
	Silka	Indian	❸②④
	Feng Sushi	Japanese	❸❸❸
	Yo! Sushi	"	⑤④④
£20+	The Table	British, Modern	❷❸④
	Meson don Felipe	Spanish	❸❸❶
	Gourmet Pizza Co.	Pizza	④④④
	Inshoku	Japanese	❸❸❸
	Wagamama	"	④❸④
£15+	Konditor & Cook	Sandwiches, cakes, etc	❶④④
	El Vergel	South American	❶❷❷
£10+	Monmouth Coffee Company	Sandwiches, cakes, etc	❶❷❷

Greenwich, Lewisham & Blackheath
(All SE postcodes, except SE1)

£40+	Chapter Two	British, Modern	❷❷❸
	Franklins	"	❷❷❸
	The Rivington Grill	"	④④⑤
	Lobster Pot	Fish & seafood	❷❷❶
	The Spread Eagle	French	❸❷❷
	Beauberry House	Fusion	④④④
	The Painted Heron	Indian	❶❶❸
£35+	Greenwich Park	British, Modern	⑤④④
	INC Bar & Restaurant	"	④④④
	Inside	"	❶❷④
	The Palmerston	"	❷❸④
	The Trafalgar Tavern	British, Traditional	④④❷
	Bar du Musée	French	⑤⑤❸
£30+	The Dartmouth Arms	British, Modern	❸❷❷
	The Sea Cow	"	❷❸④
	Le Chardon	French	❷❸❷
	Joanna's	International	❸❷❸
	Loco Locale	Italian	④❸❸
	Olley's	Fish & chips	❷❷❸
	Babur Brasserie	Indian	❷❶❶
	3 Monkeys	"	❸❸④
£25+	The Lavender	British, Modern	④❸❷
	The Sun & Doves	"	❸④❷
	Arancia	Italian	❷❷❷
	Barcelona Tapas	Spanish	④⑤❸
	Pizzeria Castello	Pizza	❷❷❸
	Zero Degrees	"	❸❸❸
	Dragon Castle	Chinese	❷❷④
	Ganapati	Indian	❸❷④

	Tandoori Nights	"	❶❶❸
	Thailand	Thai	❶❷❸
£20+	The Gowlett	Pizza	❸❹❷
	Everest Inn	Indian	❷❷❸
	Ratchada	Thai	❷❷❹
	Thai Corner Café	"	❸❷❹

Battersea, Brixton, Clapham, Wandsworth Barnes, Putney & Wimbledon (All SW postcodes south of the river)

£50+	Chez Bruce	British, Modern	❶❶❷
£40+	Naked Turtle	Australian	❸❹❹
	Balham Kitchen & Bar	British, Modern	❹❹❸
	The Greyhound at Battersea	"	❸❸❸
	Lamberts	"	❶❶❷
	Ransome's Dock	"	❸❸❸
	Redmond's	"	❸❸❹
	Sonny's	"	❹❸❸
	The Victoria	"	❸❹❸
	Le Bouchon Bordelais	French	❷❷❷
	Gastro	"	❹❺❷
	Morel	"	❸❸❺
	The Light House	International	❸❷❸
	Enoteca Turi	Italian	❷❶❷
	Frankie's Italian Bar & Grill	"	❺❺❹
	Mooli	"	❹❸❹
	Riva	"	❸❸❹
	San Lorenzo Fuoriporta	"	❹❹❹
	Zero Quattro	"	❸❸❹
	La Pampa	Argentinian	❸❹❸
	Chakalaka	South African	❸❷❸
£35+	Harlem	American	❺❺❹
	Cinnamon Cay	Australian	❷❷❷
	The Bridge	British, Modern	❸❸❸
	Buchan's	"	❹❹❹
	The Depot	"	❺❹❷
	Ditto	"	❷❸❷
	The Fire Stables	"	❹❹❸
	Grafton House	"	❹❸❹
	Phoenix	"	❷❷❷
	The Spencer Arms	"	❸❸❷
	Tree House	"	❹❸❸
	Willie Gunn	"	❹❹❸
	Ghillies	Fish & seafood	❹❹❸
	The Food Room	French	❶❷❸
	Mini Mundus	"	❸❶❷
	Niksons	"	❹❹❹
	Rapscallion	Fusion	❸❹❹
	Annie's	International	❹❷❷
	Duke of Cambridge	"	❹❹❶
	Metro	"	❹❹❷

	Name	Cuisine	Ratings
	The Sequel	"	❸❶❸
	Upstairs Bar	"	❷❶❷
	Est Est Est	Italian	– – –
	Ost. Antica Bologna	"	④④④
	La Mancha	Spanish	④④❸
	Barnes Grill	Steaks & grills	– – –
	Butcher & Grill	"	❷❸④
	Popeseye	"	❷❸④
	Bombay Bicycle Club	Indian	❷❸④
	Nancy Lam's Enak Enak	Indonesian	❸❸❸
	Tsunami	Japanese	❶❸❸
	Thai on the River	Thai	❸❸❷
£30+	Bodean's	American	❸❸❸
	The Abbeville	British, Modern	④④❷
	Alma	"	– – –
	The Aviary	"	❸❸❸
	Earl Spencer	"	❷❸❷
	The Fentiman Arms	"	④❷❷
	The Freemasons	"	❸❷❷
	The Mason's Arms	"	❸④❸
	Scoffers	"	④❷❷
	Fish Club	Fish & seafood	❶❶④
	Matilda's	"	④④④
	Emile's	French	❸❷❷
	Louvaine	"	❸❷❷
	Giraffe	International	④❸❸
	Hudson's	"	❸❷❷
	Newton's	"	❸❷❸
	The Ship	"	– – –
	Amici	Italian	④❸❸
	Antipasto & Pasta	"	❸❸❸
	Antipasto e Pasta	"	❸❷❸
	Buona Sera	"	❸❷❷
	Numero Uno	"	❸❷❷
	Pizza Metro	"	❷❷❷
	Rick's Café	"	❷❷❷
	Strada	"	④❸❸
	The Fox & Hounds	Mediterranean	❷❸❷
	Rocket Riverside	"	❸❸❷
	Rebato's	Spanish	❸❶❶
	La Rueda	"	④❺❸
	Dexter's Grill	Burgers, etc	❸❷④
	Tootsies	"	④④④
	Sea Cow	Fish & chips	❷❸④
	Basilico	Pizza	❷❸④
	Dalchini	Chinese	❷❷❸
	Royal China	"	❷❸❸
	Ma Goa	Indian	❶❶❷
£25+	The Blue Pumpkin	British, Modern	④❸❸
	The Castle	"	❸④❸
	The Lavender	"	④❸❷
	Settle Inn	British, Traditional	❸❷❷
	Real Greek Souvlaki & Bar	Greek	❺❺④

	Bread & Roses	International	④④❸
	Putney Station	"	④❸❸
	Il Cantuccio di Pulcinella	Italian	❷0❷
	Carluccio's Caffè	"	④④❸
	Ferrari's	"	④❸④
	Pappa Ciccia	"	❷0❷
	Zizzi	"	④④❸
	El Rincón Latino	Spanish	❸00
	Al Forno	Pizza	❸❷❷
	Eco	"	❸❸❸
	Dish Dash	Persian	④④❸
	Chutney	Indian	❷0❸
	Indian Ocean	"	❷❷❸
	Sarkhel's	"	❷❷❸
	The Banana Leaf Canteen	Pan-Asian	❷❷❸
	Thai Garden	Thai	❸❷❸
	Thai Square	"	④④❸
£20+	Fish in a Tie	Mediterranean	❸❸❷
	The Little Bay	"	❸❷❷
	Bar Estrela	Portuguese	❸❸❷
	Café Portugal	"	❷❷❸
	Fine Burger Company	Burgers, etc	❸❸④
	Gourmet Burger Kitchen	"	❷④④
	Brady's	Fish & chips	❸❷❸
	Firezza	Pizza	❷❷❸
	Boiled Egg & Soldiers	Sandwiches, cakes, etc	❸④④
	Hot Stuff	Indian	00❸
	Kastoori	"	00❸
	Mirch Masala SW16	"	0❸⑤
	Nanglo	"	❷0④
	Wagamama	Japanese	④❸④
	Hare & Tortoise	Pan-Asian	❸❸④
	Amaranth	Thai	00❸
	The Pepper Tree	"	❷❸❸
	Talad Thai	"	0❷④
£15+	Fuego Pizzeria	Pizza	❸❷⑤
	Sree Krishna	Indian	0❷❸
	Fujiyama	Japanese	❷④❸
£10+	Trinity Stores	Sandwiches, cakes, etc	❷❷❸

Outer western suburbs
Kew, Richmond, Twickenham, Teddington

£50+	The Glasshouse	British, Modern	00❸
	Petersham Nurseries	"	❸④❷
£40+	Smollensky's	American	⑤④④
	Canyon	British, Modern	⑤⑤❸
	The Wharf	"	⑤④❷
	Fishworks	Fish & seafood	❷④④
	La Brasserie Ma Cuisine	French	– – –
	A Cena	Italian	❷❷❷
	Kew Grill	Steaks & grills	❷❸❸

£35+	Loch Fyne	Fish & seafood	③④④
	Brula	French	❷⓿❷
	La Buvette	"	❷❷❷
	Chez Lindsay	"	❸❷❷
	Ma Cuisine	"	❸❸④
	Café Mamma	Italian	④❸❸
	Prego	"	❸④④
	Four Regions	Chinese	❸❸④
£30+	The Inn at Kew Gardens	British, Modern	❸❸❷
	Browns	International	⑤⑤④
	Nosh	"	④④❸
	Scarpetta	Italian	❸❷❷
	don Fernando's	Spanish	❸❷❸
	Tangawizi	Indian	❷❷❷
	Thai Elephant	Thai	❸❷❸
£25+	Zizzi	Italian	④④❸
	Sagar	Indian	⓿⓿④
	Fat Boy's	Thai	❸❸❸
£20+	White Cross	International	④④❷
	O'Zon	Chinese	❸⓿❸

EAST

Smithfield & Farringdon (EC1)

Price	Name	Cuisine	Rating
£60+	Club Gascon	*French*	❶❷❷
£50+	Smiths (Top Floor)	*British, Modern*	❷❸❷
	Portal	*Mediterranean*	❸❸❸
£40+	The Bar & Grill	*British, Modern*	❸❸❸
	Moro	"	❶❷❷
	The Peasant	"	④④④
	Vic Naylors	"	④④❸
	St John	*British, Traditional*	❶❷❷
	Fish Shop	*Fish & seafood*	❸❸❸
	Rudland & Stubbs	"	❸❸④
	Bleeding Heart	*French*	❷❷❷
	Café du Marché	"	❷❷❶
	Dans le Noir	"	⑤❶❷
	Malmaison Brasserie	"	❸❶❷
	Le Saint Julien	"	④❸④
	Rocco	*Italian*	❸❷④
	The Zetter	"	④④❸
	The Clerkenwell Dining Rm	*Mediterranean*	❸❷④
	Flâneur	"	❸④❷
£35+	Ambassador	*British, Modern*	❸❸④
	Coach & Horses	"	❷❸④
	Medcalf	"	❷❸❸
	The Quality Chop House	"	❸❸❸
	The Trading House	"	❸❷④
	The Well	"	❸❸❸
	Cellar Gascon	*French*	❶❸❸
	Le Rendezvous du Café	"	❷❷❸
	Alba	*Italian*	❷❷④
	Santore	"	❸❸④
	Potemkin	*Russian*	❸❸④
	Hope & Sir Loin	*Steaks & grills*	❸④⑤
	Smiths (Dining Rm)	"	❸❸❸
	Epicurean Pizza Lounge	*Pizza*	❸④⑤
	Cottons	*Afro-Caribbean*	④④❷
	Saki Bar & Food Emporium	*Japanese*	❷④④
	Cicada	*Pan-Asian*	❶❷❷
	Xich-lô	*Vietnamese*	④❷④
£30+	Abbaye	*Belgian*	④④④
	The Gunmakers	*British, Modern*	④❸❸
	Vinoteca	"	❸❶❶
	Comptoir Gascon	*French*	❶❷❶
	Bavarian Beerhouse	*German*	④❷❷
	$	*International*	④④❸
	Strada	*Italian*	④❸❸
	Carnevale	*Vegetarian*	❷❷❸
	Sofra	*Turkish*	④④④
	Tas	"	❸❷❸
	Anakana	*Indian*	❸❷❶

£25+	Fox & Anchor	British, Traditional	❸❷❷
	The Real Greek Souvlaki	Greek	❺❺❹
	Carluccio's Caffè	Italian	❹❹❸
	The Eagle	Mediterranean	❸❹❷
	Yo! Sushi	Japanese	❺❹❹
	Cây Tre	Vietnamese	❷❹❺
£20+	Smiths (Ground Floor)	British, Modern	❹❹❷
	Fish Central	Fish & seafood	❸❹❹
	Kolossi Grill	Greek	❸❶❷
	La Porchetta Pizzeria	Italian	❸❸❸
	The Little Bay	Mediterranean	❸❷❷
	Shish	Turkish	❸❸❷
	Pham Sushie	Japanese	❶❷❸
	Apium	Pan-Asian	❹❸❸
	Pho	Vietnamese	❸❷❹
£10+	Benugo	Sandwiches, cakes, etc	❷❸❹

The City (EC2, EC3, EC4)

£80+	Tatsuso	Japanese	❷❸❹
£70+	I Lombard Street	British, Modern	❹❹❹
£60+	Prism	British, Modern	❹❹❹
	Rhodes 24	"	❸❷❷
	Aurora	French	– – –
	Bonds	Mediterranean	❹❹❹
£50+	Addendum	British, Modern	❸❶❹
	Just Gladwins	"	❸❹❹
	Searcy's Brasserie	"	❹❹❹
	Paternoster Chop House	British, Traditional	❺❹❺
	Chamberlain's	Fish & seafood	❹❹❹
	Fishmarket	"	– – –
	Coq d'Argent	French	❹❹❸
	Refettorio	Italian	❸❸❹
£40+	Christopher's In The City	American	❹❸❺
	Missouri Grill	"	❸❸❹
	Bar Bourse	British, Modern	❹❹❹
	The Chancery	"	❷❶❸
	The Don	"	❷❷❷
	Home	"	❷❸❷
	Just The Bridge	"	❹❺❹
	The Rivington Grill	"	❷❸❸
	Terminus	"	– – –
	The White Swan	"	❷❸❹
	George & Vulture	British, Traditional	❺❸❷
	Gow's	Fish & seafood	❸❷❷
	Sweetings	"	❷❷❶
	Vertigo	"	❹❹❶
	Chez Gérard	French	❺❹❹
	Les Coulisses	"	❸❷❸
	Dine	"	❸❹❹
	The Royal Exchange	"	❺❹❷

	Sauterelle	"	④④❸
	Vivat Bacchus	International	❸⓿❸
	Bertorelli's	Italian	⑤④④
	Caravaggio	"	④④⑤
	Perc%nto	"	⑤⑤⑤
	Taberna Etrusca	"	⑤④④
	Boisdale of Bishopsgate	Scottish	④④④
	Eyre Brothers	Spanish	❸❸❸
	Gaucho Grill	Steaks & grills	❸④④
	Bevis Marks	Kosher	❷⓿❷
	Imperial City	Chinese	❷❸❸
	City Miyama	Japanese	❷❸⑤
	Gt Eastern Dining Room	Pan-Asian	❷❷❸
	Pacific Oriental	"	④④④
£35+	The Princess	Australian	❷❷❸
	Auberge	French	⑤④④
	Miyabi	Japanese	– – –
	Tokyo City	"	❷④④
	Sri Siam City	Thai	❸❸④
	Sri Thai City	"	❸❷❸
£30+	The Evangelist	British, Modern	❸❸❸
	The Fox	"	❸④❷
	The Sterling	"	❸❷❸
	Ye Olde Cheshire Cheese	British, Traditional	⑤④⓿
	Browns	International	⑤⑤④
	Zuccato	Italian	④❸④
	Bar Capitale	Pizza	❸❷④
	(Ciro's) Pizza Pomodoro	"	④④❷
	Savarona	Turkish	❸④④
	Kasturi	Indian	❸❷❸
	City Noto	Japanese	❸❷⑤
	Singapura	Malaysian	❸❸❸
£25+	The Diner	American	❸❷❷
	Bankside	British, Modern	④④④
	Simpson's Tavern	British, Traditional	④❸⓿
	Leon	Mediterranean	❷❸❸
	Barcelona Tapas	Spanish	④⑤❸
	La Tasca	"	⑤⑤④
	Paul	Sandwiches, cakes, etc	❷④④
	Rajasthan	Indian	❷❷❸
	K10	Japanese	❷❸❸
	Kurumaya	"	❷④④
	Moshi Moshi	"	❸❸❸
	Satu Bar & Kitchen	Pan-Asian	❸④❷
	Ekachai	Thai	❷❷❸
	Silks & Spice	"	❸❷❸
	Thai Square	"	④④❸
£20+	The Wine Library	British, Traditional	⑤❷⓿
	Maison Blanc Vite	Sandwiches, cakes, etc	❸④④
	Wagamama	Japanese	④❸④
£15+	Club Mangia	British, Modern	❸❸❷
	Hilliard	"	⓿⓿❷

Price	Name	Cuisine	Ratings
	The Place Below	*Vegetarian*	❸④❸
£10+	Apostrophe	*Sandwiches, cakes, etc*	❷❸❸
	Crussh	"	❷❷④
£5+	Fuzzy's Grub	*Sandwiches, cakes, etc*	❶❶❸
	Nuvo	"	❷❷④

East End & Docklands (All E postcodes)

Price	Name	Cuisine	Ratings
£90+	Ubon	*Japanese*	❷④④
£60+	Plateau	*French*	④④❸
	Les Trois Garçons	"	④❸❶
	Quadrato	*Italian*	❸❸④
£40+	Smollensky's	*American*	⑤④④
	Hadley House	*British, Modern*	❸④④
	Lanes	"	❸❷④
	The Morgan Arms	"	❷❸❸
	Wapping Food	"	❸❸❶
	St John Bread & Wine	*British, Traditional*	❷❷❸
	Curve	*Fish & seafood*	④❷④
	The Grapes	"	❷❸❷
	First Edition	*French*	④④❸
	Rosemary Lane	"	❶❸④
	1 Blossom Street	*Italian*	④❸❸
	El Faro	*Portuguese*	❸④❸
	Lightship	*Scandinavian*	④❷❶
	Gaucho Grill	*Steaks & grills*	❸④④
	Café Spice Namaste	*Indian*	❶❷❸
£35+	Frocks	*British, Modern*	④④④
	Winkles	*Fish & seafood*	❷❷⑤
	Bistrothèque	*French*	④❸❸
	Amerigo Vespucci	*Italian*	❸④④
	Il Bordello	"	❶❶❷
	Hawksmoor	*Steaks & grills*	– – –
	Green & Red Bar & Cantina	*Mexican/TexMex*	❷❷❷
	Royal China	*Chinese*	❷❸④
	Lime	*Indian*	❸❷❸
	Scarlet Dot	"	④④⑤
	Elephant Royale	*Thai*	④❷❷
£30+	Cat & Mutton	*British, Modern*	④④❸
	Royal Oak	"	❸❸❷
	Canteen	*British, Traditional*	④④❷
	Browns	*International*	⑤⑤④
	La Figa	*Italian*	❸❷❸
	Lilly's	*Steaks & grills*	❸❸❷
	Armadillo	*South American*	❷❶❷
	The Han of Nazz	*Turkish*	❸❸❷
	The Lotus	*Chinese*	❸④❸
	Sri Nam	*Thai*	❸④④
£25+	The Gun	*British, Modern*	❸④❸
	LMNT	"	❸❸❶
	Carluccio's Caffè	*Italian*	④④❸

	Zizzi	"	4 4 3
	Leon	Mediterranean	2 3 3
	Barcelona Tapas	Spanish	4 5 3
	Meson los Barilles	"	3 2 4
	La Tasca	"	5 5 4
	Arkansas Café	Steaks & grills	2 4 4
	Faulkner's	Fish & chips	2 3 4
	Pâtisserie Valerie	Sandwiches, cakes, etc	3 4 2
	Santa Maria de Buen Ayre	Argentinian	2 1 2
	Haz	Turkish	3 3 3
	Shanghai	Chinese	2 2 3
	Yi-Ban	"	2 3 2
	Bengal Quay	Indian	3 2 4
	Memsaheb on Thames	"	2 2 3
	Itsu	Japanese	2 3 3
	Moshi Moshi	"	3 3 3
	Namo	Vietnamese	2 3 4
	Sông Quê	"	1 4 4
£20+	S & M Café	British, Traditional	3 2 3
	Story Deli	Organic	1 4 2
	Gourmet Pizza Co.	Pizza	4 4 4
	The Drunken Monkey	Chinese	3 4 2
	The Gaylord	Indian	2 4 4
	Lahore Kebab House	"	1 4 5
	Mirch Masala	"	1 3 5
	Wagamama	Japanese	4 3 4
	Viet Hoa	Vietnamese	3 3 4
£15+	Mangal Ocakbasi	Turkish	1 2 3
	New Tayyabs	Pakistani	1 4 3
£10+	E Pellicci	Italian	3 3 1
	Crussh	Sandwiches, cakes, etc	2 2 4
£5+	Square Pie Company	British, Traditional	2 3 4
	Brick Lane Beigel Bake	Sandwiches, cakes, etc	3 4 5

MAPS

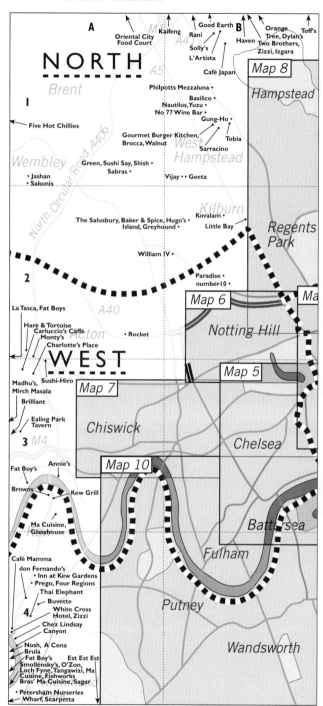

MAP 1 – LONDON OVERVIEW

A

B

NORTH

Brent

Kaifeng
Oriental City
Food Court
Rani
Good Earth
Solly's
L'Artista
Café Japan

Orange
Tree, Dylan's
Two Brothers,
Zizzi, Izgara
Haven

Toff's

Map 8

Hampstead

1

← Five Hot Chillies

Philpotts Mezzaluna •
Basilico •
Nautilus, Yuzu •
No 77 Wine Bar •
Gung-Ho •
Tobia

West
Hampstead

Wembley

• Jashan
• Sakonis

Gourmet Burger Kitchen,
Brocca, Walnut
Sarracino

Green, Sushi Say, Shish •
Sabras •

Vijay • • Geeta

Kilburn

The Salusbury, Baker & Spice, Hugo's •
Island, Greyhound •

Kovalam •
Little Bay

Regents
Park

William IV •

2

A40

Paradise •
number10 •

Map 6

Map

La Tasca, Fat Boys

Notting Hill

Hare & Tortoise
Carluccio's Caffè
Monty's
Charlotte's Place

Acton

• Rocket

Map 5

W E S T

Map 7

Madhu's,
Mirch Masala

Chiswick

Chelsea

Brilliant

Ealing Park
Tavern

Sushi-Hiro

3 M4

Fat Boy's

Annie's

Map 10

Browns

Kew Grill

Ma Cuisine,
Glasshouse

Battersea

Fulham

Café Mamma

don Fernando's
• Inn at Kew Gardens
• Prego, Four Regions
Thai Elephant

Putney

Buvette
White Cross
Hotel, Zizzi

Chez Lindsay
Canyon

Wandsworth

Nosh, A Cena
Brula
Fat Boy's   Est Est Est
Smollensky's, O'Zon,
Loch Fyne, Tangawizi, Ma
Cuisine, Fishworks
Bras' Ma Cuisine, Sagar

• Petersham Nurseries
Wharf, Scarpetta

4

North Circular Road A406

MAP 1 – LONDON OVERVIEW

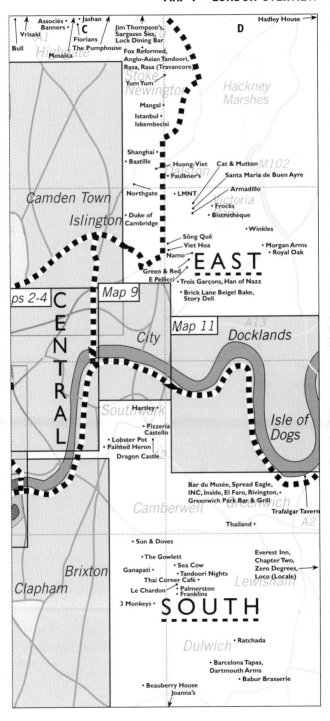

MAP 2 – WEST END OVERVIEW

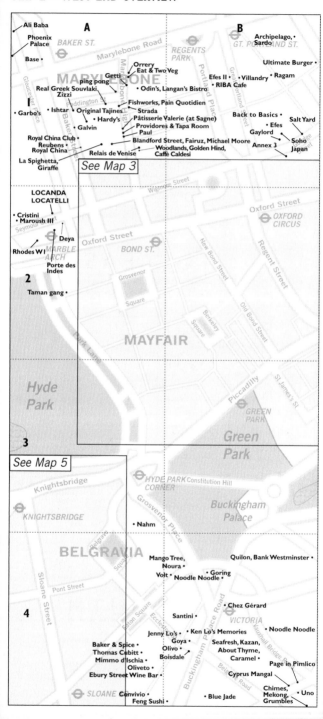

Ali Baba

A

B

Phoenix Palace

BAKER ST.

Marylebone Road

REGENTS PARK

Archipelago • Sardo

GT. PORTLAND ST.

Base •

Ultimate Burger •

Orrery
Gett Eat & Two Veg
ping pong

Efes II • Villandry • Ragam

MARYLEBONE

Real Greek Souvlaki Zizzi

• Odin's, Langan's Bistro

RIBA Cafe

Strada

1

• Garbo's

• Ishtar • Original Tajines

Fishworks, Pain Quotidien

Back to Basics •

Salt Yard

• Hardy's

Pâtisserie Valerie (at Sagne)

• Efes

• Galvin

Providores & Tapa Room

Gaylord •

Soho Japan

Paul

Annex 3

Royal China Club •

Blandford Street, Fairuz, Michael Moore

Reubens •
Royal China

Relais de Venise

Woodlands, Golden Hind, Caffè Caldesi

La Spighetta, Giraffe

See Map 3

Wigmore Street

Oxford Street

OXFORD CIRCUS

LOCANDA LOCATELLI

• Cristini
• Maroush III

Seymour

Oxford Street

BOND ST.

New Bond Street

Regent Street

Deya

MARBLE ARCH

Rhodes W1

Grosvenor

2

Porte des Indes

Taman gang •

Square

MAYFAIR

Berkeley Square

Old Bond Street

Hyde Park

Park Lane

St James's St

3

Piccadilly

GREEN PARK

Green Park

See Map 5

Knightsbridge

HYDE PARK CORNER

Constitution Hill

KNIGHTSBRIDGE

Grosvenor Place

Buckingham Palace

• Nahm

BELGRAVIA

Belgrave

Mango Tree, Noura •

Quilon, Bank Westminster •

Sloane Street

Pont Street

Volt •

• Goring
Noodle Noodle •

Eaton Square

• Chez Gérard

4

Santini •

Buckingham Palace Road

VICTORIA

• Noodle Noodle

Jenny Lo's •
Baker & Spice •

• Ken Lo's Memories

Vauxhall Bridge Road

Thomas Cubitt •
Mimmo d'Ischia •

Goya
Olivo
Boisdale

• Seafresh, Kazan, About Thyme, Caramel

Oliveto •

• Page in Pimlico

Ebury Street Wine Bar •

Ecclestone

Cyprus Mangal

SLOANE

Convivio •

Buckingham Palace Road

Chimes, Mekong, Grumbles

Feng Sushi •

• Blue Jade

• Uno

MAP 2 – WEST END OVERVIEW

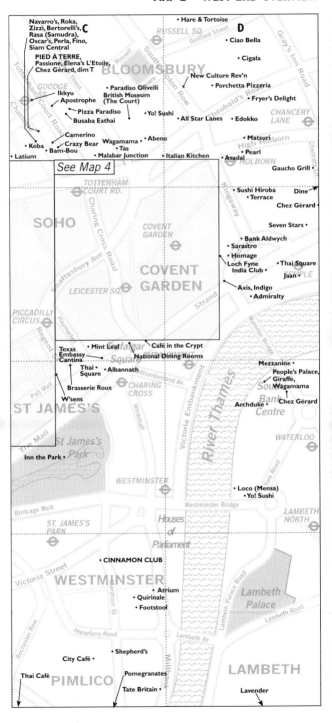

Navarro's, Roka, Zizzi, Bertorelli's, **C**
Rasa (Samudra), Oscar's, Perla, Fino, Siam Central
PIED À TERRE, Passione, Elena's L'Etoile, Chez Gérard, dim T

• Hare & Tortoise **D**

RUSSELL SQ.

• Ciao Bella

• Cigala

BLOOMSBURY

New Culture Rev'n •

• Porchetta Pizzeria

GOODGE

Ikkyu
Apostrophe

Pizza Paradiso
Busaba Eathai

• Paradiso Olivelli
British Museum (The Court)

• Yo! Sushi • All Star Lanes

• Fryer's Delight

• Edokko

CHANCERY LANE

• Matsuri

Camerino
• Crazy Bear
• Bam-Bou

Wagamama •
• Tas

• Abeno
• Malabar Junction

• Italian Kitchen

• Pearl

• Asadal

HIGH HOLBORN

HOLBORN

• Koba
• Latium

Gaucho Grill •

See Map 4

TOTTENHAM COURT RD.

• Sushi Hiroba
• Terrace

Dine →

Chez Gérard •

SOHO

COVENT GARDEN

Charing Cross Road

Shaftesbury Avenue

LEICESTER SQ.

COVENT GARDEN

Seven Stars •

• Bank Aldwych
• Sarastro
• Homage
Loch Fyne
India Club •

• Thai Square

Jaan •

TEMPLE

Axis, Indigo •
• Admiralty

Strand

PICCADILLY CIRCUS

Regent Street

Haymarket

Texas
Embassy
Cantina

• Mint Leaf

Café in the Crypt
National Dining Rooms

Trafalgar Square

Thai
Square

• Albannach

Brasserie Roux

W'sens

Northumberland Av.

CHARING CROSS

Whitehall

Pall Mall

ST JAMES'S

The Mall

Inn the Park •

St James's Park

Mezzanine •

People's Palace
Giraffe,
Wagamama

Archduke •

River Thames

Chez Gérard

South
Bank
Centre

Waterloo Bridge

Waterloo Road

WATERLOO

WESTMINSTER

Birdcage Walk

ST. JAMES'S PARK

Victoria Embankment

• Loco (Mensa)
• Yo! Sushi

Westminster Bridge

Houses
of
Parliament

LAMBETH NORTH

Victoria Street

WESTMINSTER

Marsham St.

• CINNAMON CLUB

• Atrium
• Quirinale
• Footstool

Lambeth Palace Road

Lambeth
Palace

Rochester Row

Horseferry Road

City Café •

• Shepherd's

Pomegranates

Lambeth Br.

Lambeth Palace Road

Thai Café

PIMLICO

Tate Britain •

Millbank

LAMBETH

Lavender ↓

MAP 3 – MAYFAIR, ST JAMES'S & WEST SOHO

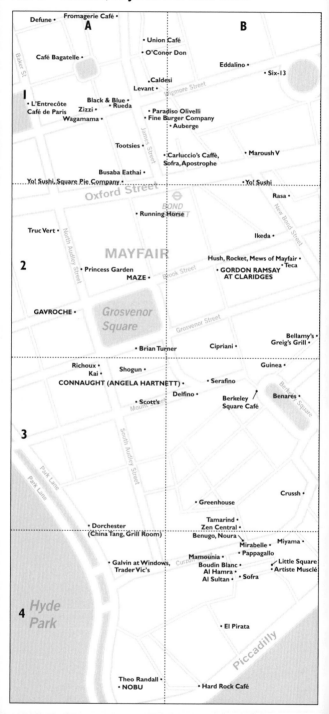

A

B

Defune •
• Fromagerie Café •

• Union Café

Café Bagatelle • • O'Conor Don

Eddalino •

• Six-13

• Caldesi

Levant •

1

• L'Entrecôte
Café de Paris
Black & Blue •
Zizzi • • Rueda
Wagamama •

Wigmore Street

• Paradiso Olivelli
• Fine Burger Company
• Auberge

Tootsies •

• Maroush V

• Carluccio's Caffè,
Sofra, Apostrophe

Busaba Eathai •

Yo! Sushi, Square Pie Company •

• Yo! Sushi

Oxford Street

Rasa •

BOND

• Running Horse

Truc Vert •

Ikeda •

MAYFAIR

Hush, Rocket, Mews of Mayfair •
• Teca

2

• Princess Garden
MAZE •

Brook Street

• **GORDON RAMSAY
AT CLARIDGES**

GAVROCHE •

*Grosvenor
Square*

Grosvenor Street

Bellamy's •
Greig's Grill •

• Brian Turner

Cipriani •

Richoux •
Kai •
Shogun •

Guinea •

CONNAUGHT (ANGELA HARTNETT) •

• Serafino

Delfino •

• Scott's

Berkeley
Square Café

Benares •

3

Mount Street

South Audley Street

Crussh •

• Greenhouse

Tamarind •
Zen Central •

• Dorchester
(China Tang, Grill Room)

Benugo, Noura
Mirabelle • • Miyama •

Mamounia •
• Pappagallo

• Galvin at Windows,
Trader Vic's

Boudin Blanc •
Al Hamra •
Al Sultan •
• Little Square
• Artiste Musclé

Curzon

• Sofra

4

*Hyde
Park*

• El Pirata

Piccadilly

Theo Randall •
• NOBU

• Hard Rock Café

MAP 3 – MAYFAIR, ST JAMES'S & WEST SOHO

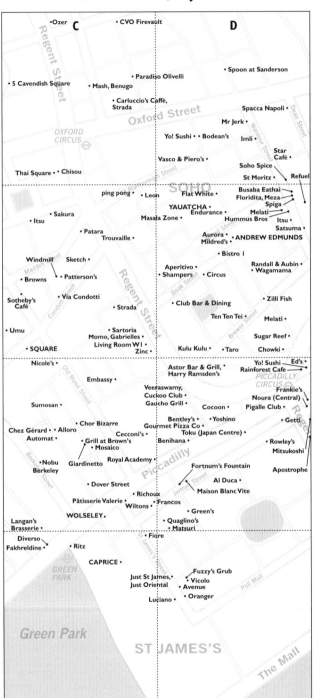

•Ozer C • CVO Firevault D

• 5 Cavendish Square

• Paradiso Olivelli • Spoon at Sanderson

• Mash, Benugo

• Carluccio's Caffè, Strada

Oxford Street

OXFORD CIRCUS

Spacca Napoli •

Mr Jerk •

Yo! Sushi • • Bodean's Imli •

Star Café •

Vasco & Piero's • Soho Spice •

Thai Square • • Chisou St Moritz • Refuel

SOHO

ping pong • • Leon Flat White • Busaba Eathai •
Floridita, Meza •
YAUATCHA Spiga •
• Sakura Endurance • Melati •
• Itsu Masala Zone • Hummus Bros Itsu •
• Patara Satsuma •
Trouvaille • Aurora • • ANDREW EDMUNDS
Mildred's •

• Bistro 1

Windmill • Sketch •
Aperitivo • Randall & Aubin •
• Browns • Patterson's • Shampers • • Circus • Wagamama

Sotheby's • Via Condotti • Club Bar & Dining • Zilli Fish
Café
• Strada Ten Ten Tei •
Melati •

• Umu • Sartoria Sugar Reef •
Momo, Gabrielles •
• SQUARE Living Room W1 • Kulu Kulu • • Taro Chowki •
Zinc •

Nicole's • Yo! Sushi — Ed's •
Astor Bar & Grill, • Rainforest Cafe •
Embassy • Harry Ramsden's PICCADILLY
CIRCUS
Veeraswamy, Frankie's •
Cuckoo Club • Noura (Central) •
Sumosan • Gaucho Grill • Pigalle Club •
Cocoon •
• Chor Bizarre Bentley's • • Yoshino • Getti
Chez Gérard • • Alloro Gourmet Pizza Co •
Automat • Cecconi's • Toku (Japan Centre) • • Rowley's
• Grill at Brown's Benihana • Mitsukoshi
• Mosaico
• Nobu Giardinetto • Royal Academy • Apostrophe
Berkeley
Fortnum's Fountain •
• Dover Street Piccadilly
Al Duca •
Pâtisserie Valerie • • Richoux Maison Blanc Vite •
WOLSELEY • Wiltons • • Francos
• Green's
Langan's • Quaglino's
Brasserie • • Fiore • Matsuri
• Diverso
Fakhreldine • • Ritz

GREEN
PARK CAPRICE •
Fuzzy's Grub •
Just St James, • • Vicolo
Just Oriental • • Avenue
Luciano • • Oranger

Green Park ST JAMES'S

The Mall

MAP 4 – EAST SOHO, CHINATOWN & COVENT GARDEN

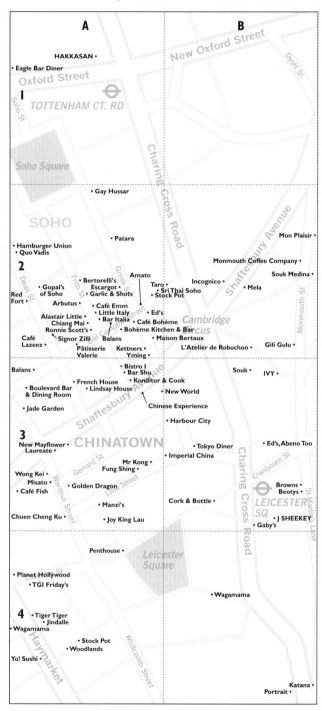

A

B

New Oxford Street

Dyott St

HAKKASAN •

• Eagle Bar Diner

Oxford Street

Soho St

1

TOTTENHAM CT. RD

Soho Square

Charing Cross Road

SOHO

• Gay Hussar

Shaftesbury Avenue

Mon Plaisir •

• Patara

• Hamburger Union
• Quo Vadis

Monmouth Coffee Company •

Souk Medina

2

Dean St

Amato

Taro •
• Sri Thai Soho

Incognico •

• Mela

Monmouth St

• Gopal's
of Soho

• Bertorelli's
Escargot •
Garlic & Shots •

Frith Street

Red
Fort •

Arbutus •

Greek Street

• Café Emm

• Stock Pot

Alastair Little •
Chiang Mai •
Ronnie Scott's •

• Little Italy
• Bar Italia

• Ed's

Old Compton Street

Cambridge
Circus

Café
Lazeez •

• Signor Zilli

Balans

• Café Bohème
• Bohème Kitchen & Bar

• Maison Bertaux

Gili Gulu •

Pâtisserie
Valerie

Kettners •
Yming •

L'Atelier de Robuchon •

Balans •

• Bistro 1
• Bar Shu

Souk •

IVY •

• French House

• Boulevard Bar
& Dining Room

• Lindsay House

• Konditor & Cook

• New World

Shaftesbury Avenue

Chinese Experience

• Jade Garden

• Harbour City

3

New Mayflower •
Laureate •

CHINATOWN

• Tokyo Diner

• Ed's, Abeno Too

Gerrard St

Mr Kong •

• Imperial China

Charing Cross Road

Wong Kei •
Misato •
• Café Fish

Fung Shing •

Lisle Street

Cranbourn St

Browns •
Beotys •

• Golden Dragon

LEICESTER
SQ

St Martin's Lane

Wardour Street

• Manzi's

Cork & Bottle •

• J SHEEKEY

Chuen Cheng Ku •

• Joy King Lau

• Gaby's

• Penthouse •

Leicester
Square

• Planet Hollywood

• TGI Friday's

• Wagamama

4

• Tiger Tiger
• Jindalle

Oxendon St

• Wagamama

• Stock Pot

Whitcomb Street

• Woodlands

Yo! Sushi •

Haymarket

Katana •

Portrait •

MAP 4 – EAST SOHO, CHINATOWN & COVENT GARDEN

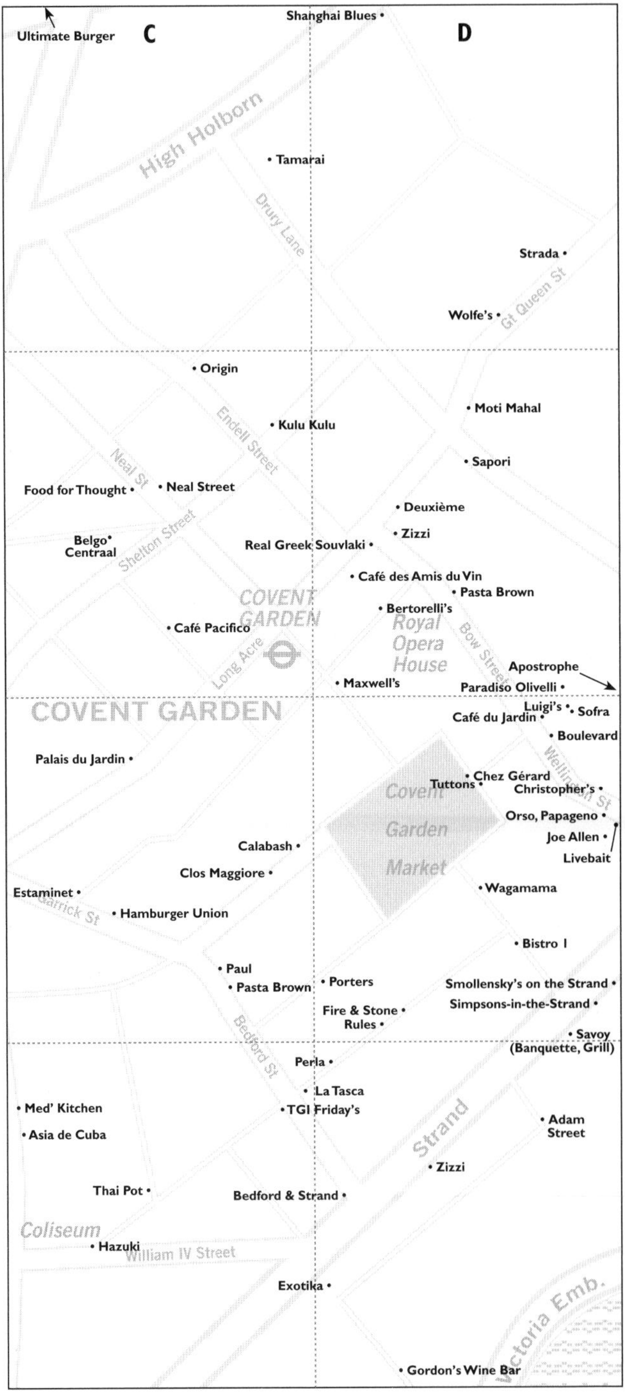

C

D

Ultimate Burger

Shanghai Blues •

High Holborn

• Tamarai

Drury Lane

Strada •

Wolfe's •

Gt Queen St

• Origin

Endell Street

• Kulu Kulu

Neal St

• Moti Mahal

• Sapori

Food for Thought • • Neal Street

Shelton Street

Belgo•
Centraal

Real Greek Souvlaki •

• Deuxième

• Zizzi

• Café des Amis du Vin

• Pasta Brown

• Bertorelli's

COVENT
GARDEN

Royal
Opera
House

Bow Street

• Café Pacifico

Long Acre

Apostrophe

• Maxwell's

Paradiso Olivelli •

COVENT GARDEN

Luigi's • • Sofra
Café du Jardin •

• Boulevard

Palais du Jardin •

Covent

• Chez Gérard
Tuttons •
Christopher's •

Garden

Orso, Papageno •

Calabash •

Market

Joe Allen •

Clos Maggiore •

Livebait

Estaminet •

• Wagamama

• Hamburger Union

Garrick St

• Bistro 1

• Paul

• Pasta Brown

• Porters

Smollensky's on the Strand •

Bedford St

Fire & Stone
Rules •

Simpsons-in-the-Strand •

• Savoy
(Banquette, Grill)

Perla •

• La Tasca

• Med' Kitchen

• TGI Friday's

Strand

• Adam
Street

• Asia de Cuba

• Zizzi

Thai Pot •

Bedford & Strand •

Coliseum

• Hazuki

William IV Street

Victoria Emb.

Exotika •

• Gordon's Wine Bar

MAP 5 – KNIGHTSBRIDGE, CHELSEA & SOUTH KENSINGTON

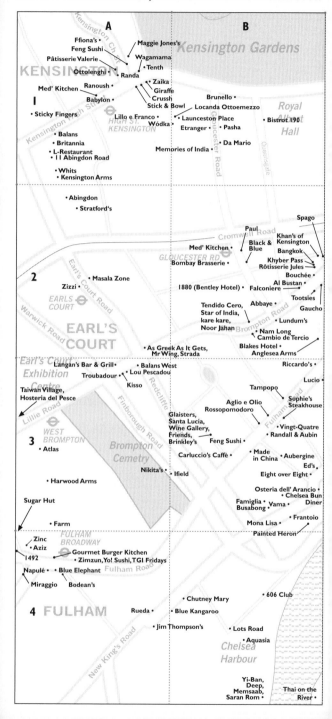

MAP 5 – KNIGHTSBRIDGE, CHELSEA & SOUTH KENSINGTON

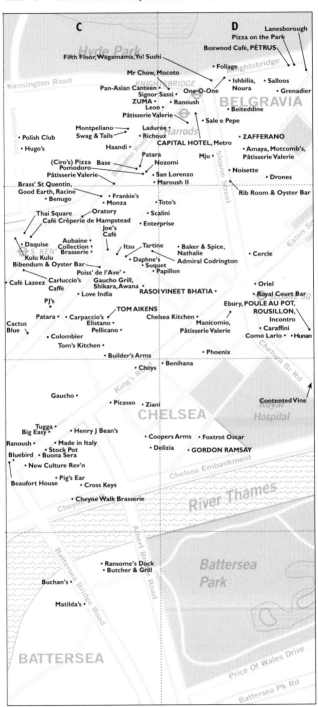

C

D

Lanesborough
Pizza on the Park

Hyde Park

Boxwood Café, PÉTRUS

Fifth Floor, Wagamama, Yo! Sushi

Foliage

Kensington Road

Ishbilia • • Salloos
Noura

• Grenadier

Mr Chow, Mocoto

KNIGHTSBRIDGE

Pan-Asian Canteen •

BELGRAVIA

One-O-One

Signor Sassi •

ZUMA •   • Ranoush

Beiteddine

Leon •

Pâtisserie Valerie

Sale e Pepe

Montpeliano   Ladurée

Swag & Tails •   • Richoux

Harrods

• ZAFFERANO

• Polish Club

Haandi •

CAPITAL HOTEL, Metro

• Amaya, Motcomb's,
Pâtisserie Valerie

• Hugo's

Patara

Mju •

Nozomi

Noisette •

(Ciro's) Pizza   Base

Pomodoro

• Drones

Pâtisserie Valerie •

San Lorenzo •

Maroush II •

Brass' St Quentin,
Good Earth, Racine

Rib Room & Oyster Bar

• Benugo

• Frankie's

• Toto's

• Monza

Thai Square

Oratory

• Scalini

Café Crêperie de Hampstead

Joe's
Café

• Enterprise

• Daquise

Aubaine •

Collection •

Itsu   Tartine

• Baker & Spice,
Nathalie

• Cercle

Kulu Kulu

Brasserie •

Daphne's

Admiral Codrington

Bibendum & Oyster Bar •

Poiss' de l'Ave' •   • Suquet

Papillon

• Café Lazeez

Carluccio's

Gaucho Grill,

Caffè

Shikara, Awana

• Oriel

• Love India

RASOI VINEET BHATIA •

• Royal Court Bar

PJ's •

Ebury, POULE AU POT,
ROUSILLON,

TOM AIKENS

Patara •   • Carpaccio's

Chelsea Kitchen •

Incontro

Cactus
Blue

Elistano •

Manicomio,

• Caraffini

Pellicano •

Pâtisserie Valerie

Como Lario • • Hunan

• Colombier

Tom's Kitchen •

• Builder's Arms

• Phoenix

• Choys   • Benihana

Gaucho •

• Picasso   • Ziani

CHELSEA

Contented Vine

Royal
Hospital

Tugga •

Big Easy •   • Henry J Bean's

Ranoush •

• Made in Italy

• Coopers Arms   • Foxtrot Oscar

• Stock Pot

Bluebird   • Buona Sera

• Delizia   • GORDON RAMSAY

• New Culture Rev'n

Chelsea Embankment

• Pig's Ear

Beaufort House   • Cross Keys

River Thames

Cheyne Walk Brasserie •

• Ransome's Dock

• Butcher & Grill

Battersea
Park

Buchan's •

Matilda's •

BATTERSEA

Price Of Wales Drive

Battersea Pk Rd

MAP 6 – NOTTING HILL & BAYSWATER

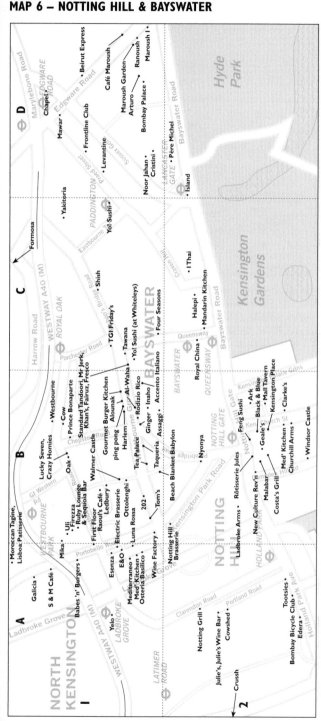

MAP 7 – HAMMERSMITH & CHISWICK

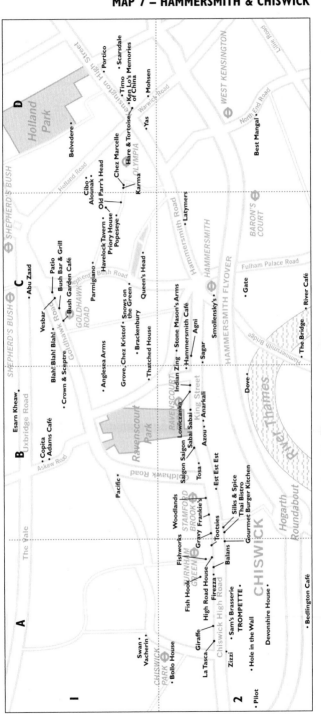

MAP 8 – HAMPSTEAD, CAMDEN TOWN & ISLINGTON

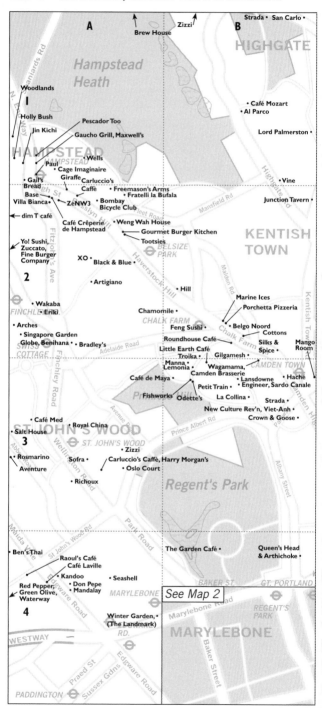

Strada • San Carlo •

Zizzi

Brew House

HIGHGATE

A

B

Hampstead
Heath

Woodlands

• Café Mozart
• Al Parco

Holly Bush

Pescador Too

Lord Palmerston

Jin Kichi

Gaucho Grill, Maxwell's

HAMPSTEAD
HAMPSTEAD

• Wells

Paul

Cage Imaginaire

• Vine

Giraffe • Carluccio's

• Gail's
Bread

Caffè • Freemason's Arms

Junction Tavern •

Base

• Fratelli la Bufala

Villa Bianca •

ZeNW3 • Bombay
Bicycle Club

Mansfield Road

← dim T café

Café Crêperie
de Hampstead

• Weng Wah House
• Gourmet Burger Kitchen

KENTISH
TOWN

Yo! Sushi,
Zuccato,
Fine Burger
Company

Tootsies

XO • Black & Blue

Marine Ices

• Artigiano

• Hill

Porchetta Pizzeria

• Wakaba
• Eriki

Chamomile •

CHALK FARM

• Belgo Noord

Feng Sushi •

Cottons

• Arches

Roundhouse Café •

Silks &
Spice

Mango
Room

• Singapore Garden

Little Earth Café

Globe, Benihana • • Bradley's

Troika •

Gilgamesh •

SWISS
COTTAGE

Adelaide Road

Manna •
Lemonia •

Wagamama,
Camden Brasserie

CAMDEN TOWN

Café de Maya •

• Lansdowne • Haché

Petit Train •

• Engineer, Sardo Canale

Fishworks • Odette's •

La Collina •

• Café Med

Royal China •

New Culture Rev'n, Viet-Anh •

• Salt House

ST. JOHN'S WOOD

Crown & Goose •

ST. JOHN'S WOOD

Strada •

• Rosmarino

• Zizzi

Aventure

Sofra • Carluccio's Caffè, Harry Morgan's

• Oslo Court

• Richoux

Regent's Park

• Ben's Thai

The Garden Café •

Queen's Head
& Arthichoke

Raoul's Café
Café Laville

• Kandoo

• Seashell

Red Pepper, • Don Pepe
Green Olive, • Mandalay
Waterway

BAKER ST.

GT. PORTLAND

MARYLEBONE

See Map 2

REGENT'S
PARK

Winter Garden, •
(The Landmark)

Marylebone Road

MARYLEBONE

WESTWAY

Baker Street

PADDINGTON

Praed St.

Sussex Gdns.

Edgware Road

MAP 8 – HAMPSTEAD, CAMDEN TOWN & ISLINGTON

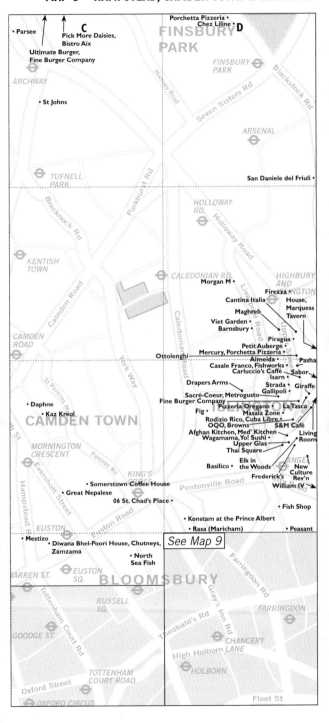

Porchetta Pizzeria •
Chez Liline • **D**

FINSBURY
PARK

C

• Parsee

Pick More Daisies,
Bistro Aix

Ultimate Burger,
Fine Burger Company

FINSBURY
PARK

ARCHWAY

Honsey Road

Blackstock Rd

• St Johns

Seven Sisters Rd

ARSENAL

*TUFNELL
PARK*

San Daniele del Friuli •

*HOLLOWAY
RD.*

Parkhurst Rd

Brecknock Rd

Holloway Road

*KENTISH
TOWN*

*HIGHBURY
AND ISLINGTON*

CALEDONIAN RD.

Morgan M •

Camden Road

Liverpool Road

Firezza •
House,
Marquess
Tavern

*CAMDEN
ROAD*

Cantina Italia •

Maghreb •

Viet Garden •
Barnsbury •

Piragua •

Caledonian Road

York Way

Petit Auberge •
Mercury, Porchetta Pizzeria •

Upper Street

Ottolenghi •

Almeida •

Pasha

St Pancras Way

Casale Franco, Fishworks •
Carluccio's Caffé •
Isarn •

Sabor •

Giraffe

Drapers Arms •

Strada •
Gallipoli •

Sacré-Coeur, Metrogusto •

Fine Burger Company

La Tasca •

• Daphne

• Kaz Kreol

CAMDEN TOWN

Fig •

Pizzeria Oregano •
Masala Zone •

ISLINGTON

Rodizio Rico, Cuba Libre •
OQO, Browns •

S&M Café

*MORNINGTON
CRESCENT*

Pancras Rd

Afghan Kitchen, Med' Kitchen •
Wagamama, Yo! Sushi •

Upper Glas •

Living
Room

Thai Square •

Hampstead Road

Evershott Street

*KING'S
CROSS*

Basilico •

Elk in
the Woods •

ANGEL
New
Culture
Rev'n

Frederick's •

William IV →

• Somerstown Coffee House

Pentonville Road

• Great Nepalese

06 St. Chad's Place •

Euston Road

• Fish Shop

EUSTON

• Konstam at the Prince Albert

• Mestizo

• Rasa (Maricham)

• Peasant

• Diwana Bhel-Poori House, Chutneys,
Zamzama

See Map 9

WARREN ST.

• North
Sea Fish

*EUSTON
SQ.*

BLOOMSBURY

Tottenham Court Rd

*RUSSELL
SQ.*

Theobald's Rd

Gray's Inn Rd

Farringdon Rd

FARRINGDON

GOODGE ST.

High Holborn

*CHANCERY
LANE*

*TOTTENHAM
COURT ROAD*

HOLBORN

Oxford Street

OXFORD CIRCUS

Fleet St

MAP 9 – THE CITY

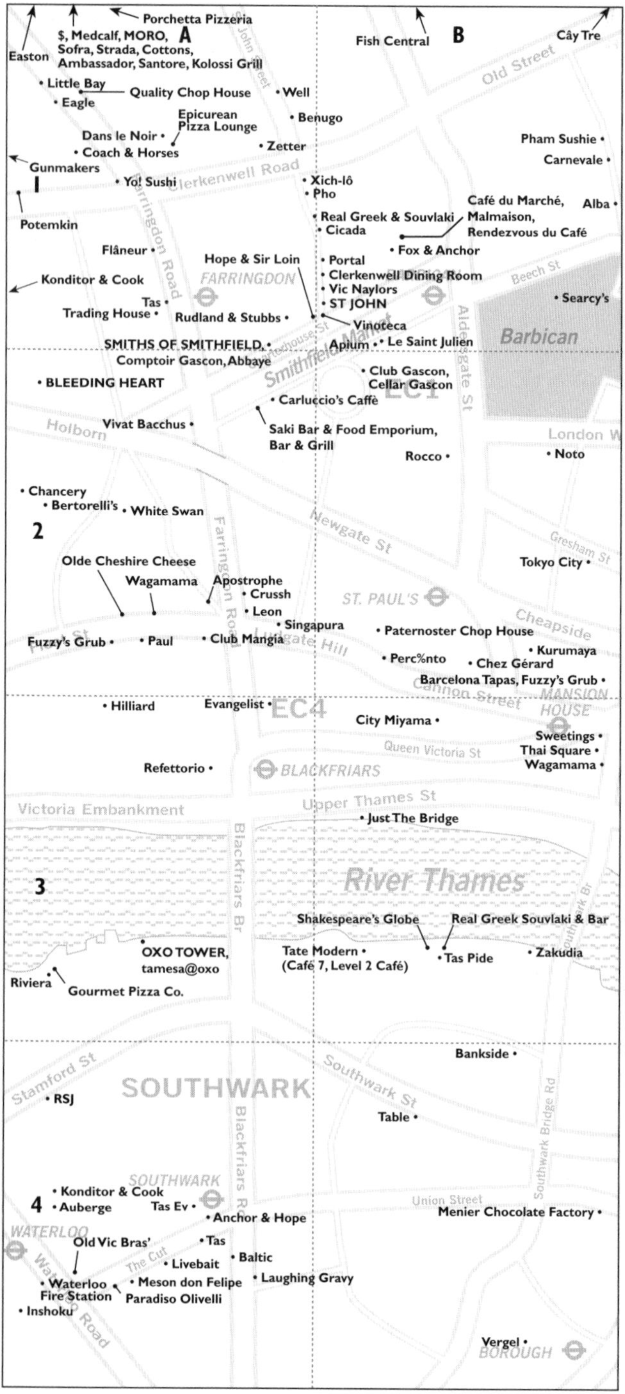

A
B
1
2
3
4
Porchetta Pizzeria
$, Medcalf, MORO,
Sofra, Strada, Cottons,
Ambassador, Santore, Kolossi Grill
Easton
Fish Central
Cây Tre
Old Street
St John Street
Little Bay
Quality Chop House
Eagle
Well
Epicurean
Pizza Lounge
Benugo
Dans le Noir
Coach & Horses
Zetter
Pham Sushie
Carnevale
Gunmakers
Clerkenwell Road
Yo! Sushi
Xich-lô
Pho
Potemkin
Farringdon Road
Real Greek & Souvlaki
Cicada
Café du Marché,
Malmaison,
Rendezvous du Café
Alba
Fox & Anchor
Flâneur
Hope & Sir Loin
Portal
Clerkenwell Dining Room
Beech St
Konditor & Cook
FARRINGDON
Vic Naylors
ST JOHN
Searcy's
Tas
Trading House
Rudland & Stubbs
Vinoteca
Aldersgate St
SMITHS OF SMITHFIELD,
Comptoir Gascon, Abbaye
Charterhouse St
Smithfield Market
Apium
Le Saint Julien
Barbican
BLEEDING HEART
Club Gascon,
Cellar Gascon
EC1
Carluccio's Caffè
Holborn
Vivat Bacchus
Saki Bar & Food Emporium,
Bar & Grill
Rocco
London W
Noto
Chancery
Bertorelli's
White Swan
Newgate St
Gresham St
Olde Cheshire Cheese
Tokyo City
Wagamama
Apostrophe
Crussh
ST. PAUL'S
Leon
Cheapside
Singapura
Fuzzy's Grub
Paul
Club Mangia
Ludgate Hill
Paternoster Chop House
Kurumaya
Perc%nto
Chez Gérard
Barcelona Tapas, Fuzzy's Grub
Cannon Street
MANSION HOUSE
Hilliard
Evangelist
EC4
City Miyama
Sweetings
Queen Victoria St
Thai Square
Refettorio
BLACKFRIARS
Wagamama
Victoria Embankment
Upper Thames St
Just The Bridge
Blackfriars Br
River Thames
Southwark Br
Shakespeare's Globe
Real Greek Souvlaki & Bar
OXO TOWER,
tamesa@oxo
Tate Modern
(Café 7, Level 2 Café)
Tas Pide
Zakudia
Riviera
Gourmet Pizza Co.
Bankside
Stamford St
SOUTHWARK
Southwark St
RSJ
Table
Southwark Bridge Rd
SOUTHWARK
Konditor & Cook
Auberge
Tas Ev
Union Street
Menier Chocolate Factory
Anchor & Hope
WATERLOO
Old Vic Bras'
Tas
The Cut
Baltic
Livebait
Laughing Gravy
Waterloo
Fire Station
Meson don Felipe
Paradiso Olivelli
Inshoku
Waterloo Road
Vergel
BOROUGH

MAP 9 – THE CITY

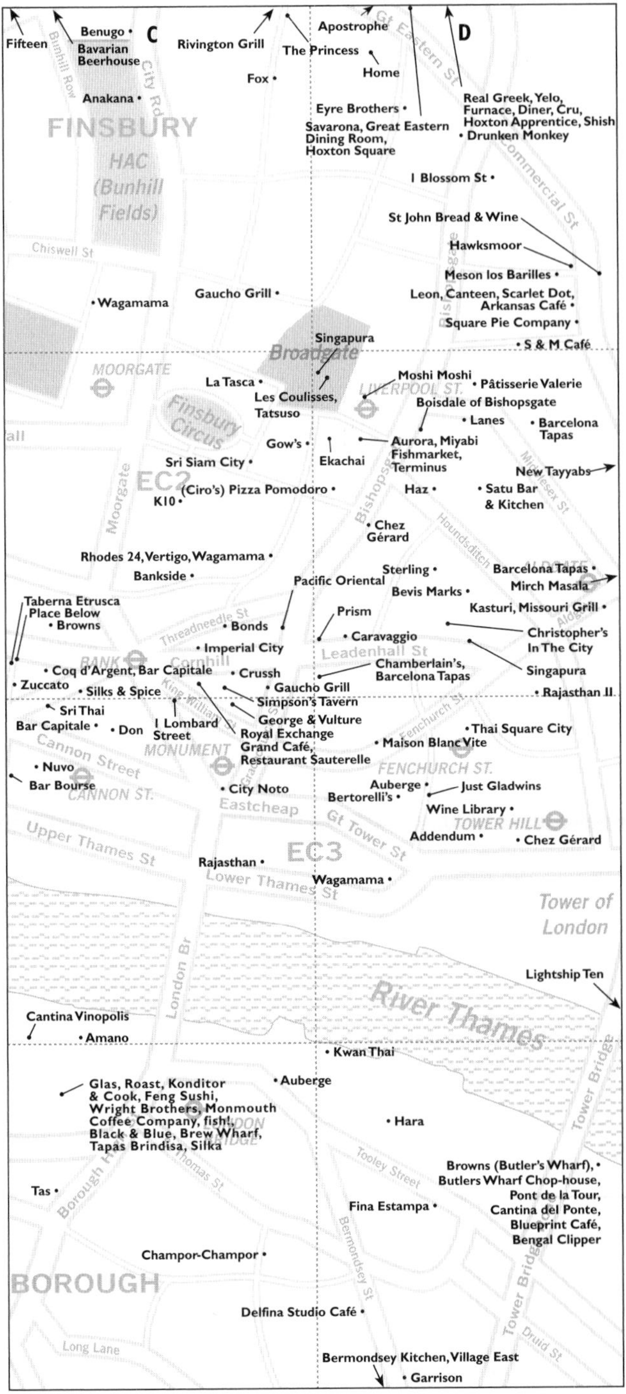

Fifteen

Benugo •
Bavarian
Beerhouse

Anakana •

Rivington Grill

Fox •

Apostrophe •

The Princess •

Home •

Eyre Brothers •

Savarona, Great Eastern
Dining Room,
Hoxton Square

Real Greek, Yelo,
Furnace, Diner, Cru,
Hoxton Apprentice, Shish
• Drunken Monkey

FINSBURY

HAC
(Bunhill
Fields)

Chiswell St

I Blossom St •

St John Bread & Wine

Hawksmoor •

• Wagamama

Gaucho Grill •

Meson los Barilles •
Leon, Canteen, Scarlet Dot,
Arkansas Café
Square Pie Company •
• S & M Café

MOORGATE

Singapura •

Broadgate

La Tasca •
Les Coulisses,
Tatsuso •

Moshi Moshi • Pâtisserie Valerie
Boisdale of Bishopsgate

Finsbury
Circus

LIVERPOOL ST.

Gow's •

Ekachai •

Lanes •
Aurora, Miyabi
Fishmarket,
Terminus

• Barcelona
Tapas

Sri Siam City •

New Tayyabs →

EC2

(Ciro's) Pizza Pomodoro •

Haz •

• Satu Bar
& Kitchen

K10 •

Moorgate

• Chez
Gérard

Rhodes 24, Vertigo, Wagamama •
Bankside •

Sterling •

Barcelona Tapas •

Pacific Oriental •

Bevis Marks •

Mirch Masala •

Taberna Etrusca
Place Below
• Browns

Prism •

Kasturi, Missouri Grill •

Threadneedle St

• Bonds

• Caravaggio

Christopher's
In The City

• Imperial City

Cornhill

Leadenhall St

Chamberlain's,
Barcelona Tapas

Singapura

BANK
• Coq d'Argent, Bar Capitale

• Crussh

• Rajasthan II

• Zuccato

• Silks & Spice

• Gaucho Grill

Houndsditch

• Sri Thai
Bar Capitale

I Lombard
Street

Simpson's Tavern
George & Vulture

• Don

Royal Exchange

• Nuvo
Bar Bourse

Cannon Street

MONUMENT

Grand Café,
Restaurant Sauterelle

• Thai Square City

• Maison Blanc Vite

Fenchurch St

FENCHURCH ST.

CANNON ST.

• City Noto

Eastcheap

Bertorelli's •

Auberge • Just Gladwins

TOWER HILL

Upper Thames St

Rajasthan •

Gt Tower St

Wine Library •
Addendum • • Chez Gérard

EC3

Lower Thames St

Wagamama •

London Br

Tower of
London

River Thames

Lightship Ten •

Cantina Vinopolis
• Amano

• Kwan Thai

Glas, Roast, Konditor
& Cook, Feng Sushi,
Wright Brothers, Monmouth
Coffee Company, fish!,
Black & Blue, Brew Wharf,
Tapas Brindisa, Silka

• Auberge

Tower Bridge

• Hara

Tooley Street

Browns (Butler's Wharf), •
Butlers Wharf Chop-house,
Pont de la Tour,
Cantina del Ponte,
Blueprint Café,
Bengal Clipper

Tas •

Fina Estampa •

Bermondsey St

Champor-Champor •

BOROUGH

Delfina Studio Café •

Long Lane

Druid St

Bermondsey Kitchen, Village East
• Garrison

MAP 10 – SOUTH LONDON (& FULHAM)

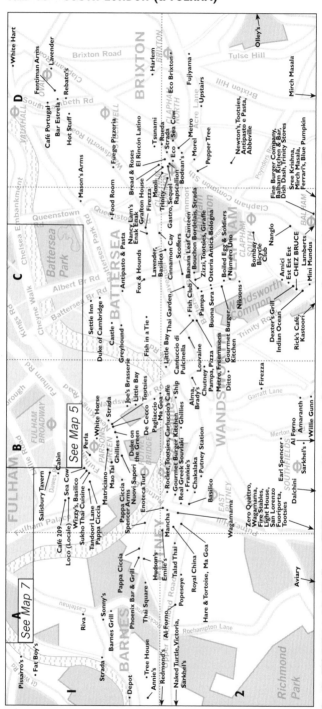

MAP 11 – EAST END & DOCKLANDS

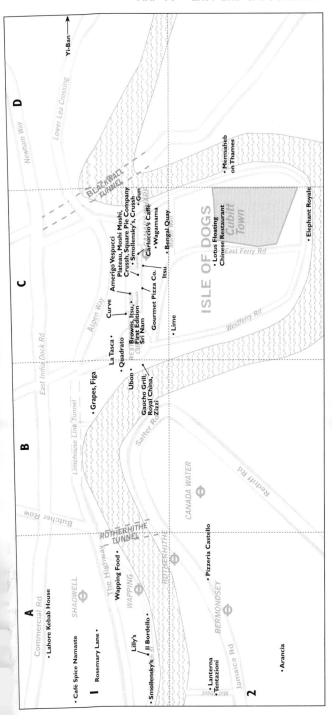

Yi-Ban →

D

Newham Way

Lower Lea Crossing

BLACKWALL TUNNEL

Amerigo Vespucci
Plateau, Moshi Moshi,
Crussh, Square Pie Company
Smollensky's, Crussh
Carluccio's Caffe
Wagamama
Itsu

Memsaheb
on Thames

Gun
Bengal Quay

ISLE OF DOGS

Cubitt Town

Lotus Floating
Chinese Restaurant

East Ferry Rd

Elephant Royale

Westferry Rd

East India Dock Rd

Aspen Way

C

Curve
La Tasca
Quadrato

Browns, Itsu,
First Edition
Sri Nam

Gourmet Pizza Co.

Lime

Limehouse Link Tunnel

B

Grapes, Figa

Ubon

Gaucho Grill,
Royal China,
Zizzi

Salter Rd

Redriff Rd

CANADA WATER

Butcher Row

Commercial Rd

ROTHERHITHE TUNNEL

The Highway

Wapping Food

SHADWELL

WAPPING

ROTHERHITHE

Pizzeria Castello

BERMONDSEY

A

Lahore Kebab House

Café Spice Namaste

Rosemary Lane

Lilly's

Smollensky's

Il Bordello

Lanterna
Tentazioni

Jamaica Rd

Arancia

Mill Street

1

2